FIREFLY ENCYCLOPEDIA OF
INSECTS
AND SPIDERS

P9-DFI-326

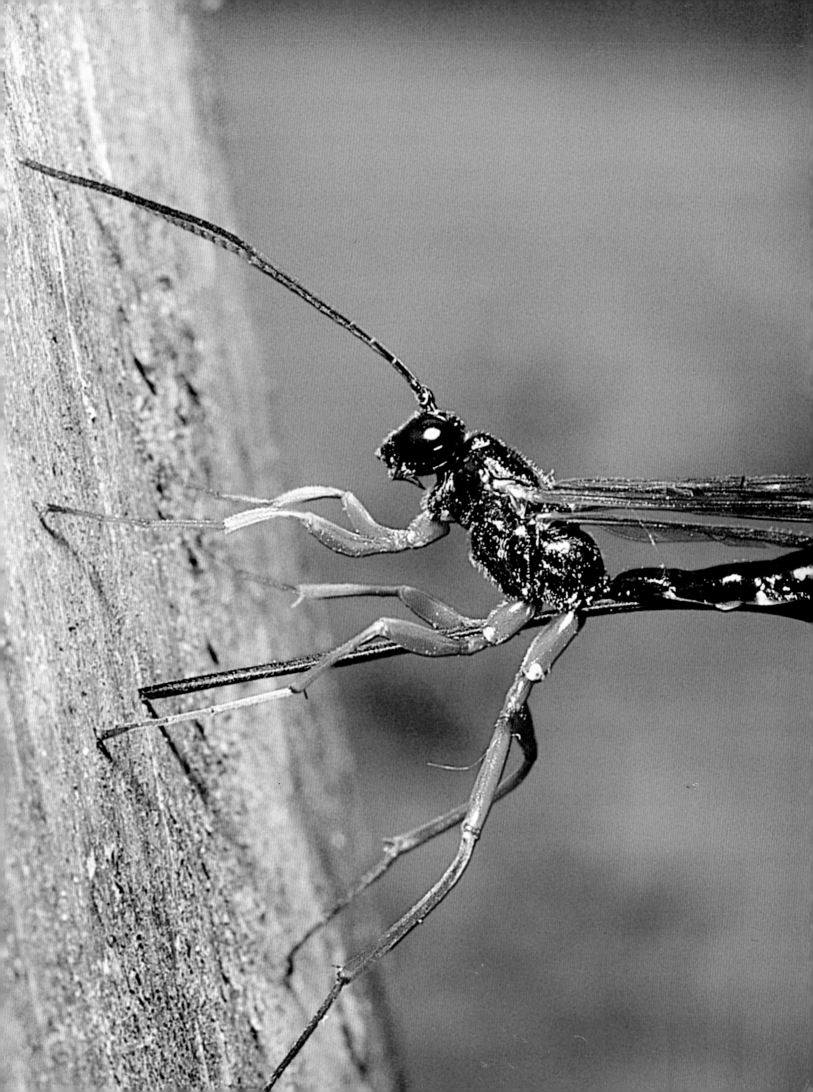

FIREFLY ENCYCLOPEDIA OF
INSECTS
AND SPIDERS

edited by CHRISTOPHER O'TOOLE

FIREFLY BOOKS

A FIREFLY BOOK

Published by Firefly Books Ltd., 2002

All rights reserved. No part of this publication may be reproduced, stored in a retrieval system, or transmitted in any form or by any means electronic, mechanical, photocopying, recording, or otherwise, without the prior permission in writing of the copyright holder, Andromeda Oxford Limited.

First Printing

National Library of Canada Cataloguing in Publication data

The Firefly encyclopedia of insects and spiders / edited by Christopher O'Toole.
Includes bibliographical references and index.
ISBN 1-55297-612-2
1. Insects—Encyclopedias. 2. Spiders—Encyclopedias.
I. O'Toole, Christopher
QL462.3.F57 2002   595.7'03   C2002-901644-4

U.S. Publisher Cataloging-in-Publication Data

The Firefly encyclopedia of insects and spiders / edited by Christopher O'Toole. –1st ed.
[240] p. : col. ill. , photos. , maps ;   cm.
Includes bibliographic references and index.
Summary: Authoritative illustrated reference on insects and spiders with contributing essays by world-renowned scientists
ISBN 1-55297-612-2
1. Entomology. 2. Insects. 3. Arthropoda.
I. O'Toole, Christopher.
595 21   CIP   QL462.3.F52 2002

First published in Canada in 2002 by
Firefly Books Ltd.
3680 Victoria Park Avenue
Toronto, Ontario M2H 3K1

First published in the United States in 2002 by
Firefly Books (U.S.) Inc.
P.O.Box 1338, Ellicott Station
Buffalo, New York 14205

AN ANDROMEDA BOOK

Planned and produced by
Andromeda Oxford Limited,
11–13 The Vineyard, Abingdon,
Oxfordshire, OX14 3PX
United Kingdom.
www.andromeda.co.uk

Copyright © 2002 Andromeda Oxford Limited

First published 2002

The moral rights of the authors have been asserted

Database right Andromeda Oxford Limited

Publishing Director Graham Bateman
Project Manager Peter Lewis
Editor Tony Allan
Art Director Chris Munday
Designers Martin Anderson, Frankie Wood
Picture Manager Claire Turner
Production Director Clive Sparling
Editorial and Administrative Assistant
   Marian Dreier
Proofreader Rita Demetriou
Indexer Ann Barrett

Originated in the Czech Republic by Global Graphics, Prague.

Printed in the United Arab Emirates on acid-free paper by Oriental Press, Dubai.

Kallima butterfly
see page 161

CONTRIBUTORS

AB   Anne Baker
Natural History Museum
London, UK

NMC   N. Mark Collins
IUCN Monitoring Centre
Cambridge, UK

PSC   Philip S. Corbet
Penzance
Cornwall, UK

PDH   Paul D. Hillyard
Natural History Museum
London, UK

JWI   John W. Ismay
Hope Entomological
Collections
Oxford University Museum
of Natural History, UK

CHCL   Christopher H. C. Lyal
Natural History Museum
London, UK

JL   John Lewis
Vice-Chairman,
British Myriapod and
Isopod Group, UK

LJL   Linda J. Losito
Oxford, UK

AWRM   Angus W. R. McCrae
Oxford, UK

GCM   George C. McGavin
Hope Entomological
Collections
Oxford University Museum
of Natural History, UK

DM   Darren Mann
Hope Entomological
Collections
Oxford University Museum
of Natural History, UK

PLM   Peter L. Miller †
Department of Zoology
University of Oxford, UK

LAM   Laurence A. Mound
CSIRO Entomology
Canberra, Australia

CO'T   Christopher O'Toole
Hope Entomological
Collections
Oxford University Museum
of Natural History, UK

KP   Keith Porter
English Nature
Peterborough, UK

KP-M   Ken Preston-Mafham
Premaphotos Wildlife
Bodmin, Cornwall, UK

RP-M   Rod Preston-Mafham
Premaphotos Wildlife
Bodmin, Cornwall, UK

HJR   Helen J. Read
Secretary, British Myriapod
and Isopod Group, UK

MJS   Malcolm J. Scoble
Natural History Museum
London, UK

SSi   Stephen Simpson
Department of Zoology
University of Oxford, UK

BW   Bernice Williams
University of Cardiff, UK

PGW   Patricia G. Willmer
University of St. Andrews
Fife, UK

TDW   Tristram D. Wyatt
Department of Zoology
University of Oxford, UK

Artwork Panels

Richard Lewington

Denys Ovenden,
Chris Shields,
Simon Mendez

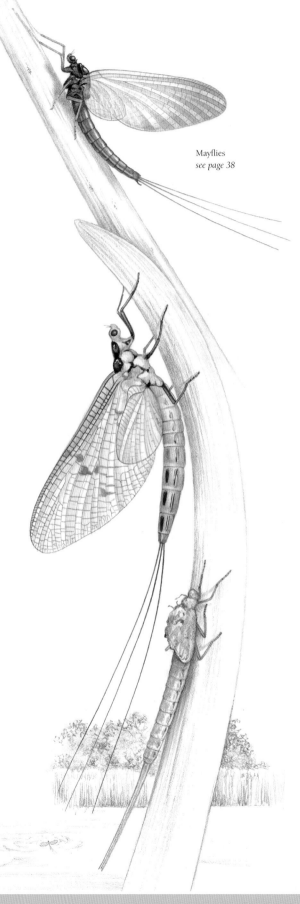

Mayflies
see page 38

Photos   page 1: Stink bug nymph (family Pentatomidae); pages 2–3: Parasitic wasp female (*Rhysella approximator*); opposite: Praying mantis nymph (*Polyspilota aeruginosa*).

CONTENTS

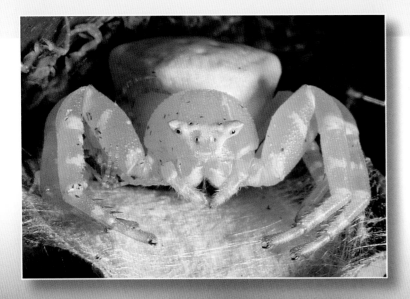

Photos main photo: Dragonfly (*Trithemis annulata*) in Sokoke forest, Kenya; inset left: Acorn weevil (*Curculio venosus*) on oak leaf; inset above: Crab spider (*Thomisus* sp.), Queensland, Australia.

PREFACE

Of the million or so animal species that have so far been described, about 85 percent are insects; there are estimated to be 200 million of them for every living person. To put it another way, there are some 10,000 million insects living in each square kilometer of habitable land on Earth, or 26,000 million per square mile. Insects also predominate overwhelmingly among the terrestrial arthropods that are the subject of this book.

What is more, the land-dwelling, jointed-limbed animals without backbones also include the millipedes and centipedes, and the spiders, scorpions, ticks and mites; for example, in rural southern England there may be as many as 5 million spiders per hectare (12.5 million per acre). These figures are for known species only: recent surveys in tropical forests suggest that there may be as many as 25 to 30 million species of arthropod in the world, most of which remain undescribed!

Until recently, most studies of arthropods were primarily or entirely descriptive – and rightly so in the face of such bewildering diversity. In the last 50 years, however, the relatively new disciplines of population and behavioral ecology have embraced the arthropods and revealed them in a new light. Population ecology has shown just how important the relationships between arthropods and other living things are. Behavioral ecology shows that many arthropods have behavior normally only associated with birds and mammals.

Arthropods, and especially the insects, are, in fact, a vital part of the survival kit of Planet Earth, having a commanding presence in the dynamic processes that maintain our ecosystems. They dispose of dead vegetation, animal corpses, and dung, and are the major herbivores, processing and returning vast amounts of nutrients to the soil. As pollinators of flowers, they are vital links in the cycle of plant generations. Yet ticks, fleas, and a variety of flies exert a negative influence on human ecology, through the diseases they transmit to humans and their livestock, while many mites and insects devastate crops and trees.

There is now a growing awareness that our survival as a species may well depend on a greater understanding of the diversity of living things and their conservation. The greatest urgency lies with the wet forests of the tropics, home of half of all plant and animal species. It is a humbling thought that our primate ancestors inherited a range of habitats largely shaped and maintained by the interactions of arthropods with plants and other animals. In a real sense we began our road to humanity by exploiting opportunities provided by courtesy of the arthropods. It is even more humbling to ponder the thought that this planet can survive without man but not, in its present form, without the arthropods.

Underlining the never-ending work of insect taxonomists is the very recent discovery of a new order of insects, the Mantophasmatodea, too recent, indeed, to be dealt with comprehensively in this volume. Comprising two known genera, *Raptophasma* from fossil material in Baltic amber and *Mantophasma* from tropical Africa, members of this order are wingless carnivores, and the modern species live in dense grass tussocks. Their evolutionary relationships are still a matter for conjecture but their anatomy suggests some affinities with either the Grylloblattodea (rock crawlers, ice crawlers) or Phasmatodea (stick insects). DNA studies may reveal molecular evidence which might help resolve the issue.

The Arthropod Success Story

The arthropod body plan comprises an external skeleton made of a remarkable horny substance called chitin, which has a high strength-to-weight ratio and is flexible and waterproof. The body plan has evolved independently at least four times. Modern systems of classification, therefore, no longer treat arthropods as a single group, "Arthropoda;" instead, they tend to divide them into different phyla with distinct origins. There are the terrestrial insects, myriapods, and their relatives (phylum Uniramia); the mainly terrestrial Chelicerata (spiders and relatives, and horseshoe crabs); and the chiefly marine crustaceans (crabs, shrimps, lobsters, and woodlice – phylum Crustacea). Smaller phyla include the terrestrial velvet worms (Onychophora), and the aquatic tongue worms (Pentastomida) and water bears (Tardigrada). Marine arthropods are not covered here.

"Arthropodization" has enabled these animals to invade a wide range of habitats. Some of their adaptations are bizarre, ranging, in insects, from flies whose larvae live in hot springs or crude oil to a Malaysian moth that sucks the blood of animals; there are even fly larvae that live as internal parasites of barnacles. The list is endless, and ultra-specialization is a recurrent theme. On the other hand there are generalists too. Consider the physiological virtuosity of larvae of the little scuttlefly *Megaselia scalaris*, which, to date, have been reared from shoe polish, emulsion paint, human cadavers pickled in formalin, and the lungs of living people.

INSECT INVENTORS

If arthropods made the evolution of the world in which we live possible, they also invented many things that humans like to take the credit for:

Tool use Female hunting wasps of the genus *Ammophila* use a pebble held between the jaws as a tamping tool to consolidate soil forming the final seal of their nest burrows.

The wheel Female dung beetles, rather than the Sumerians and Egyptians of 4,000 years ago, were the first to develop the concept of the wheel. The beetles mold dung into perfect spheres; then, balancing on their front legs, they use their two hind pairs to roll the dung back to a subterranean nest, where they lay their eggs and their larvae feed on the dung. Ironically, these scarab beetles were sacred to the Ancient Egyptians and appear frequently in their art.

Agriculture Termites and ants were in the business of cultivation millions of years before our ancestors. Many species of termites use their own feces as a medium on which to grow special fungi on which they feed. Similarly, leaf-cutter ants make a compost of leaf fragments on which they grow a unique fungus as a food supply. In addition, many ants evolved the herding instinct: they keep aphids much as we keep cows, milking them for the sweet honeydew they produce.

Chemical warfare Whether in the range of powerful venoms produced by stinging ants, wasps, and bees or in the often complex noxious substances secreted by arthropods of almost all other groups, chemical defense has evolved many times over in these versatile creatures.

Air conditioning The activities of a million or more termites in a single fungus-growing colony generate much heat in an already sun-baked savanna. To counter its effects, termites evolved cooling techniques that embodied the principles of air-conditioning millions of years before American engineer Willis Carrier filed his patent in 1902.

Antifreeze Many insect species from arctic or alpine habitats have developed a form of antifreeze to stop ice crystals forming in their body tissues. Their solution to this problem is the same as that of human automotive engineers: ethylene glycol.

If this volume has any linking theme, it is the arthropod success story. Our survey brings together a wealth of new information, hitherto buried in specialist journals and texts. An opening account of what it is to be an arthropod is followed by descriptions of all the major taxonomic groups, starting with the two superclasses of the phylum Uniramia, the myriapods (millipedes and centipedes) and the hexapods (mainly insects). Within the insects, each of the 28 different orders is treated separately, with a summary panel of salient facts, accompanied by a wider-ranging text outlining the major aspects of the group's natural history. An introduction to that other main group of terrestrial arthropods, the arachnids (class Arachnida of the phylum Chelicerata) is followed by sections on the mites and ticks, the spiders, and the scorpions and remaining subclasses. Throughout the book, boxed features, special feature spreads, and photo stories focus on topics of particular interest in behavior, morphology, ecology, or economic or medical importance.

The illustrations in this encyclopedia do more than record the stunning variety of color, form, and lifestyle in terrestrial arthropods. The photographs, almost all by Premaphotos Wildlife, were taken in the wild, in locations all over the world. Here are revealed, in the subjects' natural habitat, details of arthropod life cycles and behavior, from the egg through larval stages and molting to adulthood, courtship, mating, feeding, and defense, flight, and death. Captions expand the scope of the text and identify species by family as well as by scientific name (if not given in the accompanying text or summary panel), and any common name.

An important role is played by the artwork. Richard Lewington's color panels show the diversity and typical behavior of representatives of the major groups. The line drawings illustrate aspects of form and behavior covered in the text. The drawings in the Factfile panels are of species chosen to give some idea of the general appearance of many, if not all, members of the group in question.

It is a pleasure to acknowledge the labors of an enthusiastic team of authors, all experts in their chosen fields. My thanks are also due to the dedicated publishing team at Andromeda Oxford Ltd., led by Dr Graham Bateman, Dr Peter Lewis and Chris Munday. I hope that together we have produced a volume that does justice to the swarming hordes of arthropods, which live out their intricate lives largely unseen and often unjustly reviled.

Stalk-eyed flies
see page 132

Opposite: Seven-spot ladybird (ladybug)
see page 110

Chris O'Toole

CHRISTOPHER O'TOOLE
HOPE ENTOMOLOGICAL COLLECTIONS
UNIVERSITY MUSEUM, OXFORD

What is an Arthropod?

RTHROPODS ARE THE MOST SUCCESSFUL *animals ever to have evolved. In seas, fresh waters, and on land, they easily outnumber all other animal groups. Only humans can rival them: but still the arthropods eat our foodstuffs, materials, and buildings, parasitize our livestock, and spread disease. Nevertheless arthropods are essential to our survival: crustaceans are major food sources for the fish we eat, while terrestrial arthropods are vitally important in nutrient recycling, and also produce silk, waxes, dyes, and honey. Most crucially, they also pollinate many of our crops. The balance between arthropods and humans is finely tuned, for the arthropods constitute the vital backbone of most ecosystems.*

Why are the arthropods so successful? The answer is probably quite simple – they have an external skeleton (exoskeleton) or "cuticle." This is their single most important diagnostic feature. Most of the special adaptations and devices of the group stem from this basic characteristic.

One Origin or Several?
EVOLUTION

Arthropods first appeared in the Cambrian period 600–500 million years ago, and probably evolved from some form of worm not unlike modern marine annelids, which also have segments but are soft-bodied, with simple, lobelike appendages. Annelids and arthropods share some developmental features, and have very similar nervous systems. But there is a longstanding debate about whether arthropods branched just once from a wormlike stock, diversifying thereafter, or whether there were several separate, independent evolutionary lines. The former, monophyletic view holds "Arthropoda" to be a true phylum; but the latter implies polyphyly, arguing that arthropods are an unreal assemblage, and most commonly recognizes three principal modern phyla. These are the Crustacea (crabs, shrimps, and others), the Chelicerata (the arachnids – spiders, scorpions, mites, and horseshoe crabs), and the Uniramia (insects, plus centipedes and millipedes).

This controversy persists partly because the early arthropod fossil record is poor and cannot give final answers. There can be little doubt that arthropods do all look similar, at first glance making a satisfying grouping. They also share many design features besides external resemblance: similar guts, eyes, musculature, gonads and sperm, and an "open-plan" blood system. Monophyletic theory suggests all these likenesses must unite the groups, and cannot have arisen independently.

However, anatomical studies of the "similar" features reveal important discrepancies. Arachnids have their mouth one segment further forward than crustaceans and insects, and they have piercing

VELVET WORMS – A MISSING LINK?

The velvet worms or "walking worms" of the phylum Onychophora are an ancient group of tropical and south temperate terrestrial animals that are seemingly intermediate between annelid worms and the "proper" arthropods: some biologists choose to view them as a "missing link."

Velvet worms live in moist, damp places, such as leaf litter on the forest floor, preying on worms and insects. If attacked they exude a sticky gum, squirted from the papillae on either side of the mouth. The sexes are separate, and many of the 120 or so species give birth to live young.

The cylindrical body, usually a few centimeters long (range 1–15cm/0.4–6in) bears stumpy legs, and its whole surface is covered with periodically molted chitinous cuticle, perforated by many respiratory tracheae. There is one pair of antennae, and the stout, clawlike mandibles are suited to the worms' carnivorous diet. Internally, blood bathes the tissues directly, without blood vessels except for a dorsal heart. All these features are shared with arthropods. However, the antennae are fleshy and ringed (annulated), the body wall is thin, flexible, and permeable, not a hard exoskeleton, and the ani-mal moves by contracting sheets of muscles to affect its shape and length in a very wormlike fashion, with only limited assistance from the 14–43 pairs of short, soft, unjointed legs.

Because of these distinctions, the velvet worms are placed in their own phylum despite sharing many features, including common ancestors, with such arthropods as insects and myriapods. Onychophorans are named for the two claws on the tip of each leg (onychophora means "claw-bearers"). The best-known genus is *Peripatus* (shown below).

⬥ **Above** *A male two-striped jumping spider (Telamonia dimidiata; Salticidae) goes hunting in a Sulawesi rain forest. Like all arthropods, spiders depend for their survival on an armor of cuticle that shields their vulnerable internal organs.*

chelicerae rather than chewing mandibles as jaws. Even the mandibles of crustaceans and insects are developmentally dissimilar, and have different biting actions. Similarly, crustaceans have two-branched (biramous) limbs, the secondary branch usually forming gills, while uniramians and chelicerates now both have uniramous limbs, but with different origins. Again, three separate designs are indicated. The different growth patterns of crustaceans and insects may also be incompatible with a common evolutionary history.

Despite this evidence for multiple origins, two critical problems remain. Firstly, can the extensive similarities between groups really be dismissed as

ARTHROPODA

Recent work, especially in the field of molecular phylogeny, tends to support the view that arthropods are a single phylum (monophyletic). However, to reflect continuing uncertainty, the groups are referred to below both as phyla and as classes.

UNIRAMIANS

Phylum (or Class) Uniramia
About 1 million species described (may be 5–30 million in existence) in 2 major groupings.

SUPERCLASS MYRIAPODA   p16

The many-legged myriapods, comprising 4 classes: the centipedes (Chilopoda), millipedes (Diplopoda), Pauropoda, and Symphyla.

SUPERCLASS HEXAPODA   p22

The 6-legged hexapods, comprising 4 classes: insects (Insecta), springtails (Collembola), Protura, and Diplura.

CHELICERATES

Phylum (or Class) Chelicerata
About 70,000 species.

CLASS ARACHNIDA   p196

The 8-legged arachnids, comprising 11 subclasses including the terrestrial spiders (Aranae), scorpions (Scorpiones), mites and ticks (Acari).

Also the aquatic horseshoe or king crabs (class Merostomata), sea spiders (class Pycnogonida), and probably the extinct trilobites (class Trilobita) – not covered here.

VELVET WORMS

Phylum (or Class) Onychophora. About 120 species.

CRUSTACEANS

Phylum (or Class) Crustacea. Some 30,000 species, mostly aquatic (crabs, shrimps etc.), some terrestrial, e.g. woodlice, land crabs – not covered here.

TONGUE WORMS

Phylum (or Class) Pentastomida. About 90 aquatic species – not covered here.

WATER BEARS

Phylum (or Class) Tardigrada. About 180 species, mostly aquatic – not covered here.

convergence? It may be that different groups have evolved separately but arrived at very similar endpoints because they are the only feasible solutions to common problems, given the constraints of an exoskeleton. So, for a worm to evolve a stiff cuticle inevitably entrains all the other changes, including the appearance of appendages (legs) required for locomotion, and the capacity to molt, allowing growth, that result in the evolution of what we call an arthropod. Furthermore, there are classic examples of indisputable arthropodan convergence, since both tracheal and Malpighian tubules have arisen independently in different groups, thus permitting life on land. In other words, remarkably precise convergence does happen. Arthropods merely show it so clearly because their design severely limits the number of possible solutions to common problems.

◑ **Left** *This schematic diagram, based on numbers of species, demonstrates that arthropods make up a strikingly high proportion of all animal life on Earth. By far the greatest part of the arthropods is accounted for by the million or so species so far described in the class Insecta. New insect species are constantly being discovered and classified. There are currently about 300,000 known species of beetles in the largest insect order, the Coleoptera; in comparison, science has identified fewer than 5,000 species of mammals.*

The second objection is why "arthropodization" should have happened several times over. To answer this, polyphyleticists argue that exoskeletons are a major evolutionary advance, likely to be preserved by natural selection whenever they evolved. In that case, several evolutionary prototypes with a cuticle are to be expected, each diversifying into a separate group of "arthropods."

It might have been hoped that molecular analysis would settle the matter. Most analyses of RNA and DNA sequences have in fact suggested reasonably close relationships between the arthropod groups, but they do not clearly separate them from other invertebrate taxa; nor does the molecular evidence as yet draw clear lines within the classes, for example tending to put myriapods very distant from insects (contrary to morphological evidence). So the jury is still out on these key problems, and the arthropods may be one phylum with 4–5 classes, or several phyla.

The following pages consider arthropod design in the light of possible multiple origins, since the very number of arthropods attests to the success of the basic body plan and lends weight to the idea of multiple origins from wormlike ancestors.

Living in a Cuticular Tube
EXOSKELETON

The evolution of an exoskeleton of hardened cuticle had several implications for the evolution of arthropods. One major effect of an exoskeleton is to keep an animal small. An external tube provides the best mechanical support with limited material, but for large animals internal rods (i.e. endoskeletons, like vertebrate bones) are a better solution. Also, exoskeletons necessitate growth by molting. Large animals would collapse under their own weight before a newly-secreted skeleton hardened.

Yet small size has its advantages. The number of individuals can be greater, and rates of reproduction

○ **Above** Myriapods like this false flat-backed millipede (Nanogona polydesmoides) are classed in the phylum Uniramia alongside the insects.

(and hence of evolutionary adaptation) can be higher. Small arthropods also have an enormous range of niches available to them – they experience the world as an incredibly variable place. Hence they can develop great diversity, precisely because of the "constraint" imposed on their dimensions by an exoskeleton.

Arthropod skeletons are central to the animals' success, so the design of the cuticle itself must be critical. All arthropod cuticles have a similar, three-layered structure, all have joints and articulations of similar types, and all have glandular and sensory specializations within the cuticle. The various groups also share a common microstructure and chemistry; the bulk is made of the polysaccharide chitin, with the long, tough, chain-like chitin fibrils laid down in characteristic patterns for maximum multidirectional strength within a matrix of proteins. But the groups differ in their methods of hardening the newly-secreted cuticle after molting, and in the surface layers added (for example, only terrestrial arthropods use waxy, waterproofing layers).

Besides this variation between groups, arthropod cuticle also varies between species. It is this versatility that has made it such a successful material. It can be thick for strength or thin for flexibility, even elastic in wing and leg hinges; heavy for negative buoyancy or light for flight; colored for camouflage or warning; permeable for aquatic breathing, or extraordinarily resistant to water loss on land. These properties can exist in different parts of the same individual, but they can also occur differentially at each stage of the life cycle, contributing to the drastic metamorphosis seen in the most successful of all groups, the insects.

GROWTH AND MOLTING

Perhaps the most important drawback of an exoskeleton is that it restrains growth. Arthropods must therefore grow intermittently by producing a new and larger cuticle at intervals, shedding the old one. Many arthropods avoid the waste of good biological material by eating their own discarded shell.

Molting involves a complex sequence of changes; most of the old, unhardened endocuticle is first broken down and resorbed **a**, **b**, then the new epicuticle is laid down, somewhat crinkled **c** to allow for later expansion **d** under a layer of molting fluid. Some of the bulk protein and chitin is added below the new epicuticle **c**, **d**; when the new cuticle is reasonably

thick, the older cuticle outside it splits along specific lines **e**, and the animal pulls itself out of and sheds the old case. Then it may swallow air or water to expand its own volume and stretch the new skeleton before it hardens. Extra endocuticle may then be added, and in some cases (for example in insects) surface waxes or cements are added.

Molting must be carefully controlled and coordinated over the whole body, so it is always governed by hormones. Actual cuticle secretion and the molt cycle are due to ecdysone, a steroid hormone found in all arthropods. In insects this hormone is secreted by a gland in the thorax, which is in turn controlled

by a hormone from the brain – whenever the brain receives appropriate stimuli from the insect's environment, the entire hormonal cycle is therefore triggered and the animal molts.

Insects also have an extra chemical called "juvenile hormone" (JH) to regulate metamorphosis. When this is released from a small gland in the head, the new cuticle retains larval characteristics; but once the secretion stops, the insect produces adult cuticle instead and metamorphosis is complete. Insects do not molt after reaching maturity, unlike crustaceans, which may molt throughout their lives.

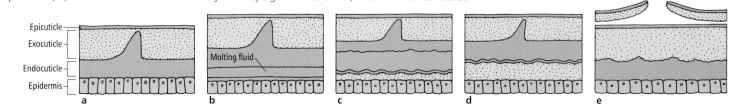

The cuticle is the arthropod's barrier against the world, giving physical protection to soft tissues and defense against parasites, pathogens, and predators, and providing a chemical barrier controlling exchanges of respiratory gases, salts, water, and other molecules. Thus, heavily-armored marine lobsters are almost invulnerable (except when molting); freshwater mosquito larvae use their cuticle to assist osmotic balance and prevent swelling; and terrestrial insects and spiders rely on the cuticle to prevent desiccation and to limit the damage from blows and falls.

A rigid exoskeleton has profound effects on locomotion; jointed legs are required for swimming, walking, and jumping. Each joint is operated by antagonistic flexor and extensor muscles, and joints operate in different planes for maximum maneuverability. All arthropod gaits are based on waves of leg movements, with the opposite legs of a pair alternating; many forms have several gaits for different speeds. Arthropods also have a characteristic posture, very unlike that of most vertebrates, with legs arising from the sides of the lower surface; the body sags between the suspending legs, for greater stability. Cuticle is also an ideal material, light but strong, for wing construction, thus enabling insects to take to the air.

The huge versatility of cuticle as a biological building material is perhaps best shown by the range of its uses for feeding. On land, the variety of mouthparts is proverbial, from the hard chelicerae and mandibles of predators to the piercing and sucking proboscis of biting flies, the delicate, flexibly-coiled "tongue" of a nectar-feeding butterfly, and the fleshy, lapping labellum of a housefly. In aquatic arthropods it can form hard, crunching mandibles and pincers, capable of breaking mollusk shells or the carapace of other crustaceans, but it can also be modified as finely-structured filtering setae to net microscopic plankton.

A Versatile Building Material
REPRODUCTION AND HOMEOSTASIS

Marine arthropods can disperse numerous eggs and sperm randomly into the sea and rely on chance fertilizations, but in other habitats specializations are needed. Freshwater crustaceans commonly produce yolky, cuticularized (shelled) eggs, or brood the young in special cuticular pouches. On land arthropods must bring egg and sperm together without either drying out, so copulation is required. Hence terrestrial arthropods usually

Below Cottonstainer bugs (Dysdercus flavidus; Pyrrhocoridae) feeding on kapok seeds. Several different instars (developmental stages) are represented here.

have complex genitalia that require a precise physical match of male and female appendages (impossible in soft-bodied animals) to ensure that only matings between members of the same species occur. They also use cuticle for egg shells (with elaborate architecture to let the embryo breathe) and, often, to make ovipositors, used to lay the eggs into suitable humid habitats – very long, sharp, and sensitive to insert eggs into host animals, or strong and sawlike to penetrate tough plants.

All animals benefit from a stable internal environment (homeostasis) to keep their biochemical systems functioning optimally. Arthropods are greatly assisted by their cuticle, since it regulates rates of exchange (for example of heat, gases, and other substances) with the outside world; but they are also hindered by their necessarily small size, since the temperature and chemical content of smaller bodies inevitably tend to fluctuate more rapidly. So arthropods need very efficient apparatuses for gas exchange and for salt and water balance, and a good fluid distribution system to keep supplies and wastes in balanced circulation.

Thus, in almost every aspect of their lives, cuticle is what makes the arthropods. It led to their evolution and constrains their design and size, but above all has contributed to their enormous diversity in virtually every habitat on Earth.   PGW

THE ARTHROPOD BODY PLAN

Cuticle

Central to arthropods' success, cuticle comprises chiefly fibrils of the polysaccharide chitin, laid down in thin layers and embedded in a matrix of proteins. The fibrils are parallel within a layer but slightly rotated between successive layers, giving great strength for minimum weight. The exocuticle is hardened by cross-linking ("tanning") of the proteins (with quinones in insects, with sulfur bridges in arachnids), and by impregnation with calcium salts in crustaceans and some myriapods. The endocuticle remains unhardened and is recycled at each molt. On top is the thin epicuticle, made of proteins and lipids. In terrestrial arthropods the epicuticle includes a waterproofing waxy layer and usually also a tough, protective cement layer.

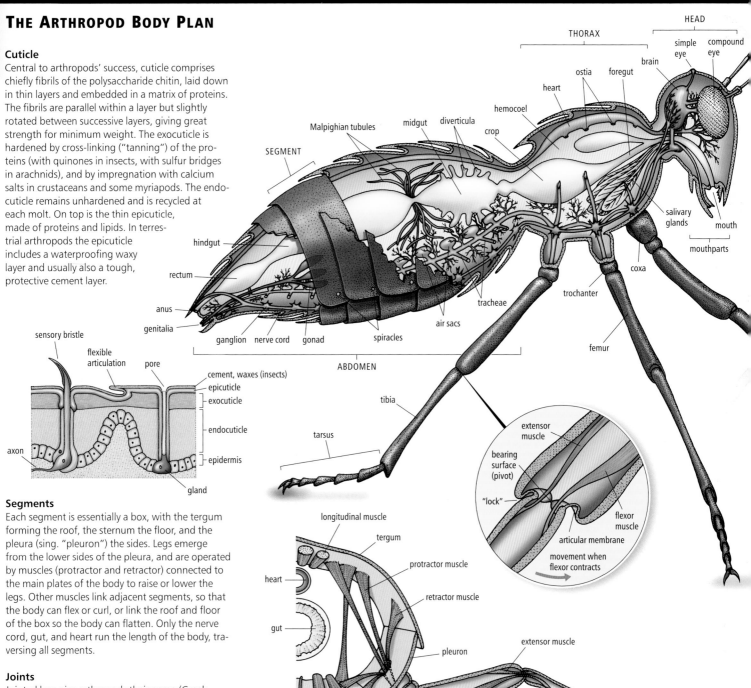

Segments

Each segment is essentially a box, with the tergum forming the roof, the sternum the floor, and the pleura (sing. "pleuron") the sides. Legs emerge from the lower sides of the pleura, and are operated by muscles (protractor and retractor) connected to the main plates of the body to raise or lower the legs. Other muscles link adjacent segments, so that the body can flex or curl, or link the roof and floor of the box so the body can flatten. Only the nerve cord, gut, and heart run the length of the body, traversing all segments.

Joints

Jointed legs give arthropods their name (Greek *arthron* – joint, *pous* – foot), with joints usually moving in only one plane, so that several joints per leg are needed to give full maneuverability. The hard cuticle "tubes," linked at the joint by softer, flexible cuticle, fit one within the other, so that when fully extended, as shown, one tube "locks" inside the other. When flexed, the outer segment rotates about a pivot formed by a cuticular extension, usually giving about 90° of movement. Internal extensions of the cuticle, termed apodemes, provide surfaces where the joint-manipulating muscles can attach.

Sensory systems

Most arthropod sense organs are modifications of the cuticle itself. The commonest form occurs as bristles (setae), which may be articulated; thus, the nerve ending within the bristle shaft is stimulated

when it moves (if touched, or vibrated by water or air movements). Or the bristle may carry chemical sensory endings (the latter are particularly common on legs, mouthparts, and antennae). Other sense organs involve canals or pits in the exoskeleton, with thin, nerve-packed membranes beneath that detect strains and tensions, especially at joints. There may also be internal position detectors (proprioceptors) attached to the cuticle or muscles.

The most obvious sense of arthropods, however, is vision. Many arthropods have simple eyes (ocelli) with only one or a few receptors, but in insects and most crustaceans, true compound eyes occur also,

with many long, cylindrical receptors (ommatidia). The cuticle always contributes the outer, transparent lens-cornea; hexagonal arrays of these occur in most compound eyes. Behind these are the crystalline cones (helping to focus light), and then the retinular cells, with highly folded inner surfaces bearing the visual pigment and uniting to form the rhabdome. These cells connect to the optic nerve fibers (axons), and thence to the brain. Such eyes produce mosaic images, more coarsely grained than our own vision, but also far more sensitively attuned to high-frequency flickering (in other words, to movement). Moreover, arthropods' eyes are convex and often

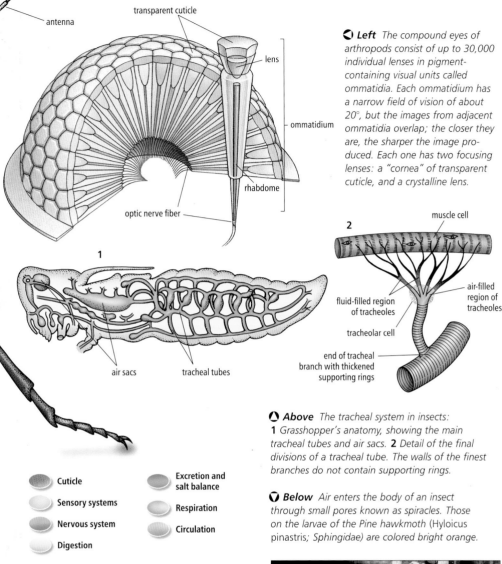

antenna

transparent cuticle

lens

ommatidium

rhabdome

optic nerve fiber

1

air sacs   tracheal tubes

muscle cell

2

fluid-filled region of tracheoles

air-filled region of tracheoles

tracheolar cell

end of tracheal branch with thickened supporting rings

◁ **Left** *The compound eyes of arthropods consist of up to 30,000 individual lenses in pigment-containing visual units called ommatidia. Each ommatidium has a narrow field of vision of about 20°, but the images from adjacent ommatidia overlap; the closer they are, the sharper the image produced. Each one has two focusing lenses: a "cornea" of transparent cuticle, and a crystalline lens.*

◔ **Above** *The tracheal system in insects:* **1** *Grasshopper's anatomy, showing the main tracheal tubes and air sacs.* **2** *Detail of the final divisions of a tracheal tube. The walls of the finest branches do not contain supporting rings.*

◔ **Below** *Air enters the body of an insect through small pores known as spiracles. Those on the larvae of the Pine hawkmoth (Hyloicus pinastris; Sphingidae) are colored bright orange.*

- Cuticle
- Sensory systems
- Nervous system
- Digestion
- Excretion and salt balance
- Respiration
- Circulation

very large, endowing them with an enormous field of vision; they work at many different light levels, adapting by movements of shielding pigments around the retinular cells; they can also be extremely sensitive to color (often extending into the ultraviolet range), and to the polarization of light.

Nervous system
All arthropods have similar nervous systems, centered on a brain in the top of the head. Insect brains are made up of three parts, the first two largely receiving inputs from the eyes and antennae respectively. Chelicerates (e.g. spiders) lack antennae, so have no obvious second segment. From the brain, nerves pass around the gut and unite underneath as the paired longitudinal nerve cord, which has ganglia in each segment (though these are fused in many forms). Each ganglion sends a constant pattern of nerves into the muscles within the segment, and receives sensory information; motor patterns generated centrally can thus be repeated slightly out of phase in adjacent segments to achieve coordinated locomotion.

Digestion
The arthropod gut is a simple tube in three parts; the fore- and hindgut are formed of the same material as the epidermis, so have cuticular linings that are molted, while the midgut is unlined and is the main center for enzyme secretion and nutrient absorption. Most arthropods have salivary glands to lubricate foods; venom and saliva may be ejected onto prey to paralyze and predigest the food. In some, the crop of the foregut is a complicated storage and crushing area. The midgut often has blind offshoots (diverticula) to increase its surface area. The hindgut is an important site for regulating excretory wastes, most of which leave as a solid paste via the anus.

Excretion and salt balance
The gill-less insects, arachnids, and myriapods regulate the salt and water content of their bodies internally. They have Malpighian tubules (blind-ending, branching off the gut) that secrete salts and wastes in solution, and a complex hindgut that takes back salt and/or water according to need.

In marine crustaceans, ammonia can diffuse away rapidly, and their blood is roughly in osmotic balance with their surroundings. Estuarine and freshwater crustaceans also use ammonia, but regulate their salt and water contents by salt uptake at the gills, and in special "green glands" near the mouthparts. In terrestrial groups, soluble ammonia is replaced with uric acid as the main nitrogenous waste.

Respiration
Most aquatic forms have gills – finely-folded extensions of permeable cuticle. These are borne on the legs in crustaceans, and usually on the end of the abdomen in aquatic insects. Some arachnids retain a gill-like structure (book gill), while others have a similar breathing apparatus tucked inside a pocket of the body (book lung). But most terrestrial arthropods – insects, myriapods, some spiders – have instead developed a system of fine cuticular tubes (tracheae) that spread inward from breathing vents (spiracles) on the surface of the thorax and the abdomen, enabling oxygen to travel directly to the tissues. This system is ideal on land (where gills would collapse and dry out) because the closeable spiracles limit water loss, and the oxygen supply can be very fast: but tracheae do have to be replaced at each molt.

Circulation
In all arthropods the blood circulates within the body cavity (hemocoel) through few vessels apart from the dorsal heart. This has holes (ostia) that take in the blood before passing it forward to the head and other active areas. The blood then returns to the open cavity of the body, although it may be directed through the legs and around the gut by partitioning of the cavity.

The blood (hemolymph), which is usually colorless or yellow-green, carries vital nutrients, wastes, and hormones to and from all tissues. (In arthropods other than insects and spiders it also carries oxygen from gills to tissues.) Blood also carries cells to defend against disease and to make repairs; and in soft-bodied forms it may transmit forces from the muscles, to allow a "hydrostatic" type of locomotion.

Millipedes and Centipedes

dESPITE THEIR APPARENT SIMILARITIES, *the four classes of the superclass Myriapoda – Chilopoda, Diplopoda, Symphyla, and Pauropoda – are not closely related. They are characterized by having at least nine pairs of simple walking legs arising from a uniform trunk, not divided into thorax and abdomen. Millipedes and centipedes are familiar animals, but they display a greater variation in shape and color than most people expect and have some surprising characteristics.*

Millipedes (Diplopoda) and centipedes (Chilopoda), two of the four classes of the many-legged Myriapoda, include some 95 percent of all myriapod species. They are found under stones, logs, bark, and in litter and soil. Unlike the insects, they lack a waxy layer on the cuticle and "breathe" through uncloseable spiracles. As a result, they are at risk of desiccation and generally, but not always, remain in humid sites, restricting their activity to the nighttime. They also differ from insects in lacking true compound eyes, and, most obviously, in having many more legs and no wings. Nevertheless, they are extremely common and successful animals, found from the arctic circle to the tropics and even in deserts. Some have adapted to life on the seashore.

Of the other two Myriapod classes, symphylans are pale, blind animals that resemble small centipedes. They have 12 pairs of legs, and feed mainly on fragments of dead vegetation and sometimes the roots of plants. Pauropods are tiny creatures, only about 2mm (0.08in) long, with nine pairs of legs. Both symphylans and pauropods have one pair of legs per body segment.

Secretive Burrowers
FORM AND FUNCTION

Most millipedes are secretive detritivores, burrowing through soil and leaf litter. By contrast, the centipedes are largely carnivorous and are much more active and predatory in their lifestyle. Apart from their very different habits, the two groups are readily distinguished by the presence of "displacements" in millipedes, with two pairs of legs corresponding to each segment, whereas centipedes have only a single pair per segment. Millipedes have simple chewing mouthparts, but centipedes have in addition large poison claws on the underside of the head.

Sight is rarely needed as the soil-dwelling myriapods mostly shun light. Only the fast, surface-dwelling scutigeromorph centipedes have complex eyes; others rely on a few simple eyes

◐ **Above** *The presence of two pairs of legs to a segment is clearly visible in this* Pararhacistus potosinus *flat-backed millipede (Polydesmida) climbing the trunk of a pine tree in a mountain forest in Mexico. This brightly colored species also lives in caves.*

◐ **Right** *In this large* Scolopendra cingulata *centipede (Scolopendromorpha), the modified front legs that function as poison claws can be seen curving closely round the sides of the flattened, platelike head. It has only a single pair of legs on each segment.*

LIFE IN THE SOIL

In order to thrive, the soil-dwelling myriapods have had to overcome the problems posed by the medium in which they live. They move either in crevices (flattened centipedes), or between soil particles (tiny millipedes), or by pushing soil aside (larger millipedes); geophilomorph centipedes burrow deep down. The direction and speed of movement are partly controlled by the sensitivity required to locate food (whether prey or vegetation) and mates.

In the soil the chemical and mechanical senses are preeminent, so myriapod antennae have abundant receptors for scent and touch, and the feet or mouthparts may also respond to such stimuli. Sometimes the rearmost legs are particularly sensitive, almost like additional antennae. Commonly a region near the antennae is also specialized to serve as the "organ of Tömösvary," thought to detect vibration. Myriapods may also have receptors to monitor the humidity and temperature of their surroundings.

The soil may seem at first sight a pleasantly stable, moist habitat in comparison with more open terrestrial areas, but it is still liable to drought or flooding, and its surface layers can be bakingly hot or frozen solid. Myriapods attempt to keep in favorable regions by migrating vertically – burrowing deeper to cool, damp layers in summer droughts or winter frosts, and rising to the surface, or even climbing vegetation and walls, when the soil is waterlogged. They have to use such behavioral mechanisms to locate suitable microhabitats because their cuticle (unlike those of insects) is not waterproof and they could otherwise easily dehydrate or drown; they might even asphyxiate if the uncloseable spiracles leading to the breathing tubes (tracheae) became water-filled. Breathing would also be difficult in soils relatively lacking in oxygen, even for herbivorous millipedes with their rather slow metabolism.   PGW

(ocelli) that merely detect light and shade; alternatively, the sensitivity to light may be spread over the cuticle. Many millipedes lack eyes altogether. The antennae bear chemical and tactile receptors, and the animals' mouthparts and legs may respond to these stimuli.

There are five orders of centipedes. The Geophilomorpha are very elongated soil dwellers with many short legs that can burrow like earthworms. The Scolopendromorpha have 21 or 23 pairs of legs; this order contains very large, often brightly-colored tropical species up to 30cm (12in) long. The shorter Lithobiomorpha are fast-running, with only 15 pairs of legs and flattened bodies. The Craterostigmomorpha are crevice-dwellers, found only in Tasmania and New Zealand, that appear in some ways intermediate between the lithobiomorphs and scolopendromorphs. Finally, the Scutigeromorpha are, in contrast, not well adapted to hiding in tight crevices.

They are fast runners with 15 pairs of very long legs and have tracheal lungs opening through slits on the upper surface of their bodies.

The millipedes are much more variable than centipedes, ranging from tiny, soft, tufted penicillates like *Polyxenus* that are less than 4mm (0.15in) long, to bulky, hardened, tropical spirostreptids up to 30cm (12in) long, with as many as 90 segments. They can be long, thin, and threadlike or relatively short and wide and able to roll into a tight ball.

Millipedes have been divided into five main ecomorphological types according to their behavioral patterns. The bristly millipedes or Penicillata are predominantly bark dwellers. These species differ from all other millipedes in having a soft body wall that is not impregnated with calcium, and they are covered with tufts of serrated bristles. They are tiny in size and live under bark, in among lichens, or in the soil.

FACTFILE

MILLIPEDES AND CENTIPEDES

Superclass: Myriapoda

Classes: Diplopoda, Chilopoda, Symphyla, Pauropoda

Approximately 15,000 species, grouped in 4 classes and 21 different orders.

DISTRIBUTION From the arctic circle to the tropics; there are even desert-dwelling species.

SIZE Length ranges from 0.5mm–30cm (0.02–12in)

FEATURES The 4 classes are not closely related, but all myriapods have 1 pair of antennae, 1 pair of mandibles, and 1 or more pairs of maxillae, as well as at least 9 pairs of walking legs (often many more).

LIFE CYCLE Unlike insects, most species have indirect copulatory methods. The young, which hatch from eggs, mostly resemble adults but have fewer segments. Millipedes pass through a legless pupoid stage into various stadia (equivalent to insect instars), the number varying between species. Longevity can be as much as 11 years or more.

CONSERVATION STATUS A single centipede species – the Serpent Island centipede (*Scolopendra abnormis*) – is currently listed as Vulnerable.

See classes table ▷

The most typical of the snake-shaped millipedes are probably the rammers. They are cylindrical in cross section, with a very hard cuticle, and the body rings are incompressible. They move through the soil by lowering their strong head-capsule and pushing hard with their many legs.

The rollers are relatively short millipedes with 13 body segments. They too are good bulldozers, but they can also roll into a tight ball by tucking their heads under their telson (see Rolling Up for Protection). Some species in the southern hemisphere can reach 10cm (4in) in length.

Wedge-type millipedes have laterally expanded keels (paranota) on each segment and are sometimes referred to as flat-backed millipedes. They may be found among leaf litter and have relatively long legs. These animals typically move by putting their heads into crevices and pushing upward, widening the gaps as they go; they are thus well adapted to living among decaying leaves.

Finally, the borers are domed in shape, have small, pointed heads, and their body segments are not as solid and incompressible as the bulldozers. As they walk into a crevice, muscles pull the posterior segments onto the anterior ones. The body is strongly tapered, so the crevice is gradually enlarged. Apart from these generalized types, there are also species of millipedes that live in caves and rocky places or up trees.

One might expect creatures with anything from 9 to 375 pairs of legs (the maximum number so far recorded) to run a serious risk of tripping over themselves. Clearly this is not the case with centipedes and millipedes, which have both evolved a range of gaits, from scuttling to wavelike movements of the legs. The more flexible and extensible burrowing geophilomorph centipedes move either by walking or by extending and contracting the trunk like earthworms, with the legs used mainly for anchorage.

ROLLING UP FOR PROTECTION

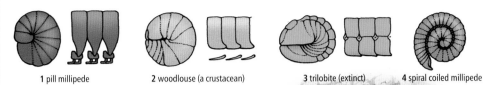

1 pill millipede   **2** woodlouse (a crustacean)   **3** trilobite (extinct)   **4** spiral coiled millipede

Curling into a tight ball (conglobation) is an excellent defense for a small arthropod with thick back plates. All the softer parts and the vulnerable sense organs can be tucked in and protected against predators, and water loss can be reduced. So it is not surprising that many forms have developed this trick. The pill millipedes or glomerids like these *Glomeris marginata* RIGHT and the woodlice or "pill bugs" – actually crustaceans – are the best-known examples, but other living arthropods also curl up, and millions of years ago many trilobites were equally expert at the defensive roll.

All of these animals are hemispherical in section, and they curl up around their flat undersurface, stretching apart the overlapping back plates (tergites) and enclosing the legs in a small central space. Pill millipedes tuck the head in **1**; the tergites are shaped to create a smooth, exposed surface, and are also staggered relative to the plates on the underside (sternites), so improving flexibility.

In contrast, woodlice **2** cannot tuck the head in. They achieve the necessary trunk flexing with normally shaped segments that overlap backward dorsally but in the opposite direction underneath, so the belly concertinas together as the back extends.

The extinct trilobites **3** achieved their roll using special peg-and-socket joints between segments; but the head was not tucked into the body, being itself heavily armored.

Longer millipedes are unable to achieve a globe shape by rolling, but still rely on spiral coiling for defense. They use a similar technique to the pill millipedes to arrange themselves as a flat spiral **4**, like a catherine wheel, with the head in the center and all legs tucked away, leaving only tough, unpalatable surfaces exposed to would-be predators. PGW

○ *Below* Representative myriapods: **1** Cylindroiulus silvarum (Julida), a European millipede. **2** Flat-backed millipede (Polydesmus sp.; Polydesmida). **3a** Giant millipedes of the order Spirostreptida at full stretch and **3b** curled up into a defensive coil. **4** Haplophilus subterraneus (Geophilomorpha), one of the largest of the many-legged, soil-dwelling geophiomorphid centipedes; common in fields and gardens, where it can damage roots. **5** Megarian banded centipede (Scolopendra cingulata; Scolopendromorpha), a burrowing centipede found throughout southern Europe that eats crickets and even small lizards. **6** House centipede (Scutigera coleoptrata; Scutigeromorpha), a species from the USA and Mexico so called for its liking for indoor environments; an agile hunter, it preys on spiders and insects in basements and crawl spaces. **7** Lithobius forficatus (Lithobiomorpha), a common small centipede often found under logs and stones.

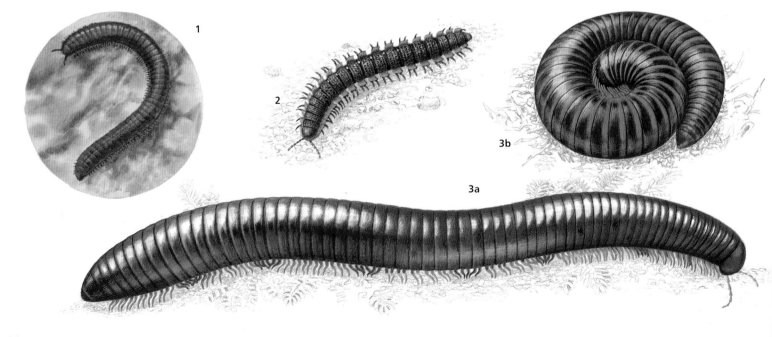

1

2

3b

3a

Herbivores and Carnivores
FOOD AND FEEDING

The vast majority of millipedes feed on plant material, most using their stout jaws to chew it into small pieces. Often they prefer leaves that have been partly decomposed by bacteria and fungi, which may increase the availability of nutrients. Thus millipedes are important nutrient recyclers. Some will eat living plants such as young shoots or fine roots, and occasionally they may be important pests of crops such as sugar beet. A few species are carnivorous or will eat the remains of dead animals such as snails. Some have developed sucking mouthparts, which they insert into plant roots or use to feed on fungi.

Centipedes are largely carnivorous and are sometimes carrion feeders. Generally they feed on small soil invertebrates (worms, snails, and various arthropods), but the large tropical scolopendrids prey on vertebrates such as lizards, toads, mice, and nestling birds. They detect prey through their antennae or legs and capture and paralyze it with their poison claws, holding it with the forelegs while they chew it up. The venom of some large scolopendromorphs can be extremely painful to humans and can cause tissue damage. Geophilomorphs are sometimes suctorial feeders. Some centipedes may be able to help control agricultural pests.

The Chemical Armory
DEFENSIVE BEHAVIOR

Millipedes, being generally slow-moving, rely on physical or chemical means of defense. The usually thick cuticle is very strong and is impregnated with calcium carbonate, while the ability to roll up or coil ensures that its strongest parts are held outermost. Most groups of millipedes have defense or "repugnatorial" glands, usually one per diplosegment. The secretions produced from these glands

○ **Above** The chemical armory available to this Sigmoria aberrans flat-backed-millipede (Polydesmidae) crawling across moss in North Carolina is advertised by its bright warning colors. Unsurprisingly, this colorful species is active on the surface in daytime.

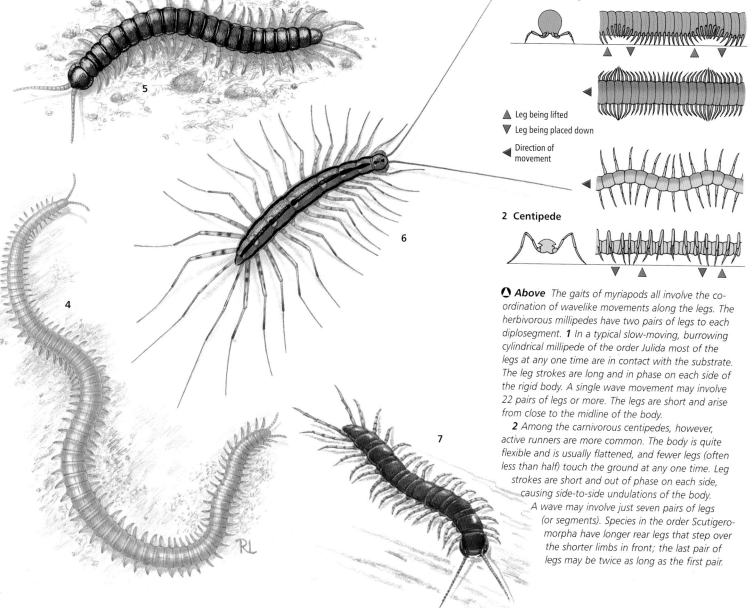

1 Cylinder millipede

▲ Leg being lifted

▼ Leg being placed down

◀ Direction of movement

2 Centipede

○ **Above** The gaits of myriapods all involve the coordination of wavelike movements along the legs. The herbivorous millipedes have two pairs of legs to each diplosegment. **1** In a typical slow-moving, burrowing cylindrical millipede of the order Julida most of the legs at any one time are in contact with the substrate. The leg strokes are long and in phase on each side of the rigid body. A single wave movement may involve 22 pairs of legs or more. The legs are short and arise from close to the midline of the body.

2 Among the carnivorous centipedes, however, active runners are more common. The body is quite flexible and is usually flattened, and fewer legs (often less than half) touch the ground at any one time. Leg strokes are short and out of phase on each side, causing side-to-side undulations of the body. A wave may involve just seven pairs of legs (or segments). Species in the order Scutigeromorpha have longer rear legs that step over the shorter limbs in front; the last pair of legs may be twice as long as the first pair.

can kill lizards and blind humans; some jungle tribes use millipede extracts as poison on arrowheads. The chemical constituent of the secretions varies between different groups and species, but the range of substances includes the sedative glomerin, a terpenoid smelling of camphor that acts as an irritant, and cyanide.

Centipedes use their poison claws to defend themselves against predators. In addition, geophilomorphs have ventral glands that produce a sticky toxic secretion that is sometimes luminescent. In some lithobiomorphs, the end legs produce a sticky, threadlike protective secretion; in a few species they readily detach and wriggle to distract predators.

Many-legged Mating Systems
REPRODUCTION AND LIFE CYCLE

In most millipedes sperm is transferred from the males to the females by means of specially modified legs (gonopods) that collect the sperm and insert it into the female. In some species the male may have various other structures that help him hold onto the female when they come together for copulation. Mating is stimulated by touch (antennal tapping and leg stroking), pheromones, and sometimes by sound signals (leg stridulations). Most millipedes then either lay their eggs in a prepared nest, made of earth mixed with a secretion produced by glands in the rectum, or else coat each egg with the mixture. One group of millipedes uses silk to make the nest. Usually the eggs are left to hatch on their own.

In centipedes there is a complex courtship ritual that involves tapping with the antennae; a drop of sperm or a spermatophore (packet of sperm) is then deposited on a web, from which it is picked up by the female. Male scutigeromorphs, however, do not produce a web. Lithobiomorphs and scutigeromorphs lay their eggs singly in the soil, but in other groups the female broods the eggs and guards the young until they are able to fend for themselves.

Symphylans have a very special method of mating that resembles that of centipedes in that the sperm transfer is indirect and there is no copulation. The males deposit between 150 and 450 packets of sperm on tall stalks. The female will eat up to 18 of these a day; some are swallowed, but others are stored in a pouch in her mouth. When the female lays her eggs, she places them in her mouth first to transfer the sperm onto them.

Millipedes hatch from their eggs into a legless pupoid stage. The pupa then molts into the first true "stadium" (equivalent to the insects' instar),

◑ **Right** Using his gonopods (modified legs), a male Epibolus pulchripes millipede (Spirostreptida) from Kenya transfers sperm to a female (below). In the course of courtship the male rides on the female's back, nibbling her face.

◁ **Left** *Like many chemically-protected animals, millipedes often seek safety in numbers. These platy-desmids grazing on fungal hyphae on a fallen tree in a Costa Rican rain forest have the flattened bodies and multiple body-rings typical of the order.*

which in most cases has three pairs of legs and no ocelli. The second molt adds more segments and legs, a single ocellus (in non-blind species), and a pair of defense glands. At subsequent molts more segments, legs, ocelli, and defense glands are added. The first active stadium to leave the nest varies between species, but by the third stadium all young millipedes are actively walking and feeding. When molting, millipedes make special chambers into which they can retreat for safety; these refuges may also be used to survive periods of drought. In some millipedes molting will continue until a maximum number of segments is reached, after which growth stops. In others, molting continues after sexual maturity is reached, with more segments and body parts still being added. Some millipedes are annuals, but others may take two, three, or more years to become mature. They may live a surprisingly long time; the common British pill millipede has been known to survive for 11 years.

Lithobiomorphs and scutigeromorphs hatch with less than their full complement of legs and gradually increase the number by a series of molts. Molting continues after the full leg number is attained, and there may be several mature stadia. Geophilomorphs and scolopendromorphs hatch as immobile larvae, but with a full complement of legs. After leaving the brood chamber they pass through several molts to reach maturity in one to several years. In *Craterostigmus*, the female broods the eggs but the larvae do not hatch with the full leg number. HR/JL

The Classes of Millipedes and Centipedes

Millipedes
Class Diplopoda

11,000 species in 14 orders and 2 subclasses; slow-moving herbivores, between 2mm–30cm (0.08–12in) long, with at least 11 leg-bearing segments, all but the first 3 of which are "diplo-segments" with two pairs of legs; 2 pairs of true mouthparts.
SUBCLASS PENICILLATA (1 order): Tiny, with soft cuticle, tufted hairs, and 13–17 pairs of legs. Cryptic, in humus, soils, and crevices.
SUBCLASS CHILOGNATHA (13 orders): Larger forms, with hard cuticle containing calcium salts. Includes the **pill**

millipedes (orders Glomerida and Sphaerotheriida) with 11–12 arched segments, allowing rolling-up; **flat-backed millipedes** (order Polydesmida), with usually 20 trunk segments bearing lateral keels; **snake millipedes** (orders Julida, Spirobolida, and Spirostreptida), with 40 or more segments bearing short legs; in humus, litter, and beneath stones or logs.

Centipedes
Class Chilopoda

3,000 species in 5 orders; active carnivores, mostly 1–6cm (0.4–2.4in) long, with at least 15 leg-bearing segments (always an odd number), 3 pairs of true

mouthparts, and large poison claws (first pair of "legs").
Order **Geophilomorpha**: Long, thread-like, soil-dwelling burrowers with 27–191 pairs of short legs.
Order **Scolopendromorpha**: Flattened burrowers or crevice-dwellers, with 21–23 pairs of legs.
Order **Craterostigmomorpha**: Flattened crevice-dwellers with 15 pairs of legs but 21 dorsal plates. 1 or 2 species confined to Tasmania and New Zealand.
Order **Lithobiomorpha**: Flattened crevice-dwellers with 15 pairs of legs.
Order **Scutigeromorpha**: Fast runners with 15 pairs of legs; in varied habitats.

Symphylans
Class Symphyla

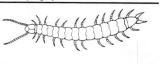

200 species of small, pale herbivores, 2–10mm (0.08–0.4in) long, with 12 leg-bearing segments (but extra tergites or back plates) and 3 pairs of mouthparts resembling those of insects; eyeless. Not common. In soil and leaf mould, under stones, in rotting wood.

Pauropods
Class Pauropoda

700 species of tiny, soft-bodied scavengers, 0.5–2mm (0.02–0.08in) long, with 9 leg-bearing segments (but fewer tergites), 2 pairs of mouthparts, branched antennae; whitish in coloration; eyeless. Not common. In soil and leaf mold.

INSECTS

IF ARTHROPODS ARE THE SUCCESS STORY OF *the planet, then pride of place among them must go to the insects. While nearly a million species have been described, several million more await discovery. About 7,000 new insect species are described every year, but this figure is probably exceeded by the annual losses of unknown species that result from the destruction of habitats, mainly tropical forests.*

Most authorities now agree that the wingless Collembola (the springtails), Protura, and Diplura are not insects; they are best viewed as separate classes within a superclass (Hexapoda) of the phylum Uniramia (see Hexapods Other Than Insects). Hexapods are distinguished from the much less numerous myriapods (centipedes and millipedes) by having bodies divided into three distinct regions (head, thorax, and abdomen), the presence of six legs (hence "hexapod") on the three-segmented thorax, and the possession of a tracheal system.

The insects themselves are divided into the small, wingless subclass Apterygota (archaeognathans and bristletails), and the winged Pterygota, which comprises the other 99.9 percent of known insect species. The wings are borne on the second and third thoracic segments, which are often fused together to form a rigid box that withstands the mechanical forces exerted in flight.

There are several theories about the origins of insects, but it is likely that they evolved from myriapods, and that their immediate ancestors resembled symphylans. Besides the arthropod

HEXAPODS OTHER THAN INSECTS

Three groups of hexapods are distinguished from insects in having their mouthparts enclosed (entognathous) within a cavity formed by the sides of the head fused to the labium. Most, unlike insects, have muscles in their antennae, and none can fly. Representatives of all three classes bear appendages on at least some segments of the abdomen.

The **proturans** (class Protura) **1** are minute, white animals, usually less than 2mm (0.08in) long, that live in soil. They have no antennae, but the forelegs function for sensory purposes, while the mid- and hindlegs are used for locomotion. The legs have five joints, and there is a single process (telson) at the tip of the abdomen. Their tracheal respiratory system is simplified, and some species possess only a single pair of spiracles. Segments are added to their body as they mature. Proturans are retiring animals and not much is known of their biology, although they occur widely. They have sucking mouthparts and feed mainly on fungi. There are some 70 species in 7 or 8 genera, including *Acerentomon* and *Protapteron*.

The **diplurans** or two-pronged bristletails (class Diplura) **2** number about 400 species, some of which are widespread and common. *Campodea* reaches a length of 7mm (0.3in), but *Heterojapax*

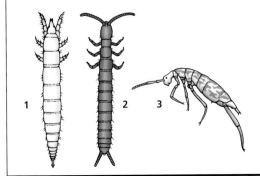

can be up to 50mm (2in) long and has its cerci modified as prey-catching pincers; the biting mouthparts are reduced. Diplurans live in damp places under logs or stones, and appear to be blind. They have a tracheal system usually with two or four spiracles, but up to 11 pairs in *Heterojapax*. The antennae and (usually) the cerci are long, and there may be rudimentary abdominal legs in addition to the three pairs of five-jointed thoracic legs. The male places his sperm in a stalked packet on the ground and the female then picks this up.

Worldwide, more than 2,000 species of **collembolans** (class Collembola) **3** occur in concealed, damp places and on the surface of ponds. They are usually less than 3mm and never more than 5mm (0.1–0.2in) long. In addition to the six four-segmented legs of the thorax, most species bear on the fourth abdominal segment a forked tail, which, when released by an appendage on segment three, springs downward, causing the insect to leap up – hence their alternative name of "springtail."

Springtails eat decomposing organic matter, and many also feed on living plants, using their biting mouthparts. Some collembolans are serious pests of sugarcane, tobacco, or mushrooms, and one common species feeds on duckweed; others feed on pollen, fungi, bacteria, or algae. They are often very abundant – for example, almost 2.5 million individuals may occur in 1ha (2.5 acres) of meadow, and some soils contain 2,000 per liter. They may suddenly appear in vast numbers on snowfields, where they may look like soot. Some construct elaborate chambers from their own fecal material, which they occupy in times of drought.

Most collembolans have a tracheal system with a single pair of spiracles, and there are two groups of up to eight simple eyes (ocelli) on the head. Genera include *Achorutes, Anurida,* and *Smithnurus*.

exoskeleton, the main features of early insects included mouthparts not enclosed in a cavity (ectognathous), a hypognathous head (with the mouthparts facing downward), one pair of antennae with muscles only at the base, six legs with more than five segments, a thorax with three and an abdomen with 11 segments (one or more usually fused), and a genital opening (gonopore) on the eighth abdominal segment of the female and the ninth segment of the male. All of these features distinguish insects from other hexapods.

The Many Uses of Cuticle
BODY COMPOSITION

The success and great diversity of insects depend on a number of key features, including: adaptations to prevent or withstand desiccation; fast,

INSECTS

○ *Above* As in all insects, this warningly colored leaf-footed bug (Laminiceps sp.; Coreidae) from Argentina has six legs, each with more than five segments. In common with most insects, but in contrast to other terrestrial arthropods, this bug also has wings.

maneuverable flight, which may be sustained for long periods; and a usually short life cycle that includes metamorphosis, a high reproductive rate, and the capacity to survive unfavorable seasons. The cooperation between individuals of the social termites, ants, wasps, and bees is a major contribution to the success of these groups.

Modern insects have been able to radiate into a very great number of terrestrial habitats largely as a result of their characteristic combination of a waterproof cuticle and a respiratory system of valved tracheae. So important and versatile is cuticle that the adaptive radiation of insects can be viewed as the radiation of the cuticle and the structures it forms, not least the exoskeleton that is typical of all arthropods. It varies from being very hard in claws and mandibles to soft and pliant in leg joints, intersegmental membranes, and, within the insect, in the linings of the tracheal system, the fore- and hindguts, parts of the genital system, and the ducts of skin glands. Although increase in an insect's size is normally limited to a short period just after a molt, caterpillars and other soft larvae can increase in length between molts. Even some adult insects can enlarge: the abdomen of a queen termite may elongate 10 times after she has founded a nest and raised an initial brood of workers.

Cuticle forms the many types of hair, bristle, and scale that adorn the external surfaces of insects, and that are responsible for such features as the exquisite colors of butterflies' wings, the furry coats of bees, and the protective spines of beetles. It also forms many types of sensory structure, including the lenses of eyes, the tympanic membranes of ears, and the perforated hairs that serve for olfaction and taste.

Cuticle can be elastic and rubbery so as to store and release energy for jumping or to assist in flapping the wings. This rubbery cuticle is made from a special protein, resilin. In addition to providing the exoskeleton, cuticle may also form an extensive endoskeleton, particularly in larger insects, providing sites for the attachment of jaw or body muscles, bracing thoracic walls internally, and forming long, tendonlike apodemes for the remote control of tarsi or claws.

Letting In Air
RESPIRATORY SYSTEMS
Like other arthropods, insects breathe by means of air-filled, cuticle-lined tubes that ramify throughout the body and open to the outside, usually in insects through 10 pairs of spiracles

positioned along the sides, each controlled by a small valve. The main tubes (tracheae) that open to the exterior give rise to myriads of smaller, blind-ending tracheoles tapering to less than 0.1mm (0.004in) in diameter. The terminal portions of tracheoles may contain a liquid, sucked into the tubes from surrounding tissues by capillarity: the liquid retreats toward the tip when the tissues become active as a result of changing osmotic pressure or pH.

The tracheal system can both meet the very high oxygen demands necessitated by flight and also minimize water loss during periods of inactivity. In flight, some insects burn more than 0.1 liters of oxygen per gram of body weight per hour (100l/kg/h), a higher metabolic rate than occurs in any other multicellular organism. Air sacs and tracheae are very abundant in the thorax, which automatically ventilates itself as a result of the wing movements; in the locust, for example, it exchanges about 20ml (0.002cc) of air with each stroke. Some large beetles have in addition two pairs of giant tracheae in the thorax through which air is ducted in flight: their presence not only helps to supply oxygen but also cools the thorax, as in an air-cooled engine.

Tracheal systems function well in aquatic environments, allowing insects either to depend on dissolved oxygen through the use of gills or to acquire it at the water surface, allowing them to exploit anaerobic habitats. Modified tracheae also serve as reflecting tapeta behind the eyes, as sound resonators, as heat insulators, and even as buoyancy tanks in some freshwater species.

Mates and Metamorphoses
REPRODUCTION AND DEVELOPMENT
The metamorphosis, complete or incomplete, that is characteristic of most insects allows the adult to act primarily as a reproductive and dispersal stage, whereas the larva is a development and feeding stage. It also allows larva and adult to exploit very different habitats and sources of food.

Although parthenogenesis (asexual reproduction) occurs in a few insects, most reproduce sexually. Early terrestrial arthropod males protected their sperm in a special covering, the spermatophore, which was deposited on the ground and taken up by the female. Some primitive hexapods (for instance Collembola or Diplura species) still use this method. In those modern insects that continue to use a spermatophore, however, the

◑ **Left and above** *These moth caterpillars clustered together on a tree in Madagascar belong to the order Lepidoptera, one of the more advanced insect orders exhibiting holometabolous development. Many moth caterpillars pupate within a silken cocoon. Butterfly pupae are generally placed in the open, fixed to a firm substrate such as a tree trunk; the Papilio pupa shown above is supported head upward by a silken girdle.*

◑ **Above right** *As in all holometabolous insects, the larvae and adults of neuropterans are quite dissimilar in appearance. The extremely flattened, wingless body and huge, sickle-shaped jaws of this antlion larva are quite different from the slender, small-jawed, fully-winged adult.*

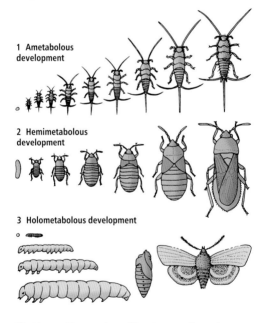

1 Ametabolous development

2 Hemimetabolous development

3 Holometabolous development

◑ **Above** *The number of larval stages (instars) ranges from 33 in some stoneflies to the five molts common in advanced orders. 1 Ametabolous development: in primitive insects such as silverfish; there is little change between first stage and adult. 2 Hemimetabolous development: the larva (nymph) of exopterygote insects such as bugs resembles a miniature, wingless adult; as it grows, the wings develop externally. 3 Holometabolous development: more advanced insects go through a complete metamorphosis – the larva undergoes a pupal stage before an adult (imago) emerges that may be quite different in form, habitat and feeding habits. Internally developing (endopterygote) wing buds occur in the later larval stages.*

male places it within the female. Females produce eggs either in one large batch or in a succession of clutches, and they may mate again between clutches. In some cockroaches the eggs hatch within the female and emerge as first-stage larvae; in the tsetse fly a single larva develops within the female, emerges when fully grown, and pupates immediately; in the live-born female Black bean aphid, embryos are already developing, parthenogenesis and telescoping of generations combining to produce a very high rate of population growth.

In some species the sexes encounter each other at feeding or egg-laying sites. Dung flies may meet on dung, tsetse flies on mammals, dragonflies by the waterside. Other species use landmarks such as hilltops, bushes, or trees to rendezvous with the opposite sex. Large, smokelike swarms of midges over church towers have even resulted in calls for the fire department! In parts of East Africa, where lake flies swarm in thousands of millions, they are gathered, compressed into cakes,

◑ **Above** *In hemimetabolous development, the nymph looks much like a small version of the adult, but without wings. Here the adult of a Venustria superba cicada (Cicadidae) from Australia is seen emerging from a large split in the nymphal skin.*

and eaten by the local people. The sexes of many species "call" to each other to mate. Fireflies flash their lanterns, cicadas, crickets, and grasshoppers stridulate noisily, deathwatch beetles tap out their own version of the Morse code, and many moths release pheromones.

Courtship, widespread in insects, can be a prolonged and complex sequence of activities. It may be more important for allowing the female to assess the "fitness" of a male than for ensuring correct species and sexual identification between the pair. Courting males may display prominent colored wings or other structures; or they may sing, perform courtship dance flights, or release chemicals. Males also compete for females by fighting; some horned beetle males, for example, will try to overturn a rival, and such battles can lead to the death of the loser. In most species conflicts are ritualized, and males may be able to assess the size or strength of a rival while displaying, without resorting to physical contact.

A male sometimes guards a female before copulation, waiting until she becomes ready to mate. He may continue to guard her afterward while she lays eggs, thus ensuring his paternity, for a male's sperm may be displaced by that of a male that mates subsequently. Alternatively, a male may insert a plug into the female, or inject a chemical that renders her unattractive or unreceptive to other males.

Data Processors
NERVOUS SYSTEMS

The insect head contains a brain and a subesophagal ganglion, each formed from the fusion of three or more primitive ganglia. Fusion also occurs among thoracic and abdominal ganglia. Fusion probably allows incoming information to be integrated more rapidly, and may economize on the number of neurones (nerve cells) required.

The brain of some species contains over a million neurones, most of which (97 percent in some flies) analyze information from the eyes and antennae. A pair of mushroom-shaped bodies in the front part (protocerebrum) contains an abundance of tiny neurones, and this region may not only integrate input from sense organs but also initiate some behavior patterns. In bees and other social insects, whose mushroom bodies are much larger than in solitary species, it may also act as a storehouse for memories.

The most striking features of insect nervous systems are the relatively small numbers of neurones available for the complex behavior insects show, the high degree of specificity and individuality of neurones, and their structural complexity, with branching processes (dendrites) sometimes spreading across half a ganglion, allowing interaction with hundreds of other neurones.

Most sensory neurones are closely associated with minute cuticular structures, upon which they depend for their functioning. Among these are mechanoreceptors including hairs, bristles, deformable caps (or campaniform sensillae), and tympanic membranes sensitive to sound waves. Some mechanoreceptors respond to strains within the cuticle or to stretch across joints arising from movement of the insect itself.

Bug Eyes and Chemoreceptors
SENSES

Insects are exceptionally well endowed with visual organs, whose responsiveness extends well into the ultraviolet, to which humans are blind. Many insects locate food, mates, rivals, nests, egg-laying sites, and predators visually, and they may be able to learn the geography of their neighborhood.

The eyes, which may occupy much of the surface of the head, can provide all-round vision, color discrimination, high acuity (in other words, resolution of fine details), and good sensitivity (ability to see at night), as well as functioning well at different light intensities. Many species can also detect the plane of polarized light – useful for orientation – while in others the overlapping fields of vision of widely separated eyes give good stereoscopic vision and the ability to judge distances. In addition, most flying insects have three small simple eyes (ocelli) near the top of the head, each with a single lens. These provide a highly sensitive and fast-reacting system that helps the insect to preserve stability in flight.

More difficult for us to appreciate is the insect world of scents and tastes. Insects also respond to gravity, to the earth's magnetic field, to temperature and humidity. Furthermore, while vision is the prime sensory system of some species, chemoreception is dominant in others. Chemoreceptors are located mainly on the antennae, mouth-parts, feet, and in some cases on the egg-laying tube (ovipositor). Insects may taste food with tarsal receptors, or smell it at a distance with receptors on the antennae. Chemicals (pheromones) released by members of some species are also detected by the antennae, sometimes at very low concentrations.

Multiple Niches
HABITAT AND ENVIRONMENT

Adult insects range in length from less than 0.2mm (0.08in) in tiny parasitic wasps – smaller than some protozoans – to over 30cm (12in) in some stick insects; the largest insects reach weights of 70g (2.5oz). The question arises why no modern species exceed this size, since much larger species did occur 30 million years ago. The explanation may be that niches for larger species are now occupied by more successful vertebrates such as birds. But if insects are limited in size, they are not limited in the diversity of habitats that they successfully colonize, nor in the multitude of ways of life they exemplify.

By perfecting a waterproof cuticle and by the development of valved spiracles, insects have been

able to colonize dry terrestrial habitats including both very hot and very cold regions. Relatives of crickets can be found living very actively in snow, while various beetles and cockroaches colonize the hot sands of deserts. Many other insects survive adverse periods by hibernation or estivation, sometimes in the egg or pupal stage and sometimes as inactive larvae or adults. Frost resistance may be improved by the addition of anti-freezes such as glycerol, while dry seasons can be overcome by burrowing and remaining inactive, or, as in the case of larvae of the African chironomid midge *Polypedilum vanderplancki*, by allowing the tissues to dry out completely. These remarkable larvae can revive quickly when placed in water after years in a dry cryptobiotic state.

Flies, including midges and several other orders, have become secondarily aquatic as larvae and even in the adult stages of some species, inhabiting a variety of freshwater habitats. In addition, thanks to rapid dispersal and a short generation time, many insects are also adept at exploiting newly-formed habitats, such as those created by retreating glaciers, volcanic eruptions, earthquakes, or fires.

Eating Up the Scraps
DIET AND DIGESTION

Evolution of the ability to fly has enabled insects to reach small and scattered habitats, such as piles of dung, dead carcasses, or rare plants, where they can feed and lay eggs. Every part of higher plants may be consumed by some insect, including roots (by cicadas), stems (stem borers), trunks (timber beetles), leaves (moth larvae), flowers (butterfly larvae), fruit (tephritid flies), and seeds (bruchid

⬗ **Above** *With its large, widely spaced eyes, this Large red damselfly (Pyrrhosoma nymphula; Coenagriidae) enjoys excellent stereoscopic vision and a fine ability to judge distance, enabling it to catch other insects on the wing.*

⬗ **Right** *Insects are well adapted to the habitat niches that they occupy. Camouflaged by their highly cryptic coloration, these Acanthodis aquilina katydid nymphs (Tettigoniidae) blend imperceptibly into the trunk of a tree in the Peruvian rain forest.*

beetles). Other insects specialize in feeding on conifers (spruce budworm), ferns (sawflies), cycads, mosses (some lycaenid beetle larvae), algae and lichens, fungi (termites), and bacteria.

The breakdown of intractable animal or plant material may be carried out either by internal gut symbionts or by the cultivation of external fungal gardens (as in the case of ants and termites). Although many plants produce an assemblage of toxic chemicals with which to deter herbivores, or are armed with thick cuticles, spines, prickles, and viscous fluids, there always seems to be at least one insect species that has overcome their defenses and that may thereby have gained exclusive grazing rights. Sometimes the plant toxins are taken over by insects for their own defenses, as in the case of burnet moths. Even the parasites of such insects may in turn utilize the same toxins.

While some insects feed on plants, others devour animal products such as hoof, horn, skin, hair, feathers, scales, wax, or dung. Parasites, many of which have lost the wings of their ancestors, may specialize on certain tissues such as blood, while predators normally consume the greater part of their prey.   PLM/CO'T

THE POWER OF FLIGHT

A major factor in the success of insects

ANYONE CAUGHT IN A SWARM OF BITING MIDGES is acutely aware of the flying abilities of insects. And the frustrated householder, failing yet again to swat that annoying bluebottle, may stop to ponder on the aerobatic skills that enable the elusive quarry to land upside-down on the ceiling.

There is no doubt that flying dominates the adult life of most insects. It allows them to exploit otherwise inaccessible habitats, to colonize islands, and to be highly active in a three-dimensional world. The ability to fly evolved early in the Carboniferous period, 354–295 million years ago. One theory is that early large insects glided on fixed side-extensions of the body, which then came to be twisted for greater control, and finally to be flapped. Another suggestion is that wings evolved in smaller species from the use of structures already flapped for other functions, such as gills for ventilation or extensions of the thorax for sexual signaling. Flight probably arose only once, and it made use of muscles whose equivalents can in the main be identified in the flightless bristletails of the order Thysanura.

Several trends mark the evolution in flying insects toward greater speed and maneuverability. The originally netlike wing venation became simplified, with fewer of the corrugations or flutes that gave longitudinal stiffness to the wings. A single pair of beating structures evolved, either by the coupling of the two wings on one side, or by a reduction in the size of one pair of wings to form either wing shields (as, for instance, in earwigs and beetles) or else the balancing organs known as halteres (as in dipteran flies). Power-producing muscles came to be distinct from controlling muscles, whereas both functions had primitively been carried out by the same muscles (as in dragonflies). There has also been a tendency toward a shorter and thicker body, with a consequent reduction of inherent stability but a great increase in maneuverability. Finally, success in flight owes much to the development of a specialized type of wing muscle that is able to contract at much higher rates than is normal for other muscle – for example, at up to 1,000 times a second in some small flies.

The form of a wing stroke is complex. The leading edge of the wing is tilted down during the down stroke and up during the upstroke. In flies, wing-twisting at each end of the stroke is automatic, but the degree of twisting can be adjusted by small muscles. In all but the most primitive insects, much of the power is developed indirectly by muscles that act on the plates (sclerites) of the cuticle exoskeleton of the thorax.

The wingbeats are assisted, first, by hinges of a rubbery protein called resilin, which cause the wings to bounce at the top and bottom of the strokes; second, by elasticity resulting from a click mechanism that makes the wings unstable at about the mid-position (like a light switch); and, third, by elasticity within the muscles themselves. Power can be raised by increasing the amount of wing twist and by increasing the beat frequency. Turns in flight are achieved usually by altering the amplitude or twist on one side, and they may be aided, as in locusts, by using the long abdomen or legs as rudders.

Some insects can hover, using a helicopterlike stroke with the body nearly vertical and the wings turning over on the upstroke. Other species clap the wings together at the top and then separate the leading edges, so causing the circulation of the air vortices upon which lift depends. Dragonflies, hoverflies, and some wasps hover with the body horizontal, using a shallow stroke whose aerodynamics are not yet fully understood.

In terms of energy costs for distance traveled, flight may be relatively cheap, perhaps cheaper than walking or running. However, in cost per unit of time it is expensive, particularly during hovering when heavy loads are carried (as in the case of wasps carrying prey), or at very high speeds – some insects may fly at up to 20m (65ft) a second (72km/h, or 45mph). Bees may have a power output of 150 watts per kilogram (0.15w/g), and hence flight muscles are furnished with a very efficient system for supplying oxygen. Adequate fuel supplies are ensured by having high concentrations of carbohydrates in the haemolymph and by using hormones to boost fuel mobilization.

⬤ **Right** *A colony of Monarch butterflies (Danaus plexippus) takes to the air from a wintering ground in Mexico. The species is famous for its migrations; some Monarchs from Mexico fly as far as Canada.*

⬤ **Below** *Mechanism of the basic wing stroke in a stylized neopteran insect. On the upstroke **1** the vertical dorso-ventral muscles pull down the tergum, raising the wings: the thoracic box is lengthened, stretching the horizontal muscles. **2** When these contract, the tergum is moved up, pushing the wings into the down stroke. These indirect flight muscles are supplemented in some insects by muscles that vary the slope or pitch of the wings.*

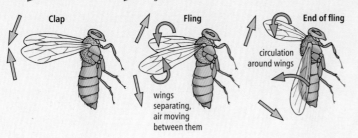

→ air movements   → wing movements

Clap   **Fling**   **End of fling**

circulation around wings

wings separating, air moving between them

⬤ **Left** *Some hovering insects use a clap-and-fling technique to create the air vortices that generate uplift. The circulation of air around the wings as they separate following the clap gives enhanced lift.*

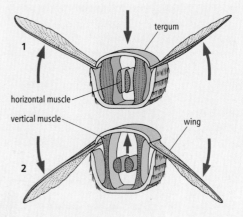

tergum

horizontal muscle

vertical muscle

wing

1

2

The high rate of energy use in flying produces considerable heat, which may be quickly dissipated in small species but which accumulates in large ones. Flight muscles are adapted to working at temperatures of up to 40°C (104°F), and many insects have to warm them up, by basking in the sun or by shivering, before take-off is possible. Bumblebees have a more sophisticated mechanism: they are warm-blooded and generate heat chemically to reach the threshold temperature for flight. This factor is particularly important in getting started on a cold morning.

Once in flight, some species can avoid overheating by shunting hot blood from the thorax into the abdomen, which operates, therefore, rather like a car's radiator. In species that lack this mechanism, flight may be confined to cool periods such as the night. Daytime fliers, such as butterflies, dragonflies, and locusts, may both save energy and prevent overheating by making glides between intermittent wing flaps, and they often have an

expanded posterior lobe of the hindwing that assists gliding.

Flying insects must have mechanisms that counter tendencies to roll, pitch, or yaw, yet allow maneuverability. Sense organs that help to preserve stability include the compound eyes and ocelli, and various mechanoreceptors on the antennae, head, wings, and the cerci at the tip of the abdomen. Many cup-shaped campaniform sensilla occur on the club-shaped halteres of flies, organs that act like gyroscopes registering deviations in all three planes. Scale insects and strepsipterans may use a similar mechanism in their reduced forewings.

Wing design in insects is, therefore, a mix of compromises. Wings must be sufficiently light to keep the inertial load on the muscles at sustainable levels. At the same time, they must be robust enough not only to withstand aerodynamic forces but to support the weight of the body and any additional loads, such as prey or pollen. They also

need to combine structural strength with flexibility. The fact that the mechanisms of insect flight and their associated physiology are so finely tuned is a tribute to the power of natural selection to drive the evolution of complex, functional wholes.

Many insect orders have flightless species, and a few have become entirely flightless, among them the fleas. Flight comes at a high cost, both to develop for pre-adult stages and in terms of energy expended in adults, and is quickly selected out when no longer valuable. Insects that have lost the power of flight include those that have become aquatic, those that burrow and have deformable bodies, parasites on vertebrate hosts, and inhabitants of small islands, where winds endanger flying forms. In other insects, flight may be limited to a certain phase of adult life, after which the flight muscles may atrophy and the wings be discarded (as in termites); or some generations may fly and others be flightless according to season (as is the case with some water bugs and aphids).　　CO'T

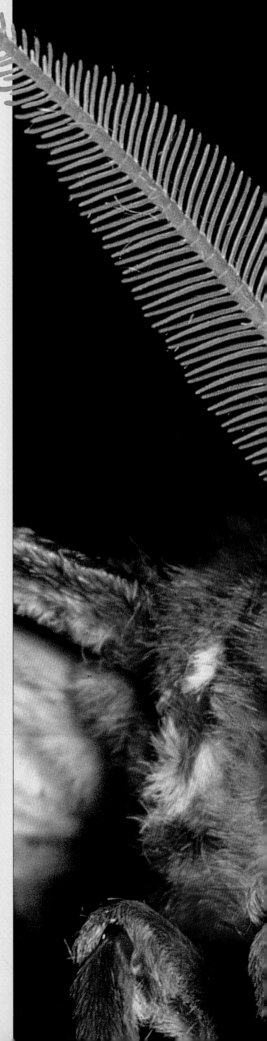

PHEROMONES

Chemical messengers between individuals of a species

PHEROMONES ARE NATURAL CHEMICALS USED
for communication between members of a
species. An alternative name is semiochemicals
("signal-chemicals"). Chemical communication
evolved early in the history of life, and pheromones
are important for almost all kinds of animals, but
they are particularly spectacularly developed, and
best understood, among insects.

The functions of the chemical messages sent
between insects range from the attraction of
mates (sex pheromones), attracting other members of the species (aggregation pheromones),
warning of danger (alarm pheromones), marking
after laying eggs (marking pheromones), or laying
a trail to follow (trail pheromones). All these classes of pheromones trigger, or "release," an immediate response from the receiver. Still others, known
as "primer pheromones," act on the receiver's
physiology, leading to a slower and more profound change, such as maturing into an adult.

Insect pheromones tend to be specific mixtures
of relatively common chemicals, with the precise
quantities of ingredients differing between
species. The ratio between the parts of the mixture
must be within a few percentage points of the
norm if there is to be a response. Periplanone, the
sex pheromone of the American cockroach *Periplaneta americana*, is a rare example of a unique
and complex chemical structure.

Insect pheromone systems have become so
finely tuned through evolution that their components are synthesized to a high degree of chemical
purity. Moreover, different geometric configura-
tions of the same molecule (isomers) can evoke
very different behavior patterns, so that discrimination between these molecules must occur at the
molecular level, whether in the antennae or the
central nervous system.

Pheromones evolve their communication function from the chemicals found naturally in the
environment, and frequently appear to be comprised of molecules (or, more often, sets of molecules) that originally served other, related
functions. For example, many of the chemicals
now used by ants and bees as alarm pheromones
are derived from, or similar to, chemicals used by
these species to defend themselves from predators. Thus, when an ants' nest is being attacked,
these chemicals are in the air. If other ants in the
nest can respond to these warnings and mount a
more successful defense, then these chemicals will,
over time, evolve an alarm pheromone function.

In most insect species, the pheromones are synthesized by the animal from compounds found in
its diet. In others, such as certain species of tropical bees, the males must collect their sex
pheromones from particular flowers; without
these collected chemicals the males cannot attract
females. As a caterpillar, the North American tiger
moth *Utethesia ornatrix* stores defensive poisons

⟁ **Below** *In Nepal, a newly-emerged female*
Odontotermes obsus *termite adopts a special
"calling" stance during which the wings are flapped
vigorously in order to disseminate a pheromone that
will attract males.*

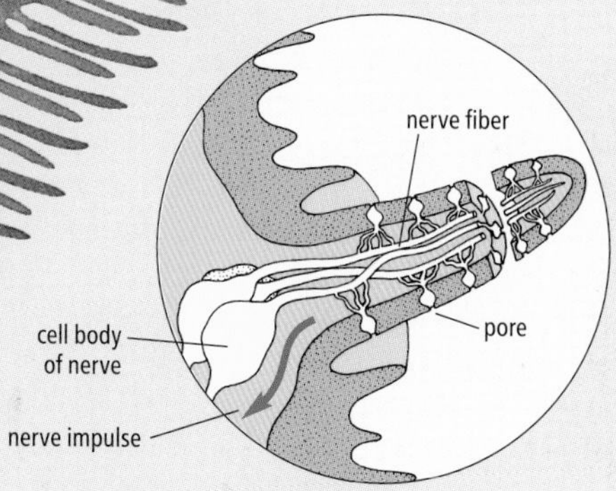

◁ Left and above *The antennae of some male giant saturniid moths like this* Attacus atlas *from Southeast Asia are finely branched, increasing the surface area and enhancing efficiency. Pheromones are detected through the olfactory sensillae (above), cuticular pegs or hairs on the antennae that contain sensory nerve fibers transmitting impulses to the central nervous system. The chemicals penetrate the thin walls of the sensillae through pores in their surface.*

from its poisonous host plant, a milkweed. Males convert some of the poison into a pheromone. Females use the pheromone in mate selection, choosing the male with the most poison (which he will transfer to her at mating, and which she will use to protect her eggs), as the concentration of the male's pheromone is proportional to his protective toxic load.

The characteristics of pheromones can often be related to their function. Alarm pheromones, which need to spread their message quickly and then fade away once the danger is gone, tend to be composed of smaller, more volatile molecules. Sex pheromones also tend to be volatile, but the molecules are larger (heavier) than in alarm pheromones. In marking trails, ants use short-lived, volatile chemicals to indicate temporary routes to food that will soon be used up, but long-lived, less volatile compounds to designate almost permanent "highways."

A male moth can locate a female of its own species "calling" with a sex pheromone from an impressive distance upwind, perhaps even from kilometers away. The males detect the pheromone with their antennae, the insect "nose." The males compete to be the first to reach the female, and this competition has led to the evolution, over millions of years, of extraordinary antennae, covered with thousands of pheromone-sensitive sensory hairs. The hairs trap the vanishingly small quantities of pheromone in the wind; nerve cells in the hairs then send the signal to a finely-tuned brain, large parts of which are specialized to respond to

Continued overleaf ▷

31

pheromone signals. The male responds to the transient signal millisecond by millisecond, flying upwind each time it identifies the right pheromone but zigzagging from side to side if it loses contact. This behavior leads it to the female.

Insect behavior is typically very stereotyped or programmed. A female moth may release a pheromone only for one or two hours each night, and the males may respond over a similarly narrow time period. The behavior of the two sexes may therefore be synchronous, but each is often controlled independently by outside stimuli, such as temperature or light. If a male moth encounters a female sex pheromone outside the appropriate response period, no response will be triggered even if it is at the optimum concentration.

The social insects – ants, bees, and wasps – use pheromones to coordinate almost every aspect of their complex social behaviors. Remarkably, termites (which are more closely related to cockroaches than to the Hymenoptera) have independently evolved very similar behavior and use of pheromones.

Many of the pheromones used by social insects are detected at a distance in the same way as female moth sex pheromones, but one important class – those used for colony recognition – are detected by contact, when one ant taps another with its antennae. These contact pheromones take the form of chemicals in the cuticular coating on the surface of the animal. Such chemical cues are used to recognize fellow nest-mates – a necessary step as members of different colonies of the same species frequently fight on contact.

The pheromones for colony recognition are in

◁ **Left** *Some insects derive their pheromones at second hand from plants. This Soldier butterfly (Danaus gilippus nivosus; Danaidae) in Peru is feeding on the remains of a heliotrope plant. Heliotropes are a favored source of pyrrolizidine alkaloid precursors.*

part produced by the individual itself and in part derived from the secretions of other individuals in the colony. All the different stages of the social insect life cycle can also be recognized by pheromone, such that old and young larvae, adults and larvae, and males and females can all be distinguished by colony members.

Complex behavior such as the foraging activities of 500,000 Blind army ants (*Eciton burchelli*) sweeping through the South American rainforest may be explained in terms of simple responses by individual ants to pheromone trails. It can be modelled mechanically by laying down and following pheromone trails while applying simple sets of rules. Similarly, despite being tiny and blind, termites use these kinds of responses to build complex mounds tens of meters high.

The same pheromone may have both releaser and primer effects in different contexts. For example, the queen mandibular pheromone of the honey bee *Apis mellifera* acts as a sex-attractant releaser to attract mates. For the majority of the queen's life, however, the pheromone acts instead as a primer pheromone acting on the physiology of her workers. The queen bee's pheromone

appears to signal to the workers that she is well and producing eggs. So long as the queen pheromone is present, workers remain sterile and do not produce their own eggs; but as soon as the workers detect that the queen is not producing the pheromone (for example, if she dies) they will immediately start to rear one of the young larvae as a new queen. Interestingly, the queen pheromone is passed from worker to worker by mouth. Pheromones may have some role in the alteration of solitary migratory locusts into the gregarious or plague form.

Eavesdropping and Deception

Pheromone communication is so powerful and important in the insect world that many kinds of animals and plants have evolved ways of exploiting it. Chemical messages may be eavesdropped; alternatively, messages may be counterfeited for deception or propaganda purposes.

Broadcast messages can be "overheard" by predators and parasites. For example, some bark beetle species use aggregation pheromones to attract enough members of their species to overcome the defenses of live trees. However, some insect predators are as sensitive to bark beetle aggregation pheromones as the bark beetles themselves. By announcing themselves to the world, the bark beetles thus make themselves vulnerable to these predators.

Pheromones can also be used for deception. Certain orchids rely on a particular species of solitary bee or wasp for pollination. The orchid flower looks and smells just like a female insect, with exactly the same pheromone as a real female. Male

the stingless bee *Trigona* – by releasing massive quantities of the prey species' alarm pheromone and, in the ensuing confusion, carrying back stolen honey and pollen.

Putting Pheromones to Use

Pheromones offer a powerful way to manipulate the behavior of insect pests, and thus have an important role to play in pest control. Pheromone-baited traps may be used to detect and monitor the populations of pest insects, enabling control measures to be deployed more effectively. This technique has been widely use with stored-grain-eating beetles such as *Prostephanus truncatus*, which is now sweeping across Africa after having been introduced from Central America. Similarly, a honey-bee pheromone is used to detect the spread of the Africanized honey bee across the USA. In crops, conventional pesticide spraying can be limited, or timed, to periods when the pest is actually present, as shown by trap catches.

More directly, the mass application of synthetic pheromones can be used to prevent male and female pest insects from finding each other, thereby reducing the next generation of caterpillars. This approach has been effective in controlling populations of the Pink bollworm moth, *Pectinophora gossypiella*, on cotton in the USA, Egypt, and Pakistan. Mating disruption is also showing great success in controlling the Tomato pin worm moth *Keiferia lycopersicella* without killing its natural enemies, such as spiders and parasites, which control other potential pests. Thus, pheromones offer the exciting prospect of highly specific, "greener" methods of control.

TDW

◐ Above *The brilliant metallic male* Euglossa *orchid bees (Apidae) from Central and South America collect naturally occurring scents from specific orchids. They use these in modified form, applying them as territorial markers, usually in rainforest light-gaps.*

◑ Below *By laying down and following a specific trail-pheromone, these blind army ants (Eciton burchelli; Formicidae) in Trinidad are able to keep to a relatively narrow pathway through the rain forest. Gaps are spanned using "bridges" made of ants.*

bees are fooled into trying to mate with the flower, picking up pollen in the process and transferring it to another orchid of the same species the next time that the bee is fooled.

Deception is also carried out by ant-nest "guests" such as beetles and some specialized species of butterfly, notably lycaenids. By stealth adoption of the colony odor, or, in the most advanced cases, synthesis of the ants' chemical signature, these guests fool the nest guards. Once inside, they parasitize the nest, even eating the young ant larvae. Similarly, South American robber bees such as *Lestrimelitta limao* use pheromone "propaganda" to overcome their prey – species of

MIMICRY: DEFENSE THROUGH PRETENSE

1 *Mimicry, by which non-noxious species evolve to resemble noxious ones in order to deter predators, is widespread in insects. One remarkable example occurs in the* Scaphura *katydids (Tettigoniidae) from South America, which closely echo the appearance and behavior of large pompilid wasps on the prowl. The resemblance extends to adopting a jerky, wasplike gait, with the abdomen curved down and the wings partly raised.*

2 *The Bee beetle (*Trichius fasciatus*) from Europe is a convincing mimic of a number of large, furry bumblebees of the genus* Bombus. *The beetle flies with a loud, beelike buzz and feeds openly on flowers.*

3 *Mimicry of various kinds of wasps, both social and parasitic, occurs widely in the clearwing moths in the family Sesiidae. This is* Felderolia canescens *from South Africa, a highly credible mimic of a polistine paper wasp. Like their models, the sesiid moths are active in daytime and move in an abrupt, jerky manner.*

5

4

⑤ *The first-instar nymphs of various tropical orthopteroid species – mantids, katydids, and crickets among them – are convincing mimics of ants. In mantids such as these African* Polyspilota aeruginosa, *the young, antlike nymphs gather on or near the oothecae from which they emerged. Ant mimicry often continues into the second instar, but is usually lost by the third because of the increasing size and changing shape of the larvae.*

6

❹ *The treehopper* Heteronotus reticulatus *(Membracidae) from the Neotropics is one of a number of species in which elaborate rearward extensions of the pronotum enable the bug to become a back-to-front mimic of an ant sitting with its jaws agape. Ant mimics benefit from their models' reputation among predators as distasteful prey with a fearsome array of defenses that include biting, stinging, and spraying formic acid.*

❻ *Like insects spiders often display mimicry, and the parallel even extends to exhibiting back-to-front simulation of ants, as shown here in a southeast Asian jumping spider* (Orsima ichneumon; *Salticidae). Unlike the stationary treehopper, however, the spider is constantly on the move, bobbing its abdomen, which bears a pair of spinnerets resembling antennae, up and down in imitation of the questing motion of a foraging ant* KP-M

Bristletails

t HE BRISTLETAILS THAT FORM THE SUBCLASS *Apterygota are small, agile insects that differ from all others in one crucial respect: they do not have wings, and have never had them in all their long evolutionary history. They owe their common name to the three threadlike appendages at the end of their small, tapering bodies, which are possibly used as sensory probes. For creatures less than 2cm (0.8in) long, they are surprisingly long-lived; some are thought to survive for up to 7 years.*

Above *Seen here negotiating a carpet, the silverfish (Lepisma saccharina; Lepismatidae) gets its name from its fishlike covering of minute silvery scales. These give it a slippery texture that helps it to break free from the grasp of enemies such as ants and spiders. Silverfish are common in houses throughout the world, living on starchy materials or such substances as the glue used in bookbindings. If necessary, they can go without food for months.*

Right *Large aggregations of the Shore bristletail (Petrobius maritimus; Machilidae), shown here surrounding a whelk, can often be seen on smooth, flat, sheltered areas of rock within the splash zone of the upper shore. Highly mobile insects, they can jump a considerable distance in order to escape danger.*

FACTFILE

BRISTLETAILS

Class: Insecta

Subclass: Apterygota

Orders: Archaeognatha, Thysanura

About 720 species in 6 families and 2 orders

BRISTLETAILS Order Archaeognatha
Approximately 350 species in 2 families: Machilidae and Meinertellidae. Worldwide.

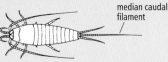

median caudal filament

Features: Head hypognathous; jaws, uniquely among insects, have a single point of articulation; compound eyes large, often touching; ocelli usually present; antennae long, threadlike, and multi-segmented; tarsi 3-segmented; body cylindrical, tapering towards the posterior; thorax somewhat humped dorsally; 11th abdominal segment elongated to form a median caudal filament; cerci present, shorter than median caudal filament; short, lateral styli (rudimentary appendages) present on abdominal segments 2–9. **Life cycle:** Ametabolous (without noticeable metamorphosis). **Conservation status:** Not threatened.

BRISTLETAILS AND SILVERFISH Order Thysanura
370 species in 4 families: Lepidothrichidae, Lepismatidae, Maindroniidae, and Nicoletiidae. Worldwide.

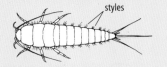

styles

Features: Head hypognathous; jaws dicondylic (with two points of articulation with the head) and with transverse action; compound eyes small or absent; antennae long, threadlike, and multi-segmented; abdomen with 10 complete segments; body relatively flat, tapered, and often covered with scales; 11th abdominal segment elongated to form a median caudal filament; cerci present, often as long as median caudal filament; abdominal segments 2–9 sometimes with styli. **Life cycle:** Ametabolous (without noticeable metamorphosis). **Conservation status:** Not threatened.

Insects as a class may be divided into two main subclasses of very unequal size, the winged Pterygota and the much smaller Apterygota (*apteros* meaning "not winged" in classical Greek). The latter group includes all of the primitively wingless insects whose ancestors have never borne wings since their first known appearance in the Devonian period, 417–354 million years ago. (Secondarily wingless insects, such as fleas and some flies, have become wingless due to a parasitic lifestyle; such loss of wings has occurred independently many times and in many insect orders, and for a variety of reasons.)

The Apterygota comprises two orders of three-pronged bristletails, the Archaeognatha and the Thysanura. At one time three other orders were included: the proturans, the two-pronged bristletails or Diplura, and the springtails or Collembola. However, these groups lack the projecting mouthparts that today are taken to characterize insects, and so are now given separate status within the superclass Hexapoda (see Insects).

Bristletails

ORDER ARCHAEOGNATHA

The Archaeognatha owe the name "bristletails" to their three-pronged tails. They are the most primitive – in other words, the least derived – of living insects. They first appear in the fossil record during the Devonian period, along with the first arachnids. The name Archaeognatha is derived from the Greek *archaeos*, meaning "ancient," and *gnatha*, meaning "jaw," referring to the primitive way in which their mandibles are connected to the head capsule by a single (monocondylic) articulation. All other insects have two points of articulation (dicondylic).

Archaeognathans have cylindrical, tapering bodies, ranging in length from 3 to 20mm (0.1–0.8in). The mouthparts are partly retracted (hypognathous) into the head, which bears three ocelli and two large contiguous compound eyes, which in life are often colorful. The antennae are long and filamentous, often having more than 30 segments, and the palps characteristically extend beyond the head. The thorax is characteristically humped, and the abdomen ends with a long caudal filament, with two shorter cerci. Segments 2–9 of the abdomen possess small ventral styles, which are thought to represent rudimentary legs. Most species have one or two pairs of eversible vesicles on segments 1–7, which are used to absorb water from moist surfaces.

Reproduction is sexual, and involves primitive sperm transfer. In the Machilidae, the male places small droplets on a thread, which is then gathered up by the female. In one machilid species, *Petrobius maritimus*, the male deposits sperm directly into the female's ovipositor. Males of Meinertellidae place the spermatophore on silk stalks. The female lays batches of 2–30 eggs, using her ovipositor to place them in crevices or in holes. The development of the immatures is slow and may take up to two years, passing through ten molts; unlike in most other insects, molting continues throughout adult life.

Bristletails are mostly nocturnal, although some meinertellid species are strongly diurnal. They feed on vegetable debris, algae, and lichens, and also scavenge on dead insects. The bristletails are worldwide in distribution; some species are even found in the Arctic Circle, where they live in leaf litter, grass tussocks, and rock crevices, often in coastal habitats. Some Meinertellidae are known from the arid parts of Africa and Australia.

Silverfish, Firebrats, and Others
ORDER THYSANURA

Sometimes known as fishmoths, the Thysanura or Zygentoma are also often referred to as bristletails, thus sharing their vernacular name with the Archaeognatha. Silverfish and firebrats are the common names of two of the best-known species. The name Thysanura itself derives from the Greek *thysanos*, meaning "fringed," and *ura*, meaning "tail," referring to the long, fringed filaments at the end of the abdomen. Thysanurans first appeared during the Carboniferous period 354–295 million years ago, and although they superficially resemble the Archaeognatha they are in fact dicondylic, in that the mandibles have two points of articulation with the head.

Thysanurans are more or less flattened; the body tapers towards the rear, ending in a central filament with cerci on either side that are often covered with scales and may be as long as the central filament itself, ranging in size from 5 to 20mm (0.2–0.8in). The head is hypognathous, and the compound eyes are never contiguous (as in the Archaeognatha); ocelli are absent, and the antennae are filamentous. The abdomen often bears styles on segments 2–9, and segments 2–7 may possess eversible vesicles or sacs.

Reproduction is sexual, although some species of Nicoletiidae are parthenogenetic – that is, there is no male sex, and females reproduce without mating. Mating behavior has been observed in only a few common species; it comprises simple to elaborate foreplay in the form of a "dance" by the male, after which he deposits a spermatophore on a silk thread, which the female picks up between the valves of her ovipositor. Females lay eggs in cracks and crevices. After emerging, the immatures molt 10 times before becoming adult, the length of time being dependent on both temperature and food availability; adults continue to molt throughout their lives.

Thysanurans are free-living and occur in a wide range of habitats. Members of the families Lepidothrichidae and Lepismatidae are often cryptically colored and live under the bark on tree trunks or in leaf litter, whereas members of the Nicoletiidae are mainly subterranean or else live in caves. Some species are commensals sharing the nests of termites and ants, and these include some of the smallest species, most of them in the subfamily Atelurinae of the Nicoletiidae. Most thysanurans are omnivorous, although species in the family Nicoletiidae are for the most part vegetarian. Some species, such as the common silverfish (*Lepsima saccharina*) and the firebrat (*Thermobia domesticum*), both in the family Lepismatidae, have invaded human dwellings, where they feast on starchy substrates and can cause damage to wallpaper, books, and photographs.   DM/GCM

Mayflies

◁ Left *Representative species of mayflies:* **1** *The subimago or preadult stage of* Leptophlebia marginata, *known to fly fishers as the Sepia dun.* **2** *The Pond olive* (Cloeon dipterum), *a common European species often found in garden ponds and other small bodies of standing water.* **3** *The Green drake* (Ephemera danica), *shown with its last-instar subimago stage; its nymphs take two years to reach maturity.*

OGETHER WITH DRAGONFLIES, MAYFLIES ARE *the most ancient surviving flying insects. Because both lack a wing-flexing mechanism, the two orders are classed together as the only representatives of the infraclass Palaeoptera; all other winged insects are grouped in the Neoptera.*

Palaeopterans first appeared in the Carboniferous era, 354–295 million years ago, when there were probably more species than there are now. Forms similar to modern genera are found in the subsequent Permian epoch (to 248 million years ago), at which time their larvae, originally terrestrial, may have become aquatic. The adult life of a mayfly, as of a dragonfly, is spent mostly in the air.

One-Day Flies

FORM AND FUNCTION

The small, delicate, soft-bodied adult mayflies of the order Ephemeroptera rest with the wings held vertically over their back. The typically large forewings have a rich venation, including many triple-branched veinlets. The hindwings are much reduced, even absent, in some species, but the forewings are highly fluted, with alternating convex and concave veins. The wing surfaces lack scales or setae (hairs). The adults do not feed, and live for no more than a few days, sometimes even for less than an hour, their energies being devoted almost entirely to an airborne quest for mates. The brevity of the adult stage, reflected in the scientific name Ephemeroptera and in the German common name *Eintagsfliegen* ("one-day flies"), is a characteristic of the order; the gonads are often already mature in the final-stadium larva.

Some of the briefest adult lives of all are exhibited by species of the aberrant genus *Prosopistoma*, the males of which live only for the 45 minutes immediately following the sunrise of the day on which they are born; the females have a similarly short lifespan, and are among the few mayflies that never molt from the subimaginal stage. The larva of *Prosopistoma* resembles a shield or carapace pressed tightly against the substrate, usually a stone in a rapidly flowing stream. Because of its superficial resemblance to a branchiopod, the larva was assigned to the Crustacea at the time of its first discovery in 1785, and it was not until 1871 that it was recognized as a mayfly larva. The small, delicate, short-lived adult was not discovered until 1954. It has atrophied legs and dies after completing the mating flight.

⊙ **Above** *A late-stage larva of a mayfly of the genus* Leptophlebia *clings to pondweed in a bog in Northern Ireland. The larvae of all but one of the 2,000-plus mayfly species are aquatic, living off particulate matter in the water or scraping algae off rocks. They may go through as many as 25 or more molts over a period of a year or more before eventually making the dramatic switch from the water to the air when they emerge, first in a penultimate "subimago" winged stage and then for their brief adult life.*

From Molt to Molt
DEVELOPMENTAL STAGES

Mayfly larvae are found in a wide variety of freshwater habitats, most species occurring in lotic (actively moving), temperate waters. A few occur in brackish water, however, and one is even terrestrial. The aquatic larva may take several weeks to a year or more, and pass through 10–50 (usually 15–25) molts, before being ready to emerge as a subimago, the winged, terrestrial, pre-adult stage that is unique to mayflies. In most species the subimago survives for a period ranging from just a few minutes to a day or two before molting to disclose the sexually mature adult. Besides the Prosopistomatidae, other mayflies that fail to molt after the subimaginal stage belong to the families Polymitarcidae, Palingeniidae, and Behningiidae.

The biological function of the subimaginal stage is unknown, but two suggestions have been advanced: first, that the extra molt enables the tails (which give stability during flight) and the long male forelegs (used by the male during copulation) to reach a length that they could not attain during a single molt; and second, that, by molting during the winged stage, mayflies retain water-repellent short hairs (or setae) on the surface of the wings that prevent them becoming trapped in the water at the time of emergence. Neither suggestion has received general acceptance, and the matter remains open for speculation.

In external appearance mayfly larvae somewhat resemble bristletails (silverfish) of the insect order Thysanura. The larvae possess two or three long "tails" (cerci) at the tip of the abdomen, somewhat shorter than the tails of adults. They have a closed tracheal system, and breathe by means of gills, which are typically platelike, richly furnished with tracheoles, and inserted along each side of the abdomen. Mayfly larvae possess up to nine pairs of gills, which are either freely exposed or concealed under an operculum in a branchial chamber through which water is drawn by gill movements. The gills in some species, for instance in the family Siphlonuridae, are used as paddles to assist locomotion, which was perhaps their original function, whereas in others (for example in the Heptageniidae) they are expanded to form an adhesive disc; they can also serve as ventilatory organs, increasing the flow of water over other respiratory surfaces. Mayflies with immovable gills are usually restricted to environments with high current velocities, where their oxygen consumption can be related to current speed. Movements of the gills generate a water current that assists the process of food gathering in species that are filter feeders. Respiratory tufts may be developed on other parts of the body besides the abdomen, such as the leg bases. Mayfly larvae normally require one to three years to develop, although some small species in warm regions may complete three generations in a year. In temperate regions a generation is usually completed in one year.

FACTFILE

MAYFLIES

Class: Insecta

Subclass: Pterygota

Order: Ephemeroptera

About 2,000 species in 19 families, among them the **Ephemeridae** (including the Green drake, *Ephemera danica*); **Baetidae**; **Caenidae**; **Siphlonuridae**; **Heptageniidae** (including the Pond olive, *Cloeon dipterum*, and Lake olive, *C. simile*); **Ecdyonuridae**; and **Leptophlebiidae** (including the Sepia dun, *Leptophlebia marginata*).

DISTRIBUTION Worldwide except Antarctica, the high Arctic, and some oceanic islands.

SIZE Medium-sized; wingspan from under 1cm to 5cm (0.4–2in).

FEATURES Delicate insects with biting mouthparts; general structure homogeneous within order; mouthparts vestigial in adult, which does not feed; antennae bristlelike (setaceous); two pairs of richly veined clear wings (hindwings smaller, may be absent) held vertically when at rest; adults

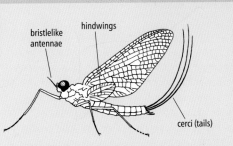

and larvae typically with three threadlike "tails" (cerci) at the tip of the abdomen, those in the adult being as long as or longer than the rest of the body; wings develop externally (exopterygote).

LIFE CYCLE Larvae (sometimes called nymphs) aquatic; unique pre-adult winged stage (the subimago, or dun); incomplete metamorphosis (hemimetabolous).

CONSERVATION STATUS Two species – the Pecatonica River mayfly (*Acanthometropus pecatonica*) and the Robust burrowing mayfly (*Pentagenia robusta*) – are recently extinct. The Large blue lake mayfly (*Tasmanophlebi lecuscoerulei*) is listed as Vulnerable.

Some mayfly larvae live in still water and swim by vertical undulations of the body, aided by the gills and tails. Others crawl about on the muddy bottom of their habitat or live in U-shaped burrows that they excavate with the aid of special tusks attached to the mandibles. Burrowing larvae tend to be filter-feeders, producing a feeding current in the burrow by undulatory movements of the body. Species that live in fast streams may be flattened (for example *Rithrogena*); their shape makes it easier for them to crawl into crevices and offers little resistance to the water flow as they adhere to stones on the stream bed.

Most mayfly larvae are primary consumers: some are filter feeders, collecting suspended matter with setae on the forelegs and mouthparts, whereas others are fine-particle detrivores or scrapers, rasping algae from rocks and other surfaces; a few are predatory. Larvae and pupae of some dipteran species in the Chironomidae and Simuliidae families attach to certain running-water mayfly larvae. They seem not to harm them, and may benefit by enjoying access to a feeding current and by hitching lifts away from exposed situations when streams are in spate. Parasites of larvae include nematode worms and flukes, the final hosts of the latter being fish. A species of *Symbiocloeon* (Baetidae) lives inside the mantle cavity of a freshwater bivalve mussel, where it profits from food filtered by its host. Larvae are eaten mainly by fish but also by various freshwater invertebrates, including snails, beetles and bugs as well as the larvae of caddisflies, dragonflies, and stoneflies. Because of their role as prey of insectivorous fish, many species have been given vernacular names by fly fishermen

Larvae of some species, including the burrowing Ephemeridae, may exist at very high densities in habitats where the substrate is extensive and uniform. In large North American lakes such as Lake Erie or rivers like the Mississippi, and in some Swiss lakes also, their intermittent, synchronized emergences can constitute a serious nuisance to waterside communities, as the mayfly adults settle on foliage or accumulate to a depth of a meter or more beneath street lamps, to which they have been attracted, impeding traffic.

In temperate regions different species emerge throughout the summer; in the tropics emergence may be seasonal, or it may occur throughout the year in time with phases of the moon. To complete the penultimate molt (emergence), the last larval stage either climbs out of the water or, in small species, may emerge directly from the water surface. It molts first into a subimago, the fisherman's smoky-winged dun. This flies a short distance and then, in most species, molts again, in some after only a few minutes but in others after several hours, to form the clear-winged, sexually mature adult familiar to anglers as the "spinner."

The Rush to Mate
ADULT MORPHOLOGY AND BEHAVIOR

Adults do not feed, and their digestive tract remains air-filled after the molt, thus increasing their aerial buoyancy. Before the last molt, the midgut is sealed off from the two ends of the digestive tract to form a sausage-shaped balloon filled with air, causing the larva to float up to the surface. When this happens en masse it produces the so-called "rise," a phenomenon that is particularly conspicuous in members of the genus *Caenis*, when the arrival of large numbers of insects at the surface can give the appearance of raindrops on the water.

Males assemble in swarms in calm weather and perform striking aerial dances, alternately flying up and slowly gliding down, their rate of descent being moderated by their three long cerci. The males have compound eyes with a specially adapted dorsal region, often forming a separate eye, in which the large lenses (ommatidia) face upward and have high acuity, being specialized for detecting movement – an adaptation for seeing females flying above them. The lower lenses face sideways and down, being specialized for seeing detail.

When a female enters a swarm she is promptly seized from below by a male, whereupon he passes his elongated forelegs around her thorax, locking the tarsal claws into special recesses in her pleura. The genitalia then link together and the couple mate as they sink slowly towards the ground. The male inserts paired penes side by side into the two female genital openings. Copulation takes only a few seconds and insemination is internal, no spermatophore being produced. The female then releases her fertilized eggs into the water, either in a large mass or more usually in small packets, as she repeatedly touches the water surface with the tip of her abdomen. In a few species that inhabit streams, the female descends below the water surface to lay eggs. Eggs of species inhabiting running water sometimes bear sticky threads or adhesive discs able to arrest their movement downstream. About 50 species are known to reproduce parthenogenetically, and in five of these males are unknown, parthenogenesis being the only method of reproduction. In parthenogenetic species such as *Cloeon*, the final-stadium larva already contains fully-formed embryos, ready to hatch as first-stadium larvae.

Pollution Takes a Toll
CONSERVATION AND ENVIRONMENT

Because many mayfly species are very sensitive to a lack of oxygen and to acidity, the species composition of a habitat can provide a valuable measure of pollution. Acid rain has probably eliminated mayfly larvae from many habitats in North America and Europe, and thus contributed indirectly to the diminution of fish stocks, because mayfly larvae form a major constituent of the diet of fish. When in 1675 the great Dutch biologist Jan Swammerdam gave the first accurate description of a mayfly, he chose a species of *Palingenia*, a genus then abundant in Holland but now extinct in western Europe. Because mayfly larvae are so sensitive to pollution, the presence of certain families is taken into account in the evaluation of water quality. PSC

○ *Above* Mayflies emerge from a lake at the start of the short adult stage that culminates their lives. Adults are necessarily in a hurry; they often have a lifespan of a day or less in which to find a partner and mate to reproduce the species.

◗ *Right* Mayflies are unique in having a winged pre-adult stage, the subimago, which bridges the gap between larval life and the final molt to adulthood. This female subimago or "dun" belongs to a common European species, the Autumn mayfly (Ecdyonurus dispar).

Dragonflies and Damselflies

fOR SEVERAL CENTURIES DRAGONFLIES HAVE *been valued for their esthetic qualities, especially in the Orient. They have been depicted in medieval manuscripts and Flemish flower paintings, on Dutch tiles and Japanese postage stamps, and have provided themes for many songs and poems. Generally, however, Western folklore has tended to imbue them with inauspicious properties.*

Dragonflies are indeed dragons of the air, possessing superlative powers of flight, acute vision, and often brightly colored wings. Some dragonflies of the Carboniferous Era reached a wingspan of 75cm (30in). The largest Odonata species today, rather surprisingly a damselfly of the *Megaloprepus* genus, is only a quarter of that size.

Damsels and Dragons
FORM AND FUNCTION

The order Odonata is divided between the delicate, weakly flying damselflies of the suborder Zygoptera, in which the fore- and hindwings are similar in shape, and the usually larger and more robust dragonflies (suborder Anisoptera) in which the shape of the two wings differs. An apparently relict family of primitive dragonflies has extant representatives in Japan and Nepal. The two species in this family, adults of which possess some characteristics of each of the other two suborders, were on this account formerly assigned to the suborder Anisozygoptera. Now, however, it is recognized that the Anisozygoptera are confined to the Mesozoic Era, and do not include the rather aberrant members of the Epiophlebiidae, which are more appropriately placed in the Anisoptera.

The aquatic larvae or nymphs of dragonflies and damselflies have exploited a great variety of habitats. The larvae pass through anything from 8 to 18 stadia (sometimes known as instars) and may grow to a length of 6.6cm (2.6in). Life as a larva may last 5–6 years in the primitive Petaluridae, but can be as short as 30–40 days in some darters or damselflies that inhabit temporary pools. Temperate-region hawkers, skimmers, and damselflies typically spend one or two years as larvae, whereas some of their tropical counterparts can complete all their stages of development in less than 30 days.

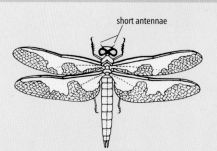

short antennae

FACTFILE

DRAGONFLIES AND DAMSELFLIES

Class: Insecta

Subclass: Pterygota

Order: Odonata

About 6,000 species in 27 families, grouped into 2 suborders: Anisoptera (dragonflies) and Zygoptera (damselflies). Dragonfly families include: **Aeshnidae** (US darners; UK hawkers; e.g. Emperor dragonfly, *Anax imperator*); **Gomphidae** (US clubtails, forceptails, spinylegs, dragonhunters, and sanddragons; UK clubtails; e.g .Club-tailed dragonfly, *Gomphus vulgatissimus*); **Corduliidae** (emeralds; e.g. Downy emerald, *Cordulia aenea*); **Libellulidae** (US skimmers, meadowflies, gliders, pennants, pondhawks, dashers, dragonlets, whitetails, and shadowflies; UK chasers, darters and skimmers; e.g. Broad-bodied chaser, *Libellula depressa*). Damselfly families include: **Calopterygidae** (US jewelwings; UK demoiselles; e.g. *Calopteryx* species); **Lestidae** (US spreadwings; UK emerald damselflies; e.g. *Lestes* species); **Coenagrionidae** (forktails, firetails, bluets; e.g. Large red damselfly, *Pyrrhosoma nymphula*); **Petaluridae** (petaltails; e.g. *Petalura gigantea*); and, in the Oriental region, **Epiophlebiidae** (ancient dragonflies; e.g. *Epiophlebia superstes*).

DISTRIBUTION Worldwide except Antarctica and the high Arctic; especially abundant in tropics and Far East.

SIZE Generally large and robust; **bodylength** up to 15cm (6in); **wingspan** to 19cm (7.5in).

FEATURES Powerful, biting mouthparts retained in predatory adults; antennae very short, compound eyes very large; two pairs of richly veined wings, sometimes brightly colored; fore- and hindwings of similar shape, narrow at base and held vertically at rest (damselflies) or of different shapes, broadly attached at the base, and held out horizontally at rest (dragonflies); legs directed forward; abdomen long and usually slender, in male bearing secondary genitalia beneath the 2nd and 3rd segments; wings develop externally (exopterygote).

BREEDING Metamorphosis incomplete (hemimetabolous); larvae (sometimes called nymphs) aquatic, predatory, capturing prey by explosive extension of hinged labium (mask).

CONSERVATION STATUS The IUCN lists 17 Odonata species as Critically Endangered, 73 as Endangered, and 40 as Vulnerable. In addition, 2 island species – *Jugorum megalagrion*, a dragonfly from the Hawaiian Islands, and *Sympetrum dilatatum*, a damselfly from St. Helena – are recently extinct.

▷ Right *All dragonflies hold their wings out more or less horizontally when at rest. The rich wing venation typical of odonates is clearly visible in this Red skimmer* (Libellula saturata) *in Mexico.*

Development times depend largely on food availability and temperature. Temperate-region damselflies that take two years to complete development in the northern parts of their range can achieve up to three generations a year in the southern parts. Some spring species normally overwinter in the last larval stadium and then emerge synchronously in spring, whereas others – the summer species – overwinter in a stadium before the last and emerge later, sometimes over an extended period.

Dragonfly larvae occupy many types of habitat, including lakes, ponds, bogs, marshes, tree holes, and bromeliad leaf-bases, as well as rivers, saline marshes, burrows in moist soil, and even waterfalls. The larvae of one species of the libellulid genus *Zygonyx*, for example, develop in the spray zone beside the Victoria Falls in Zimbabwe and among submerged roots in whitewater rapids in Uganda, while the adults patrol the edges of the torrents. A few tropical species are virtually terrestrial, occupying moist leaf litter on the forest floor.

Damselfly larvae swim by side-to-side body undulations, often assisted by three leaflike appendages at the tip of the abdomen. These appendages often function also as tracheal gills. Dragonfly larvae, in the first few stadia, swim in similar fashion, but later acquire the ability to use jet propulsion, which provides them with an effective highspeed escape mechanism. The rectal chamber of dragonfly larvae also contains the tracheal gills, which are ventilated by inhalation and exhalation of water through the anus. The main predators of larvae are water bugs, water beetles, fish, and other dragonfly larvae, from which they seek protection by camouflage, antipredation behavior, and choice of microhabitat. Some dragonfly larvae seek protection from predators (mainly fish) by burrowing in mud or sand, and a few deep-burrowing clubtails have the last abdominal segment elongated to form a respiratory siphon comprising 30 percent or more of their total body length; its tip occupies the sediment-free water above which water for respiration can be drawn.

Some damselfly larvae establish home ranges among vegetation and defend these against conspecifics. Such behavior probably enhances their survival by allowing them to develop more rapidly and become larger adults, by obtaining more food (on account of greater prey availability in the shelter of vegetation), and by reducing detection by predators. As the larvae grow they undergo approximately 10–20 molts over a period of between 3 months and about 6–10 years depending on the species. As the time approaches for the

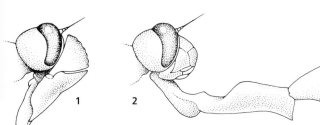

final molt (emergence), the internal organs of the larva change into those of the adult (metamorphosis): some of these changes, such as enlargement of the compound eyes, swelling of the wing sheaths, and retraction of musculature within the labium, can be detected externally. Shortly before emergence the larvae cease to feed, and move close to sites where they can emerge, such as water plants, rocks, floating leaves, or the shore itself. Tropical species, especially the larger dragonflies, normally leave the water at sunset, transform during the night, and make their maiden flight shortly before sunrise; smaller tropical species, and most species in temperate regions, emerge as early in the daytime as temperature permits, and leave on the maiden flight promptly afterwards. On warm nights some temperate hawkers, the Emperor dragonfly among them, may complete emergence during the night.

The newly emerged (teneral) adult flies away from the water, and spends anything from a few days to several weeks feeding and maturing; the range is from one day to two months or, if a dry season and/or a winter intervenes, up to as much as nine months. This prereproductive phase of adult life, known as the maturation period, is normally spent in protected, prey-rich sites away from water. Teneral adults can be identified by a glassy sheen of the wings, and it is during this phase that most species develop their full adult color.

An important dichotomy among adult Odonata is the one between perchers and fliers. When active, perchers, which include darters, skimmers, chasers, and clubtails as well as almost all damselflies, make short, investigatory flights from a perch, to which they promptly return. In contrast, fliers, which include hawkers, emeralds, and a few libellulids, remain continuously on the wing. The distinction is not invariable within a species, but has searching implications for behavior, especially with respect to the regulation of body temperature (thermoregulation).

Thermoregulation is a major component of dragonfly behavior. All dragonflies sometimes need to warm the thoracic flight muscles before takeoff. Heat can be absorbed economically by basking in the sun, or it can be generated by shivering (wing whirring). Perched libellulids avoid overheating by pointing the abdomen directly at the sun (the obelisk posture). In flight, hawkers reduce their body temperature by making long glides, or by diverting hot blood from the thorax into the abdomen, where it is cooled before being returned. Some blue-colored dragonflies, such as *Anax* and *Aeshna* species, turn gray when cold as a result of pigment movements in the hypodermal cells, allowing them to absorb more radiation from the sun. As they warm up, the blue color returns.

○ **Above** When folded at rest, the "mask" of a dragonfly larva **1** covers the other mouthparts. The mask can be extended very rapidly **2** to grasp prey and bring it within reach of the powerful jaw.

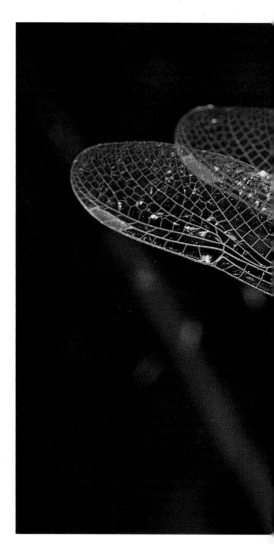

○ **Above** Dragonflies are among the fiercest carnivorous insects. The Emperor dragonfly (Anax imperator) *is known to feed on the Large red damselfly* (Pyrrhosoma nymphula).

○ **Right** Dragonflies have characteristically large eyes, set close together on the top of the head, as seen on this Golden-ringed dragonfly (Cordulegaster boltonii). By contrast, damselfly eyes are widely spaced.

○ **Below** In hot weather dragonflies such as this American Low-flying amberwing (Perithemis tenera; Libellulidae) adopt the obelisk pose, pointing their tails at the sun to minimize heat absorption.

DEFENDING A PATCH

A male territorial dragonfly commonly takes control of a stretch of the margin of a river, stream, or pond that includes suitable egg-laying sites. He normally allows only the female with which he has most recently mated to oviposit on the patch he is defending. The patch or territory may extend for tens of meters along the bank, or be limited to a much smaller area centered on a water plant, tree hole, or bromeliad leaf-base. In some species one individual may hold the same territory for many days or even weeks – the recorded maximum is 90 days – but in other species there can be a rapid turnover of males at the same spot.

Contests between the territory holder and an intruding male sometimes escalate, and clashes may develop that occasionally result in one of the males being knocked into the water, where it becomes vulnerable to fish and other predators. Sometimes conflicts are highly ritualized, involving a variety of peculiar flight patterns: two males may fly toward each other displaying brightly-colored abdomens or gaudy legs, or one may fly in circles around the other as it hovers, or the two may perform elaborate, zig-zagging dances, spiralling upward.

Copulation often occurs in the middle of the territory, the male hovering or remaining perched where he is highly visible to approaching males. In some species only a few males, usually the largest, are able to hold territories; most other males either act as satellites, residing, apparently unobserved, in the territories of other males, or else wander with no fixed address, seizing females whenever opportunity offers, sometimes even away from the water (these individuals are termed "sneakers"). Territorial males normally obtain many more matings than do others; indeed, in some territorial species, a very high proportion of all copulations during the flight season are secured by very few males, constituting a compelling selective force favoring successful territorial defense.

Gaudy Hunters
DIET

Dragonfly larvae are typically opportunistic hunters, their diet including oligochaete worms, gastropods, crustaceans, tadpoles, and fish, as well as a wide variety of small invertebrates, including members of their own species. Most species are ambush feeders, detecting approaching prey mainly by sight. Their compound eyes develop early, and increase rapidly in size as growth proceeds. A hawker larva, when foraging, typically remains motionless until prey approaches. Then the larva stalks the prey slowly until it comes within range, the correct distance being gauged stereoscopically. The larva then shoots out its labium (mask), whose long basal segments are folded beneath the head when at rest; full extension of the labium takes only 25 milliseconds, being effected by a forward surge and sudden release in blood pressure that has been built up using muscles and an abdominal diaphragm, synchronized with the release of a locking device beneath the head. This pressure system is used also by dragonfly larvae as an emergency means of locomotion, by repeatedly expelling jets of water from the anus. The labium is furnished with terminal, hinged hooks that grasp the prey and drag

it back to the mouth as the labium retracts. Other species detect moving prey by sensing the vibrations they generate, using fine hairs (setae) on the antennae, body, or legs. All larvae use the labium for prey capture, and its shape and size can vary considerably according to the microhabitat and the type of prey commonly sought. Indeed, the general body shape, pigmentation, behavior, rate of growth, and eye development in dragonfly larvae closely reflect a species' lifestyle (for example, whether active or sedentary) and microhabitat occupancy (which might be among submerged plants, fine or coarse sediment, or submerged leaves and debris).

Like the larvae, adults of almost all species of Odonata are generalized, opportunistic feeders, often being quick to congregate where prey is abundant, for example around swarming termites or near beehives. Some species forage among swarms of flies or other small insects at twilight; indeed, a few tropical hawkers forage only at these times. Dragonflies are able to catch small midges at such low illuminations that a human observer can barely see the dragonflies themselves. Non-flying prey may also be included in the diet; some damselflies pluck aphids or beetle larvae off plants, whereas hawkers may glean small frogs from the ground.

Only one family of Odonata contains adults that are specialized feeders. This is the Pseudostigmatidae, the largest living damselflies, found mainly in the forests of tropical Central America. Adults prey exclusively on spiders, which they pluck from webs while hovering in forest clearings.

MATING AND SPERM COMPETITION

Mating in dragonflies and damselflies begins with the male grasping the female with the paired claspers at the tip of his abdomen, on her prothorax in damselflies and on the head in dragonflies, thus forming the tandem position. Then, if the female accepts his advances, she will bend the tip of her abdomen downward and forward until her genitalia (located at the tip of her abdomen) engage with his secondary genitalia (beneath the 2nd and 3rd abdominal segments). Copulation in what is known as the wheel position can then commence.

The female typically begins to lay eggs immediately after copulation, often with her former partner guarding her, either by retaining hold of her in the tandem position or by hovering close to her. Male dragonflies and damselflies compete intensely for females, but competition does not end with success or failure in securing a mate. A female can store live sperm in her body for days, and one mating may provide enough sperm to fertilize a lifetime of eggs.

As each successive egg batch matures, the female needs to visit the water again to lay the eggs, whereupon she is liable to be intercepted by the male in residence there. Thus, females have to mate many times in order to gain access to egg-laying sites controlled by males. The sperm a female receives during copulation takes precedence in fertilizing any eggs she lays during the next 24 hours. After this, the sperm mixes with any other sperm in her store and therefore no longer enjoys precedence. This fact explains why a female's copulation partner defends her so resolutely after copulation: if she were to mate with another male before laying all the eggs in her current batch, her first partner would forfeit the parentage of those eggs.

Initiatives available to the male in influencing sperm competition depend on the structure of his intromittent organ, or penis. In damselflies the penis (on the 2nd abdominal segment) is hard and robust, bearing an array of hooks and backwardly-directed bristles, enabling it to scoop out rival sperm from the female's body before acting as a conduit for transferring fresh sperm. In dragonflies the penis is a four-segmented, inflatable structure 1 in which the first (basal) segment stores sperm. When the terminal segment expands, it can act as a ram, pushing rival sperm into places where it commands a low priority for fertilizing eggs. In a few species the terminal segment extends a barbed, whiplike flagellum 2 which may be able to enter the female's sperm-storage organs and withdraw their contents. Thus the intense competition that males show for exclusive access to females is known as sperm precedence and sperm competition.

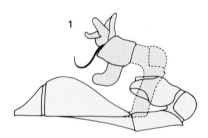

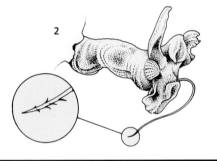

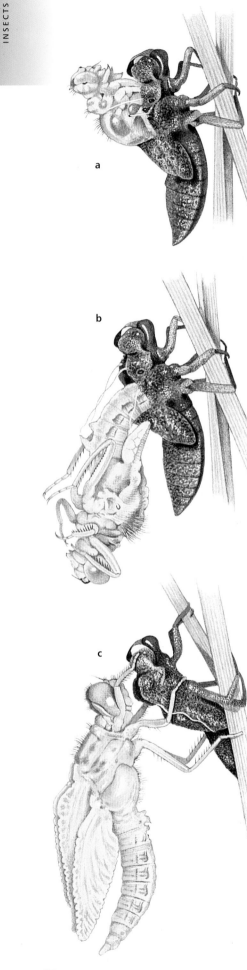

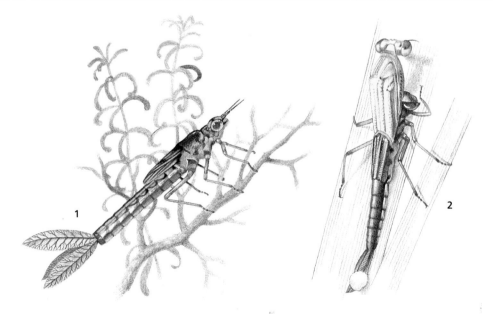

◁ **Left** The final-instar or -stadium larvae of dragonflies and damselflies climb out of the water on emergent vegetation just before the adults hatch: here **a-c**, Orthetrum coerulescens (Libellulidae) emerges from its typically squat and flat larva.

◑ **Above** The larvae of narrow-winged damselflies such as Coenagrion puella (Coenagrionidae) develop three tail "fins" or gills 1 to allow them to breathe underwater. The gills are no longer needed when they emerge from the water to hatch 2.

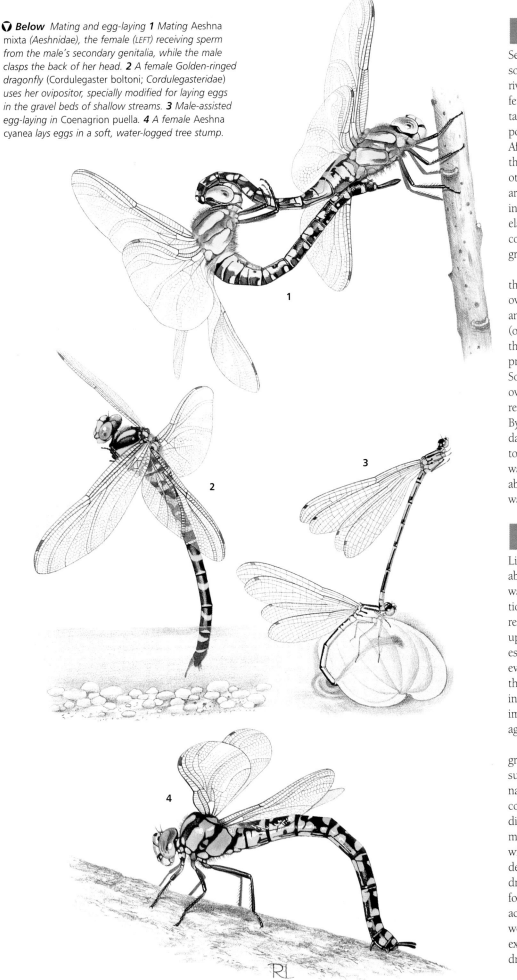

Below *Mating and egg-laying* **1** *Mating* Aeshna mixta *(Aeshnidae), the female (*LEFT*) receiving sperm from the male's secondary genitalia, while the male clasps the back of her head.* **2** *A female Golden-ringed dragonfly (*Cordulegaster boltoni; *Cordulegasteridae) uses her ovipositor, specially modified for laying eggs in the gravel beds of shallow streams.* **3** *Male-assisted egg-laying in* Coenagrion puella. **4** *A female* Aeshna cyanea *lays eggs in a soft, water-logged tree stump.*

The Struggle to Mate
SOCIAL BEHAVIOR

Sexually mature males return to the water, and in some species they may defend territories against rivals along the shore (see Defending a Patch). The females arrive later. The arrival of a female precipitates intense competition among males for her possession (see Mating and Sperm Competition). After mating, she lays her eggs in the territory of the successful male, while he guards her from other males. There are many variations on this arrangement in different species; for example, in some damselflies and a few dragonflies an elaborate courtship precedes copulation. Such courtship contrasts with the more usual rush-and-grab tactics of the males of many other species.

A female produces successive batches of eggs throughout her life, and is normally ready to oviposit immediately after copulation. Damselfly and hawker females possess egg-laying tubes (ovipositors) that can pierce plant tissues and then insert eggs into them – a relatively slow process that protects the eggs from desiccation. Some damselflies crawl beneath the water and oviposit well below the surface, sometimes remaining submerged for over an hour to do so. By contrast, many dragonflies, including chasers, darters, skimmers, and clubtails, lack an ovipositor and tend to scatter their eggs widely onto the water or nearby. They may repeatedly dip their abdomens into the water, or extrude eggs onto the water surface or floating vegetation.

Losing Habitat
CONSERVATION AND ENVIRONMENT

Like mayflies, Odonata larvae are affected unfavorably by pollution. If quantities of nutrients in the water rise, in the process known as eutrophication, a consequent increase in algal growth may result in the disappearance of the higher plants upon which some larvae depend. By far the greatest threat to the survival of dragonflies today, however, comes not so much from pollution as from the destruction of larval habitats by draining, infilling, or deforestation of the catchment area – impacts that commonly accompany intensive agriculture, forestry, or urbanization.

On the credit side, recent years have seen a greatly raised profile for dragonflies in countries such as Britain. Burgeoning interest among many naturalists, not just specialists, has given rise to a considerable effort towards compiling detailed distribution maps of the British species and their most important breeding sites. This development will be of enormous help in influencing planning decisions that could have a negative impact upon dragonfly habitat. The presence of a breeding site for rare species will now customarily be taken into account when planning sites for new building works. In addition, many landowners now create expensive new ponds with the aim of encouraging dragonflies.   PSC/PLM

Cockroaches

nOT ONLY ARE COCKROACHES FOUND JUST
*about everywhere, they also eat just about any-
thing. They have adapted successfully to an
enormous range of habitats, from sea level up to
almost 2,000m (6,500ft). They inhabit the deserts,
tundras, grasslands, swamps and forests. They live in,
on, and under trees. They burrow in the ground and
live in caves. Some southeast Asian species are even
semi-aquatic.*

The versatile cockroaches are among the most
ancient of all insect groups, and fossils are known
from the Carboniferous period, 354–295 million
years ago. Each species is built for its particular
habitat. Burrowing cockroaches tend to be stocky
and wingless, with strong, spadelike limbs. Tree-
dwelling insects are slim, with well-developed
wings and long, slender legs for fast running.
Species living under bark are highly flattened.

Omnivorous and Ubiquitous
FEEDING AND DIGESTION
Many cockroaches are true omnivores, feeding
with their relatively unspecialized chewing
mouthparts on living or dead plant and animal
material. More specialized feeders include the
wood-eating *Cryptocercus* species (Cryptocerci-
dae) from China and North America. Although
many insects feed on wood, most are unable to
digest its major component, cellulose. *Cryptocercus* has solved this problem by keeping a population of protozoans in a special sac off its gut.
These micro-organisms digest cellulose for the
cockroach and release the nutrients back into the
gut in a form that the insect can absorb. In return
for their services, the cockroach provides the protozoans with food and a secure environment.

The only other group of insects (apart from
some beetles) that have this relationship with
protozoans are the termites, which have exactly
the same types of gut organisms as *Cryptocercus*.
Structural similarities, and the greater age of
known cockroach fossils, suggest that termites
may have evolved from cockroaches.

Cryptocercus nymphs are not born with the protozoans in their gut. They acquire them by feeding
on droplets of fecal material exuded from the anus
of adults. This behavior requires young and adults
to live together, and it has been suggested that a
similar requirement may have led to the development of true sociality in termites. Yet although
Cryptocercus and some other cockroaches live in
aggregations, none exhibits the termites' communal care of young and other divisions of labor.

Courting by Sound and Smell
REPRODUCTION
The mating behavior of cockroaches varies from
simple contact stimuli to complex dances and the
release of pheromones. In some species the males
run around pumping their wings up and down in
order to attract a mate; in others they have specialized glands on the dorsal surface of their abdomen
that secrete attractants: as the female mounts the
male's back to claim this secretion, the male takes
the chance to copulate.

In these species, the female starts the courtship
sequence by adopting a "calling" posture, with
the tip of her abdomen lowered to aid the release
of a sexually attractant pheromone. The male
responds by approaching the female and rubbing
antennae with her. He then turns his back and
raises his wings at an angle of roughly 60°, revealing a pheromone-releasing gland of his own,
known as the "excitator." She then mounts his

Above *Representative species of cockroaches.
1 The American cockroach (Periplaneta americana),
2 German cockroach (Blattela germanica), and **3**
Common cockroach (Blatta orientalis) are all pest
species that have learned to live in close proximity
to people. **4** The Madagascan hissing cockroach
(Gromphadorhina portentosa) is very different; as
its name implies, this heavily-armored species uses
sound for contact and also as a sexual stimulant;
males that do not hiss do not copulate.*

RATS AND MICE OF THE INSECT WORLD

Although cockroaches are among the most despised of insects, thanks largely to their habit of entering our dwellings, less than 1 percent of all known species are pests; flies, fleas, and beetles all in fact cause more problems for humans than cockroaches in terms of spreading food spoilage and disease. The simple fact is that species such as the large American and the smaller German and Oriental cockroaches are the insect equivalent of rats and mice. Like those rodents, they have become extraordinarily successful at living in association with humankind, thriving in the same warm, humid, sheltered environments that we ourselves enjoy. It is believed that cockroaches started this human association when man first moved into caves.

Because of their flattened bodies, cockroaches are able to crawl into narrow crevices, behind cupboards, under floorboards, and into drains and sewers, where they hide during the day. At night they become active and roam around in search of food. Being catholic in their tastes, they will eat any accessible household foods as well as papers, documents, and book bindings.

More seriously, cockroaches foul with their excreta and dirty feet those sites where they walk and feed. A cockroach that has crawled out of a drain or sewer and then wanders over exposed foodstuff may transmit disease. Cockroaches have been reported to carry poliomyelitis virus as well as the food-poisoning *Salmonella* bacterium, and they are also known to cause allergic reactions such as asthma in some people.

Cockroaches are exceptionally difficult to eradicate. They are very adaptable and, after one unpleasant but not fatal experience, will learn to avoid areas where poisons have been placed. They are also difficult to catch. They are extremely sensitive to any vibration of the surface on which they stand, being able to detect a movement of less than one-millionth of a millimeter. They also respond to very slight air movements, which they sense through hairs on the two appendages (cerci) that project from the tip of the abdomen. A cockroach can detect the vibration of air movements long before a would-be attacker can get anywhere near it, and can run swiftly for cover in inaccessible cracks and crevices.

Cockroaches are also long-lived and produce large numbers of offspring. The American cockroach holds the record. It can live for over 4 years, during which time a female may lay more than 1,000 eggs. It is little wonder, then, that they are such successful pests and are so unpopular with their unwilling human hosts.

back to feed upon the secretions from the gland, permitting the male to thrust back to achieve the necessary position for copulation to take place.

In a number of species the use of sound signalling has been developed. In the blaberid subfamily Oxyhaloinae, all of the species produce sound. In the genera *Nauphoeta*, *Leucophaea*, and *Henschoutedenia*, the base of the wings and the underside of the base of the pronotum have a row of stridulatory pegs, so when the pronotum is moved it makes a squeaking noise. In the Gromphadorhini group, which includes the hissing cockroaches of Madagascar such as the *Gromphadorhina*, *Elliptorhina*, and *Princisia* species, the male actually produces an audible hissing noise by expelling air out of its spiracles. This hissing plays a part in both territorial, mating, and defensive behavior.

The reproductive life of cockroaches shows as much diversity as other aspects of their biology. The six families are divided on the basis of differences in the wing venation, the shape of the tip of the abdomen, the internal genitalia, egg-laying behavior, and foregut structure.

The reproductive biology of cockroaches consists of four types. Most are oviparous, depositing their eggs along with glandular secretions that harden to form a tough protective capsule called the ootheca, which may be stuck to the substrate and concealed with bits of debris. The females of a number of species in the family Blattellidae carry the ootheca around on the end of the abdomen, where it receives vital water from the female. In contrast, some of the Blattellidae and most of the

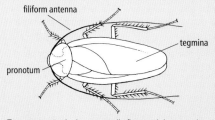

FACTFILE

COCKROACHES

Class: Insecta

Order: Blattodea (also known as the Blattaria)

3,500 species in 6 families

DISTRIBUTION Worldwide, except polar regions.

SIZE Body length ranges from 3 to 80mm (0.1–3in).

FEATURES Body dorsoventrally flattened; long, multi-segmented, filiform antennae; mouthparts mandibulate, hypognathous; large, shieldlike pronotum; frontwings (tegmina) leathery; hindwings membranous, folded fan-wise at rest; wings can be either full, brachypterous, or absent; multi-segmented cerci; males possess styles on the last abdominal segment (reduced or absent in some groups).

LIFE CYCLE Most species oviparous, although some exhibit false ovoviviparity and at least 1 species is viviparous. Nymphs resemble adults in appearance except for smaller size and lack of reproductive organs and wings; there is no pupal stage. Larvae go through a number of molts; the number of stages between the intermediate molt and adulthood ranges between species from 5–13.

CONSERVATION STATUS Not threatened.

See families table ▷

⊘ **Below** A cluster of nymphs exploit the safety-in-numbers principle: the larger the aggregation, the lower the risk of predation to the individual. In their case the protection is enhanced by their bright colors, which signal to would-be predators that they are distasteful to eat. Cockroach larvae, which resemble small adults in appearance, go through a number of molts.

Blaberidae show false ovoviviparity, where the ootheca is extruded by the female, then rotated through 90° and withdrawn into a special brood chamber. Here the eggs remain until they hatch, producing live young. Members of the Australian endemic subfamily Geoscapheinae (Blaberidae), which includes the large cockroaches in the genera *Macropanesthia*, *Parapanesthia*, *Geoscapheus*, and *Neogeoscaphaeus*, exhibit a different form of false ovoviviparity, whereby no ootheca is formed; instead, the eggs pass directly from the oviduct into the brood chamber. Finally, the Pacific beetle roach *Diploptera punctata* (Blaberidae), and probably other members of the same genus, goes one step further and is viviparous. The tiny eggs are laid directly into the brood chamber, where they

◑ **Below** *In Trinidad, a* Homalopteryx laminata *mimics a dead leaf on the rainforest floor. Camouflage is one of many defensive mechanisms deployed by cockroaches to escape predators; most long-legged species are fast runners, relying on speed to get away.*

grow though receiving nutrients in the form of a sort of milk from the female. In this species only a few nymphs are eventually produced, but they are much larger than those of other cockroaches of an equivalent size, thereby giving them a head start.

Unlikely Carers
PARENTAL CARE
One of the largest cockroaches in the world is *Macropanesthia rhinocerus* (Blaberidae), which can reach up 70mm (2.8in) in length and weigh as much as 20g (0.7oz). This species is only found in northern Queensland, Australia, where it lives in burrows that can be up to 6m (20ft) in length and 1m (3.3ft) in depth. The adults are completely wingless and live in family groups, even practising parental care. The nymphs, which are paler and softer than the adults, would be an easy target for predators, so they remain in the nest chamber until they reach maturity, which may take as long as 9 months. The adult pair make nightly forages outside and drag leaves and grass back into the burrows for the nymphs to live on.

There are other interesting cases of parental

care within the cockroaches. In the South American genus *Paratropes* (Blaberidae), the female has a concave abdomen and convex wings, forming a chamber for the nymphs to hide in. In the Malaysian genus *Perisphaeria* (Blaberidae), some species of which are metallic green, the adult females look like pill-bugs and have the ability to roll up into a ball when threatened. Even more amazing is their maternal behavior. They have small pits on the underside of their bodies, into which the specialized mouthparts of the first instar nymphs fit perfectly. The result is that the nymphs are protected on the underside of the female, even when she rolls up into a ball. It has also been hypothesized that the nymphs receive nutrients from these pits; if this is the case, it would be the first recorded case of "suckling" in the insect world.

Expert Survivors
ANTI-PREDATOR DEFENSES
The eggs of cockroaches are parasitized by a number of other insect species, most commonly wasps (for example species in the family Evaniidae). Oothecae that are left in exposed positions are particularly at risk. In addition, cockroaches are parasitized by a number of mites, worms, and even amoebas. As young and as adults, they are also considered tasty morsels by insects and other arthropod predators, as well as by frogs, toads,

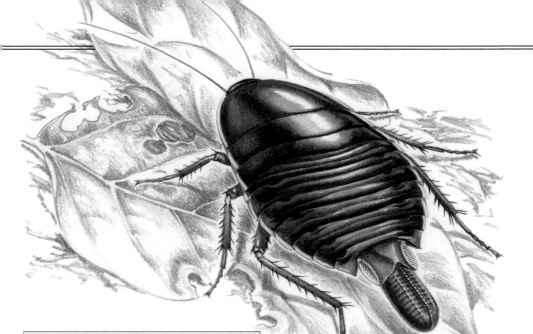

Cockroach Families

Family Blattidae

550 species, mostly occurring in Africa, Asia, and Australia. Generally medium-sized. This family includes some of the most familiar cockroach species, including the American cockroach (*Periplaneta americana*) and the Common cockroach (*Blatta orientalis*).

Family Blattellidae

The largest family of cockroaches, with some 1,750 species. Most often small and delicate, with an average body length of 15mm (0.6in), although the South American blattellid *Megaloblatta longipennis* is one of the largest cockroaches in the world, with a wingspan up to 20cm (8in). The German cockroach (*Blatella germanica*) and the Brown-banded cockroach (*Supella longipalpa*) are widespread domestic pests.

Family Blaberidae

Approximately 1,000 species. This family includes some of the largest cockroaches; many are stout, wingless, and burrow in the soil and in rotting logs. Some, such as the Madeira cockroach (*Leucophaea maderae*), live in association with humans. The Madagascan hissing cockroach (*Gromphadorhina portentosa*) is commonly kept as a pet.

Family Polyphagidae

Approximately 200 species. Small to medium-sized, these cockroaches are often hairy, and have a preference for arid habitats, although several species (e.g. *Ergaula capucina*) live in caves. The American *Attaphila fungicola*, which is just 3mm (0.1in) long, lives in ants' nests, where it feeds on fungus.

Family Cryptocercidae

7 species in 1 genus, *Cryptocercus*, of which 5 are found in North America and 2 in China. All species live in dead wood.

Family Nocticolidae

20 species in 2 genera: *Nocticola* (18 species), found in Africa, Australia, and Asia, and *Spelaeoblatta* (2 species), found in Asia. Most species are associated with cave habitats, although some are associated with termites.

⬆ **Above** *A female Pale-bordered cockroach (Polyzosteria limbata) with an egg-filled ootheca extending from its abdomen. This Australian species is one of a number in the family Blattellidae that carry these secreted egg-chambers with them rather than depositing them on the ground.*

⬇ **Below** *A cockroach of the genus* Pseudomops *feeds on berries at dusk in the Mexican desert. Most cockroaches are omnivorous scavengers, feeding off living or dead animal or plant matter; fruit-eating is one of the less common forms of nutrition, although it has also been observed in a South African species.*

lizards, snakes, birds, and insectivorous mammals. Many cockroaches have evolved different mechanisms to avoid predation. For example, in the genus *Ergaula* (Polyphagidae), both the adults and nymphs feign death, remaining motionless when attacked. In the adults the pretense of death is taken one step further; once stimulated, tiny sacs are everted on the side of the abdomen that release a chemical that smells like rotting flesh. Members of the blaberid subfamily Oxyhaloinae squeak or hiss when attacked.

Chemical defenses are used in a number of cockroach groups, including all species of the subfamily Polyzosteriinae (Blattidae), some of which (such as the Australian *Platyzosteria*) also exhibit bright warning colors. The chemicals are mostly aliphatic compounds, often *trans* 2-Hexanal, which can be propelled from glands in the abdomen. Certain *Eurycotis* species, found in Florida and in tropical America, produce the chemicals in the form of an acidic, milky fluid that can either be exuded as an oozed deposit or, alternatively, squirted backward for 20cm (8in) or more.

The Philippine cockroach genus *Prosoplecta* (Blattellidae) is striking in that it is brightly colored and mimics ladybirds, thereby gaining protection from predators that find ladybirds distasteful. There are several other brightly-colored cockroaches whose gaudy hues show off their ability to produce unpleasant chemical defense secretions.   DM

Termites

tERMITES LIVE IN COLONIES RANGING IN SIZE *from a few hundred to as many as seven million individuals. They not only feed, groom, and protect each other, but the offspring of one generation assist the parents in raising the next – the mark of truly social animals.*

Each termite society is divided between several castes – the winged and sighted reproductives (queen, king, and young reproductives, the vast majority of which will perish without mating), and the wingless and usually blind workers and soldiers, which feed, maintain, and protect the colony. The termites share this characteristic of social life with the ants, but in each termite caste either sex may occur, whereas ant, wasp, and bee workers are always female.

The Cockroach–Termite Convergence
EVOLUTION

The similarities between colonies of termites and ants are all the more remarkable because the termites in fact evolved quite independently, and much earlier than ants. What is more, ants are also termites' worst enemies (see below).

Another striking similarity is that between termites and cockroaches. For example, the primitive Australian Darwin termite and the colonial, wood-feeding Brown-hooded cockroach (*Cryptocercus punctulatus*) of North America share an array of morphological and other characteristics, including not only the general structure of their wings, genitalia, and jaws, but even the habit of laying batches of eggs in a double row of 20–35. Moreover, both species have similar colonies of protozoa (xylophagous flagellates) in their intestines, giving vital assistance in the digestion of food. Both the cockroach and termite adults pass these beneficial protozoa on to young individuals in their feces. (This reliance of the younger on the older members of the colony has been a key factor favoring the evolution of social behavior in termites.)

These similarities were long held to be evidence of a common ancestry of termites and cockroaches in the early Mesozoic, some 220 million years ago. However, more recent DNA analysis has led many entomologists to conclude that these shared characteristics result from convergent evolution.

Founding a Colony
REPRODUCTION AND NEST-FOUNDING

A termite colony begins when a flying, sexually mature male is attracted to a female by an odor secreted from a gland on her underside. If they

○ **Above** *Harvester termites like these* Hodotermes *from Namibia are such efficient gatherers of plant material that they present serious competition for domestic livestock such as cattle or sheep.*

○ **Below** *The flight period of alate (winged) males and females from termite nests is a time of plenty for many predators, from hawks to ground beetles. Before mating, this throng will need to shed their wings.*

FACTFILE

TERMITES

Class: Insecta

Subclass: Pterygota

Order: Isoptera

About 2,300 species in 7 families

DISTRIBUTION Worldwide from the Equator to 45–50° N and S, but mostly in the tropics (e.g. only 41 species in N America).

SIZE Mostly slender, 2–22mm (0.1–0.9in) long, reaching to 14cm (5.5in) in some queens.

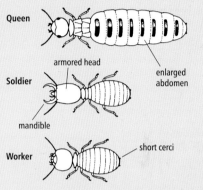

FEATURES Highly social, living in large, permanent communities with various "castes," each distinct in form; reproductive adults darker, with 2 similarly-shaped pairs of wings that drop off after the swarm flight; head with biting mouthparts, set at right angles to rest of body.

LIFE CYCLE Larvae resemble adults; no pupal stage.

CONSERVATION STATUS Not threatened.

---

have not already done so, they then shed their wings, whose brief function of dispersal from the parent nest is now over. They run off in a "tandem pair," the male close behind the female, in search of a good location to build a nest and raise young.

The first larvae are always destined to be workers in one form or another. In the six families of more primitive "lower termites," even the immature forms can behave like workers and contribute to the well-being of the colony.

Once a few workers have been raised and are able to build, nurse young, and finally collect food, soldiers are reared to defend the colony. Soldiers are usually armed with enlarged biting or snapping jaws and armored heads, and are sometimes capable of squirting defensive secretions at their enemies from special head glands. However, they are wholly dependent upon the workers for their food, which is regurgitated or fed in an anal secretion. The original two flying termites, surrounded by their subjects, have now truly earned the titles of "king" and "queen" of the colony.

In most termite species both soldiers and workers are blind, although they are sensitive to light directly through the cuticle of the head capsule. In a mature colony, fully-developed adults capable of

Termite Families

Darwin termite

Family Mastotermitidae
1 species (*Mastotermes darwiniensis*). Australia; primitive, nests in tree stumps; food mainly wood, but a pest of many materials.

Sawtooth termite

Family Serritermitidae
1 species (*Serritermes serrifer*). Brazil; nests in walls of mounds of other termites (usually the *Cornitermes* snouted termites); food not known.

Dry-wood termites

Family Kalotermitidae
350 species, distribution as order; nests in dead branches; food dry, mainly dead, wood; also pests in plantations, building timbers. Includes the genera *Kalotermes* and *Neotermes*.

Harvester termites

Family Hodotermitidae
17 species in drier areas of Africa, Arabia, Asia; nests underground; food grass; pests of grasslands.

Damp-wood termites

Family Rhinotermitidae
Some 210 species, same range as order; nests in, and feed on, rotten wood; some very destructive in buildings and crops.

Termopsidae

17 species in Australia, Asia S Africa, USA, Chile; nests in stumps and logs; food rotten wood; pests of timber.

Higher termites

Family Termitidae
About 1,700 species (over 70 percent of all termite species) in tropical and subtropical regions worldwide; nests very variable, in trees, surface mounds, or underground chambers; food very variable: dead wood, grass, leaves, soil, humus, and other organic matter. Four large subfamilies: soldierless termites and relatives (subfamily Apicotermitinae, including the genera *Ateuchotermes* and *Alyscotermes*); termitines or subterranean termites (Termitinae, including *Cubitermes* and *Procubitermes*); snouted termites, some harvest termites (Nasutitermitinae, including *Nasutitermes*, *Syntermes*, *Trinervitermes*, *Longipeditermes*, and *Constrictotermes*); and fungus-growing termites (Macrotermitinae, including *Macrotermes* and *Odontotermes*).

reproduction (reproductives) are raised, equipped with wings and proper eyes unlike their brothers and sisters. At this stage the queen may be laying over 30,000 eggs a day, her body hugely enlarged into an egg-producing machine up to 14cm (5.5in) long and 3.5cm (1.4in) across. Her king, still constantly in attendance, retains his normal size, by now dwarfed by his huge, white, pulsating spouse.

When conditions are right, often after a heavy storm, the workers open holes in the nest (or in some cases, as in *Armitermes euamignathus*, construct special hollow towers) and release the young reproductives, which fly off in all directions to complete the cycle of renewal. At this stage, the exposed and weak-flying termites are at their most vulnerable, falling victim to a range of predators – ants, spiders, geckos and other lizards, shrews and similar mammals, a host of birds from francolins to falcons, and even people. Perhaps fewer than one flying termite in a thousand survives to raise a mature colony.

Designed to Digest
FOOD AND FEEDING
The Isoptera is the only order of insects with a general ability to digest cellulose, the main chemical constituent of all plants. The secret of the termites' success is their ability to enter into cooperative associations with protozoa, bacteria, and fungi that can produce the enzymes they need to digest plant material.

The presence of such protozoa in the gut is a feature of all "lower termites," most of whose members feed on dead wood. Nevertheless, much of the material consumed by termites remains undigested; the copious feces are often used in nest building, or are simply ejected onto heaps from the wood or soil in which the termites are living.

The "higher termites," the seventh family, lack special gut protozoa, but have a range of more sophisticated associations that include bacteria and fungi. These alliances partly explain the family's evolutionary success, in terms of both diversity of species and adaptations to a wide range of feeding habits. In three of the four higher termite subfamilies (Apicotermitinae, Nasutitermitinae, and Termitinae), large bacterial cultures grow in the hindgut, where they help ferment plant material.

Most termites prefer to eat dead plant material that has already been attacked by fungi, which help to break up the cells, releasing the nutrients. In the savanna regions of Africa and Asia the long dry seasons greatly slow down the activities of fungi and of the termites that depend upon them, but one group, the subfamily Macrotermitinae

(including the genera *Odontotermes* and *Macrotermes*), has overcome food shortage in a unique way. They have developed a symbiotic association with fungi of the genus *Termitomyces*, which the termites cultivate inside the nest on "fungus combs" made of their own feces. The fungus, which is found nowhere else, breaks down the feces, which the termites then consume. These fungus-growing termites are of very great ecological importance. Their activities dominate decomposition processes in most seasonally dry areas of the Old World.

Keeping Out Intruders
DEFENSIVE STRATEGIES
Several mammals are specialist feeders on termites, including the aardvark and aardwolf of Africa, the pangolins of Africa and Asia, and the anteaters of South America. The termites' greatest enemies, however, are ants. Many ant species specialize in raiding termite foraging parties. Termites are highly variable in their foraging patterns, and those that travel furthest tend to be most vulnerable to predators. Some termites, such as the dry wood genera *Kalotermes* and *Neotermes*, never leave the branch in which they are nesting. Others, such as the fungus-growers, may travel over 50m (165ft) from the nest through a semipermanent network of tunnels in order to reach new sources of food. They defend themselves in a number of ways: by building fortified nests, by covering their food in a protective sheet of mud while they feed underneath, and with the specialized caste of soldiers.

Among the soil-feeding higher termite subfamily Apicotermitinae are a number of genera such as *Ateuchotermes* and *Alyscotermes* that have no soldiers; instead, the workers defend the colony by bursting their slimy gut contents over marauding ants, killing themselves in the process. Most termite species have soldier castes with large armored jaws, but in the most advanced form of soldier these have become redundant. The Nasutitermitinae (snouted termites) have a specially-developed frontal gland that produces sticky and irritating chemicals from the tip of an extended snout. This strategy is so successful at warding off the attention of ants that most snouted termite soldiers have very reduced jaws, and a number of nasute genera forage in open columns, defended at the sides by snouted soldiers; examples include the grass-gathering "harvester" termites of the genus *Trinervitermes*, and also *Longipeditermes*.

Recyclers with Voracious Appetites
ECONOMIC AND ECOLOGICAL IMPACT
Except during their annual swarms, termites are secretive insects, (although many harvester termites form conspicuous foraging columns in daylight), yet they are all too familiar to people in tropical and subtropical regions because of the extensive damage they can cause. Termites depend on dead plant material for food, and often for a nesting place too. Man usually replaces natural vegetation with crops, forestry plantations, factories, and homes, all of which can provide the

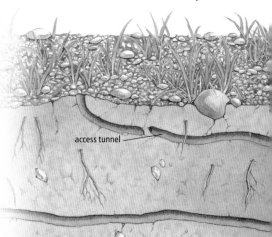

access tunnel

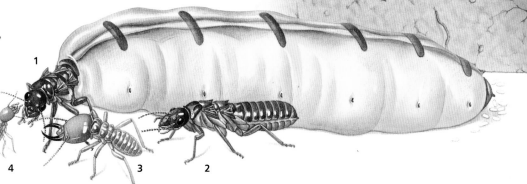

Right The queen *1* keeps tens of thousands of eggs in her abdomen, and is many times larger than the king *2*, who remains in constant attendance by her side. Large workers *3* forage; smaller ones *4* work inside the nest.

◑ **Left** *The chimneys atop the nests of* Macrotermes subhyalinus *(Termitidae) are a conspicuous sight in semi-desert regions of north Kenya. They help vent the heat generated by the colony and its fungus combs.*

◐ **Below** *Mounds built by termites of the African savanna may rise 6m (20ft) high and also sink 3m (10ft) below ground. Towers with chimneys provide cooling and ventilation, aided by cellars. Workers bring back food through the nest's many tunnels, which provide protection from predators, while soldiers serve as guards outside. Internal air circulation is an essential part of the design, as demonstrated in the cross-section of a* Macrotermes *mound shown below right.*

NATURE'S FINEST BUILDERS

Most species of termite hide their nests underground or inside dead wood, but a few higher termites build bizarre mounds and tree nests that can be a significant component of the tropical landscape. In the African savannas, high temperatures and low rainfall pose a real threat; exposed to the midday sun, termites would survive for only a few minutes. To protect the colony, the fungus-growing species *Macrotermes bellicosus* builds a towering earth mound up to 7.5m (25ft) high, most of the above-ground portion being hollow to allow circulation of air. Its function is to maintain an equable temperature in the nest below ground level, preventing it from overheating during the day or cooling too far at night. Much of the nest itself is occupied by the fungus combs, which themselves produce substantial amounts of heat.

Around Darwin in arid northern Australia, the remarkable Compass termite (*Amitermes meridionalis*) builds wedge-shaped nests 3.5m (11.5ft) high that run north to south, so that in the morning and evening sunshine on the flat surface helps warm up the nest, but at midday the knife-edge, pointed toward the sun, prevents overheating. Also in Australia, the snouted termite *Nasutitermes triodae* builds huge nests up to 6m (20ft) high that can become a permanent feature of the landscape; some are known to have been occupied continuously for over 60 years. The greatest diversification of the snouted termites has occurred in South America where, at the opposite extreme, grass-feeding *Syntermes* species build nests that extend 3.4m (11ft) underground!

In rain forests, changes in air temperature are less of a problem than sudden cloudbursts. In African forests, soil-feeding *Cubitermes* species (subfamily Termitinae) build mushroom-shaped nests with a series of caps or tree-side roofs to shed the rain. In the same forests, species of *Procubitermes* plaster their nests to a tree and protect them by building up to 40 water-shedding mud barriers in a herringbone pattern above the nest. In South America, species of the snouted termite genus *Constrictotermes* do precisely the same thing.

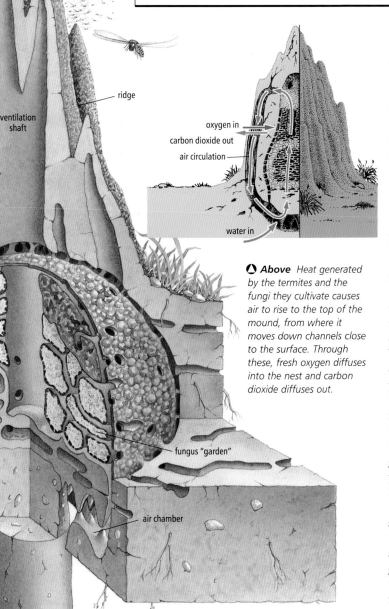

ridge

ventilation shaft

nuptial chamber

brood chamber

access to water

fungus "garden"

air chamber

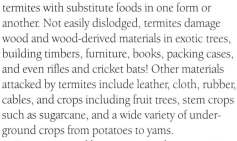

oxygen in

carbon dioxide out

air circulation

water in

◑ **Above** *Heat generated by the termites and the fungi they cultivate causes air to rise to the top of the mound, from where it moves down channels close to the surface. Through these, fresh oxygen diffuses into the nest and carbon dioxide diffuses out.*

termites with substitute foods in one form or another. Not easily dislodged, termites damage wood and wood-derived materials in exotic trees, building timbers, furniture, books, packing cases, and even rifles and cricket bats! Other materials attacked by termites include leather, cloth, rubber, cables, and crops including fruit trees, stem crops such as sugarcane, and a wide variety of underground crops from potatoes to yams.

Damage caused by termites can be very serious indeed. The entire village of Sri Hargobindpur in the Punjab region of India was abandoned in the 1950s because of the harm done by the termite *Heterotermes indicola*. A similar threat may have faced the village of Popayán in Colombia, where the church cross bears the inscription, "A Paternoster to Jesus that we may be free of termites."

Yet the capacity for destroying dead plants that is so troublesome to us is also the reason for termites' unrivaled ecological importance. In any ecosystem it is essential that plant material should be broken down, incorporated into the soil, and once again made available for the growth of living plants. Bacteria and fungi play the largest part in this process of decay, but in tropical savannas and forests termites also have an important role. In the tropics, termites may consume up to one-third of the total production of dead wood, leaves, and grass. Their populations can attain 2,000–4,000 per square meter of soil surface (approximately 200–400/sq ft), sometimes reaching as high as 10,000 (1,000/sq ft), and they dominate other soil animals. Their biomass, usually in the range of 1–5g/sq m (0.04–0.2oz/sq ft), can reach as high as 22g/sq m (0.8oz/sq ft), over twice that of the greatest densities of vertebrates on earth, found in the migrating herds of wildebeest and other mammals on Tanzania's Serengeti Plains.   KP-M/NMC

Mantids

SUPERBLY DESIGNED AS SIT-AND-WAIT AMBUSH *predators, mantids have large, widely spaced compound eyes and chewing mouthparts. Their triangular heads swivel freely atop a long, narrow prothorax (the first section of the thorax), which also carries the highly modified, grasping forelegs bearing an array of hooks and spines, arranged to form a gin-trap from which prey has little chance of escape.*

All mantids are carnivores, feeding mainly on a variety of insects including other mantids. Cannibalism on young of their own species is frequent. They are solitary creatures, and it is possible that this observed tendency toward cannibalism is partly responsible. In species that guard their ootheca, however, it is essential that the female should not attack her offspring during their mass emergence from the eggs. It is not known whether her predatory instinct is entirely "switched off" during this period, or whether she is able to discriminate between her own progeny and other potential prey.

Masters of Disguise
CAMOUFLAGE AND MIMICRY

In addition to their keen eyesight and formidable offensive armory, most mantids are cryptically colored to resemble the plant on which they lie in wait. In Africa, many green species can change to brown at the onset of the dry season, thereby responding to an equivalent switch in the main background tones. This environmental transformation can be even more drastic and sudden in areas of Africa and Australia, where bush fires frequently sweep through the landscape, changing it instantly to an all-pervading black. Within a few days mantids from both these regions are able, thanks to the phenomenon known as fire melanism, to change color to match the charcoal tints that now prevail around them.

◁ *Left* The typical triangular shape of the mantis's head is very evident in this female Polyspilota aeruginosa, a widespread species from Africa. The large compound eyes jutting out from the top corners of the head are very sensitive to movement.

FACTFILE

MANTIDS

Class: Insecta

Subclass: Pterygota

Order: Mantodea

About 1,800–2,000 species in 8 families. By far the largest family is the Mantidae, which includes the **European praying mantis** (*Mantis religiosa*) and all of the common North American mantids.

DISTRIBUTION All warmer regions; best represented in tropics.

SIZE Adults medium to large, 1–15cm (0.4–6in) long.

FEATURES Downward-directed triangular head on flexible neck; large eyes; long first segment of thorax (prothorax); large, grasping forelegs; form and coloration often cryptic in imitation of plants. Day-active carnivores, mostly found on shrubs, tree trunks, tall herbs, taking chiefly insects for food;

other terrestrial species may also take spiders and other terrestrial arthropods. The Amorphoscelididae, best represented in Australia, differ from the Mantidae in having a short dorsal plate (pronotum) covering the prothorax, and no spines in the crook of the forelegs.

LIFE CYCLE Eggs laid in capsules (oothecae), whose shape characterizes the species.

CONSERVATION STATUS 1 Spanish species, *Apteromantis aptera*, is currently listed by the IUCN as Lower Risk/Near Threatened.

◖ Left The male of this Dead-leaf mantis (Acanthops falcata) *is fully winged and, as its common name suggests, resembles a flattened dead leaf. The female, being wingless, has to adopt a different disguise, and instead resembles a leaf that has shrivelled up.*

◗ Below Although highly modified for raptorial purposes, the front legs of mantises such as this Parasphendale agrionina from Africa can still be used for walking. The swollen abdomen of this individual indicates that it is a female that is probably close to making its ootheca.

Some species go further than merely matching their background color and actually become a mobile part of their environment. Many mantids provide passable imitations of blades of grass or green, living leaves, but it is in the incredibly accurate imitation of dead leaves that certain mantids excel. In species of *Phyllocrania* from Africa and Madagascar, for example, elaborate projections of the cuticle of the head, body, and legs create an extraordinary degree of resemblance to a tattered dead leaf, an illusion enhanced by the insect's habit of perching in an inverted posture while awaiting prey. Many twiglike species refine their act by protracting the front legs directly forward with the head sunk down between them, thereby creating an uninterrupted, sticklike profile; in *Danuria buchholzi* from Africa, there is even a notch in the fore-coxa into which the head fits snugly. A number of tropical species mimic flowers with varying degrees of verisimilitude. In the African *Pseudocreobotra* it is the nymphs that do this best, as they can change color (within limits) over the space of a few days to match their chosen

bloom, usually colored pink, yellow, or white. Even when perched on a plant stem, these nymphs are sufficiently flowerlike to deceive nectar-seeking insects into making a fatal visit.

The rather squat, wingless members of the family Eremiaphilidae inhabit desert regions of North Africa and Asia, where their persuasive resemblance to stones makes them almost invisible unless they move. They are particularly abundant on the flat areas of compacted pebbles known as *reg* or desert pavement, where their long legs let them cover the baking ground with amazing speed and agility. The first instar nymphs of many African mantids mimic ants, often staying together in a group for maximum effect. This mimicry may be remarkably specific; for example, the nymphs of *Tarachodes afzelii* mimic the ant *Camponotus acvapimensis*, while *Miomantis paykulii* mimics various *Pheidole* species. In *Miomantis aurea* the first three instars mimic the weaver ant *Oecophylla longinoda*, although neither the later instars nor the adults are at all antlike; increasing size obviously precludes the continued use of the device.

Surprise Attackers

PREY CAPTURE AND DEFENSE

While waiting for a prey insect to pass, the mantis remains motionless, or gently rocks from side to side as if swaying in the breeze. It holds its forelegs folded against the prothorax, suggesting an attitude of prayer – hence the common name "praying mantis." When an insect passes, the mantis slowly turns its head and prothorax toward it (static insects are not normally recognized as prey, and the mantis may walk past or even over them without responding). If the insect strays within range, spined forelegs suddenly shoot forward to seize it. Some mantids have such lightning reactions that they can snatch a passing fly or other flying insect out of the air. Held in a pincerlike grip, the prey is brought to the mantid's jaws and devoured. The vicelike hold of the legs is so secure

THE RISKY BUSINESS OF MATING

Female mantids are famous for eating their suitors, but while this behavior does occur it is not nearly as common as once thought. In one American species it never occurs at all, not because males are adept at avoiding being eaten or because females are not cannibalistic, but because no males are known to exist. All the offspring are female and are produced from unfertilized eggs. This phenomenon, known as parthenogenesis, is common, although sexual reproduction usually occurs in most species.

Nevertheless, male mantids are sometimes eaten by females, before, during, or after mating. Under natural conditions, this behavior only seems to take place on anything like a regular basis in a very small number of species, especially *Mantis religiosa*. The most obvious benefit for the female is that she gets a nutritious meal, although by only mating with males that court her appropriately and by eating those that do not (as sometimes occurs), she may also help ensure that her male offspring will inherit the successful courtship behavior shown by their father and thus live to sire offspring of their own. As for the male, if he survives mating he could in theory mate with other females and sire more offspring, although not enough is known about patterns of sperm priority in mantids to reveal how effective this strategy would be. Observations of males trying to unseat mating rivals, however, indicate that second matings must have some reproductive benefit.

In order to maximize reproductive success, males have evolved a number of forms of behavior that minimize the risk of being eaten. They approach a female very slowly and cautiously, generally from behind, and, when close, leap onto her back. It may be vital for the male to take up a position from which he cannot be reached by the female's grasping forelegs, a task made easier by the fact that he is the smaller of the two. Even so, matings between mantises of different genera have been observed in which the males could not possibly have correctly performed any necessary courtship "insurance," so perhaps the risks involved are not as great or as general as has previously been thought.

The risks are also minimized by the fact that in some (perhaps most) mantids the males do not have to "try it on" with an unwilling and aggressive mate who is not expecting them, but instead arrive in response to active "calling" behaviors by the females. In *Acanthops falcata*, a dead-leaf mantis from Central and South America, the wingless females solicit the fully winged males by releasing a pheromone from glands on the abdomen. The incoming males are assured of a threat-free welcome, while the females "play fair" by switching off their pheromone production once they have mated.

During copulation the male transfers a spermatophore to the female, who goes into a trancelike state. On completion the male is in danger and in at least some species he leaps off as soon as the act is finished and runs away very quickly.

that there is no need to dispatch the prey before feeding commences, so the mantis can afford to begin casually nibbling away strips of flesh from its living victim until it eventually succumbs.

The cryptic coloration and behavior that serve mantids so well as hunters also protect them from falling prey themselves to birds, lizards, and insectivorous mammals. Once disturbed, mantids utilize a variety of defensive strategies. They may run away very quickly, or even launch into flight. Some species stand their ground and rear back to display brightly-colored marks on the insides of their forelegs. Others suddenly expose bright markings or eyespots on their hindwings, or on the top of the abdomen. If approached too closely by a predator (or an entomologist!), they will immediately strike out, and the spined forelegs can inflict a very painful jab. Colorful defensive displays are frequently withheld when the mantis is confronted by a large predator such as a human, but displays will be instantly unleashed against a smaller and potentially more easily impressed enemy, such as a bird, monkey, or lizard.

If picked up, a mantis will bend its mobile forelegs backwards over its prothorax and use the spines to ensure that it is either dropped by its tormentor or else held more carefully. Mantids will also sacrifice one or more mid- or hindlegs in

order to escape. This shedding of limbs is known as autotomy and results from the contraction of a special muscle at the base of the leg. The grasping front legs are very rarely autotomized, for a mantis without its front legs soon dies of starvation. Regeneration of lost appendages may occur if the limbs are shed early in the life of the mantis.

Protecting Baby Predators

REPRODUCTION AND DEVELOPMENT

Depending on the species, female mantids lay anywhere from 10 to 400 eggs in a frothy mass produced by glands in the abdomen. This froth hardens on contact with the air, so that the developing eggs are protected by a horny capsule, and often also by a tough, spongy coat. The size and shape of this structure, called the ootheca, depends on the species. Many species, including the *Mantis religiosa* of Europe and North Africa, attach the ootheca to a flat surface such as a tree trunk, fence post, or rock. In others species it surrounds twigs or stems, and in some species it is even deposited in the soil.

Despite the protective coat, parasitism of the eggs, particularly by certain wasps, is common, and often few if any larval mantids emerge from an ootheca. The young larvae leave the egg case via a series of exit holes that lie along its upper midline. In some genera such as *Galepsus* and *Tarachodula*, the mother stands guard until the young emerge, and in these species the ootheca is elongate in form so that the mother can straddle it with her body for maximum protection. The highly cryptic *Galepsus* females choose a well-concealed location, but *Tarachodula pantherina* mothers guard their eggs on exposed twigs. It is possible that their presence may help guard against attack by predators such as birds that hunt by sight, as this is one of the few mantis species that appears to flaunt warning (aposematic) colors.

Newly emerged larval mantids eventually disperse and commence their predatory existence as small, vulnerable versions of their parents. After passing through several molts, during which they increase in size and their developing wing buds become progressively larger, the larvae go through a final molt to become adults. Adult male mantids usually have fully developed wings, while the wings of the females of many species are reduced or absent.

The earliest known fossil mantids date from the Oligocene, 34–24 million years ago. Mantids are often confused with stick insects. The two orders, while superficially similar in appearance, are in fact easy to tell apart; most notably, the prothorax is extremely elongate in mantids but not in phasmids. Also, stick insects, which are herbivores, lack the armored, grasping forelegs and the mobile triangular heads of mantids.   KP-M/SSi

◐ **Below** For the first few days after they emerge from their ootheca, young mantids remain closely packed together. They then make their first molt and disperse. These are Stagmatoptera septentrionalis on a rainforest leaf in Trinidad.

◑ **Right** Like all mantids, this Harpagomantis discolor *female* has forward-pointing eyes whose binocular vision permits accurate judgement of distances – vital for successful hunting. This is one of several African species that sit in wait on flowers.

Earwigs

t HE BELIEF THAT EARWIGS ENTER THE EARS OF *sleeping people and bore into their brains is completely unfounded; some earwigs can indeed bite, but the effect would be hardly noticeable on humans. The legend may, however, have contributed to their common name, which is generally derived from the Old English* earwicga, *meaning "ear creature;" in fact, however, the word could equally well be a corruption of "earwing," referring to the shape of the insects' fanlike, membranous hindwings.*

◑ **Above** *The Linear earwig (Doru lineare) from North America is typical of earwigs the world over. The slender, flattened body ends in a pair of large pincers, relatively straight in females but much more curved in males. The large and delicate hindwings are intricately folded away for protection beneath the short, horny elytra (forewings).*

The insects, which are sometimes also called pincer bugs, owe their ordinal name Dermaptera rather to their leathery forewings; in classical Greek, *dermatos* meant "skin" and *pteron* "wing." The earwigs are known from the Jurassic period (205–144 million years ago), and are thought to be most closely allied to the Grylloblattodea.

Prowlers with Pincers
FORM AND FUNCTION

Earwigs are easily recognizable by the presence of abdominal pincers or forceps, which are derived cerci. The forceps are present in most of the 1,900 or so species, although completely absent in the suborders Arixeniina and Hemimerina. Both sexes have these forceps, although they vary in shape and size between the two. The forceps are multi-purpose structures, being used in courtship and defensive behavior, for grooming, and in the folding of the hindwings.

Earwigs are dorsoventrally flattened, elongate, slender insects, ranging in size from 4 to 50mm (0.2–2in), and, exceptionally, to 80mm (3in) in one species. The mandibulate mouthparts point forward (in other words, they are prognathous), and the antennae are slender and often beadlike. The senses of touch and smell play important roles in earwigs, so the antennae are continually moving and sensing the environment. Earwigs have large, compound eyes, and the ocelli are lacking. The forewings are short, usually not reaching beyond the third abdominal segment, and the hindwings are fanlike and folded under the forewings when in repose; some species are completely wingless (apterous). The abdomen is highly flexible due to the telescopic nature of its segments, and bears cerci that are usually unsegmented and in the form of forceps. Generally earwigs are uniformly brown or black in color, or are patterned with a mixture of brown, black, orange-brown, or cream.

Dermaptera are found throughout the world except for the polar regions, and are most diverse in the tropics. They occur in all habitats from the snowline at the tops of mountains to the marine shorelines. The favorite habitats of the European lesser earwig (*Labior minor*) are dung piles and rubbish heaps. A few species are ectoparasites of bats and rats (see Weird Earwigs).

Most earwigs are omnivores that eat plant and animal remains. Some species prey on small invertebrates such as aphids, and certain ones, such as *Labidura truncata*, are encouraged into crops to help keep down pests such as the caterpillars of Codling moths. However, a number of earwig species are themselves crop and garden pests. These include the European earwig, *Forficula auricularia*, and the Australian *Nala lividipes* (Labiduridae). The biology and ecology of most earwigs, however, remain poorly known.

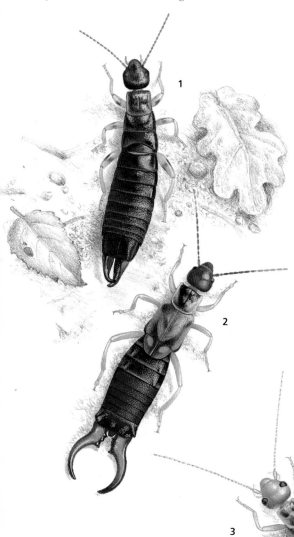

◑ **Above** *Three species of earwigs exhibit the elongated bodies and abdominal pincers, used for many different purposes, that are typical of the order. From top to bottom, these are **1** the Ring-legged earwig (Euborellia annulipes), **2** the European earwig (Forficula auricularia), and **3** the Tawny earwig (Labidura riparia).*

WEIRD EARWIGS

Two suborders of Dermaptera have very strange lifestyles: these are the Arixeniina and Hemimerina, and they live as ectoparasites on mammals. Except for the males of two species of Arixeniina, these two groups, unlike all other earwigs, have no developed forceps, but instead have weakly sclerotized cerci.

The Arixeniina **1** contain just one family, Arixeniidae, consisting of five species in two genera. These atypical earwigs are completely wingless, hairy, and flattened. Their eyes are strongly reduced or even absent, no doubt because they live in the dark. The family is known from only a few caves and hollow trees in the Malaysian region, where they are associated with free-tailed bats of the family Molossidae. The earwigs feed on the bodily exudates and skin debris of the bats; they will also eat bat fecal matter and dead insects, although usually only when

threatened with starvation. The arixeniids exhibit pseudoplacental viviparity, which basically means they give birth to live young that, unlike other, more typical earwigs, have only four instars.

The Hemimerina **2** are restricted to sub-Saharan Africa, where they are found on pouched rats; *Araeomerus* species associate with the Lesser pouched rat (*Beamys hindei*), while *Hemomerinus* species live on the two giant *Cricetomys* species. These insects, which look more like cockroaches than earwigs, average about 10mm (0.4in) in length, and are blind and wingless. They are smooth and flattened in shape, with strongly developed tarsi for gripping the hairs of their hosts, enabling them to move rapidly through fur. Unlike the arixeniids, the hemimerines never leave their hosts, feeding exclusively on skin fragments and body exudates. It is possible that the relationship is more mutualistic than parasitic, because the insects are thought to help clean the rats and thus reduce the risk of skin infections.

Another species that lives in association with bats is *Chelisoches bimammatus*. These earwigs live in bat caves in Thailand and Malaysia and feed on the accumulated guano of the fruit-eating Lesser dawn bat, *Eonycteris spelaea*. The earwigs piggyback on the bats as a way of getting into new cave systems, and it is thought that this kind of phorectic behavior may have led to the more specialized associations found in the arixeniids.

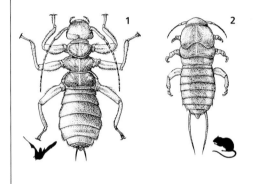

FACTFILE

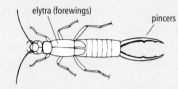

EARWIGS

Class: Insecta

Subclass: Neoptera

Order: Dermaptera

Approximately 1,900 species in 10 families, divided between 4 suborders: the **Archidermaptera**, known only from Jurassic fossils; **Hemimerina**, (1 family, 2 genera, 11 species), found only in southern Africa; **Arixeniina** (1 family, 2 genera, 5 species), found only in SE Asia; and **Forficulina** (8 families, approximately 1,800 species), with a worldwide distribution

DISTRIBUTION Worldwide.

SIZE Elongate and slender; length 4–50mm (0.2–2in).

FEATURES Antennae slender, often beaded (6–15 segments); mouthparts mandibulate, prognathous; tarsi 3-segmented; forewings short and leathery; hindwings semicircular and pleated; cerci enlarged to form forceps.

LIFE CYCLE Hemimetabolous (featuring incomplete metamorphosis, with larval but no pupal stage). Larvae (4–5 instars) resemble adults, except that wings are small or absent.

CONSERVATION STATUS One species – the St. Helena earwig (*Labidura herculeana*) – is currently listed as Critically Endangered, and may well be extinct.

Caring Mothers

SOCIAL BEHAVIOR

The males of many species use the forceps in courtship behavior, and in some species the female often chooses to mate with the male with the biggest pair. Mating takes place end-to-end, and in almost all species the male takes no further role in care of the young once the spermatophore has been delivered.

Maternal care, however, is well-developed in most species. According to species, the female lays from 30 to 50 eggs in a "nest," often under rocks or logs or at the end of a tunnel, defending them against predators and licking them regularly to keep them clean and free from fungal infection. Once the eggs hatch, the female will carry on looking after the young, in some cases bringing suitable food into the nest or even regurgitating her own meals to feed them. Once the nymphs have passed through a couple of instars (growth stages), however, the females lose their maternal instinct and may in fact eat any of the young that are unfortunate enough not to have left the nest. The nymphs will pass through up to five instars before becoming adult, and this process may take as long as a year, although in tropical areas the period can be a short as six weeks.

Some earwigs such as *Doru taeniatum* (Forficulidae) have developed chemical defense secretions. When attacked, this species maneuvers its abdomen in such a way that it can simultaneously

use its pincers and spray a mixture of noxious quinones from a pair of glands in the fourth abdominal segment.

The world's largest earwig, *Labidura herculeana*, is endemic to the island of St. Helena in the South Pacific, but it has not been seen since 1965. A number of expeditions have tried unsuccessfully to find it, but only remains have been located; it is now thought to be extinct.   DM

🔊 **Below** Mothers generally stay with their eggs until they hatch, licking off fungal spores that could cause infections and guarding them against predators. They then spend some time with the larvae, feeding them with food brought to the nest or else regurgitated from their own meals.

Stoneflies

tHE PLECOPTERA OR STONEFLIES ARE AN ancient order of insects that first appeared during the Permian period, some 250 million years ago, and have changed little since. They first evolved in the southern hemisphere, where the older of the two suborders (the Antarctoperlaria) still only occur in the Australasian region and South America.

The stoneflies are believed to be the earliest group of the Neoptera; although they are sometimes regarded as being most closely related to the orthopteroid orders and the Embioptera, it may well be that in fact they form a sister group to the whole of the Neoptera. The group occurs throughout all continents except for Antarctica, from sea level to over 5,500m (18,000ft) up in the Himalayas.

Three Weeks of Adult Life
FUNCTION AND DISTRIBUTION

Plecopterans are delicate, soft-bodied insects that are rather uniform in appearance, ranging in length from 3 to 50mm (0.1–2in). The adults of most species are fully winged, although there are a number of species that are brachypterous or even apterous. The name Plecoptera is derived from the Greek words *plectos*, meaning "pleated," and *pteron*, "wing;" the reference is to the way in which the hindwings are folded when at rest.

Although winged, the stoneflies are poor fliers and are generally not found too far away from water, in which they develop. The adults spend most of the time sitting on waterside rocks or vegetation, their membranous wings folded flat across the body. During their 2–3 weeks of adult life, the delicate, brownish or yellowish flies generally do not feed, although some species scrape algae from rocks and trees or take pollen.

The suborder Antarctoperlaria contains just four families, found only in the southern hemisphere. The Austroperlidae, Eustheniidae, and Gripoterygidae are distributed throughout Australasia and South America, whereas the Diamphipnoidae, containing just five species, some of which are brightly colored, are endemic to South America only. The single species in the genus *Acruroperla* (Austroperlidae) is particularly spectacular; it has an iridescent, metallic blue or black body and dark wings with a red or yellow costal margin.

The eleven families of the suborder Arctoperlaria are restricted to the northern hemisphere, except for one family – the Notonemouridae – that is widespread in the southern hemisphere. The Leuctridae includes the needleflies or rolled-wing flies, which bend their wings round the sides of the body when at rest, and the angler's February red (*Taeniopteryx nebulosa*). The Perlodidae are predatory; among their ranks is the genus *Isoperla*, the largest in the order with some 50 species. The largest family is the Perlidae, which includes the

○ **Right** A Yellow sally pair (Isoperla grammatica; Perlodidae) mating on waterside vegetation. Males of many species also have greatly reduced wings.

○ **Below** Members of the family Perlidae include some of the largest stoneflies, most of which breed in fast-flowing rivers with stony beds, often in upland areas. The cerci at the body's rear are unusually long.

Large stone fly (*Dinocras cephalotes*) and *Perla bipunctata*, also well-known to anglers. The Taeniopterygidae are known as winter stoneflies and are commonly seen to come out in the early part of the year when snow may still be on the ground. Other families include the Isoperlidae (including the Yellow sally, *Isoperla grammatica*) and the Chloroperlidae, known as the green stoneflies.

Drumming Up a Partner
REPRODUCTION AND LIFE CYCLE

Mating usually takes place during the day, and may involve a duet of drumming between the male and the female. The male taps his abdomen on the substrate to make a species-specific drum beat that attracts the female; in turn she may sound back a recognition beat. In some species this acoustic mating behavior is reduced to transmitting sound through the substrate, thereby avoiding predators that may otherwise be attracted by the noise.

Typically, a female lays her eggs, which may number up to 1,000, by dipping her abdomen, while in flight, under the surface of the water. The spherical eggs become sticky on contacting the water and stick to rocks and gravel in the stream. Some species actually crawl into the water to lay their eggs on the underside of rocks, and in some of the Notonemouridae the female has a long ovipositor that is used to insert the eggs deep into rock crevices. In these stoneflies the eggs are usually flat and disklike, with one adhesive surface.

Stonefly larvae, sometimes called naiads, survive best in cool, well-aerated, unpolluted water with a gravel bottom. Stoneflies pass through a large number of molts before becoming adult. Over a period of usually one, but up to four, years, they may molt more than 30 times. The larvae either breathe simply by diffusion or else have external tufted gills on the mouthparts, thorax, legs, abdomen, or, often, extruded from the anus. A very few species have terrestrial larvae that live in cool, moist areas away from water; in marked contrast, one bizarre, wingless species of the family Capniidae spends its entire life 60m (200ft) beneath the surface of Lake Tahoe in North America. The larvae of most species feed on detritus, although some families are omnivorous or are predatory on small aquatic invertebrates such as midge larvae. At the last instar, the larvae leave the water, sometimes in great numbers, to molt into their adult form.

Both adult and larval stoneflies are an important part of the freshwater food web, providing food for many other insects and fish. Since stoneflies are very sensitive to pollution, they are used by scientists as indicators of water quality.   DM

FACTFILE

STONEFLIES

Class: Insecta

Subclass: Neoptera

Order: Plecoptera

2,000 species in 15 families, divided between 2 suborders: Arctoperlaria (11 families) and Antarctoperlaria (4 families).

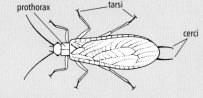

DISTRIBUTION Worldwide except Antarctica, especially in temperate climes.

SIZE Delicate, medium-sized; body length 3–50mm (0.1–2in).

FEATURES Cylindrical body, sometimes flattened; prothorax well developed; 2 pairs of membranous wings (hindwings broader) held flat across body at rest; antennae long, threadlike; cerci multisegmented, threadlike; tarsi 3-segmented.

LIFE CYCLE Hemimetabolous (incomplete metamorphosis); larvae aquatic.

CONSERVATION STATUS 1 species – Robert's stonefly, from the USA – is listed as recently extinct; 2 other Australian species are classed as Vulnerable.

Crickets and Grasshoppers

t HE CRICKETS AND GRASSHOPPERS OF THE
large order Orthoptera are noted for jumping
(to escape predators) and singing (to potential
mates). Powerful hindlegs, special noise-producing
equipment, and ears to receive the sounds produced
are characteristic features of most members of this
large insect order.

The orthopterans also demonstrate a huge range
of lifestyles, from free-living species exhibiting
camouflage or warning coloration (or most often
both) to near-blind burrowers with shovel-like legs
such as the mole-crickets. Even within a single
species, some individuals may be solitary while
others group in massive swarms.

Straight-winged Jumpers
FORM AND FUNCTION

The first fossil Orthoptera appear in the Upper
Carboniferous, with the first Ensifera appearing in
the Permian (295–248 million years ago) and the
first Caelifera in the Triassic (248–205 million
years ago). The Orthoptera are grouped in the
Orthopteroidea, which also includes the cockroaches, mantids, and earwigs, and are thought to
be most closely related to the Phasmatodea (stick
insects). The name Orthoptera is derived from the
Greek orthos, meaning "straight," and pteron, "a
wing," and refers to the structure of the forewing.

Broadly speaking, the Orthoptera have evolved
into two ecological types: those species that are
adapted to a life in the open and those that live a
largely concealed existence, often below ground.
Insects that live in the open are in constant danger
of being eaten by all manner of predators, both
invertebrate (for instance spiders or other insects)
and vertebrate (lizards, frogs, birds). These free-
ranging orthopterans have evolved many ways of
minimizing this risk. A common strategy is to
blend with the surroundings. Many members of
the order bear a striking resemblance to living,
dead, or even diseased leaves, and to bark, burned
tree trunks, twigs, lichens, stones, or sand. Other
species have become highly distasteful to predators, often by incorporating toxins from food
plants into their bodies. Such insects are usually

🔽 *Below* Warningly-colored
grasshoppers are widespread
in warm regions of the world.
The Variegated grasshopper
(Zonocerus variegatus;
Pyrgomorphidae) is often
a pest of crops in West and
Central Africa.

FACTFILE

CRICKETS AND GRASSHOPPERS

Class: Insecta

Subclass: Pterygota

Order: Orthoptera

22,000 species in 39 families, divided into 2 suborders: Ensifera and Caelifera

DISTRIBUTION Worldwide, except for polar regions.

SIZE Medium to large; body length 10–150mm (0.4–6in)

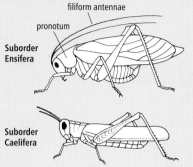

FEATURES Stout or elongate insects; mandibulate mouthparts; antennae filiform, short or long; pronotum shield- or saddle-shaped; forewings (when present) narrow and hardened, to protect hindwings (when present) that fold fanlike; hindlegs usually modified for jumping; tarsi 3- or 4-segmented; cerci short, unsegmented; hearing organs and sound-producing (stridulatory) organs (usually only in males) often present

LIFE CYCLE Hemimetabolous; large nymphs more or less resemble wingless adults.

CONSERVATION STATUS 8 species are currently listed as Critically Endangered and 8 as Endangered; 50 are considered Vulnerable. In addition, 2 US species are now listed as extinct, and a third as Extinct in the Wild.

See superfamilies table ▷

brightly colored, so that predators learn to associate an unpleasant taste with a distinctive pattern of bright warning (aposematic) colors. Yet other orthopterans have evolved to resemble other insects; by mimicking unpalatable or dangerous species, they reduce the chance of being eaten. As larvae (nymphs), certain species of long-horned grasshoppers or bush crickets (Tettigoniidae) mimic other insects and even spiders, but subsequently develop into cryptically-colored adults.

Most crickets and grasshoppers that live above ground have keen eyesight and hearing. They are very wary and are quick to leap away if disturbed, using their highly developed hindlegs. The adults of many species also fly. In escaping, brightly colored areas of the body that are normally hidden may be exposed; such flashes of color may serve to startle or to mislead predators.

A variation of this behavior is the distracting flash display of certain grasshoppers. For example the Australian Yellow-winged locust *Gastrimargus musicus* (Acrididae), when disturbed, leaps into the air and flies a short distance. It has brightly colored hindwings that are only visible during flight, and its wings also produce a clicking sound. During the escape flight the grasshopper suddenly shuts its wings and drops to the ground. The predator, having suddenly lost sight and sound of the quarry, follows its brightly-colored trajectory. In fact, the camouflaged grasshopper is sitting very still some meters back from this point.

Should the predator manage to seize it, an orthopteran will kick out with its powerful and often spiny hindlegs and regurgitate the contents

○ **Above** *If molested, the Armored ground katydid (*Acanthoplus armativentris; *Tettigoniidae*) from southern Africa can release a noxious yellow liquid from its thoracic glands. Even so, hungry mongooses will eat it.*

of its foregut. Many of the distasteful species also release offensive secretions from glands that open onto their body surface. A number of species in the family Pyrgomorphidae, such as the Australian genus *Monistria*, have toxins that are probably sequestered in the hemolymph from plants. These poisons act as a defense against diurnal vertebrate predators and are advertised by bright warning (aposematic) coloration. If held by a hindleg, a grasshopper will sacrifice the limb by

○ **Right** *Many crickets (*Gryllidae*) are wingless and cannot fly. This male has raised his forewings, inviting the female to mount and feed on secretions from his metanotal glands.*

the contraction of a special muscle at the base. A small diaphragm immediately closes the wound and prevents infection or massive blood loss.

Orthopterans that spend most of their time concealed fall into one of three types. The first includes crickets and grasshoppers that burrow in the soil or else live in rotting wood or beneath bark or stones. These species also spend some time in the open, usually at night. Some are extensively modified for digging; their legs are often short, with the first pair shovel-like. In addition, they often have reduced wings, and their bodies are generally cylindrical and smooth.

Cave-dwelling species are dull-colored, delicate insects. Their eyesight is poor, but they have extremely long legs and antennae that endow them with excellent senses of touch, smell, and heat detection. The family Rhaphidophoridae contains the majority of the cave-dwellers, some of which have now become so adapted to life in the permanent dark that they have completely lost their eyes. Some species can take up to two years to complete their lifecycle. The North American cave cricket *Euhadenoecus insolitus* is known to have parthenogenetic populations, making males redundant. As with the cockroaches, which initially shared human cave dwellings, some cave crickets have followed us into our homes.

Finally, a few orthopterans live their entire lives underground, never coming into the open; this group includes the Cooloola monsters (Anostostomatidae – see box) and several of the Jerusalem crickets of the genus *Stenopelmatus* (Stenopelmatidae). Some live in the soil and are soft, blind, unpigmented creatures, whose legs are highly modified for digging. The strange sand-groppers (Cylindrachaetidae) are found from Papua New Guinea to Australia, with a single species in Patagonia, South America. The members of this wingless family look more like beetle larvae than orthopterans; all of the known 18 species construct tunnels in sandy soils.

Although most orthopterans do not live as commensals with other animals, the bizarre ant-loving crickets (Myrmecophilidae) are an exception. These very small, flattened, wingless insects live in ants' nests. They feed on secretions produced by their hosts and behave very much as members of the colony. The Indian *Homeogryllus cincticornis* is known to inhabit termite mounds.

The family Anostostomatidae contains the New Zealand weta and the Australian and South African king crickets, which are amongst the bulkiest of all the orthopterans. The tusks of the

○ **Right** *Camouflage is an effective defensive technique employed by some orthopterans. Truxalis species (Acrididae) closely resemble the grass in which they live; this individual has wandered onto a leaf, making it more conspicuous. When hunched up among quartz pebbles, Trachypetrella andersonii (Pamphagidae – inset) becomes part of its surroundings.*

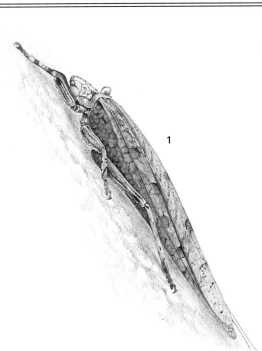

tusked weta, such as *Hemiandrus monstrosus* and *Motuweta isolata*, are long, forward projections from the base of the mandibles, the size of which is variable. In some species the tusks have stridulatory pegs that permit the insects to produce audible sounds by making a pincer movement. Approximately 16 of the New Zealand weta species are in serious decline, partly due to predation by introduced animals such as rats. Current research on their conservation involves captive breeding programs and translocation studies, all aimed at saving them from extinction.

Mouthparts for Chewing
DIET

Most grasshoppers feed on the foliage of plants; some are restricted to a small number of plant species, while others are less choosy. The crickets and katydids are generally omnivorous and will eat both living plants and dead plant and animal material. Soil-dwelling species feed on the roots of plants or on algae and other microorganisms, which they ingest along with mud. Certain groups are predacious, catching other insects with their grasping forelegs in a manner similar to mantids.

All orthopterans have chewing mouthparts, modified according to the species' diet. For example, the structure of the mandibles of different short-horned grasshoppers varies with the toughness of their chosen food plants. The endemic

Australian tettigoniid subfamilies, the Zaprochilinae and the Phasmodinae, are unusual in the group in that they feed exclusively on flowers. The wingless phasmodines resemble stick insects (Phasmatodea) and feed on a range of flowers, often causing serious damage, whereas the zaprochilines feed only on nectar and pollen.

Singing for a Mate
STRIDULATION

The production of sound (stridulation) is a notable feature of orthopteran life. Sounds may be used in territorial and defensive behavior; the mating calls, however, are the most noticeable to human ears. Stridulation, normally by males, plays an important role in courtship. The songs are species-specific, thus ensuring that only females of the correct species are attracted for mating. The song may also be important for males in distancing one from another. Many orthopterans have courtship dances involving intricate patterns of leg and body movements.

There are two basic mechanisms used to produce courtship songs. In one, the insect rubs specialized veins on the bases of the forewings. This tooth-and-comb technique is found mainly in species of the suborder Ensifera (crickets, katydids, and long-horned grasshoppers). The other mechanism, used largely by the suborder Caelifera (short-horned grasshoppers and locusts), could be termed a washboard technique as it involves friction between a ridge or row of pegs on the inside of the hindleg and one or more pronounced veins on the forewing. Many other techniques are employed, but these are the most

8a

8b

◁ **Left** *All orthopterans are equipped with biting and chewing mouthparts. This last-instar nymph of a* Microcentrum *katydid (Tettigoniidae) is feeding on a hibiscus flower.*

◆ **Above** *1 A Neotropical* Acanthodis *katydid (Tettigoniidae) 2* Ommatopia pictifolia *(Tettigoniidae) from Brazil resembles a dead leaf. 3* Brochopeplus exaltatus, *from Sri Lanka, and 4* Sasima spinosa, *from New Guinea (both Tettigoniidae) are impressive leaf mimics. 5 Black cricket (*Gryllus bimaculatus; *Gryllidae). 6 House cricket (*Acheta domestica; *Gryllidae). 7 European mole cricket (*Gryllotalpa vinae; *Gryllotalpidae). 8a At rest, this European grasshopper (*Oedipoda miniata; *Acrididae) resembles mottled stone, but if disturbed 8b it flies off with a flurry of colored wings to startle its attacker.*

characteristic of the order. In some families both the male and the female may be able to sing mating duets, whereas in others only the male sings.

The Oak bush cricket (*Meconema thalassinum*; Tettigoniidae) produces sound in a particularly unusual way. It raises one of its hind legs and drums with its tarsi on the substrate, producing a sound that almost resembles purring. A number of other species click their mandibles together to create "teeth-gnashing" sounds; these are often used by grasshoppers when threatened.

The ears of the orthopteran are found on the abdomen or the front legs, and consist of a thin membrane connecting internally to specialized receptors. Sounds cause the membrane to vibrate

◯ **Right** *A female katydid (Eupholidoptera chabrieri; Tettigoniidae) carrying a very large spermatophore transferred to her by the male during copulation. She will ultimately eat the spermatophore.*

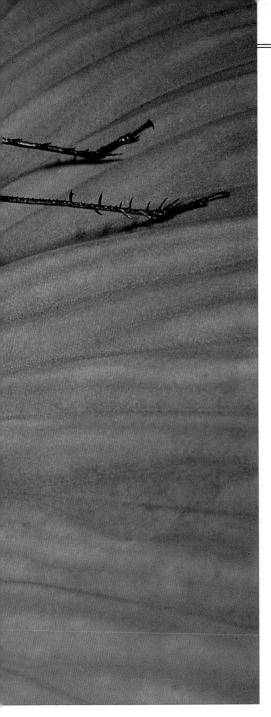

◐ **Left** *During courtship, the male (right) of this* Nisitrus *diurnal cricket (Gryllidae) from Sumatra serenades the female with a series of chirps. Courtship in this species is lengthy and elaborate, and includes an unusual leg-waving signal.*

◑ **Above** *In katydids (Tettigoniidae) such as this* Stilpnochlora *species from Peru, the "ears" consist of a slit at the base of the front tibia (in the foreground above), covered by a thin membrane that vibrates in sympathy with sound waves.*

and so stimulate nerve cells in the receptors. In some species, the ears of the male and female may be of different shapes. In a number of bush crickets (Tettigoniidae), hearing is used to avoid predation by bats. One such species, *Phaneroptera falcata*, is able to detect bats up to 30m (100ft) away, allowing individual insects to escape long before the bats have even located them.

The sounds produced by orthopterans may be surprisingly loud; the cone-headed katydids (Tettigoniidae; Copiphorinae) are some of the loudest insects known. Normally this is because of the design of the sound-producing apparatus itself. However a number of families including the mole crickets (Gryllotalpidae) actually build their own amplifiers. The shape of the male mole cricket's burrow magnifies the insect's song so that on a still evening it may be heard up to 2km (1.2mi) away! The most sophisticated advances in loudspeaker design have recently produced, by the use of computers, forms that seem to copy almost exactly the burrow of a mole cricket.

Not all the sounds made by crickets can be heard by human ears, however. Many species produce sounds at the ultrasonic level, and since human hearing only reaches about 20kHz, any sounds above that limit are beyond our range. In the Australian katydid genus *Kawanaphila* (Tettigoniidae), the males of two species produce songs consisting of brief, pure-tone sound pulses at ultrasonic frequencies lasting for up to 1 millisecond. These frequencies differ between the two species – *Kawanaphila yarraga* emits pulses at 40 kHz, *Kawanaphila mirla* at 70 kHz – enabling females to recognize the correct mates. Entomologists often use these ultrasonic songs to capture orthopterans by using modified "bat-detectors."

The surrounding ambient temperature often affects orthopteran sound production. In some species the males will not sing until the air temperature is optimal. This can be so finely tuned that, for example with the Snowy tree cricket (*Oecanthus fultoni*; Gryllidae), the temperature can be calculated in degrees Fahrenheit by adding 40 to the number of chirps in a 15-second period!

In the North American Sagebush cricket (*Cyphoderris stripitans*; Haglidae), the males come out from hiding at night, climbing to the top of sagebush plants to begin singing. Studies have shown that virgin males are better singers than older males, whose deficiencies are partly due to the attentions of the female during mating, but also to a depletion in energy reserves because of the reduction in time spent feeding.

During copulation, the female, who is on the male's back, begins to feed on his fleshy hind wings. The female will also eat the spermatophore – the capsule in which sperm transfer occurs – after mating. This sexual cannibalism is thought to give the female extra protein for egg production.

pronged ovipositor, and specialized muscles between segments allow her to extend her abdomen down to more than twice its normal length before depositing her eggs. In general, egg pods are laid in the soil; in temperate regions some species may deposit their pods into grass tussocks, while in the tropics rotten logs may be used. The European *Chrysochroa dispar* of the Acrididae lives in damp meadows where the female lays her eggs in plant stems or dead wood, but never at ground level, in order to avoid them drowning in winter floods. Numerous insects use these pods as a source of food; in Africa the pods of *Zonocerus* species are used by oil beetles (Meloidae), bee flies (Bombyliidae), and parasitic wasps (notably the Scelionidae). These parasites often keep pest grasshoppers in check.

The larval orthopterans (nymphs) that emerge are usually similar in appearance and behavior to adults, although in some species they may be of a different color, or else bear a color pattern unlike that of the adults. They pass through from three to five molts before becoming adults.

As a whole, the orthopterans are not notably gregarious or destructive, but some species of the family Acrididae occur in two phases, one solitary and one gregarious. In the latter form they may mass in swarms of many millions and devastate huge areas of crops. Such acridids are referred to as locusts. DM/SSi

◁ **Left** *Most grasshoppers lay their eggs in soft ground. While doing so, this female Elegant grasshopper* (Zonocerus elegans; *Pyrgomorphidae*) *from Africa is accompanied by her mate.*

Concealing the Eggs

REPRODUCTION AND LIFE CYCLE

Most orthopterans lay their eggs either in the soil or in plant tissue; in some burrowing forms, they are laid in specially-dug chambers. Species in the suborder Ensifera have a well-developed, sword-shaped or cylindrical ovipositor, which can be short and broad like a scimitar or long and thin, often longer than the entire body. This ovipositor is introduced into an appropriate site for egg-laying, such as plant tissue or bark crevices, the locality being dependent on the species. The shape of the ovipositor is often diagnostic for site preference; in species with long and thin ovipositors, eggs are normally deposited in the soil, whereas those with short, scimitar-shaped ovipositors lay them in crevices or in plant tissue. In species that deposit their eggs in plants, the female chews an initial entry hole, and the tip of the ovipositor is often toothed or serrated to help the female "saw" into plant tissue. Most ensiferans lay their eggs singly, although suitable cracks and cavities are often full of eggs.

The caeliferans, however, lay eggs in batches, or "pods," of 10–200, surrounded by protective foam. The female digs down with her short,

THE COOLOOLA MONSTER

In 1976, a strange creature was collected from a pitfall trap set on the rainforest floor in the Cooloola National Park in Queensland, Australia. The Cooloola monster (RIGHT; *Cooloola propator*), as it came to be known, created a sensation among entomologists.

The new discovery was an adult male, about 3cm (1.2in) long and extremely robust in appearance, with a broad body and shovel-like legs and head. It had very short antennae and was almost blind. The wings were very short and nonfunctional (females are completely wingless). Such features strongly suggested that the insect was a burrower.

The beast was obviously an orthopteran, but it did not fit into any of the known families, or even clearly into either of the two suborders. Taxonomists finally agreed that it should be placed in the suborder Ensifera, but that it represented a new family, the Cooloolidae. This family has since been made a subfamily of the Anostostomatidae, based on new scientific evidence, although not everyone agrees.

The Cooloola monster burrows in the sandy, moist soil of coastal rain forest and open eucalypt forest in central Queensland. Adult males appear above ground only at night, apparently after rain, as this is the time when they are most commonly collected. Females, on the other hand, seem to live

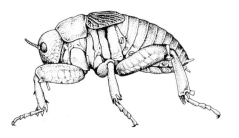

their entire lives underground. They can barely walk on the surface, having a large, swollen abdomen and very small feet and claws.

The shape of the mouthparts suggests that the Cooloola monster is a predator. Possibly it feeds on beetle larvae and other insects that live among the tangled roots of plants near the surface of the forest soil. Unfortunately, little is known of the biology or ecology of the group.

In recent years another three species have been discovered, all in Queensland. The Dingo monster (*Cooloola dingo*) was found burrowing in sandy soil. The Sugarcane monster (*Cooloola ziljan*), which was accidentally plowed up, is the largest species known so far. The final species, *Cooloola pearsoni*, was found in 1991 on South Percy Island, an uninhabited island some 85km (50mi) offshore.

SOLITARY OR GREGARIOUS?

Phase changes in Desert locusts

TWO DISTINCT LIFESTYLES, EACH OF WHICH IS geared to different prevailing environmental conditions, characterize the Desert locust (*Schistocerca gregaria*). When lush, green plants are plentiful, it lives a solitary life, widely dispersed throughout the vegetation. In this solitary phase, developing nymphs are green, to match their background, and develop into solitary living adults.

However, when drought comes and food resources dwindle to isolated patches of browning vegetation, the nymphs become more brightly and warningly colored through successive molts. At the same time, they become gregarious, and their population density increases dramatically. These changes are associated with changes in body chemistry: when solitary and green, the nymphs are protected from predation by resembling their background and are relatively palatable to those predators (lizards, birds) that find them. When gregarious and warningly colored, the nymphs will have started to ingest toxins from poisonous plants, making them distasteful to all predators. Moreover, being gregarious reflects the fact that there is safety in numbers: by adopting a similar livery of black, yellow, and orange markings, relatively fewer nymphs are killed, since predators soon learn to associate these colors with a very unpleasant experience.

If the weather changes, rains fall, and vegetation re-establishes itself, then these phase changes in color and behavior are reversible, even within the developmental lifespan of an individual. If, however, the drought persists and nymphs remain crowded, then they eventually become gregarious adults and the dreaded swarm is born and soon on the wing in search of pastures new.

A Desert locust swarm may contain 50 billion individuals, and strip vegetation over a vast area (1,000sq km/c.400 sq mi). There is much incentive, therefore, to understand the factors leading to swarm formation and to find environmentally friendly alternatives to dousing much of Africa and the Middle East with insecticides.

Scientists at Oxford University have recently identified some of the factors involved in the determination of phase changes. Their research revealed that phase change from solitary to gregarious takes place under maternal and, to some extent, paternal influence.

A solitary female will produce gregarious offspring if she herself was recently crowded. If a solitary female mates with a gregarious male, then her hatchlings will be gregarious too. Although it is not yet clear how a female gains indirect evidence of population density during courtship and mating, pheromones are known to play a key role in her passing on gregariousness to her offspring.

A female lays 30–100 eggs in a hole she digs in the ground, and surrounds them with a frothy secretion from her accessory glands. This dries to form a pod that protects the eggs from desiccation. Gregarious females, or recently crowded solitaries, produce a pheromone in the accessory glands that is incorporated into the egg pod and induces gregariousness in the emerging nymphs. There is no evidence to suggest that solitaries that have never been crowded produce a corresponding "solitarizing" pheromone.

A female "knows" she has been crowded when tactile sensors on her hind femur are jostled by other locusts during the course of her own nymphal development or as an adult, shortly before her egg-laying phase. This sense of crowding can be induced experimentally in females that have been kept totally isolated by stroking the femur with a paintbrush. Females stimulated in this way produce egg pods impregnated with the gregarizing pheromone. This might explain the observation that solitary females caught in a heavy downpour of rain become temporarily gregarious after a bombardment of their legs by raindrops.

The remarkable phase changes of the Desert locust comprise a multi-stranded response to a changing environment. It is just one of many examples of the elegant fine-tuning of which insects are capable. CO'T

⊘ **Below** *Desert locust swarms can devastate crops. A swarm once consumed 167,000 tons of grain, enough to feed 1 million people for a year.*

Cricket and Grasshopper Superfamilies

THE CLASSIFICATION OF THE ORTHOPTERA is presently in a state of flux, with no single definitive system being generally accepted. The placement of some genera, subfamilies, and even families within the 13 superfamilies varies between authors. Taxonomic authorities at least agree, however, in dividing the group into two suborders, the Caelifera and the Ensifera. At its most basic, the division is based on the number of antennal segments, the caeliferans having less than 30 and the ensiferans more than that number.

SUBORDER CAELIFERA

About 10,500 species, grouped in 31 families and 10 superfamilies. Principal characteristics include: hearing organs on the first abdominal segment; stridulatory mechanisms (when present) on the forewings and legs; ovipositor consisting of paired, pronglike valves.

Proscopioidea

130 species in 1 family, the Proscopiidae. S America. Very elongate in form (up to 165mm/6.5in in length); in appearance they resemble twigs or stick insects (Phasmatodea), with which they are sometimes confused.

Eumastacoidea

About 1,000 species in 9 families, of which the Thericleidae and the Eumastacidae are the largest. The eumastacids are known as monkey grasshoppers; most species in this family are wingless and have bulging eyes.

Xyronotoidea

About 4 species in 2 families, the Xyrotonotidae and the Tanaoceridae. N America.

Pampagoidea

4 families, of which the Pamphagidae is the largest, with about 300 species. Most occur in arid environments. The southern African species *Trachypetrella andersoni* is one of the bulkiest of all orthopterans, reaching up to 70mm (2.8in) in length.

Pyrgomorphoidea

About 450 species in a single family, the Pyrgomorphidae. Worldwide, with Africa being the most species-rich area. Some species are brightly coloured and very poisonous; if eaten, they can even be fatal to children. Others, e.g. *Zonocerus* species, are pests of crops, including melon, peanut, cotton. *Phymateus* species are large and brightly colored, often having flash colors on their hindwings.

Trigonopterygoidea

15 species in 2 families, the Bornearcrididae (narrow-leaf bush hoppers) and the Trigonopterygidae (broad-leaf bush hoppers). SE Asia.

Acridoidea

The largest and most widespread of the superfamilies, with some 7,500 species in 6 families. The largest of the families is the Acrididae, which contains the familiar common grasshoppers and the locusts; species include the **toad grasshoppers** and the **Yellow-winged locust** (*Gastrimargus musicus*). The subfamily Cyrtacanthacridinae contains some of the largest grasshoppers and the most destructive locusts, e.g. *Schistocerca gregaria*; one of the commonest features of this group is a peg between the front legs, which is absent in most other acridids. The subfamily Acridinae contains the most familiar grasshoppers as well as the remaining very destructive species, e.g. the **Migratory locust**, *Locusta migratoria*. The family Romaleidae is found worldwide and contains some of the largest grasshoppers, such as females of the genus *Tropidacris*, which can exceed 120mm (4.7in) in length.

Tetrigoidea

About 850 species in 2 families, the Tetrigidae and the Batrachideidae. Generally small in size, the Tetrigidae are sometimes called **pygmy** or **grouse grasshoppers** or **ground hoppers**. Most species are found near water or in damp conditions; some are capable of swimming underwater, and one subfamily is even partially aquatic.

Tridactyloidea

2 families, the Tridactylidae and the Ripipterygidae. Small insects, from 4–15mm (0.15–0.6in) in length, associated with mud or sand at the edge of water. The tridactylids are sometimes called **pygmy mole crickets**; most species occur in the tropics.

Cylindrichaetoidea

2 genera in 1 family, the Cylindrichaetidae. One genus is found in Patagonia, the other in Australia; such a disjunct, relict distribution is strong evidence for the primitive nature of the group. Sometimes called **sandgroppers** or **false mole crickets** as, like their namesakes, they live in tunnels in damp soil and sand.

SUBORDER ENSIFERA

The ensiferans are the long-horned orthopterans. Main characteristics include: hearing organs on the front tibia; stridulatory mechanisms (when present) on the forewings; ovipositor often in the form of a long, needle- or sicklelike projection. The suborder contains three superfamilies, the Stenopelmatoidea, the Grylloidea, and the Tettigonioidea.

Stenopelmatoidea

About 1,500 species, now classified in just 3 families, the Anostostomatidae, the Rhaphidophoridae, and the Stenopelmatidae. The classification of this superfamily, which is sometimes referred to as the Gryllacridioidea, has recently undergone major changes; previously 6 families (Cooloolidae, Gryllaceidae, Mimnermidae, Rhaphidophoridae, Schizodactylidae, and Stenopelmatidae) were recognized. Regarded as one of the most primitive of the superfamilies.

Family Anostostomatidae

Contains 8 subfamilies: Anabropsinae, Anostostomatinae (the Mimnermidae of the old Gryllacridoidea), Cooloolinae (the Cooloolidae of the old Gryllacridoidea), Cratonelinae, Deinacridinae, Leimelinae, Lezininae, and Lutosinae. The Cooloolinae include 4 Australian species collectively known as "monsters" (see The Cooloola Monster). The Deinacridinae include some of the largest and strangest orthopterans. The **wetas** (18 species in 2 genera, *Heideina* and *Deinacrida*), from New Zealand, are often found in tunnels in dead wood or on the ground, from where they venture out at night to feed on plant foliage.

Family Rhaphidophoridae

Around 500 species in 7 subfamilies: Aemodogryllinae, Ceuthophilinae, Dolichopodinae, Gammarotettiginae, Macropathinae, Rhaphidophorinae, and Troglophilinae. Commonly known as **cave** or **camel crickets**. Includes North American **cave cricket** (*Euhadenoecus insolitus*).

Family Stenopelmatidae

5 subfamilies: Oryctopinae, Siinae, Stenopelmatinae, Schizodactylinae and Gryllacridinae, the last 3 of which were given family status in the old Gryllacridoidea. The 38 or so Stenopelmatinae species, often called **Jerusalem crickets**, are found in N and C America. The 600 species of the Gryllacridinae occur throughout the southern hemisphere, although rarely in the northern half; they range in size from just 10mm (0.4in) to 150mm (6in).

Grylloidea

Generally known as the true crickets. Contains nearly 4,200 species worldwide.

Family Gryllidae

The largest family, including the well-known **House cricket** (*Acheta domestica*). A number of the subfamilies in this group are sometimes given family status, such as the **tree crickets** (Oecanthinae) and the **scaly crickets** (Mogoplistinae).

Below *The Hedgehog katydid (Cosmoderus erinaceus; Tettigoniidae) from Uganda is one of many African species in which the pronotum (dorsal shield) is defended by an array of spines.*

Family Gryllotalpidae

About 50 species worldwide. Commonly called **mole crickets**, all have developed molelike front legs for digging in the soil. The **European mole cricket** (*Gryllotalpa gryllotalpa*) is sometimes a pest in greenhouses.

Family Myrmecophilidae

65 or so species with a worldwide distribution. Small, flattened, apterous crickets that live in association with ants.

Tettigonioidea

The largest of the ensiferan groups, with over 6,000 species.

Family Tettigoniidae

Contains around 23 subfamilies, with most of the species concentrated in the Conocephalinae, Phaneropterinae, Pseudophyllinae, and Tettigoniinae. Commonly called **katydids**, **long-horned grasshoppers**, or **bush crickets**. Tettigonids occur worldwide, although most species live in the tropics, where they feed on a variety of plant and animal substances. Some species are highly predacious and are known to bite people, e.g. the aptly named **Wart biter** (*Deticus verrucivorus*). Other tettigonid species include: **Oak bush cricket** (*Meconema thalassinum*); the **armored katydids**, including *Acanthoplus armativentris* and *Cosmoderus erinaceus*; **cone-headed katydids** (Copiphorainae); *Eupholidoptera chabrieri*; and *Stilpnochlora incisa*.

Family Haglidae

4 species in 2 genera. N America, Asia. **Hump-backed crickets**, also known as the Prophalangopsidae. Contains mostly extinct species; thought to be the ancestral family of the Tettigonidae.

DM

Leaf and Stick Insects

a MONG THE MOST SPECTACULAR OF ALL insect groups, the leaf and stick insects are unusually large, and exhibit a striking mimicry of plants that depends on a unique range of adaptations in color, shape, and behavior. The name Phasmatodea is derived from the Greek phasma, meaning "phantom," in reference to the insects' cryptic appearance and behavior.

The longest insect ever recorded was a stick insect: the Malaysian *Pharnacia kirbyi* was measured at an overall length of 555mm (nearly 22in). There are a number of other phasmid species that can reach great length; the Titan stick insect (*Acrophylla titan*) can reach 270mm (10.6in), and even larger are members of the genus *Ctenomorpha*, which can attain lengths of up to 300mm (11.8in). The bulkiest stick insect on record is the Malaysian jungle nymph *Heteropteryx dilatata*, which can reach lengths of 150mm (6in) and weigh 60g (2oz).

Nocturnal Foliage-eaters
FORM AND FUNCTION

The phasmids, which first appeared in the fossil record during the Triassic period 251–205 million years ago, are closely related to the Orthoptera. They possess, however, several unique anatomical features that distinguish them from all other neopterans and indicate that they are a monophyletic group. For example, all species possess a pair of exocrine glands inside the prothorax, and the males of many species possess a unique sclerite termed the vomer. This structure is located above the genitalia and permits the male to clasp the female during copulation.

The 2,500 species are predominantly nocturnal and are mostly found in the tropics, where they live in and on plant foliage. There are just six families in three suborders, two of which are the Anareolatae (containing the families Heteronemiidae and Phasmatidae) and the Areolatae (Bacillidae, Pseudophasmatidae, Phyllidae). The sixth family, Timematidae, is sometimes considered not to belong to the Phasmatodea at all, although where else it might belong is open to question. It contains a single genus, *Timena*, and just 13 small, mostly wingless species commonly known

○ **Right** *In a number of* Circia *stick insects from Madagascar, outgrowths on the head, body, and legs resemble tufts of moss. During the day the insect rests on mossy tree trunks or on rainforest leaves.*

FACTFILE

LEAF AND STICK INSECTS

Class: Insecta

Order: Phasmatodea (or Phasmida)

2,500 species in 6 families: Heteronemiidae, Phasmatidae, Bacillidae, Pseudophasmatidae, Phyllidae, Timematidae

DISTRIBUTION Worldwide, particularly in the tropics.

SIZE Maximum body length normally 300mm (12in).

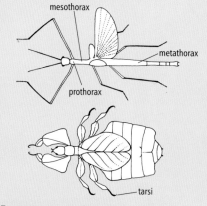

FEATURES Antennae long, slender; mouthparts mandibulate, prognathous; body form usually cylindrical; prothorax shorter than meso- or metathorax; leg segments long and slender; tarsi 5-segmented; two pairs of wings, but often reduced or absent; cerci short, unsegmented.

LIFE CYCLE Hemimetabolous; nymphs more or less resemble adults.

CONSERVATION STATUS 1 Australian species – the Lord Howe Island stick insect (*Dryococelus australis*) – is now listed as recently extinct.

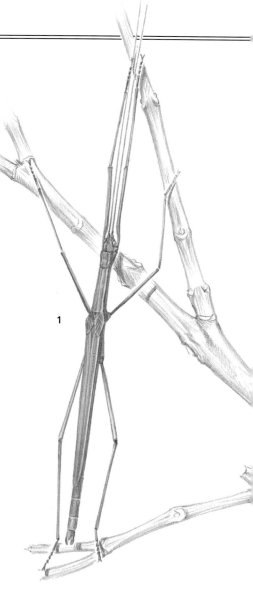

1

○ **Above** *Stick insects from around the world.* **1** *A* Necroscia *species from Malaysia.* **2** Acanthoclonia paradoxa *from Trinidad is so sticklike it can sit safely on leaves in full view, like a fallen twig.* **3** Acrophylla titan *is the longest species in Australia, sometimes reaching 25cm (10in).* **4** *A South American species of* Stratoctes *from Peru.* **5** *A female Giant Australian stick insect,* Extatosoma tiaratum.

as trimens, all of which are found in the mountainous areas of northern America.

In contrast, the family Heteronemiidae contains about 1,000 species distributed worldwide; the well-known Laboratory stick insect, *Carausius morosus*, belongs to this group. The Phasmatidae contain about 750 species, including most of the giant stick insects. The Bacillidae include about 300 species, most of them in southeast Asia, while the 300 species of Pseudophasmatidae are found throughout the world. The Phyllidae are commonly known as leaf insects, and the 30 species are all from southeast Asia.

Phasmids feed solely on foliage, using their chewing mouthparts. Many species will only feed on a small number of plant species and are normally choosy when young. In captivity, a large percentage of species can be encouraged to feed on non-natural host plants, especially bramble.

Changing Hue
COLORATION

Most phasmids are mottled green or brown. However, there may be a wide variation in coloration within a population of a species at a single site, with, for example, some of the insects being all green, while others are brown. Coloration also varies in the same species at different locations.

Population density may influence the color of developing phasmids. While the majority of species are relatively solitary creatures, some reach plague densities. In Australia, species including *Didymaria violescens*, *Padocanthus wilkinsoni*, and *Ctenomorphodes tessulatus* can, when swarming, become pests as defoliators of eucalypt forest. As density increases, developing insects become, like locusts, more brightly colored. For the solitary insect it is probably better to be inconspicuous, while as one of a group it is advantageous to see the others clearly and stay together.

Some stick and leaf insects also change color with temperature, humidity, and light intensity. The cells of the epidermis beneath the cuticle contain granules of pigment, which migrate within the cells in response to environmental conditions. On hot, sunny days the pigment granules clump

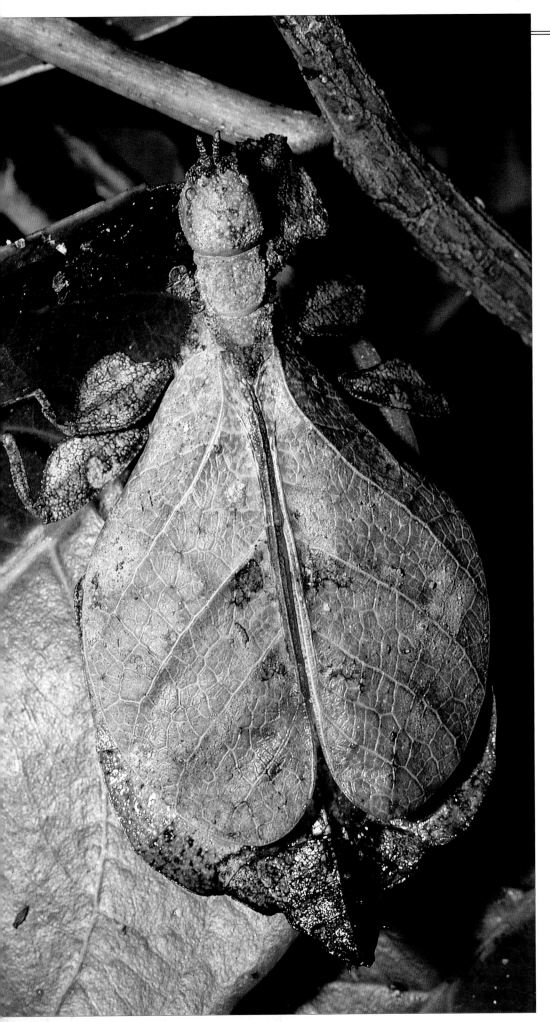

together, forming larger light-colored areas, with the result that the insect reflects more heat. When the environment is cool and humid and light intensity is low, the granules disperse within the epidermal cells and the insect darkens in color. It is then able to absorb more heat and keep warm.

Leaves with Legs
CAMOUFLAGE

Stick insects are generally long and slender, with cuticular knobs and bumps that give them the same shape and texture as the twigs of a species' host plant. The head, body, and legs of certain species also bear leaflike flanges and extensions. These features are most extremely developed in the leaf insects of the family Phyllidae, in which the body is also flattened laterally; the whole insect takes on an extraordinary likeness to a leaf, complete with midrib and veins.

A perfectly camouflaged phasmid would not last long if it drew attention to itself by moving rapidly about its host plant. In fact, most leaf and stick insects are incapable of running quickly; instead, they spend most of their time sitting motionless, their long forelegs extended in front of them. They would, however, also become conspicuous if they remained stationary while their surroundings were moving, as happens when a breeze ruffles the foliage of a tree. The rhythmic, side-to-side swaying movements of stick and leaf insects may have evolved in response.

The resemblance of phasmids to parts of plants is not limited to the adult and immature insects. The eggs of stick and leaf insects look very similar indeed to plant seeds. They are usually oval, and have a thick shell that may either be smooth or else intricately sculptured and patterned. The exact shape and ornamentation of the egg depends on the species, and is often used as an aid to classification.

In many species the eggs bear a knoblike protuberance known as a capitulum; these lumps are found only in those stick insects species that drop eggs freely onto litter, and not in the species that bury eggs or glue them to vegetation. The capitula resemble elaiosomes, lipid-rich appendages found on some seeds that are known to be an adaptation for burial by ants. In similar fashion the capitula encourage ants to remove the eggs to their nests, where they are buried. Buried eggs suffer reduced rates of predation and parasitism by wasps. Elaiosomes and capitula are both adaptations to put ants to use for burial purposes, and are among the most amazing examples of evolutionary convergence between plants and animals.

◐ **Left** *Adult leaf insects (Phyllidae) bear an extraordinary resemblance to leaves, both living and dead. In this* Phyllium *species from New Guinea the lateral flattening of the body is clearly evident, as is the very leaflike venation on the wings. Even the legs bear flanges suggesting smaller leaves.*

◁ Left *This mating pair of* Megaphasma *stick insects from Mexico clearly show how much smaller and slimmer the male is than the female. Such a marked size differential is normal in phasmids.*

◑ Below *Long, slender, stiltlike legs are typical of most phasmids, such as this* Megaphasma *male in the Mexican desert. Unlike most rainforest phasmids, which mainly rest on leaves, it spends the day in the open.*

Dropping Out of Trouble
PREDATION AND DEFENSE

Despite their fantastic disguises, the eggs, nymphs, and adults of phasmids often fall prey to other animals, with birds being the main predators. In addition, tiny *Paranastatus* wasps (Hymenoptera: Eupelmidae) are known as egg parasitoids of stick insects. Species of biting midge (Diptera: Ceratopogonidae) and mites (Arachnida: Acari) can feed on their hemolymph, while there are also flies (Diptera: Tachinidae) and nematode worms that parasitize phasmids.

If disturbed, many species take avoiding action; they become momentarily cataleptic and fall from their perch. During the fall the legs are thrown back and the insects temporarily resemble shuttlecocks. Other phasmids will attempt to deter an attacker; *Heteropteryx dilatata* nymphs rustle and expose brightly-colored hindwings from beneath their horny, camouflaged forewings.

Some species regurgitate their gut contents. The North American two-striped or Florida stick insect, *Anisomorpha buprestoides*, can squirt irritating chemicals from glands in the prothorax. Many species will jab their attacker with the spines on their legs; the Papua New Guinea *Eurycantha* genus, for example, uses this kick defense. The males of *Eurycantha calacarata* are particular aggressive; when stimulated, they raise themselves up, spreading there hind legs apart, and emit a foul-smelling odor from their abdomens. The hind legs are well armored, and the femora bears a large spine, which can penetrate even human skin.

Stick on Stick
BREEDING AND REPRODUCTION

Mating behavior in wild phasmids is little known, although it is thought that pheromones may play an important role. The fact that many males have long wings and are capable of flight adds weight to this idea. Copulation usually takes place by the male mounting the female and then moving the end of his abdomen into place by rotating it through 180°. Mating usually occurs at night, and can last from 30 minutes to 24 hours. In a number of species the male may stay on the female's back to prevent other males from mating with her.

The female normally lays her eggs one at a time. She either lets them drop to the ground below or catapults them away by flicking her abdomen. In some species, such as the Pink-winged stick insect (*Sipyloidea sipylus*), the eggs are cemented into cracks and crevices or onto the underside of leaves of their host plant. In a number of stick insect species, the female possesses a short ovipositor that is inserted into the substrate, where the eggs are buried. Female stick insects may produce from 100 to 1,300 eggs, depending on the species.

On the ground, the eggs are protected either by being buried or by their seedlike appearance, and may lie for one, two, or even three years. There is a short hatching period of several weeks every spring. Young phasmids are miniature versions of their parents. They hatch by pushing the specialized lid off the egg and, because they tend to move against gravity and towards light, they then climb up the nearest vertical object. Since eggs are deposited beneath the mother's host plant, there is a good chance that the young nymphs will find appropriate food to eat. In the Australian species *Extatosoma tiaratum*, commonly known as Macleays' spectre or the Spiny leaf insect, the first instar nymphs both resemble and mimic the behavior of the ants from whose nests they have emerged. The first instar nymphs of *Timena chumash* are able to jump in the air up to several times their own body height, presumably as a predator-avoidance behavior.

The nymphs pass through a number of molts before becoming adult. Adult females are ready to mate soon after the last molt, while males require longer before becoming sexually mature. Normally males go through five molts, one less than females, and this abbreviation ensures that they are ready to mate when females bred from eggs laid at the same time become adult.

The production of offspring from unfertilized eggs is common among the phasmids. This phenomenon is known as parthenogenesis, and in most species it seems to operate as a fail-safe device. Adults are often widely dispersed and, despite the fact that males are usually able to fly and females emit a sex-attractant pheromone, there is a risk that mating might not occur. In a few species such as the Laboratory stick insect, however, parthenogenesis is obligatory – males have never been found in the wild. Normally unfertilized eggs develop to become females, but in at least one Australian species, *Ctenomorphodes tessulatus*, males may be produced as well. DM/SSi

Booklice and Webspinners

INSECTS OF THE ORDER PSOCOPTERA ARE FAST *runners, commonly known as booklice, barklice, dustlice, or psocids. In contrast, the webspinners or Embioptera are dull-colored, soft-bodied tunnel-dwellers that live gregariously in webs of silk.*

The psocids' ordinal name derives from the Greek *psokos*, meaning "rubbed" or "gnawed," and *ptera*, meaning "wings," which, roughly translated, conveys "winged insects that gnaw." Webspinners owe their common name to the silk, secreted by glands in their fore tarsi, that they use to build the network of tunnels in which they live.

Booklice
ORDER PSOCOPTERA

The psocids first appeared during the Permian (295–248 million years ago), and are often found as fossils, or even in amber. Because their mouthparts show the least modification from the primitive mandibulate condition, they are often regarded as the most primitive hemipteroid order.

Psocids range in size from 1 to 10mm (0.04–0.4in) in length, and have a characteristic appearance, with a round, mobile head, bulbous eyes, long, threadlike antennae, an enlarged pterothorax, and wings (when present) that are held rooflike over the abdomen. Some psocids can have apterous, brachypterous (short-winged), and winged forms in both sexes. The legs are long and slender, and in some species the hind legs are modified for jumping. In some psocids the hind coxae have a ridged area adjacent to a membranous tympanum; this is known as Pearman's organ, and the insects use it to produce sound during courtship behavior; in certain species, these sound patterns can be quite elaborate. Facultative and obligatory parthenogenesis are known, and some species are even viviparous. Depending on species, eggs are laid singly or in clusters, and may be hidden by a covering of silk or detritus; the females of some species guard their eggs. Once hatched, the nymphs go through five or six instars and may stay together or disperse, depending on species.

Psocids are generally free-living in moist environments, in leaf litter, beneath stones, on vegetation, and on or under the bark of trees. Some species in the family Archipsocidae live gregariously in silken sheets, the silk being produced by specialized labial glands. At least one Australian species has developed a wood-boring habit.

The classification of the psocids is not yet fully established because there have been recent advances in their study that have not been fully integrated into the existing system. However, three main suborders are currently accepted: Trogiomorpha, Troctomorpha, and Psocomorpha, the latter containing some 75 percent of all known species. The separation of the suborders and families relies on antennal and tarsal structure and wing venation. Species of one family in the Trogiomorpha, the Lepidopsocidae, have the body and wings clothed in scales, making them look like small moths. The family Psocidae (Psocomorpha), which contains the typical barklice, is by far the largest in the order.

Psocids feed on microflora such as algae, lichens, fungi or their spores, and naturally occurring yeasts. Their mandibulate mouthparts are basic, which is to say that the lacinia (a subdivision of the maxilla) has become a separate, rodlike structure that is pushed against the substrate as a brace while the mandibles scrape off surrounding food particles. The pharynx and hypopharynx are also modified for grinding food, rather like a mortar and pestle.

A number of barklice species in the family Psoquillidae are associated with the nests of birds; it is possible that the true lice (Phthiraptera) evolved from these commensal barklice. Recently a species was discovered on St. Helena that is completely blind and has a subterranean lifestyle. Some members of the family Trogiidae and Liposcelidae have become pests in houses. The latter family includes the common booklice, a vernacular name that usually refers to members of the genus *Liposcelis* (Liposcelidae); these insects infest stored products such as cereals or grains that have become damp and attracted mold, on which the insects feed. They also feed on fungal spores associated with damp wallpaper and bookbindings.   DM

FACTFILE

BOOKLICE AND WEBSPINNERS

Class: Insecta

Subclass: Pterygota

Orders: Psocoptera (booklice) and Embioptera (webspinners)

BOOKLICE Order Psocoptera
Approximately 3,000 species in 35 families, grouped in 3 suborders: Trogiomorpha (5 families), Troctomorpha (8 families), and Psocomorpha (22 families). **Size:** Small; 1–10mm (0.04–0.4in) long.

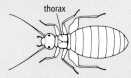

Features: Head prominent, with threadlike antennae; ocelli present in winged forms only; bulbous post-clypeus; narrow "neck" between head and thorax; 2 pairs of wings, although some species are wingless; front wings larger than hind wings; venation reduced; wings held rooflike over the body; tarsi 2- or 3-segmented; cerci absent. **Life cycle:** Reproduction sexual or asexual; some give birth to live young (viviparous); hemimetabolous development, with usually 6 adultlike larval stages. **Conservation status:** Not at risk.

WEBSPINNERS Order Embioptera
170 species in 8 families. **Size:** Small to medium-sized; 5–12mm (0.2–0.5in) long.

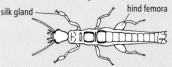

Features: Elongated, cylindrical body adapted for living in tubular silk tunnels; antennae with 12–32 segments; eyes kidney-shaped; no simple eyes (ocelli); biting mouthparts; males have 2 pairs of long, narrow wings; all females (and males of some species) wingless; legs short, thick, with 3-segmented tarsi; swollen basal tarsal segment of forelegs bears silk gland; hind femora enlarged; abdomen 10-segmented, with 2-segmented cerci at tip. **Life cycle:** Nymphs adultlike, without wings or genitalia; wings develop externally. **Conservation status:** Not at risk.

⬘ **Above** *Embia ramburi (Embiidae), a common European webspinner, is wingless in both sexes. It lives under stones and logs, inhabiting tunnels made from silk produced from glands in the swollen front legs.*

⬘ **Left** *Tropical booklice tend to be much larger and more brightly colored than those in temperate regions. These* Thyrsopsocus *species (Psocidae) are grazing the surface tissues from a leaf in a Peruvian rainforest.*

Webspinners
ORDER EMBIOPTERA

The silken tunnels in which webspinners live protect the insects from predators and desiccation, and provide safe runways from a central nest or retreat to sources of food such as decaying leaf litter, lichen, and mosses. In the humid tropics, where desiccation is less of a problem, the network of tunnels radiating out from the retreat can be very extensive and cover large areas of bark or lichen and moss-covered stones. The secretion of silk seems to be involuntary; thus, there is a continuous accretion to the tunnel walls.

The Embioptera are highly gregarious. A colony usually consists of several adult females and offspring of varying ages and sizes. After laying a batch of eggs within the tunnel, a female may guard them and newly hatched nymphs for a short time. Each individual passes through four nymphal instars. The sexes are indistinguishable until the final two male instars, which have wing buds. Although the short-lived males have well-developed jaws, they do not feed, but use their jaws to grasp the female during mating. Newly-emerged males leave their colony of origin for a short dispersal flight and later enter a new colony, where they seek mates. However, the males of species specialized for life in arid regions are often wingless. Females may eat the males after mating.

Both sexes can run rapidly back as well as forward. The males' wings are adapted for this activity, being highly flexible, and can be bent forward over the head. For flying, they are stiffened by the inflation of a blood sinus formed by the radial vein. Males are often attracted to light at night.

Because the Embioptera show so many specialized characters, it is difficult to assess their affinity with other insect groups. However, they are now thought to share ancestry with the orthopteroid orders, and probably represent a very early divergence from them, a view that is supported by their structural similarities to the earwigs (Dermaptera) and stoneflies (Plecoptera).   CO'T

Zorapterans and Thrips

EXCEPT FOR THEIR SMALL SIZE, ZORAPTERANS and thrips have little in common. While the zorapterans number just 33 species and for the most part live harmlessly on rotting wood, the thrips total as many as 5,000 species and are significant pests of many different crops.

The zorapterans or angel insects were only discovered in 1913, and they are still one of the least-known of the insect orders. The single family Zorotypidae contains just two genera, *Formoso-zoros* and *Zorotypus*, although one recent study has separated the genus *Zorotypus* into seven separate genera. Zorapterans are possibly closely related to the cockroaches, while some entomologists have suggested that they form an evolutionary link between the orthopteroids and hemipteroids.

Thrips, in contrast, are related to the bugs and parasitic lice. They probably evolved like booklice as fungus or detritus feeders in plant litter.

Zorapterans
ORDER ZORAPTERA

Zorapterans are small, delicate insects that vary in color from pale brown to dark brown or black. The adults of most species are dimorphic, which is to say they occur in two forms, winged and wingless. The wingless one, from which the order takes its name (*zoros* meaning "pure" in classical Greek, and *apteron* "without wings"), is generally pale brown and has no eyes; the winged is darker and has both simple and compound eyes. These winged adults are likely to be the dispersal stage, although flying zorapterans are seldom seen.

Although both sexes can be winged or wingless, winged males are extremely rare. The sex ratio within a single colony is more or less even in the wingless form, suggesting that the females actually mate before leaving the nest to form a new colony; winged males would thereby become redundant. As with termites and ants, the mated female casts off her wings after reaching a suitable new habitat, leaving small stubs. The nymphs are paler than the adults, and go through between four and five molts before becoming mature.

Zorapterans live gregariously under bark and in rotting wood, where they feed on fungal spores and hyphae as well as on small invertebrates such as mites; in crowded conditions they may be cannibalistic. They have occasionally been found in termite nests, although it is uncertain if they are simply nest associates or are inquilines, feeding on the termites' fungus gardens (see Termites). Zorapterans are found in tropical and subtropical areas of all continents, with nearly half the known species in Central and South America; one species was recently discovered in Australasia.

Recent detailed studies of a few species have revealed some elaborate mating behavior, with the male offering the female a precopulatory gift of a secretion from a gland in the head (the cephalic gland); the female's mate choice is based on the quality of this gift. A female may mate two or three times, sometimes with the same male, to ensure that she imbibes enough of this nutritional secretion to help in the production of eggs.

Mating takes place end-to-end, sometimes with the male lying on his back, and can last for up to an hour. In *Zorotypus hubbardi*, where in some colonies males are rare, females are able to reproduce without mating, by parthenogenesis. Zorapterans spend a great deal of time grooming themselves, using their mouthparts and front legs in stereotyped movements. DM

Thrips
ORDER THYSANOPTERA

Among the several groups of tiny insects that have wings fringed with hairlike cilia, the thrips of the order Thysanoptera (meaning "fringe-winged") are unique for their sucking mouthparts. Thrips

⬦ **Above** *Tropical thrips, such as this species from Thailand, are usually very much larger than their counterparts from the temperate zones. Here, numerous bright red nymphs belonging to various instars are accompanied by shiny black adults.*

◗ **Below** *Zorapterans are tiny insects – this* Zorotypus hubbardi *1 measures only 2–3 mm in length.* **2** *At 1–2 mm, the Western flower thrip (Frankliniella occidentalis), a feared horticultural pest, is even smaller. In general, however, thrips are larger than zorapterans.*

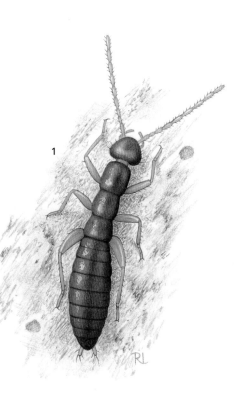

1

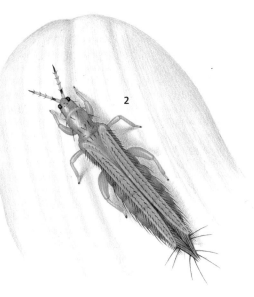

2

FACTFILE

ZORAPTERANS AND THRIPS

Class: Insecta

Subclass: Pterygota

Orders: Zoraptera (zorapterans or angel insects); Thysanoptera (thrips)

ZORAPTERANS Order Zoraptera
33 species (plus 1 known from fossil record) in 2 genera (*Formosozoros, Zorotypus*) and 1 family: Zorotypidae. Worldwide, tropics and subtropics. **Size:** Tiny, under 4mm (0.2in) long.

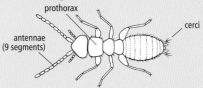

Features: Soft-bodied; antennae 9-segmented; mouthparts mandibulate, hypognathous; prothorax well developed; wings often absent, 2 pairs with reduced venation when present; femora enlarged and broad, bearing spines; tarsi 2-segmented; abdomen 11-segmented; cerci 1-segmented. **Life cycle:** Hemimetabolous (incomplete metamorphosis), so no pupal stage; eggs are ovoid, and the nymphs hatch by means of an egg burster; nymphs resemble small adults in structure, diet, and habitat; one species can reproduce without mating. **Conservation status:** Not threatened.

THRIPS
Order Thysanoptera
About 5,000 species in 9 families and 2 suborders. Worldwide. **Size:** 0.5–15mm (0.02–0.6in) long.

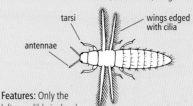

Features: Only the left mandible is developed; maxillae in form of stylets forming a sucking tube; wings have fringe of hairlike cilia; tarsi tipped with extrusible bladder, used to cling to smooth surfaces. **Life cycle:** 2 larval and 2–3 pupalike, pre-adult stages; some reproduce without mating. **Conservation status:** Not threatened.

feed by punching a hole in their food (often a leaf, flower, or pollen grain) with their single mandible, inserting the syringe-like stylets, and sucking out a cell's contents. The stylets are usually 1–3 micrometers across, but in Idolothripinae that take in whole fungal spores they are 5–10 micrometers. Some thrips feed on small arthropods such as scales and mites, and one Brazilian species is ectoparasitic on a homopteran bug.

Thrips are divided into two suborders. The Terebrantia is made up of 8 families, including the Thripidae, and contains 2,000 species worldwide. Some of these are predatory, but most feed in flowers or on leaves, like the Greenhouse thrips (*Heliothrips haemorrhoidalis*), the Onion thrips (*Thrips tabaci*) and the Grain thrips or thunderfly (*Limothrips cerealium*). In contrast, the suborder Tubulifera consists of just one very large family, the worldwide Phlaeothripidae, although this in turn is divided into two subfamilies. The Idolothripinae takes in 600 species feeding on fungal spores on dead leaves and twigs. The 2,400 species of the Phlaeothripinae mostly feed on fungal hyphae; a few are predatory, some in flowers but many, like the Laurel thrips (*Gynaikothrips ficorum*), on green leaves.

Some thrips in the suborder Terebrantia retain a primitive, sawlike egg guide, but in the Tubulifera the ovipositor is soft and eversible. The life cycle, with two larval and two or three pupal stages, is intermediate between those of primitive and advanced insects. Thrips may take just three weeks to develop from the egg to the adult state. Some species produce several generations a year, but others have only one. Species specific to the male cones of plants such as pine trees or cycads, whose pollen is available for only a few days, remain dormant for 11 months of the year. In contrast, fungus-feeding thrips can be found at all times when there is sufficient moisture.

Most thrips are bisexual, but males develop from unfertilized eggs and have half the number of chromosomes of females. Some thrips never have males, and they are rare in the two pest species, Greenhouse and Onion thrips. Such thrips reproduce rapidly without mating, although the severe horticultural pest, the Western flower thrips (*Franliniella occidentalis*), is always bisexual.

Most thrips live in the tropics, but a few species can be abundant in temperate areas. In Europe, when warm, thundery conditions follow cool summer weather, vast numbers may suddenly take to flight, a behavior pattern that has earned them the common name of "thunderflies." Wingless thrips may similarly be distributed by winds, even across the ocean from Australia to New Zealand.

In many species males fight over females, large and small males differing greatly in the size of their front legs. Some Australian gall-inducing thrips have a soldier caste that protects the gall from invaders. Other Australian thrips construct domiciles by gluing leaves together, or even weave a silken tent, and then breed inside safe from ants and the sun.

Some species feed on a wide range of plants, breeding rapidly, dispersing widely, and hiding on transported plants. Such thrips can be pests on many crops, for the loss of cell sap debilitates plants and fruits. Some carry plant diseases, notably tomato spotted wilt virus, causing severe losses in flower and vegetable crops.   LAM

Parasitic Lice

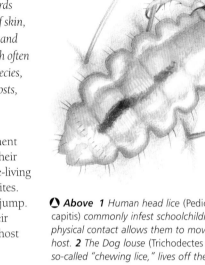

PARASITIC LICE LIVE OUT THEIR LIVES IN A *forest comprising the fur or feathers of birds and mammals. They feed on fragments of skin, the fur or feathers themselves, the host's blood, and possibly even the remains of other lice. Although often unregarded, there are thousands of different species, and they may have a dramatic effect on their hosts, even to the extent of causing their deaths.*

Lice spend their entire lives in the environment provided by the skin and fur or feathers of their host, the "dermecos." No louse has any free-living stage – all are obligate permanent ectoparasites. They have no wings, and cannot, like fleas, jump. Instead they rely on walking, clinging to their host, and can change hosts only when two host individuals are in contact.

At Home in the Dermecos
FORM AND FUNCTION

The ancestor of the parasitic lice probably lived in the nests of early mammals or birds, feeding on fungus and pieces of feather or skin shed by the nest builder. Ancestral lice may have had wings, but subsequently lost them, probably because they are a hindrance to nest-dwelling insects. Thereafter they must have relied on hitching rides on the nest builders to reach other nests, a habit known as phoresy.

Adaptation to the dermecos as a permanent home subjected the evolving parasites to novel selective pressures; factors playing a part would have included the food available, the grooming or preening activities of the host, and the composition of the feathers or fur. One particularly strong pressure must have been for methods of staying on the host. Modern lice are attracted to warmth, ensuring they keep close to the skin of the animal they live on. Most louse species use their claws and the broadened end of the tibia or tarsus to hold onto the hair or feathers of their host, although members of the family Gyropidae (amblyceran rodent lice found in South America) hold onto the hair by wrapping their strongly-ridged legs around it. For unknown reasons, most mammal lice have only a single claw on each leg, while bird lice (like most other insects) have two.

In the dermecos sight is unimportant, and the eyes of lice have become small or absent. Other senses are more valuable, however, and most lice are thickly covered in sensory hairs. The "skin" of lice is tough and flexible, the body and head dorsoventrally flattened (unlike fleas, which are laterally flattened), and their legs and antennae

⬧ Above 1 *Human head lice* (Pediculus humanus capitis) *commonly infest schoolchildren because close physical contact allows them to move from host to host.* **2** *The Dog louse* (Trichodectes canis), *one of the so-called "chewing lice," lives off the blood of its host.*

⬧ Below *This scanning electron micrograph shows a Crab louse at approximately 80 times lifesize. The louse uses the claws on its six legs to hold itself in place while it sucks blood with its biting mouthparts.*

have become much shorter than those of their ancestors. These adaptations help minimize the risk of destruction by the grooming or preening activity of the host, and help easy movement through the feathers or fur.

Although most lice still take the ancestral diet of skin flakes or feathers, others feed on exudates of the host, or on blood. One of the guinea-pig lice of South America (*Gliricola porcelli*) has serrated mouthparts with which it cuts into hair follicles to extract the oils and waxes contained within

them. Many chewing lice, such as the Dog louse, have sharp, pointed mandibles with which they make small wounds and thus extract blood. Some hummingbird lice also feed on blood, but they have developed long stylets to pierce the skin of the host. Many lice have an association with bacteria that live in specialized cells or tissues next to their gut and enable the insects to digest blood and skin protein (keratin). One species of *Cebidicola*, a chewing louse, has even been found with fragments of other lice inside its gut, suggesting it scavenges for dead parasites.

Most lice have only one or two host species, and are thus very host-specific. There are a few with large numbers of hosts, up to a maximum of about 30; conversely, some tinamous (South American guineafowl-like birds) host up to 16 different varieties of lice, though a more usual number is 2–3. Since lice are so tied to their hosts, the geographical distribution of the two is often the same. There are exceptions, however, like the dog louse *Heterodoxus spiniger*, which originally infested wallabies but has spread around the world between 40°N and 40°S on its new host. Even so, distribution patterns of lice are largely unknown.

The distribution of lice on the body of the host is as interesting as the geographical pattern. Lice are very susceptible to grooming, which itself was probably evolved at least in part to kill parasites, and have adapted to meet the challenges of different grooming behaviors. Most birds use their beaks a great deal, but naturally are unable to do so on their heads and necks, so some lice live only on these parts of the bird; these species are slow-moving, with broad heads and round abdomens that are only slightly flattened. Birds can preen their wings very easily, however, and lice living there are fast-moving, long, and slender, and can slip sideways through the feathers with ease.

Keeping the Eggs in Place
REPRODUCTION AND DEVELOPMENT

Courtship behavior has not often been observed among lice. However, some male lice, in order to hold onto the female, will wrap their antennae tightly around the base of her abdomen while they mate with her. The antennae can be clearly adapted for this purpose, with enlarged segments and even teeth. Males may mate from beneath the female, or even back to back.

Female lice cement their eggs directly onto the hairs or feathers of the host. They do not require a developed ovipositor, and the ovipositor lobes found in other insects are reduced or absent. The Sheep chewing louse has small, hooklike lobes, which it uses to "catch" the hair upon which the egg will be laid; many other mammal lice probably do the same. These small lobes are also used to mold cement, which is produced with the eggs, into a suitable shape to attach the egg to the hair or feather. This cement is quick-setting and dries very hard; the female lice sometimes become

FACTFILE

PARASITIC LICE

Class: Insecta

Subclass: Pterygota

Order: Phthiraptera

About 3,150 species in 27 families, grouped into 4 suborders.

DISTRIBUTION Cosmopolitan

SIZE Length 0.5–11mm (0.02–0.4in)

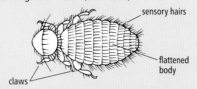

sensory hairs

flattened body

claws

FEATURES Permanent external parasites of birds and mammals; wingless, do not jump; flattened body with inconspicuous coloration; short antennae, usually with 5 segments; 1 pair of spiracles (breathing holes) on thorax; abdomen may be distinctly segmented.

LIFE CYCLE Larvae resemble adults in shape (incomplete metamorphosis).

CONSERVATION STATUS The Passenger pigeon louse (*Lipeurus extinctus*) is recently extinct.

SUCKING LICE Suborder Anoplura
500 species in 43 genera and 15 families. **Features:** Small heads with minute compound eyes, or none at all; piercing mouthparts with 3 stylets; all 3 segments of thorax fused; a single claw on each leg. **Hosts:** Placental mammals. **Food:** Blood. Includes Human crab louse (*Pthirus pubis*), Human body louse (*Pediculus humanus*), Human head louse (*P. h. capitis*), and seal lice (family Echinophthiriidae).

ELEPHANT LICE Suborder Rhyncophtherina
3 species in 1 genus. **Features:** Front of head prolonged into rigid, cylindrical snout (rostrum) with biting mouthparts at tip. **Hosts:** Elephants, warthogs. Includes Elephant louse (*Haematomyzus elephantis*), Warthog louse (*H. hopkinsi*).

CHEWING LICE Suborder Ischnocera
1,800 species in 120 genera and 5 families. **Features:** Unique spongy pad (pulvinus) between front of head and biting mouthparts. **Hosts:** Birds, placental mammals. **Food:** Feathers, skin, skin secretions, blood. Includes Dog louse (*Trichodectes canis*), Sheep chewing louse (*Bovicola ovis*).

CHEWING LICE Suborder Amblycera
850 species in 75 genera and 7 families. **Features:** Maxillary palps present; biting mouthparts; third segment of antennae cup-shaped. **Hosts:** Birds, mammals. **Food:** Feathers, skin, skin secretions, blood. Includes guinea-pig lice (e.g. *Gliricola porcelli*), hummingbird lice (e.g. *Trochiloecetes* species), Curlew quill louse (*Actornithophilus patellatus*), pelican lice (*Piagetiella* species), rodent lice (family Gyropidae).

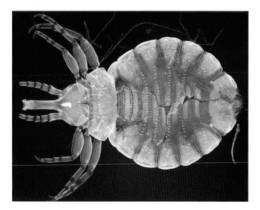

○ **Above** A female Warthog louse (Haematomyzus hopkinsi; Rhyncophtherina); its snoutlike beak has biting mouthparts that enable it to penetrate the thick skin of its host. This image is shown in false color.

caught in it and find themselves stuck to a hair.

The eggs are laid in clumps in protected positions on birds' heads and necks, in the grooves between the barbs of flight feathers, or at the base of mammalian hairs. Moisture is taken up by the eggs via the cement and numerous small holes at the base. There is also a cap on the egg, which allows the nymph to exit when developed, and this can bear prominences and tubercles and be pierced by small holes to admit air. Many species of lice have long, complex outgrowths from the egg, but the function of these is not known.

The young louse breaks out from the egg by swallowing air, which it passes through its alimentary canal, so that pressure is built up in the egg behind the hatching nymph. This force removes the cap of the egg and, in some species, causes the

nymph to be "fired" from the egg like a cork from a bottle. After hatching, the nymph feeds on the same food as the adult, and as it grows it sheds its skin three times before becoming adult; there is no pupal stage. The Human body louse can become adult eight days from hatching, while some of the seal lice take almost a year. Adult longevity is probably less variable, lasting from two or three weeks to several months.

Lice on the Line
CONSERVATION AND ENVIRONMENT

Although most lice have not been shown to transmit disease, their effects can in some cases be disastrous. The Human body louse in particular spreads typhus and relapsing fever, and has thereby caused the death of many millions of people. In contrast, the Human head louse and Crab louse are not known to spread disease. In some domestic animals, such as the dog, lice can transmit parasites that are at least debilitating.

Lice themselves can also be at risk. The most numerous animal to become extinct last century was the Passenger pigeon louse, *Lipeurus extinctus*. The millions of Passenger pigeons were accompanied by far more lice, which fell extinct along with their more visible hosts.

Although lice to most eyes are not as attractive as their furred or feathered hosts, they have as much intrinsic interest and an equal claim to protection. In most cases they do not materially damage their hosts; indeed it has been suggested that they may have played an important part in the evolution of such important behaviors as social grooming in apes and display in peacocks. CHCL

Bugs

PIERCING AND SUCKING MOUTHPARTS housed in a long, beaklike rostrum distinguish bugs from all other insects. Most bugs tap plant juices, but some suck blood from other insects or higher animals. The resulting damage to crop plants, and the transmission of diseases that can result from their blood-sucking activities, both have serious implications for humans.

The Hemiptera is the largest order in the Neoptera, with over 82,000 species in four suborders: the Heteroptera, or true bugs, and the Auchenorrhyncha, Coleorrhyncha, and Sternorrhyncha, the latter three being sometimes referred to collectively as the Homoptera. Making their first appearance in the Permian period 295–248 million years ago, the Hemipterans' nearest relatives are the thrips of the order Thysanoptera.

Piercing and Sucking
FORM AND FUNCTION

The Hemiptera are highly variable in size, structure, color, and biology. The sucking mouthparts are similar throughout the order, only varying in length and number of segments. The legs are mainly adapted for walking and running, although

○ **Above** Two species of Brazilian treehoppers (Membracidae) have contrasting defensive mechanisms. The black and white bugs (Membracis foliata) employ aposematic (warning) coloration, while the green bug with twin horns uses crypsis (camouflage).

◑ **Right** The segmented rostrum (beak) is very obvious in this cottonstainer (Pyrrhocoridae) of the genus Dindymus from Sumatra. It is feeding on a caterpillar; most cottonstainers feed on seeds. Bugs of the Heteroptera hold the wings flat across the body.

some species have hind legs modified for jumping or swimming. Some predators have raptorial front legs resembling those of mantids. The legs may also have spines and leafy extensions.

The two pairs of wings are generally membranous, although in all Heteroptera and in some other groups the forewing is horny, protecting the hindwings. In some Aradidae and in males of the Coccoidea, hindwings may be absent.

The abdomen has 11 segments, but in some species it is always reduced or modified. In the Cicadidae the first two segments are modified for sound production. The eighth and ninth are usually modified in connection with the external genitalia; in the female, they often take the form of an ovipositor, the shape reflecting the mode of use.

Mostly Sexual
REPRODUCTION AND LIFE CYCLE

Hemiptera eggs vary greatly from simple ovoids to eggs on stalks or with complex microsculpture. Bugs lay eggs on or in plant tissue and soil, or else they attach them to stones. In some species both parents may guard the eggs.

The nymphs resemble small, wingless adults, but usually have fewer antennal and tarsal segments. However, in some groups such as the Coccoidae and Cicadidae, nymphs and adults do differ considerably. The number of instars varies from just two to six, and there is no true pupal stage. However, in the aleyrodids and in male coccoids, a resting stage occurs that is often referred to as the pupa.

The suborders Coleorrhyncha, Heteroptera, and Auchenorrhyncha nearly all reproduce bisexually, whereas the Sternorrhyncha employ a number of strategies, such as viviparity, parthenogenesis, and alternative host plants.

MECHANISMS FOR FEEDING

Bugs are specialized to feed by piercing the outer surface of their food source in order to suck up liquid and liquified products. The majority of bugs are plant-feeders, using all parts of a diverse array of plants, but many are predators on other insects, and some may suck blood from mammals and birds. While many bugs feed on liquid food products, those that utilize seeds may secrete enzymes to liquify or semi-digest the seed before ingestion.

The most obvious feature of a bug's head is its segmented, movable rostrum or labium (a squash bug is shown at right). The tip of the rostrum contains sensory cells that may aid the insect in choosing its preferred food source. Along its length the rostrum carries four thin threads or stylets in a groove (see cross-section). The outer pair (mandibles) have sharp teeth near the tip that allow a hole to be cut in the plant or animal surface. The inner pair (maxillae) are grooved along their length and fit closely together, so that their inner surfaces form the food canal and the salivary canal.

In bugs that feed from small plants in which the vascular system is close to the surface, the rostrum may be shorter than in those feeding from large plants whose vascular tissue is farther back. When not in use, the rostrum is held pointing backward, close to the body and between the front legs. In

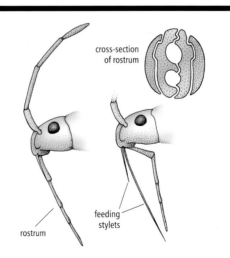

cross-section of rostrum

feeding stylets

rostrum

plant-feeding forms the rostrum is brought down to the surface of the plant. In many predatory bugs the rostrum may be held forward in front of the head in order to be able to attack prey.

When feeding, the outer labium is pulled away from the feeding stylets. Salivary fluid, including enzymes such as amylase and pectinase, is pumped down the salivary canal and semi-digested food is pumped back up. The pump consists of a series of plates at the base of the stylets. **MRW**

Mating behavior in hemipterans is varied, from the simple find-and-copulate to courtship movements, sexual scents (pheromones), and acoustic signalling. The males of some lygaeid bugs offer the female a nutritional seed as a nuptial gift, which she feeds on during copulation.

Peloridiids

SUBORDER COLEORRHYNCHA

The Coleorrhyncha is an unusual group, exhibiting a mixture of both ancestral and specialized characteristics found in both the heteropterans and homopterans. The exact status of this suborder has long been debated, but it is currently regarded as affiliated to the Heteroptera.

The suborder consists of a single family, the Peloridiidae, which includes about 25 species occuring in Australia, New Zealand, and South America, where the insects are found in Chile and Patagonia. The adults are small (2–5mm/0.08–0.2in), greenish-brown in color, have tiny antennae and a broad head with laterally placed eyes, and live cryptically in mosses and liverworts in temperate forest regions.

Aphids and Scales

SUBORDER STERNORRHYNCHA

Made up of aphids including the greenfly and blackfly, the Sternorrhyncha is characterized by the placement of the rostrum between the first pair of legs. Sternorrhynchans are usually very small insects, made conspicuous only because many species form large colonies.

Dense infestations may seriously weaken or kill host plants, and the damage caused is recognized by farmers and growers as "blight" or "wilt." Some species disfigure fruit or flowers sufficiently to render them unsaleable. Many transmit virus diseases from plant to plant. Feeding by some species causes deformations of host plants, ranging from simple pits in the stem or curled edges on leaves to large and elaborate galls.

The Sternorrhyncha are a monophyletic group forming the sister group to the rest of the Hemiptera. The suborder contains four superfamilies, the Aleyrodoidea, the Aphidoidea, the Coccoidea, and the Psylloidea.

The Aleyrodoidea contains the single family Aleyrodidae, with approximately 1,200 species.

FACTFILE

BUGS

Class: Insecta

Order: Hemiptera

Over 82,000 known species, grouped in 4 suborders: Coleorrhyncha, Sternorrhyncha, Auchenorrhyncha, and Heteroptera.

DISTRIBUTION Worldwide

SIZE From 0.8–110mm (0.03–4.3in)

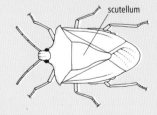

scutellum

FEATURES This large group includes a vast range of forms, habitats, lifestyles, and behaviors, but all species (both adults and nymphs) have piercing and sucking mouthparts in a beaklike rostrum bearing threadlike stylets. Coloration varies greatly, from cryptic browns and greens to metallic purple and blue.

LIFE CYCLE Eggs vary greatly in size and shape; from 2 to 6 nymphal instars; no true pupal stage.

CONSERVATION STATUS Not threatened.

See suborders table ▷

Commonly referred to as whiteflies, the adults are fragile, midgelike insects with a wingspan of approximately 3mm (0.1in). The two pairs of equal-sized wings have a characteristic dusting of white, powdery wax.

The sexes of whiteflies are similar and only distinguishable by the genitalia, although the males tend to be slightly smaller. Reproduction may be either sexual or asexual. Eggs are laid in small groups, often arranged in arcs or circles on the underside of leaves, and are borne on short stalks. Although long-legged, the first-instar nymphs are not very mobile; the legs are much shorter in second- and third-instar nymphs, which resemble scale insects. The nymphs feed on sap. Fourth-instar nymphs cease to feed after a while, and each forms a puparium in which the adult develops.

The Cabbage whitefly, *Aleyrodes proletella*, can often be disturbed in clouds from cabbages and related brassica crops, but it seems to do little damage. However, its relative the Glasshouse whitefly, *Trialeurodes vaporariorum*, is a major pest of tomatoes and houseplants. This tropical species was accidentally introduced to Europe from Central America. A tiny parasitic wasp, *Encarsia formosa* (Hymenoptera: Aphelinidae), attacks the nymphs and is used to control this species.

The Tobacco whitefly, *Bemisia tabaci*, is a vector of over 60 plant viruses, many of which cause damage to a large number of crops. It is increasing its worldwide distribution, and its presence must be reported to the government in some countries.

The superfamily Aphidoidea contains three families, the Adelgidae, the Aphididae, and the Phylloxeridae. Currently, around 4,700 species are known throughout the world, although the greatest diversity is in temperate regions; many are important crop pests. Aphids are polymorphic, with winged and wingless forms, and are predominantly parthenogenetic, although

Above *Representative species of bugs. 1 Most aphids are green, which acts as camouflage on plants. One of the most common species, the Peach-potato aphid (Myzus persicae; Aphididae) feeds on more than 200 plants. 2 The spiked shape and green-and-red coloration of these treehoppers (Umbonia spinosa; Membracidae) both serve to deter predators. 3 Bright colors signal that this shield bug (Catacanthus anchorago; Pentatomidae) is protected by a foul smell. 4 An assassin bug (Acanthaspis spp; Reduviidae) feeds on a caterpillar. 5 A fulgorid (Phenax variegata; Fulgoridae) roosts on lichen-covered bark, which it resembles. 6 The Lesser water boatman (Corixa punctata; Corixidae), 7 the Saucer bug (Ilyocoris cimicioides; Naucoridae), and 8 the Back swimmer (Notonecta glauca; Notonectidae) are all active predators. 9 The water stick insect, Ranatra linearis, and 10 the water scorpion, Nepa cinerea (both Nepidae), hang from the surface film by their respiratory siphons and wait to grasp passing prey with their raptorial front legs. The water's surface provides a living for 11 this pond skater (Gerris lacustris; Gerridae) and 12 water strider (Hydrometra stagnorum; Hydrometridae).*

evacuate honeydew. The abdomen also carries two siphunculi – paired tubes used for secreting wax or defensive chemicals.

Aphids have diverse and often complex life histories that vary according to subfamily. A number of generations are produced each year, one of which produces sexually and gives rise to overwintering eggs. Other generations are parthenogenetic and ovoviviparous (giving birth to live young). Host alternation is common, especially in the Aphidinae, where winter hosts are woody and spring and summer hosts are herbaceous. These traits, and the ability to produce large numbers of offspring in short periods of time, are the reasons aphids are such a successful group.

The Peach-potato aphid, *Myzus persicae*, uses peach or plum as the primary hosts, and a number of herbaceous plants, potatoes among them, as a secondary host. As a vector of the fungal disease potato blight (*Phytophthora infestans*), this species helped cause the Irish potato famine of the 1840s, which was responsible for the deaths of almost 1 million people.

The 50 Adelgidae species are called woolly or conifer aphids and are almost entirely confined to the northern hemisphere. Adelgids may be parthenogenetic, but do not bear live young. All adelgids feed on conifers, where some species cause galls. The females of the apterous forms and the nymphs are often covered with a woolly wax, which is secreted from abdominal glands. Some species can cause unwelcome economic damage in conifer plantations.

The Phylloxeridae are a small family of 70 species, occurring mostly in the northern hemisphere. Phylloxerids have three antennal segments (in winged forms or alates) and no ovipositor. Their life history is similar to that of adelgids, but there is no alternation of generations. Most feed on deciduous trees, although a number feed on vines. One such species, the Vine or Grape phylloxera, *Daktulosphaira vitifoliae*, was responsible for the near-destruction of the European wine industry in the late 19th century, when it was introduced from North America.

The 2,200 species of the worldwide Psylloidea are often known as jumping plant lice, so-called because a number of species can jump as an escape behavior. The group is very widespread in the southern hemisphere. Adults are small, no larger than 6mm (0.2in), with two pairs of wings (when present) held rooflike over the body. The antennae are ten-segmented, the sexes are similar, and reproduction is bisexual. The eggs are stalked, like those of the aleyrodids, and the base of the stalk is inserted into plant tissue, from which water can be absorbed. Some species have a specialized ovipositor and insert eggs directly into plant tissue. The nymphs are similar to the adults, but are often flattened and lack the enlarged hind legs used for jumping. In a number of Spondyliaspidinae (Psyllidae), the nymphs form protective

they exhibit a number of reproductive strategies.

Aphids produce feces in the form of honeydew; gall-inhabiting species also produce quantities of wax, which prevents the honeydew from wetting and drowning them. Voided honeydew is attractive to many insects, including bees; some species of ants tend aphid colonies, driving away predators and carrying the honeydew producers to the most nutritious parts of the plants. In extensive areas of conifer forests the honeydew of tree-

dwelling aphids may be the main ingredient of the honey produced by hive bees. This "forest honey" is greatly prized by connoisseurs.

The Aphididae, known as true aphids, range in size from 1–6mm (0.03–0.2in) and have from four to six antennal segments. They are soft-bodied insects, green, black, or sometimes even pink in color, usually with two pairs of transparent wings. The wings are held rooflike over the body, which ends in the cauda that the aphid uses to

coverings from anal secretions; called lerps, they take the form of variously-shaped cones, bivalves, or even intricately woven baskets.

Jumping plant lice disperse on the wing, and the females are very discriminating in the choice of plant species on which they lay their eggs. Thus, almost all psyllid species are restricted to a single host, or to a few closely related species.

The Psyllidae are by far the largest family, with approximately 1,200 species, of which a large number are pests. *Diaphorina citri*, which originated in Asia, is one of two species recently found attacking citrus crops in the USA. In a reversal of roles, the psyllid *Boreioglycaspis melaleucae* is being tested as a potential biological control agent of the persistent Broad-leaved paperbark tree (*Melaleuca quinquenervia*; Myrtaceae), which is regarded as a weed species in Australia.

The worldwide Triozidae comprise 650 species, a number of which are gall-inducing. The nymphs of some species secrete long, waxy filaments from the abdomen. Triozids have very distinctive wing venation, which separates them from all other psyllid families. The genus *Trioza* is cosmopolitan and includes a number of pest species, among them the Citrus psylla (*Trioza erytreae*) a vector of greening disease in South Africa.

The Coccoidea contain about 20 families that are often very difficult to separate from one another. Around 7,000 species are known worldwide. These are the scale insects or mealy bugs, so called because of the waxy or toughened scalelike

structures that females secrete. Morphologically, the Coccoidea are among the most highly modified insects; they are wingless, with a complete fusion of head, thorax, and abdomen. This body form is an adaptation for a sessile or nearly sessile lifestyle attached to a host plant. Coccids are important pests of many tropical crops, and the Soft brown scale (*Coccus hesperidum*; Coccidae), as well as some species of mealybugs (Pseudococcidae), are injurious to houseplants and glasshouse crops. Adult females are always wingless and are

○ **Left** *Soft scales (Coccidae), such as this* Ceroplastes *species in Brazil, scarcely resemble insects, but often look more like plant galls. Some members of the genus produce wax that is exploited commercially. Many species are pests of cultivated plants.*

either slow-moving or totally immobile; males are short-lived, generally winged, and do not feed, devoting their brief lives to reproduction.

The newly-hatched larvae are very active and are called "crawlers." Dispersal usually occurs in this stage; crawlers of some species can survive being blown about by the wind, and thus can travel a considerable distance before settling down on a plant to commence feeding.

Armored scales (Diaspididae) are the largest of the families, with over 2,500 described species. As their name suggests, they are covered with an armor of secreted wax. This coating begins to form when the first-instar nymph settles to its sessile life. The scale may also incorporate the molted skins (exuviate) of later instars.

The Pseudococcidae are commonly called mealybugs, and are the second largest of the coccoid families, with approximately 2,000 species worldwide. A "mealy," waxy secretion covers the body, together with protruding wax filaments. Mealybugs live in a wide range of habitats and feed on both the above- and below-ground parts of plants. A number of species are serious crop pests, including the Pink sugarcane mealybug (*Saccharicoccus sacchari*).

THE SONG OF THE CICADA

In tropical, subtropical, and warm Mediterranean regions, the song of the cicada is among the most familiar of sounds. The sound-production mechanism in cicadas is entirely different from the friction methods used by grasshoppers (for instance, the drawing of pegs over a file).

In cicadas (RIGHT) the sound-producing organ consists of a pair of thin membranes in the cuticle, the tymbals, situated on each side of the first segment of the abdomen. Each tymbal is distorted, or buckled, by a large muscle similar to a tin lid being clicked in and out. Contraction of this muscle causes the tymbal, via the connecting strut, to buckle, and relaxation returns the tymbal to rest. Every movement produces a pulse or "click," and the songs of cicadas consist of trains of pulses. Air sacs that

greatly amplify the sound may be present in the abdomen. The clicks may also vary in amplitude, depending on the way the tymbal is buckled.

Cicada calls are often very loud, some being audible to the human ear at distances of well over 1km (0.6mi) in tropical forests. Only the males produce sound, and their calls serve to attract females of the same species.

Variations in the structure of the tymbal and its associated plates are an essential basis for the classification of cicadas. Some species, however, may be more readily separated by their songs in the field than by examination of dried specimens, which may appear identical.

While the airborne sounds produced by cicadas have been known for centuries, it was only 50 years ago that it became known that the small leafhoppers and plant hoppers also produced sound for communication. Adult males, and also many females, were found to contain structures that appeared comparable to the tymbals of cicadas. It now seems that all the cicadas and hoppers of the suborder Auchenorrhyncha use sound for communication. The low-intensity sounds produced by these small insects are transmitted via the plants on which they live. In some species females may attract males by a simple series of pulses; the male then produces a more complex "courtship song" before mating takes place.   MRW

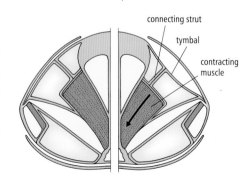

connecting strut

tymbal

contracting muscle

The Coccoidae, commonly called soft scales, number about 1,000 species. Many species produce wax in various forms, and the African genera *Ceroplastes* and *Gascardia* are often covered in a wax coating several times their body size. Many species form encrusting aggregations on host plants. The Horse chestnut scale (*Pulvinaria regalis*) a species probably introduced from South America to parts of North America and Europe, has become a serious problem on amenity trees.

The Margarodidae, with some 250 species, are the most primitive scales. Intermediate female instars are legless "cysts" that can survive periods of several years without food or water. The ground pearls live on plant roots; females of some tropical species form large wax cysts, often bronze or gold in color, which people often collect and use as beads. Adult females of the African *Aspidoproctus maximus* reach lengths of up to 35mm (1.4in), making them the largest scale insects.

The Cottony cushion scale (*Icerya purchasi*) was the first species of insect to have been controlled biologically. Californian citrus crops were nearly lost in the 1880s because of infestations of this scale, which had been introduced from Australia. The introduction of the ladybug *Rodalia cardinalis*, (Coleoptera: Coccinellidae), a natural predator of the scale in Australia, served to control the pest, and a threefold increase in the harvest was

accomplished within a few years. The Cottony cushion scale is also interesting because it is one of the few known hermaphroditic insects.

The 80 species of the pantropical Kerriidae are very distinctive because they possess brachial plates and a dorsal spine. The Lac insect (*Kerria lacca*) which lives on various fig trees, is the source of natural lac or shellac. This resinous substance has been used since at least 1200 BC as a varnish, a glaze on food, a hair dye, and as a jewellery setting. The first phonograph records were covered in shellac before vinyl was developed. Lac is still harvested by hand from trees in India, Thailand, and China, and forms an important source of income for rural communities.

The Central and South American Dactylopiidae have less than 10 species, all with elongate, convex bodies; they feed exclusively on two genera of cacti. The Cochineal insect (*Dactylopius coccus*) has been farmed since the time of the Aztecs, 500 or more years ago, for its wax and the natural dye cochineal or carminic acid, which is the source of a bright red coloring used in cooking, cosmetics, and the textile industry. Nowadays, the species has been carried all over the globe for commercial use. As well as being beneficial in terms of dye production, the dactylopids have been used as biological control agents of the prickly-pear cactus in South Africa.

◑ **Above** *The long, orange-tipped prolongation of the head of this lanternfly of the genus* Pyrops *(Fulgoridae), from the rain forests of Sumatra, is typical of the many bizarre ornamentations found on the heads of these insects.*

Cicadas and Hoppers

SUBORDER AUCHENORRHYNCHA

A distinctive feature of the Auchenorrhyncha is that the rostrum originates from the underside of the rear of the head. This group contains the planthoppers, leafhoppers, froghoppers, treehoppers, lantern bugs, and cicadas – a large and diverse grouping of predominantly plant-feeding bugs that range in size from leafhoppers just 2mm (0.07in) long to cicadas with a wingspan of 20cm (8in). The Auchenorrhynchans are less important economically than the Sternorrhyncha, especially in temperate regions, but they are nevertheless vectors of plant virus diseases. A few species are important for the direct effects their feeding habits have on plants.

The Auchenorrhyncha contains two infra-orders, the Fulgoromorpha and the Cicadomorpha. All species are free-living plant-feeders. The Fulgoromorpha contains a single superfamily, the Fulgoroidea; the Cicadomorpha contains four superfamilies: the Cercopoidea, Cicadoidea, Cicadelloidea, and Membracoidea.

Bug Suborders

Peloridiids
Suborder Coleorrhyncha

The "beak" is at the anteroventral extremity of the face, shielded by the propleura; the antennae are tiny, the head broad with laterally-placed eyes. 25 known species in 1 family, Peloridiidae, including *Xenophysella dugdalei*, *Oiophysa ablusa*, and *Xenophyes cascus*.

Aphids and Scales
Suborder Sternorrhyncha

Beak appears to arise from thorax between bases of forelegs; antennae usually well developed; usually very small, many species form large colonies. Over 15,000 known species in 4 superfamilies and 30 families.
ALEYRODOIDEA contains 1 family: whiteflies (Aleyrodoidae), including the Cabbage whitefly (*Aleyrodes proletella*). APHIDOIDEA contains 3 families: phylloxerids (Phylloxeridae), including the Vine or Grape phyloxera (*Daktulosphaira vitifoliae*); true aphids (Aphididae), including the Peach-potato aphid (*Myzus persicae*); woolly or conifer aphids (Adelgidae).
COCCOIDEA (scale or mealy insects) contains 20 families, including alcerdid or grass scales (Alcerdidae); armored or hard scales (Diaspididae); cochineal insects (Dactylopiidae); date scales (Phoenicococcidae); ensign coccids (Ortheziidae); felted scales (Eriococcidae); gall-like coccids (Kermesidae); giant coccids and ground pearls or margarodid scales (Margarodidae), including the Cottony cushion scale (*Iceryia purchasi*); lac scales (Kerriidae), including the Lac insect (*Kerria lacca*); mealybugs (Pseudococcidae), including the Pink sugarcane mealybug (*Saccharicoccus sacchari*); soft scales (Coccidae), including the Soft brown scale (*Coccus hesperidum*), the Horse chestnut scale (*Pulvinaria regalis*).
PSYLLOIDEA (jumping plant lice) contains 6 families, including psyllids (Psyllidae), triozids (Triozidae), including the Citrus psylla (*Trioza eryteae*).

Cicadas and Hoppers
Suborder Auchenorrhyncha

Beak appears to arise from "neck"; antennae very short, ending in a bristle; sound-producing structures present. Just under 17,000 species in around 30 families in 2 infraorders and 6 superfamilies. Cicadomorpha contains 4 superfamilies:
CERCOPOIDEA (froghoppers or spittlebugs), including aphrophorid spittlebugs (Aphrophoridae) and Cercopid spittlebugs (Cercopidae);
CICADELLOIDEA, including leafhoppers (Cicadellidae);
CICADOIDEA: cicadas (Cicadidae) and tettigarctid cicadas (Tettigarctidae);
MEMBRACOIDEA, including aetalionid treehoppers (Aetalionidae), treehoppers (Membracidae).
Fulgoromorpha contains 1 superfamily, FULGOROIDEA (planthoppers) including achilid planthoppers (Achilidae); cixid planthoppers (Cixiidae); delphacid planthoppers (Delphacidae); derbid planthoppers (Derbidae); dictyopharid planthoppers (Dictyopharidae); flatid planthoppers (Flatidae); fulgorid planthoppers (Fulgoridae), including the Peanut-head bug (*Fulgora laternaria*); tettigometrid bugs (Tettigometridae)

True bugs
Suborder Heteroptera

Beak can be swung down or forward from body; many species predatory; base of forewings hardened, remainder and hindwings membranous; at rest wings overlap, lie flat over body; stink glands present. 50,000 known species in 75 families in 7 infraorders:
ENICOCEPHALOMORPHA including unique headed or gnat bugs (Enicocephalidae);
DIPSOCOROMORPHA, including jumping ground bugs (Dipsocoridae);
GERROMORPHA including pond skaters (Gerridae), water crickets or broad-shouldered water striders or ripple bugs (Veliidae), water striders (Hydrometridae), water treaders (Mesoveliidae);
NEPOMORPHA including back swimmers or water boatmen (Notonectidae), giant water bugs (Belostomatidae), lesser water boatmen (Corixidae), water scorpions (Nepidae);
LEPTOPODOMORPHA, including shore bugs (Saldidae) and spiny shore bugs (Leptopodidae);
CIMICOMORPHA including assassin bugs (Reduviidae), bedbugs (Cimicidae), lace bugs (Tingidae), leaf, plant or capsid bugs (Miridae), including the Apple capsid (*Plesiocoris rugicollis*);
PENTATOMORPHA, including flat bugs (Aradidae), burrower or negro bugs (Cydnidae), ground and seed bugs (Lygaeidae), including the Chinch bug (*Blissus leucopterus*); shieldbugs or stinkbugs (Pentatomidae); squash or leaf-footed bugs (Coreidae), including the Dock bug (*Coreus marginatus*).

The 20 families in the Fulgoroidea comprise about 10,000 species. Commonly known as the planthoppers, this is a diverse group of insects, varying in size from small (2mm/0.08in) to large (80mm/3.15in). The adults feed mainly on plant sap, although some Achilidae and Derbidae feed on fungi. Some nymphs secrete wax, which forms long abdominal filaments. Fulgoroids are predominantly a tropical–subtropical group.

Globally, the Cixiidae have about 1,300 species and most are under 10mm (0.4in) in length. Cixiids are the most primitive fulgoroids. The adults resemble cicadas, with clear, membranous wings held rooflike over the body; the forewings have distinctive veins, with dark, hair-bearing spots. Females secrete white, woolly wax, which they carry as a tuft at the tip of the abdomen.

Cixiids lay eggs directly into the ground, using an awl-like ovipositor. The nymphs feed on the roots of grasses and other plants; some make small, wax-lined cells close to their host plants. The adults are usually found on trees and shrubs.

Delphacidae are worldwide, and there are 1,700 species varying in size from 2 to 10mm (0.08–0.4in). Intraspecific wing dimorphism and sexual dimorphism are common. All species live on or close to the ground, and the nymphs are free-roaming. A number of species produce sounds during courtship. Most species show some degree of host preference.

Delphacids include some major crop pests of rice, maize, and sugarcane. The Asian brown planthopper, *Nilaparvata lugens*, causes grass stunt in rice, which periodically affects much of southeast Asia. The Australian Sugarcane hopper (*Perkinsella saccharicida*) is a vector of Fiji disease, and has infected a number of countries around the world, where it causes serious problems. In Hawaii, a small mirid bug (*Tytthus mundus*) has been used as a control agent of this species in one of the most successful examples of biological control.

The Fulgoridae include the largest and most bizarre homopterans, the 800 species being mainly tropical in distribution. Ranging in length from 10 to 100mm (0.4–4in), some species have a wingspan of over 15cm (6in). All species feed on trees and shrubs, often piercing the bark directly.

Fulgorids are usually called lantern bugs, the name stemming from old, unsubstantiated accounts that their heads glow in the dark.

Fulgorids are often very brightly colored, although some have cryptic forewings and brightly-colored hindwings. Many have large extensions to their heads: that of the Brazilian *Fulgora laternaria* resembles a crocodile's! Species with brightly-colored hind wings and cryptic forewings use flash colors to ward off potential predators; when disturbed, the bug quickly opens and closes its wings repeatedly, scaring the attacker. The head extensions may also help in evading predators. When at rest, the strange head shape breaks up the outline of the body, which confuses predators.

True Bugs
SUBORDER HETEROPTERA

The true bugs differ from all other hemipterans in being able to swing the "beak" forward from its resting position on the underside of the body. Precise direction of the mouthparts makes it possible for them to exploit food resources other than the plant tissues to which other bugs are restricted. Many heteropterans are predatory and some specialize in feeding on seeds. All of the aquatic bugs are true bugs.

This diversity of biology is reflected in a great variety of body forms, and the 50,000 known species are distributed among 75 families. True bugs are characterized by nonuniform forewings, with both membranous and hardened portions.

All heteropterans have stink glands to repel predators. In nymphs they are located on the back of the abdomen. In adults, the abdomen is covered by the wings, and a different gland or pair of glands comes into use, opening on the sides or underside of the thorax. Many bugs advertise their distastefulness with bright, warning colors; others are cryptically colored and use stink glands only as a second line of defense.

The surfaces of ponds, lakes, slow-flowing rivers and streams, and even the sea literally support the water striders. These bugs exploit surface tension, standing on the surface film with water-repellent feet. A variety of predatory bugs live beneath the surface of fresh water, solving the problem of underwater respiration via a number of adaptations: some have a long respiratory siphon, while others swim to the surface from time to time to replenish air supplies either through a retractable siphon or else by trapping air bubbles on the underside of their bodies.

The Heteroptera comprise seven infra-orders: the Enicocephalomorpha, Dipso-coromorpha, Gerromorpha, Nepomorpha, Leptopodomorpha, Cimicomorpha, and Pentatomorpha. The classification of the Heteroptera is often contentious, with superfamilies, families, and subfamilies

◐ ◑ *Above and right* The broad, blunt-ended front wings typical of species in the family Flatidae show up clearly in this group of Flower-spike bugs (Phromnia rosea) at rest in Madagascar. These bugs fly well, and will scatter if disturbed by a bird. As nymphs (RIGHT), Flower-spike bugs use wax as a defensive measure, forming brushlike "tails" from long filaments of the substance. This strategy is common in both nymphs and adults in many families of hoppers.

◐ *Left* When on a tree trunk, its normal home, the large adult of the Peanut-head bug (Fulgora laternaria) is well camouflaged by its barklike coloration. If disturbed, it opens its wings and startles its attacker with these intimidating eyespots.

changing status with each new review. The characters separating the various infraorders, superfamilies, and families include the structures of the antennae, legs, and abdomen, the venation of the wings, and the shape of the male genitalia.

All 1,400 species forming the **infraorder Gerromorpha** or semiaquatic bugs are predators. Most can walk on the surface film of water, with the Gerridae and Veliidae spending their entire lives afloat. There is a constant "rain" of insects falling from the air, their struggles on the water surface sending out tiny ripples that water skaters detect from a distance of a few centimeters. Their large, prominent eyes also help them to detect prey and avoid predators.

The largest family is the worldwide Veliidae or water crickets, containing approximately 600 species. Also known as broad-shouldered water striders or riffle bugs, they occupy a wide range of standing waters, from small pools to lakes; two genera are even found on the surface of the oceans. Veliids range in size from a tiny 1mm to 10mm (0.04–0.4in); their stout bodies are covered in fine, water-repellent hairs, and the wings exhibit dimorphism, with apterous and macropterous forms occurring even in the same species. *Habrovelia*, *Tonkuivelia*, and *Veliohebria* are semiterrestrial, and at least some species of *Paravelia* and *Microvelia* live in water collected at the bases of bromeliads or in water-filled rot holes in trees. The Haloveliinae have much elongated middle legs; this subfamily contains the genera *Halovelia*, *Xenobates*, and *Colpovelia*, all of which inhabit the marine intertidal zones along the northern coast of Australia.

The Gerridae are some of the most recognizable aquatic insects. Commonly called pond skaters, water striders, or wherrymen, the group includes 500 species distributed worldwide. They range in length from 1.6 to 36mm (0.06–1.4in) and are long-legged with globular to elongate bodies. Gerrids are among the most studied bugs in terms of their ecology, biology, and behavior, mostly because a number of species lend themselves to study in artificial conditions.

The genera *Asclepios* and *Halobates* of the subfamily Halobatinae are among the most unusual of the Hemiptera order, if not of the entire Insecta class, because they are the only true marine insects. Some species remain close to the shore, but five *Halobates* species roam the ocean, being truly pelagic. The water strider *Austrobates rivularis* was recently described from a freshwater stream on Cape York Peninsula in the far north of Queensland, Australia. A new genus was proposed for this species, which is thought to represent a "missing link" between the freshwater and the marine gerrid species.

The worldwide Mesoveliidae, known as the water treaders, are the most primitive of the Gerromorpha bugs. There are 39 species, with the genus *Mesovelia* being the largest and most cosmopolitan. They range in size from 1.2 to 4.2mm (0.05–0.17in) and vary greatly in body form, although most are stout and oblong in shape, with relatively long legs. The head is longer than it is wide, and, unlike in most Gerromorpha species, is the only part of the body bearing hair. Most species are wingless (apterous), and in macropterous forms of some *Mesovelia* species self-mutilation of the wings is known. *Cryptovelia terrestris* is one of the smallest known heteropterans.

The **infraorder Nepomorpha** contains 11 families and some 1,950 species. This group includes all of the aquatic bugs that actually live underwater, as well as a number of riparian taxa. The forelegs are often raptorial, evolved for catching prey. Most species inject a mixture of enzymes to immobilize and digest their prey. The belostomatids (giant water bugs) are known to have a very painful bite, which has led to much folklore.

With about 550 species, the worldwide Corixidae are the largest family, living in streams, ponds, and acidic bogs. They are often called water boatmen because of their oarlike hindlegs. Ranging in size from 2.5 to 15mm (0.1–0.6in), they feed mainly on plant material. The males stridulate during courtship and mating.

The Notonectidae contains 340 species. This family occurs throughout the world and is well represented in temperate regions. Superficially similar to corixids, notonectids can be distinguished by the fact that they swim upside-down – hence the common name of "back swimmers."

Most species hang upside-down from the surface film and wait for prey to drop in near by; the struggling insect causes vibrations in the surface film, alerting the notonectid. Some males in the subfamily Anisopinae, including species of *Anisops* and *Buenoa*, stridulate as part of courtship. The noise produced can be heard several meters away. Some *Anisops* species living in poorly oxygenated water have specialized cells in the abdomen containing hemoglobin. These cells link directly to the breathing system, enabling the insects to extract the optimal amount of oxygen.

The Belostomatidae, containing about 150 species, are often called giant water bugs, and with good reason: one neotropical species, *Lithocerus maximus*, reaches a length of 110mm (4.3in) and is the largest known bug. Belostomatids occur worldwide, but are most diverse in the tropics. All but one species have strong, raptorial front legs, and will attempt to catch any prey that passes close by, including fish and amphibians. Most live in standing water, and, although excellent swimmers, tend to wait in ambush for their prey. All

◗ **Right** *The striking appearance of these Australian shield bug nymphs (Lyramorpha species; Tessaratomidae) is a warning to would-be predators that they produce a foul-smelling and bitter liquid from glands in the abdomen. The four gland openings are clearly visible.*

species are flattened ovoid-elongate in shape and brown in color, except for the African snail predator *Limnogeton*, which lacks raptorial front legs and has developed swimming legs instead. In one of the few examples of paternal care in insects, males of the genera *Belostoma*, *Abedus*, and *Sphaerodema* have wings modified to form a nursery, in which they carry eggs until they hatch.

There are 231 species of the Nepidae or water scorpions, most of them tropical. They range in size from 14 to 45mm (0.55–1.7in), and are brown and elongate with a long caudal breathing tube. Nepids are poor swimmers and tend to crawl along the bottoms of ponds. In some species, the dorsum of the abdomen is bright red and is visible when the bug is in flight, presumably acting as a warning color. The holarctic *Nepa* and the elongate, worldwide *Ranatra* are the best-known genera; the latter are often referred to as water stick insects.

The **infraorder Leptopodomorpha** contains just over 300 species in 5 families. Most are associated with riparian habitats, including intertidal zones, the exception being the Leptopodidae, which live in dry, tropical habitats. All are predatory and will also scavenge dead insects.

The Saldidae are the largest family, with 265 species distributed throughout the world. Often called shore bugs, they range from 2.3 to 7.4mm (0.09–0.3in) in length, are ovoid-elongate in shape, and are patterned. They are extremely agile, jumping and taking rapid flight, making them difficult to catch. They are most often found in freshwater riparian habitats, usually on stony shores.

The **infraorder Pentatomorpha** contains 29 families and nearly 9,000 species, including some of the largest terrestrial bugs. Most are plant-feeders, although some specialize on fungi or seeds, while others, such as the Asopinae (Pentatomidae) and the Geocorinae (Lygaeidae), have become secondarily predacious.

The Pentatomidae is the largest family in the Pentatomorpha and one of the four largest in the Heteroptera. Predominantly tropical, the family comprises 4,100 species including the stinkbugs and the shieldbugs, and is distributed throughout the world. Pentatomids range in size from 4 to 20mm (0.15–0.8in), and are mainly greenish or brown, although some are very brightly colored.

Pentatomids lay up to 200 barrel-shaped eggs, usually in batches of 12, in either hexagonal arrays on flat surfaces or in double rows on twigs and petioles. First-instar nymphs do not feed on plants. Instead, they cluster around the empty egg shells, ingesting symbiotic bacteria the female smeared on the eggs as she laid them. The females of some species show parental care.

These bugs are well known for the strong-smelling scents secreted from abdominal glands by nymphs and from thoracic scent glands by adults. The scents are complex, species-specific

○ **Above** *The shield-backed bugs (Scutelleridae) can be distinguished by the shape and extent of the scutellum, which covers most of the abdomen, making them look very like leaf beetles. This is a species of Callidea from Africa.*

◐ **Left** *With its flat, shieldlike shape this* Catacanthus *from Sulawesi is a typical member of the family* Pentatomidae, *commonly known as shield- or stinkbugs. Large, brightly-colored species such as this are mainly tropical, and have powerful stink glands.*

◐ **Below left** *In the Pentatomidae copulation takes place end-to-end, as typified by these Common green shieldbugs* (Palomena prasina) *from Europe. As usual, the male (left) is smaller than his mate.*

◑ **Right** *The wing-buds of this last-instar Peromatus nymph (Pentatomidae) from Brazil are clearly visible as flaplike extensions of the mesothorax. At its next and final molt it will become a fully winged and quite differently colored adult.*

blends of volatile compounds that deter predators when the insects are attacked; in some pentatomids, the scent also triggers an escape response in nearby members of the same species. In addition to chemical defenses, some pentatomids produce a noise when attacked by rubbing pegs on the inner face of the hind femora against a special ridge on the underside of the abdomen. The North American Two-spotted stink bug (*Perillus bioculatus*) makes itself useful by hunting the notorious Colorado beetle (*Leptinotarsa decemlineata*).

The 1,800 species of the remarkable Aradidae (flat bugs or bark bugs) range between 3 and 11mm (0.1–0.4in) in size. They are dorsoventrally flattened, oval or rectangular in shape, and have a roughened dorsal surface and stout antennae. Although mainly macropterous, a large number of tropical species are wingless. Most aradids are fungus-feeders, from fungal threads (mycelia) or the fruiting bodies of wood-decaying fungi; members of the Aneurinae and Calisinae subfamilies, however, feed on the sap of trees, and *Aradus cinnamoneus* (Aradinae) has been recorded feeding on conifers. Some Australian and North American

species live in termite nests, where they feed in the fungal gardens created by the termites (see Termites). *Aradus*, the largest genus with 200 species, is predominantly a northern hemisphere group, living under the bark of dead trees, where there is an ample supply of fungal mycelia.

The Acanthosomatidae have 180 species ranging in size from 6 to 18mm (0.2–0.7in). They are broadly oval in shape, tapering to the apex of the body; the scutellum is large and pointed, but does not cover the corium (the membranous part of the wing), and the tarsi are two-segmented. Acanthosomatids occur throughout the world.

Some species exhibit parental care, guarding the eggs and early-instar nymphs from predators and parasitoids. In some cases the female may guard the nymphs until their fifth instar. The genus *Elasmucha* contains a number of species in which parental behavior has been studied. The European Parent bug (*Elasmucha grisea*), which lives on birch trees, lays 30–40 eggs in a hexagonal clutch on the underside of a leaf. The female straddles the site until the eggs hatch, which may take 20 days or more. In the Japanese *Elasmucha putoni* and *E. dorsalis*, females make defensive movements, including jerking, tilting the body to the origin of attack, and wing-fanning.

The Cydnidae, generally referred to as burrower

or negro bugs, are the second largest family of the shieldbug-type pentatomorphids, with around 600 species in eight subfamilies. The family is well represented in all zoogeographic regions. The insects range in size from 2 to 20mm (0.08–0.8in), and many have a broad, flattened head and legs adapted for digging. Most cydnids are fossorial, spending much of their lives underground, where they feed on plant roots. In the majority of species, both sexes have a row of pegs on a vein in the hind wing, which, when rubbed against a ridged part of the body, produces high-pitched vibrations used in courtship. Some species produce defensive secretions that act as an irritant to any would-be attacker.

The Corimelaeninae (negro bugs), consist of 200 western-hemisphere species, the adults of which resemble small beetles. In those species that have been studied, both nymphs and adults occur on the host plant, well above ground. At least three South American species associate with ants. The Cydninae are the largest and most diverse of the subfamilies, with over 300 mostly fossorial species. Although distributed widely, this group is largely subtropical and tropical, and associated with well-drained soils.

The Podopinae have a large, elongate scutellum that often reaches the tip of the abdomen. They

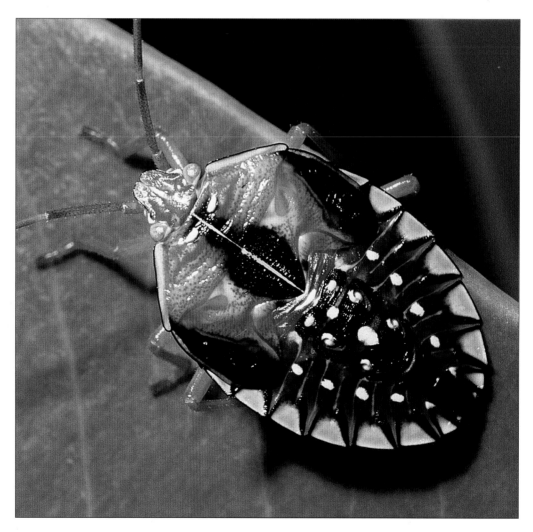

are generally yellow-brown to dark brown in color, except for some strikingly marked members of the tribe Graphosomatini, such as the red-and-black-striped *Graphasoma italicum*. The 255 species are chiefly found in damp grassland. The subfamily is associated with grasses; species in the tribe Podopini live and feed at the base of grasses, while some Graphosomatini, such as the African *Bolbocoris* species, feed on grass seeds. Species of *Scotinophora* are pests of rice and other cereal crops in Asia and Africa.

The Pentatominae are the largest group of the family and vary in form and color; in some species, the pronotum has thornlike angles. All are plant-feeders, including a number of pests. The Green vegetable bug (*Nezara viridula*) is a common, subcosmopolitan pest of a wide variety of crops, from cotton to tomatoes. In Australia, the parasitic wasp, *Trissolcus basalis* (Scelionidae), is used as a biocontrol agent to prevent outbreaks.

The Lygaeidae are a large and diverse family, with 4,000 species that are extremely varied in both size and form. The majority are small (1.2–12mm/0.05–0.5in) and dull brown or black in color, but a number are brightly colored red or yellow and black. Lygaeids exhibit forms with short wings (brachyptery), ant mimicry (myremcomorphy), and beetle mimicry (coleoptery). Many lygaeids possess stridulatory structures, located on either the forewings, hindwings, abdominal sternum, or along the sides of the head and thorax. Although most are seed feeders, there is a great deal of diversity in the feeding habits of this group. The Blissinae, for example, are sap suckers, the Geocorinae prey on other insects, and the Cleradini suck vertebrate blood. The Bledionotinae exhibit striking ant mimicry, with the pronotum adorned with bizarre ornamentation and the anterior abdominal segments fused.

The Lygaeinae are found worldwide, with most of the 500 species in the tropics. Many species in the 58 genera are large and conspicuous, with bright aposematic color patterns of red or orange and black. All known species are plant-feeders, with many feeding on seeds.

The Rhyparochrominae are by far the largest and most diverse lygaeid subfamily. They are dull bugs, often either brown or else mottled brown, black, and white, and are small to medium (2–20mm/0.08–0.8in) in size. Most are ground-dwellers living in leaf litter, where they feed on mature fallen seeds. Some climb plants to exploit maturing seeds, but only a few species are truly arboreal. The African *Stilbocoris natalensis*, which feeds on fig seeds, is remarkable in that the male presents a seed to the female as a courtship gift. As the female begins to feed, the male mates. This species is also interesting for its ovoviviparous species that give birth to live young, a rare trait among the Heteroptera. In Trinidad and Peru, the cave-dwelling *Cligenes subcavicola* feeds on seeds dropped by roosting fruit bats; one such cave had

a density of 100,000 bugs per square meter (almost 10,000 to the square foot).

The 1,800 species of Coreidae range from thin and delicate to large and robust bugs, usually elongate or elliptical, often with bizarre dilations and expansions of the hind femora or tibia and antennal segments. They range in size from 7 to 45mm (0.3–1.8in), and occur worldwide, though mostly in the tropics, which is where they reach their largest size and most elaborate designs. Although usually dull-colored, many species are warningly adorned in bright hues, which can be metallic in some tropical-forest species. Coreids are all plant-feeders, mainly on young shoots, and some species are economically important pests. They are sometimes called leaf-footed bugs, but are more often known as squash bugs, because North American species of *Anasa* feed on members of the squash family (Cucurbitaceae). Males of large species defend territories on flower heads, fighting off any trespassers. This behavior may be widespread in the family and might explain the marked sexual dimorphism in the hind legs of many species, in which males often have enlarged, spiny hind femora.

The African *Carlisis wahlbergi* can spray a defensive chemical over distances of 150mm (6in) by using its pair of scent glands, which presumably gives it some directional control. In one outbreak in a South African garden, a single gardenia tree was found to contain over 9,000 adults of this bug, weighing a total of 9.8kg (22lb).

Species of *Thasus* are among the largest of terrestrial bugs, reaching up to 45mm (1.8in) in length. *T. acutangulus* has warningly-colored bright orange, yellow, and black nymphs that feed in aggregations that are pheromone-driven: any displaced individuals can find their way back by smell. If disturbed, the aggregation pulsates, spraying jets of anal fluid into the air and exuding scent-gland secretions.

The **infraorder Cimicomorpha** is the largest group of the Hemiptera, with over 19,600 species, although more than half of its 16 families contain less than 50 species. It also includes the two largest families of true bugs, the Miridae and Reduviidae. Although it is believed that ancestral Cimicomorpha were predatory, the modern group has a large number of phytophagous species.

The Miridae are the largest single family in the Heteroptera, with 10,000 species in 8 subfamilies. Mirids are often called plant bugs or capsids, and they occur throughout the world in almost all habitats. Most of the family are phytophagous, although some, such as the Dicyhini (Bryocorinae), are omnivores and the Isometopinae eat

◐ **Right** *Although numerous very large species of leaf-footed bugs (Coreidae) are found in the tropics, few are as elaborately colored as these Pharaoh bugs (Pachylis pharaonis) sucking sap from a plant stem in the Brazilian campo cerrado.*

scale insects (Coccoidea). The tropical Cylapinae feed on fungi, but the Deraeocorinae and species of Phytocoris (Mirinae) are predacious. Mirids, which range in size from 2 to 15mm (0.08–0.6in), are among the most delicate of bugs and are often colored to blend in with the background. A four-segmented labium and the presence of trichobothria (small patches of hairs) on the mid and hind femor distinguish the mirids from most other heteropterans. In body plan, they range from ovoids to remarkably effective myrmeco-morphs (ant mimics). These last not only have antlike coloring but also mimic ants in gait, and a number of species have constrictions of the abdomen that give the impression of a petiole, the slender segment joining the rest of the abdomen to the thorax that is a distinctive feature of ants.

One of the most unusual mirids is *Hadronema uhleri*, which lives and scavenges exclusively in spiders' webs. The genus *Helopeltis* (Bryocorinae) is a pest of cultivated plants in tropical Africa and the Indo-Malayan region. The Australian *Tytthus mundulus* (Phylinae) preys on insect eggs and is used to control the Sugar-cane hopper (*Perkinsiella saccharicida*) in Hawaii.

The Tingidae, or lace bugs, contain 1,900 species worldwide in 3 subfamilies. They range in length from 2 to 8mm (0.08–0.3in), and most species are characterized by the dense reticulate or lacelike network of veins on the edge of the prono-tum and forewings. In some species the edges of these parts are greatly extended to form intricate, explanate sides.

Most tingids are free-living herbivores, usually on a single host species, where they feed on the underside of leaves. They are gregarious as nymphs, and some species show maternal care. Females lead their young between suitable feeding spots, guarding them from predators and para-sitoids. Some species indulge in "egg-dumping"; on the cuckoo model, a female lays eggs among those of another individual and leaves them to be reared by the surrogate mother.

The 500 damsel bug species (Nabidae) are divided into 2 subfamilies. Most are mid-sized, rarely exceeding 10mm (0.4in), and are mainly elongate, drab-colored insects. Wing polymorphism is common in many species and nabids can be either apterous, brachypterous, or macropterous. The rostrum is long and curved, reaching back to the pro- or mesothorax, and the front legs are gen-erally thickened. Males of most nabids possess a structure called Ekblom's organ that disperses pheromones. In the subfamily Prostemmatinae, hemocoelic insemination occurs, which is to say that the male's genitalia penetrate the vaginal wall of the female, ejaculating sperm into the hemoe-coel (insect blood cavity).

Found worldwide, the Reduviidae are the predatory assassin bugs, one of the largest and most diverse of true bug families, with 6,500 species, most of them tropical. Not only is there a variety of body forms unique to the family, but many species also mimic other bugs in the families Aradidae, Coreidae, and Pyrrhocoridae. Key characters of the family are the presence of a prosternal stridulatory sulcus, the necklike shape of the head behind the eyes, and the strongly curved rostrum. Assassin bugs range in size from 7 to 40mm (0.3–1.6in). Some species are brightly colored, typically in shades of red and black, while others are cryptic, resembling their background. Many species are hairy or spiny, and some have strange, flangelike body extensions. Unlike many other predatory bugs, reduviids are active hunters; some species seem to exhibit cooperation when attacking large prey. In Namibia a few species of the subfamily Ectrichodiinae are specific predators of millipedes, which are often over 10 times larger than the bugs themselves; in these cases, several bugs sometimes attack the prey simultaneously and drag it away, although it is unclear if the cooperation is deliberate.

At the cooler edges of its range the nocturnal fly bug *Reduvius personatus* (Reduviinae) often lives in houses; in Britain, for example, it preys on pest insects and spiders. Nymphs of this species use sticky threads to cover themselves with detritus as a camouflage measure.

The subfamily Triatominae, often called cone nose bugs or kissing bugs, is the most important group of medically significant bugs. It contains 111 species, most of which occur in the New World, from southwestern North America to Argentina, although 11 species also occur in Asia. All species are nocturnal and feed exclusively on vertebrate blood. Triatomes inhabit the nests of their hosts, such as wood rats. However, a number of species have invaded the domestic environment, where they feed on people and their livestock. The genera *Triatoma*, *Rhodnius*,

Panstrongylus, *Eratyrus*, *Cavernicola*, and *Dipetalogaster* are all recorded as biting humans. However, the species of major concern are *Triatoma infestans*, *Triatoma dimidiata*, and *Rhodnius prolixus*, all of which are vectors of the protozoan blood parasite *Trypanosoma cruzi*, which causes Chaga's disease. This is fatal in about 10 percent of cases; it is transmitted not by inoculation (in other words, through bites), but rather through fecal contamination.

The Nabinae are general predators of small invertebrates, although, unlike the reduviids, their raptorial frontlegs are hardly developed. An exception is the neotropical *Arachnocoris*, which live in spiders' webs, where it scavenges dead insects.

The Anthocoridae comprise 500 species found throughout the world. There is a single subfamily, the Anthocorinae, although the taxonomy of this group is still unclear. Anthocorids are sometimes called flower bugs or minute pirate bugs, and range in length from 1.4 to 5mm (0.06–0.2in). They are strongly flattened, elongate, and generally dark brown or black in color with pale markings. As with the Cimicidae and other more obscure bugs, male anthocorids have a genital paramere adapted for direct penetration through the side of the female's abdomen. This process is known as "traumatic insemination."

Some species feed on both plant and animal matter. Most species are, however, timid predators, selecting sessile or defenseless prey, such as insect eggs and the hemolymph of small insects. The nymphs of some *Anthocoris* species bite humans, causing severe irritation. *Xylocoris* species live under the bark of dead trees, their dorsoventrally flattened bodies adapted for narrow spaces.

The largely tropical and subtropical bed bug family, Cimicidae, includes about 90 species. Cimicids are highly evolved, flightless ectoparasites of vertebrates, especially bats. They are generally pale mahogany brown, ovoid, and between 4 and 12mm (0.2–0.5in) in length, and their wings

◆ **Above** In many tropical assassin bugs (Reduviidae) such as this Canthesancus golo *from Sumatra, the top of the pronotum – the covering of the front of the thorax – bears a stockade of sharp defensive spines. The rostrum (beak) is folded back beneath the head.*

◗ **Right** *In the USA, where they are common, bugs of the genus* Apiomerus *(Reduviidae) are called bee assassins from their habit of lying in ambush on flowers to kill visiting bees. This individual is at work on a cactus flower in New Mexico.*

◆ **Left** *The toad bugs of the family Gelastocoridae owe their common name to their hopping motion and their habit of seeking insect prey by the margins of rivers and ponds. This Big-eyed toad bug (*Gelastocoris oculatus*) is from South Carolina.*

are reduced to small pads. All cimicid males practice traumatic insemination.

Cimicids are temporary blood-feeding parasites, spending most of their time in the bedding, nest, or roost of their host, only emerging to gorge themselves on a blood meal. Apart from bat feeders, some specialize on birds (mostly swifts and swallows). Only three species feed on humans. Of these, both *Leptocimex boueti*, from West Africa, and *Cimex hemipterus*, which lives throughout the tropics, usually attack bats and (in the latter case) chickens. The notorious and now global Common or Human bed bug (*Cimex lectularius*) was, until the advent of modern insecticides, the most serious household pest. This species also feeds on bats, chickens, and other domestic animals. As with other species in the family, the Human bed bug does not stay on its host after feeding, which mostly occurs at night, but retreats to suitable nooks and crannies. Although there is no evidence that this bug transmits any diseases, its bites are a severe nuisance, and excessive feeding can cause iron deficiency in children.   DM

GROWING UP IN A HARLEQUIN BUG NURSERY

❶ *The female Harlequin bug Tectocoris diophthalmus (Scutelleridae) attaches her eggs in a broad collar around a twig of a host plant. She then perches on top of them and remains on guard until the eggs hatch. The clutch size (typically around 100) is exceptionally large for a bug that has to give effective protection to an exposed egg-batch. The eggs are at risk from parasitic wasps – hence the need for the female's presence.*

❷ *When the eggs begin to hatch, the female moves away, allowing the tiny nymphs to emerge unhindered by her body. After a day or so the nymphs will move away to a nearby leaf and begin to feed, at which point their mother finally leaves them.*

❸ *The kind of prolonged maternal care seen in certain other related bugs is probably unnecessary in the Harlequin bug. This species wears an extremely brilliant "warning" pattern in all its stages, and as a result these second-instar nymphs are likely to face few hazards.*

❹ *The final-instar nymphs are a brilliant metallic blue and red, rather than the black and red seen in all the earlier stages. Throughout their development they remain together in tightly-knit groups, intensifying the effect of their "warning" uniform and so further reducing the risk of predation.*

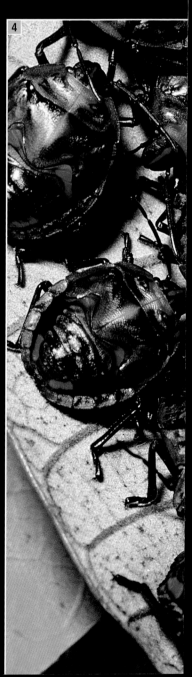

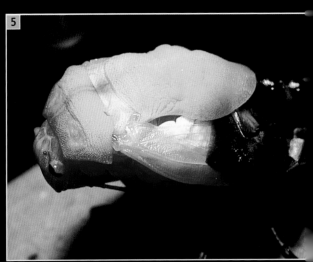

5 *For its final molt into adulthood, the last-instar nymph spreads its legs and fixes its tarsal claws firmly to a leaf. Unlike certain other bugs, it does not first adopt a head-down position. The orange of the adult is very pale at first, but soon begins to darken.* KP-M

Snakeflies and Alderflies

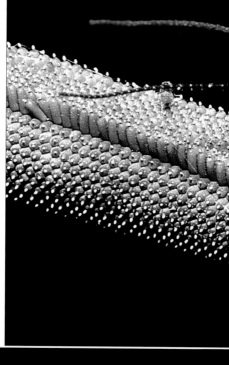

mAKING THEIR INITIAL APPEARANCE IN *the Permian 280–225 million years ago (snakeflies possibly earlier, in the preceding Carboniferous era), the snakeflies and alderflies were the first insects to have wings that develop internally. They also represent the earliest known occurrence of a pupal stage, and therefore of complete metamorphosis. Being first on the scene does not seem to have been of much evolutionary benefit to the two orders in the long term, however, for this is now a group of insects in a backwater, containing relatively few, seldom-seen species.*

◗ *Right* As a female alderfly (Sialis lutaria; Sialidae) *adds yet more eggs to her already impressively large cluster on the stem of a pondside rush, two tiny female parasitic wasps lay their own eggs inside hers. As they hatch from the eggs, the alderfly larvae will fall directly into the water below.*

◗ *Below* With its prowlike, forward-jutting head, net-veined wings, and sleek outline, an adult snakefly such as this European Raphidia notata (Raphidiidae) *can scarcely be mistaken for any other insect. The rather stout, black ovipositor protruding prominently at the rear end shows that this is a female.*

FACTFILE

SNAKEFLIES AND ALDERFLIES

Class: Insecta

Subclass: Pterygota

Orders: Raphidioptera (snakeflies); Megaloptera (alderflies, dobsonflies, fishflies)

SNAKEFLIES Order Raphidioptera
About 200 species in 2 families; species include *Erma, Glavia, Inocellia, Raphidia, Agulla*. All continents except Australia, commonest in Europe and America. **Size:** 1–2cm (0.4–0.8in) long, wingspan 1–4cm (0.4–1.6in).

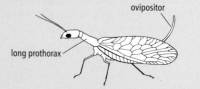

Features: Antennae bristlelike, rather short; prothorax or "neck" very long; 4 wings have pigmented patch; some veins fork at ends; cerci at tip of abdomen are very short.
Life cycle: Female has long ovipositor; larvae terrestrial, carnivorous.

ALDERFLIES, DOBSONFLIES, FISHFLIES
Order Megaloptera
About 300 species in 2 families: Corydalidae (dobsonflies and fishflies) and Sialidae (alderflies). Chiefly in temperate regions. **Size:** Wingspan up to 15cm (6in).

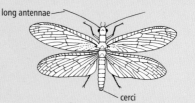

Features: Antennae usually long; prothorax short; wings without pigmented patch; hindwings fold fanwise in basal region and are coupled to forewings by jugal lobe; veins rarely fork at tip; male has 1-jointed cerci.
Life cycle: Female lacks ovipositor; carnivorous larvae are all aquatic.

Snake- and alderfly larvae, some of which may be active for several years, have well-developed legs and heads with powerful biting jaws, and they give rise to an exarate pupa (with the appendages not stuck down on the body) that can crawl about. In the adult stage they have four wings that can be folded along the body like a pitched roof. The wings are large and richly veined. Flight is fluttery and weak in most species. Adults are short-lived, and in a few species do not feed.

Snakeflies

ORDER RAPHIDIOPTERA

The snakeflies were formerly included with the lacewings and alderflies in the single order Neuroptera, but these days they are generally given their own order (Raphidioptera) within the overall neuropteroid grouping (Neuropterida). The Raphidioptera contains 200 or so very similar-looking species in two families worldwide. Most species were formerly included in the single genus *Raphidia*, which has recently been split into numerous very similar genera, none of which really merits more than subgeneric status.

Adult snakeflies have a highly distinctive appearance, although few people actually have the chance to see them as they are among the most elusive members of the Neuropterida; the adults spend much of their lives high among the upper branches of forest trees, so are seldom seen near ground level. The two pairs of transparent wings have a fishnet density of veins similar to those found in the neuropterans. The forewings are narrower but longer then the hindwings.

The prothorax is extremely long and mantislike, forming a "neck" that projects the narrow, elongate head well forward, enabling it to be held well up above the body in a lookout pose. The antennae are long and whiplike, composed of numerous beadlike segments; they are placed well forward on the shiny, flat-topped head, just above the large and powerful jaws. The legs, which are

"normal" in form, arise from the rear of the pro-thorax. The long, thin antennae and unmodified front legs are the most obvious distinction from mantisflies (Neuroptera: Mantispidae), which also have a relatively elongate pronotum and net-veined wings, but have highly modified raptorial front legs. Female snakeflies have a rather threat-ening appearance because of their long, project-ing, needlelike ovipositor, which can be mistaken for a sting; the name Raphidioptera, from the Greek *raphidas* meaning "needle," derives from this feature. Metamorphosis is complete, and the larvae are quite unlike the adults, being similar to certain beetle larvae, from which they can be diffi-cult to distinguish.

In snakeflies both the adults and larvae are predacious, using their powerful legs to run down other insects. The adults' prey often consists of soft-bodied invertebrates such as aphids and lepi-dopteran caterpillars, while the larvae are mainly predatory on the larvae of beetles and flies. As some prey items may be pests, snakeflies are con-sidered beneficial insects in orchards. The females use their long ovipositors to insert the eggs beneath tree bark, where the larvae live. Some species are only found on conifer trees, while others are mainly associated with oaks or other deciduous species, confirming the group's status as woodland-dwellers. Distribution can be rather uneven; all of the 19 North American species are restricted to the west of the continent, for exam-ple, although they do extend as far north as British Columbia.

Alderflies

ORDER MEGALOPTERA

The alderflies, dobsonflies, and fishflies of the order Megaloptera include some very large insects indeed; some American dobsonfly adults attain a wingspan of 15cm (6in). The aquatic larvae of dobsonflies bear seven pairs of unjointed tracheal gills on the abdomen and additional ventrally-placed gill tufts. The gills are regularly protracted and retracted, causing water to swish past them. The body ends with a pair of prolegs bearing large claws, which help the flies to move about.

Adult females lay their eggs near water, some-times in masses of several thousands. Different generations of some Australian species lay eggs on the same tree stump year after year. After hatching, the larvae fall into the water, where they catch prey (typically, small insect larvae) with their large jaws. They may take several years to mature before pupating in soil nearby. The nocturnal adults of some species do not feed, even though the males have huge, tusklike mandibles that can measure up to three times the length of the head; they are unable to inflict a painful bite, however, and are probably used in sexual competition with other males. By contrast, the much shorter jaws of the females are relatively powerful and can bite with some force.

The brownish, rather stout alderflies (*Sialis* species) are abundant near water in the early summer. The adults generally all look very similar and can usually only be identified to the correct species by examining the male genitalia, or the anal plates in females. The adult stage lasts only 2–3 days, during which feeding does not take place. Mating occurs at night and is assisted by the fact that emergence of the adults is closely synchronized, so that large numbers of both sexes are usually present over a brief period.

Females lay large clusters of eggs on vegetation overhanging water. Several females often choose the same plant, which may eventually bear an extensive coat of eggs. The larvae have seven pairs of gills, each with five joints rather like limbs, and there is an additional gill on the last segment. They spend 2–3 years crawling around actively in search of their prey, which consists of aquatic insects, worms, and other small invertebrates. They eventually pupate in a cell constructed in waterside soil or debris.   KP-M/PLM

Lacewings

mANTISPIDS, LACEWINGS, AND ANT LIONS, the net-veined insects of the order Neuroptera (meaning "nerve-winged"), comprise a diverse assemblage, ranging from tiny, aphidlike waxflies, with a wingspan of only 3mm (0.1in), to huge, spectacular tropical ant lions with wingspans of some 16cm (over 6in).

The most familiar members in temperate regions are the green lacewings, which often enter houses, where the beautiful golden eyes of some of the commonest species invariably attract attention.

Predatory Larvae
DEVELOPMENTAL STAGES

The larvae of most species are terrestrial predators. They feed with mouthparts formed from the maxillae and mandibles, which act as a sucking tube through which food can be imbibed under the action of a pumplike mechanism in the pharynx. The gut ends blindly and any solid indigestible material is stored. In the family Sisyridae the larvae are aquatic and are specialized to feed on freshwater sponges. The females lay eggs on branches overhanging the water, and the larvae fall in when they hatch. They are equipped with seven pairs of gills.

The brown lacewings (Hemerobiidae) are an important family whose terrestrial larvae feed on aphids and other plant suckers. In the more familiar green lacewings (Chrysopidae), the larvae are important predators on aphids. Some have developed the trick of hiding from their enemies under the empty skins of their prey. When attacked by ants, the larvae respond by swinging their flexible abdomens around to smear their adversaries with

⬆ Above *This Helicomitus sp. (Ascalaphidae) from Kenya is one of the more spectacularly colored of the owlflies. Its wings show the intricate venation that gives this group its popular name.*

a drop of defensive liquid from the anus. A female protects her eggs from parasites and predators by attaching them to long stalks. She forms a stalk by sticking a blob of "glue" onto a leaf and then quickly moving her abdomen upward, which draws the rapidly hardening glue out into a long thread, to which the egg is attached, clusters of eggs creating a pin-cushion effect.

The larvae of the Osmylidae lack gills, even though they prey on larvae of chironomid midges and other aquatic forms. In similar vein, the larvae of Myrmeleonidae and Ascalaphidae are voracious predators with large, serrated jaws, through which they inject enzymes into their prey and then suck out the juices. Ant lions are larvae of the family Myrmeleontidae; they dig pits in sand and lie concealed at the bottom, with their large jaws just protruding. Any small insect that stumbles into the pit is met by a fusillade of sandgrains propelled accurately upward by the ant-lion larva, sending the victim tumbling down into the lion's waiting jaws. Other species have larvae that live

---

FACTFILE

LACEWINGS

Class: Insecta

Subclass: Pterygota

Order: Neuroptera

About 5,000 species in some 20 families, including **spongeflies** (Sisyridae), **brown lacewings** (Hemerobiidae), **green lacewings** (Chrysopidae), **waxflies** (Coniopterygidae), **giant lacewings** (Osmylidae), **mantispids** (Mantispidae), **owlflies** (Ascalaphidae), **ant lions** (Myrmeleontidae), **butterfly lions** (Nemopteridae)

DISTRIBUTION Worldwide, mainly tropics.

SIZE Length 0.2–7.5cm (0.1–3in); wingspan 0.3–16cm (0.1–6.4in).

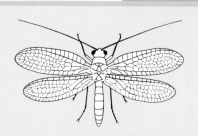

FEATURES Sometimes rather hairy; antennae threadlike or clubbed; 4 wings without pterostigma; have inefficient coupling mechanism; veins nearly all fork at tip; syringelike mouthparts.

LIFE CYCLE No ovipositor or cerci; larvae mainly terrestrial predators. 3 larval, 1 prepupal stage (hypermetamorphosis).

CONSERVATION STATUS Not threatened

◖ **Left** Lacewing larvae are voracious feeders on aphids, which they spear and hold aloft on their sickle-shaped jaws while the body-contents are drained. This Chrysoperla carnea larva will quickly decimate the aphids around it.

on tree trunks or burrow into the soil without forming pits. In nemopterid larvae the prothorax may be greatly elongated to form a long neck, which helps them to seize prey. Many mantispid larvae enter the egg-cocoons of spiders, especially wolf spiders, and feed on the eggs.

Four-winged Fly-by-Nights
ADULT HABITS AND ECOLOGY

Most adult neuropterans are nocturnal, and are often only noticed when they come to artificial lights. The membranous wings usually have a dense network of crossveins and are held rooflike over the body when at rest. Green lacewing adults possess hearing organs in large wing veins that can respond to the short, high-frequency pips emitted by bats, so helping them to avoid being eaten. Males and females both transmit sexual messages by vibrating the abdomen, sending pulses down through the legs and into the leaf on which they are perched, which broadcasts the message to nearby individuals. Each species has its own distinctive calling code, which precludes wasteful interspecific contacts.

Adult Ascalaphidae hunt prey on the wing by day. They have much better powers of flight than most other neuropterans, and they can be mistaken for dragonflies at a distance, although at close range their long, clubbed antennae (short in the very similar ant lions) immediately distinguish them. The males of some species are attractive insects with brightly colored wing markings. Others are very cryptic, and adopt a stylized pose when at rest, with the abdomen held out at an angle (often at right angles) to the substrate, usually a twig or tree-trunk, along which the wings are aligned. The abdomen is often rather bent, with a gnarled appearance and sometimes a truncated tip, giving the effect of a snapped-off twig. When caught, some tropical species not only feign death but also release the foul smell of rotting meat.

Females lay eggs on grass or twigs; some species surround the clutch with a stockade of rodlike bodies (repagula), probably for protection. Adults of the family Nemopteridae are well-known

for their extraordinary, streamerlike hindwings, which do not contribute to flight but instead trail behind and probably have a sexual function. The males dance up and down like mayflies, forming swarms that attract females.

Finally, the intriguing Mantispidae resemble small mantids with their raptorial forelegs, extended prothoraxes, and mobile heads with large, compound eyes, well suited to catching prey. Mantispids are mainly tropical but quite common also in temperate climates (excluding the British Isles). Certain species from the Americas are convincing mimics of social wasps, and may be polymorphic, so that a single species of mantispid is able to mimic several different wasps.   KP-M/PLM

◗ **Right** Representative species of lacewings: **1** A brown lacewing (Hemerobius angulatus); these small lacewings are predators on aphids. **2** Chrysopa carnea, one of the commoner green lacewings, notable for their golden eyes. **3** Libelloides coccajus, a highly predatory ascalaphid or butterfly lion. **4** With its long prothorax and raptorial forelimbs, this mantidfly (Mantispa interrupta) resembles a mantis, but is only about 2.5cm (1in) long.

Beetles

b EETLES ARE THE MOST SUCCESSFUL GROUP OF *animals on Earth, forming almost one-third of all described animal species and about two-fifths of all insects. They exploit the most extreme conditions, and they occur in all shapes and colors and sizes from less than 0.25mm (0.01in) to 20cm (8in).*

Beetles are found in virtually every habitat, from lakes and rivers to arid deserts, exploiting both rich and harsh conditions. Such is their enormous abundance that when the renowned biologist J.B.S. Haldane was asked what could be deduced about the nature of the Creator from the study of living things, he replied, "An inordinate fondness for beetles!"

300,000 Species
FORM AND FUNCTION

Beetles are extremely variable in design. They range in size from a minuscule 0.25mm long to 20cm (0.01–8in), and can be hairy or smooth, thin and delicate or horned, armored giants. They are all characterized by a tough, inflexible pair of modified forewings called elytra, which meet in the midline of the body to cover the membranous hindwings (the word "coleoptera" is Latin for "sheathwings"). This feature distinguishes them from the true bugs, which have softer, more papery elytra. Beetles hold the elytra away from the body when in flight, and at rest they fold the wings neatly beneath them. Some beetles have adopted a flightless existence, and may, like the oil beetles, have fused elytra, or rudimentary wings and flight muscles. Others, like ladybugs – more correctly, ladybug or ladybird beetles, as they are very much coleopterans and not hemipterans – are very proficient fliers and migrate over large distances to find overwintering sites.

The jointed legs that are typical of insects are modified for various lifestyles: long and slender for speed (as in tiger beetles and ground beetles), broad and toothed for digging (dung beetles, dor-beetles), curved and paddlelike for swimming (true water beetles); hopping species such as the flea beetles have expanded hind femora that house large muscles.

The mouthparts have five main components: the mandibles, the maxillae, the palps, an upper lip or labrum, and a lower lip or labium. The mandibles are the cutting, piercing, and crushing organs, while the other mouthparts deal with tast-ing and preparing the food and pushing it into the mouth. The large, sharp jaws of tiger beetles are an adaptation to a highly predatory way of life; the small, hard mandibles carried by weevils (snout beetles) at the tip of an elongated snout or rostrum are for crushing plant material. Specialized nectar feeders like species of the New World genus *Nemognatha* have tubelike mouthparts formed from elongated sections of the maxillae.

A beetle's sense organs are concentrated on its head, but tiny, vibration-sensitive hairs clothe the entire body. Some species can perceive sounds of a particular frequency using sensory structures on the legs. The majority (except for a few cave beetles and many larvae) have compound eyes and probably see in color. Those relying on vision for hunting (for example, ground beetles) or mating (fireflies) have larger, more efficient eyes. Some ground beetles can detect prey at distances of 15cm (6in). Whirligig beetles, which swim on the surface of ponds, have divided eyes, one half for vision under water, the other in air.

The antennae house receptors that are sensitive to humidity, vibration, and airborne scents, and are highly variable. Reduced in the larvae, the antennae in adults may be abruptly bent or elbowed (as in weevils of the family Curculion-idae), threadlike or filiform (for example, in the longhorn beetles, Cerambycidae), toothed (as in cardinal beetles, Pyrochroidae), or platelike or lamellate (chafers, Scarabaeidae). Beetles use their antennae to detect food and potential mates; males often have much more elaborate antennae than the females because they have to seek out the females, often over large distances.

Some beetles – usually males – have prominent "antlers" on their heads, formed from extended mandibles. Longhorn beetles have specialized structures for producing sound. They make a chirping noise by menas of stridulation, a process in which a hard edge or plectrum is rubbed against a row of toughened ridges on the underside of the abdomen.

◖ Right *A pair of shiny forewings or elytra that meet down the centre-line of the back is the distinguishing feature of beetles, as on this male Neptune beetle (Neptunides polychromus; Scarabaeidae) from Uganda. These wing casings are armored, to protect the membraneous wings.*

◖ Left *The male cockchafer beetle (Melolontha melolontha; Scarabaeidae) has comblike lamellate antennae whose uses include sensing female pheromones. When the antennae are not in use, the individual lamellae fold up like a closed fan.*

BEETLES

Class: Insecta

Subclass: Pterygota

Order: Coleoptera

About 300,000 known species in 166 families and 4 suborders

DISTRIBUTION Cosmopolitan; almost everywhere except the sea.

SIZE Length from 0.25mm (0.01in) to 20cm (8in).

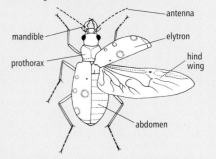

FEATURES Front pair of wings modified to form hardened cases (elytra) for rear wings; forward-projecting, biting mouthparts.

LIFE CYCLE Development includes larva and pupa, involving complete metamorphosis (holometabolous).

CONSERVATION STATUS The IUCN lists 17 species as recently extinct; in addition, 10 are currently Critically Endangered, 15 Endangered, and 27 Vulnerable.

See table ▷

Beetles have developed an impressive armory of defenses to protect themselves from a wide range of predators. The hard, shiny elytra may form the first line of defense against other insects. When threatened, many dome-shaped leaf beetles and ladybugs retract their legs and antennae under this protective shield, clamp down to the surface on which they are standing, and wait until it is safe to reemerge; even the sharp mandibles of predatory tiger beetles cannot establish a grip on the slippery surface. A number of beetles, particularly the larvae, have spiny or hairy surfaces that make them more difficult to attack. Skin beetle larvae have hairs designed to penetrate a predator's skin and set up a local irritation.

Some ladybug larvae have hollow spines that, when ruptured, release a sticky, yellow blood (hemolymph) containing distasteful chemicals. The adults produce the same substance from "kneejoints." This phenomenon is known as reflex bleeding. If, for example, an ant seizes the ladybug's leg in its jaws, the hemolymph gums up the antennae and mouthparts of the attacker, which rapidly backs away in distress.

Among beetles, the use of repellent chemicals is widespread and extremely effective (see Chemical Warfare). For example, flightless ground beetles of the genus *Anthia* squirt out jets of formic acid that can burn the skin and cause serious eye

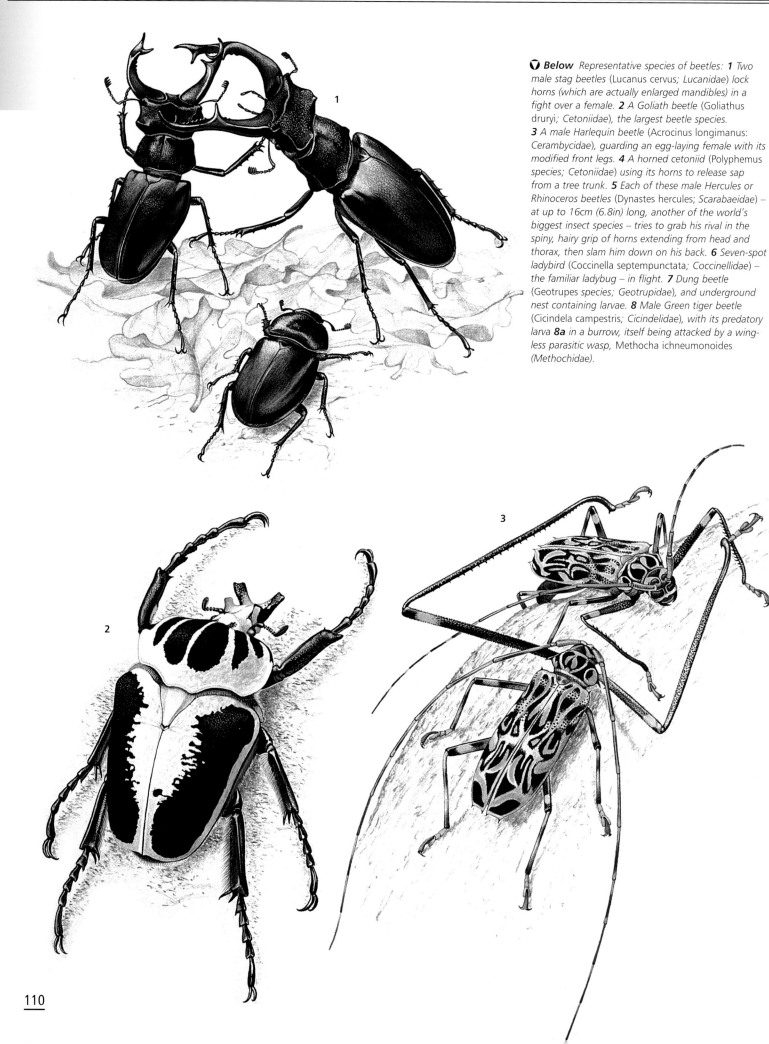

◉ *Below* Representative species of beetles: *1* Two male stag beetles (Lucanus cervus; Lucanidae) lock horns (which are actually enlarged mandibles) in a fight over a female. *2* A Goliath beetle (Goliathus druryi; Cetoniidae), the largest beetle species. *3* A male Harlequin beetle (Acrocinus longimanus: Cerambycidae), guarding an egg-laying female with its modified front legs. *4* A horned cetoniid (Polyphemus species; Cetoniidae) using its horns to release sap from a tree trunk. *5* Each of these male Hercules or Rhinoceros beetles (Dynastes hercules; Scarabaeidae) – at up to 16cm (6.8in) long, another of the world's biggest insect species – tries to grab his rival in the spiny, hairy grip of horns extending from head and thorax, then slam him down on his back. *6* Seven-spot ladybird (Coccinella septempunctata; Coccinellidae) – the familiar ladybug – in flight. *7* Dung beetle (Geotrupes species; Geotrupidae), and underground nest containing larvae. *8* Male Green tiger beetle (Cicindela campestris; Cicindelidae), with its predatory larva *8a* in a burrow, itself being attacked by a wingless parasitic wasp, Methocha ichneumonoides (Methochidae).

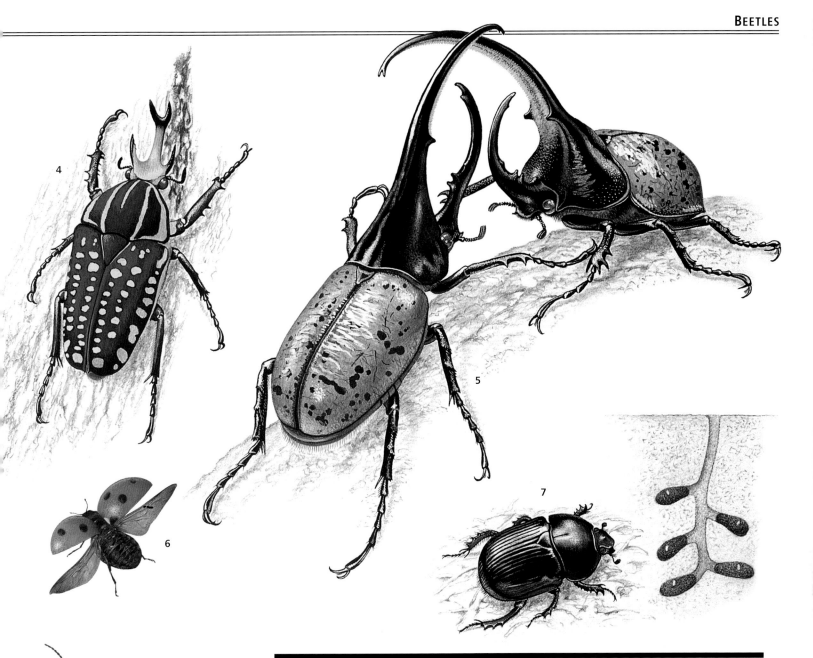

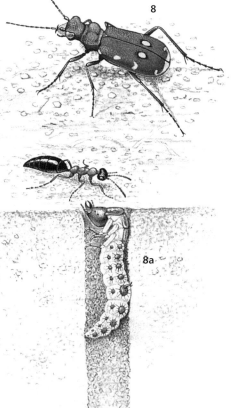

CHEMICAL WARFARE

Bombardier beetles, such as *Brachinus* species, deter would-be predators by spraying them with boiling hot quinones – noxious chemicals that blister the skin and frighten off both ants and toads. The beetle itself suffers no ill effects because the quinones are present only briefly in its body. The quinones' precursors, hydroquinone and hydrogen peroxide, are produced by special glands and stored in a cuticle-lined abdominal chamber. They are discharged as required into a second "combustion" chamber, where they are acted upon by the enzyme peroxidase. The reaction that follows produces quinones, water, and oxygen, and also considerable heat. The oxygen allows the quinones to be expelled, with some force and an audible "pop," from a nozzle at the tip of the abdomen. The heat, an added deterrent, causes much of the liquid to be converted to an irritating gaseous cloud resembling a tiny puff of smoke.

By swivelling the mobile abdominal tip, the beetle can aim its spray to either side, both forward and backward, with remarkable accuracy. It releases spray in tiny pulses, and can continue spraying for some time before its reservoir is exhausted.

Many darkling beetles also use quinone sprays. Some *Eleodes* species, less mobile than bombardier beetles, lower the head and raise the abdomen to direct the spray at the face of a vertebrate attacker. Since the rest of the beetle is not distasteful, certain mice have adopted a method for getting around the defense mechanism. The beetle is snatched up and its abdomen rapidly inserted into sand, where the quinones discharge harmlessly; the mice then eat it from the head downward.

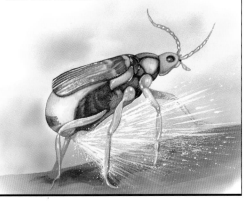

damage. The juices of crushed *Paederus sabaeus*, a rove beetle, if accidentally brushed onto the cornea, causes the painful condition known as "Nairobi eye." The larvae of the leaf beetle genus *Polyclada* are so poisonous that Kalahari bushmen use them to tip their hunting arrows.

The body fluids and elytra of oil or blister beetles contain cantharidin, a blistering agent that can be fatal to man if ingested in sufficient quantity; just 0.1gm (0.004oz) will cause the skin to blister. Strangely, the dried, powdered bodies of blister beetles are sold as the aphrodisiac Spanish fly; the Marquis de Sade experimented with it, and the Roman poet Lucretius is said to have died of an overdose. In the 19th century, an unexplained illness put many French soldiers serving in North Africa in hospital with painful priapism; the condition has only recently been ascribed to the habit of eating the legs of local frogs that had fed on blister beetles.

The forked tail of the larva of the leaf beetle *Cassida rubiginosa* allows it to carry a protective umbrella made of cast skins and feces. It waves this at an attacking ant, smearing it with feces. The ant retreats and thoroughly cleans itself. Similarly, the Hazel pot beetle (*Cryptocephalus coryli*) protects its young by laying each egg in a "pot" made of its own feces. When the egg hatches, the larva remains encased inside the pot, adding extra layers of feces as it grows. On the move, the head and legs protrude from one end, with the pot

dragging behind. With the head concealed, the larva blends into its background as a small rabbit dropping.

Beetles that are distasteful advertise the fact with bright, distinctive color patterns, usually black with red, yellow, or white. This warning coloration exploits the ability of vertebrate predators to learn from their mistakes. The inexperienced insectivore will try anything that looks potentially edible, but soon learns to associate unpleasant experiences with particular colors. The use of a limited number of colors means that the number of fatal experimental attacks on these insects is much less than if the predators had to learn a different color pattern for each species.

Sound may equally be used as a deterrent. A sudden, unexpected squeak can be enough to make a predator drop an unfamiliar beetle on a first encounter; the effect is reinforced if the beetle is also distasteful. Like many other ground beetles, *Cychrus caraboides*, which makes a protest sound if handled, also ejects butyric acid from glands opening on the tip of the abdomen near the anus (pygidium). The sound produced when a click beetle is disturbed is caused by a spring mechanism lying between the thorax and abdomen. A peg on the thorax is forced into a groove on the abdomen, where it causes a release of muscular tension that throws the insect (also known as the skipjack or snapping beetle) for some distance with an audible "click."

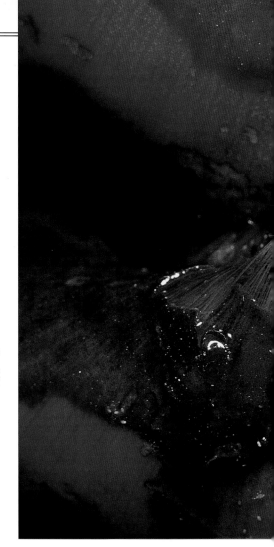

The 4 Suborders and Key Families of Beetles

Archostemata

A very ancient group comprising 2 families, the Cupedidae (35 species, chiefly fossils from the Lower Permian, beginning 280 million years ago) and Micromalthidae (1 species, *Micromalthus debilis*, with 5 larval forms).

Adephaga

30,200 species in 10 families, most of which are predatory as both adults and larvae except Haliplidae (crawling water beetles), which feed on algae, and Rhysodidae (wrinkled bark beetles), found in rotting wood. Many Paussidae live in ants' nests. Carabidae are all ground dwellers, including ground beetles, bombardier beetles, tiger beetles. Aquatic families include Amphizoidae, Hygrobiidae (screech beetles), Noteridae, Gyrinidae (whirligig beetles), and Dytiscidae (predacious diving beetles, or true water beetles). Trachypachidae inhabit wet regions and larvae may be aquatic.

Myxophaga

22 species in families Sphaeriidae, Lepiceridae, Hydroscaphidae, Torrincolidae.

Tiny beetles with aquatic larvae; mostly found in hotter regions.

Polyphaga

About 248,000 species in 150 families. Feed on a variety of plants and animals. Distinguished by absence of sixth segment in leg of larvae. Families include:

Water scavengers Hydrophilidae (water scavenger beetles), divers, in wet places.

Fungus feeders Erotylidae, Corylophidae, Cisidae, Lathridiidae.

Wood feeders Lucanidae (stag beetles, including *Lucanus cervus*), Cerambycidae (longhorn beetles, including the Old house borer or beetle *Hylotrupe bajulus* and the Harlequin beetle *Acrocinus longimanus*), Anobiidae (furniture beetles and woodworm, including the Cigarette or Tobacco beetle *Lasioderma serricorne* and the Deathwatch beetle *Xestobium rufovillosum*), Bostrychidae (e.g. Bamboo borer *Dinoderus minutus*), Lyctidae (powderpost beetles), Pyrochroidae (cardinal beetles), and Passalidae (Betsy beetles, patent leather beetles).

Predators Histeridae (hister beetles), Staphylinidae (rove beetles), Cleridae (checkered beetles, including the Red-

legged ham beetle *Necrobia rufipes*), Lampyridae (fireflies, glow-worms), and Coccinellidae (ladybugs or ladybirds or lady beetles, including the Two-spot ladybird *Adalia bipunctata* and Seven-spot ladybird *Coccinella septempunctata*) are predators. Soft-winged flower beetles (Melyridae) are predators that also feed on pollen.

Blister beetles The families Rhipiphoridae and Meloidae (oil or blister beetles, including *Meloe proscarabaeus*) are parasitic as larvae.

Dung eaters Geotrupidae (dung beetles including *Geotrupes* species dorbeetles), Trogidae (hide beetles) and Scarabaeidae (chafers and scarab beetles, including Hercules beetle *Dynastes hercules* and the Sugarcane chafer *Podischnus agenor*), all live on dung.

Carrion feeders Most Silphidae (burying or sexton or carrion beetles).

Plant feeders Apionidae, Curculionidae (including the Boll weevil *Anthonomus grandis*, Biscuit or Drugstore weevil *Stegobium paniceum*, Maize billbug *Sitophilus maidis*) – with over 50,000 species one of the largest families in the animal kingdom – and Bruchidae are all

plant-feeding weevils or snout beetles.

Root feeders Elateridae (click beetles including *Agriotes ustulatus*, skipjacks or snapping beetles, wireworms), Dascillidae, and many Buprestidae (jewel beetles).

Foliage feeders Chrysomelidae (leaf beetles), including the Colorado beetle *Leptinotarsa decemlineata*, cucumber beetles (*Diabrotica* species), Mexican bean beetle *Epilachna varivestis* and Corn flea beetle *Chaetocnema pulicaria*.

Bark dwellers Scolytidae (including Elm bark beetle *Scolytus scolytus*), living under bark.

Flower dwellers Nitidulidae (pollen beetles), Cantharidae (soldier beetles), and Oedemeridae adults are commonly found on flowers.

Leaf litter dwellers Scydmaenidae (stone beetles) and Pselaphidae, found in soil, leaf litter; Byrrhidae (pill beetles) in moss.

Household pests Dermestidae (skin beetles, carpet beetles, "woolly bears") and Ptinidae (spider beetles).

Desert dwellers Many Tenebrionidae (darkling beetles, meal worms) are adapted for desert conditions.

Voracious Feeders
DIET

The feeding habits of beetles range from predation to dung feeding and parasitism, although no species are parasitic on man. Most, however, feed on plants. Some are monophagous, feeding on only one type of food, but many others are polyphagous – nonspecialist feeders.

It would be virtually impossible to find a land plant that is not attacked by at least one beetle, although very few are destroyed in the process. A number of larvae (for example those of the Elateridae and Curculionidae families) feed below ground on plant roots. Wireworms, the larvae of click beetles, eat grass roots, reducing the plant's productivity, while the huge larva of the Atlas beetle is likely to kill the palm tree on which it feeds.

Beetles feed on plant leaves in a multitude of different ways. Some eat them from the outside, others (the leaf miners) from the inside. The second method gives greater protection to a developing larva, although Blue tits are adept at opening leaves with their beaks, much like peeling back the ringpull on a can. On the surface, species like the Willow leaf beetle (*Phyllodecta vitellinae*) graze in aggregations on the outer layers of the leaf. Other species nibble away at the leaf margins.

Stem feeders are more likely to inflict serious damage on a plant, eating into the vessels that transport food and water. "Witchetty grubs," a number of which are prized as food by Australian aboriginals, are the larvae of cerambycid beetles, and they feed in woody stems. Bark beetles normally feed closer to the surface of a tree, just beneath the bark, while the larvae of timber beetles tend to bore deeper into the wood, where

● **Above** *Weevils of the huge family Curculionidae feed on all parts of living plants. This Banded ginger weevil* (Cholus cinctus) *is feeding on a* Heliconia imbricata *flower in a Costa Rican rainforest.*

● **Below** *The numerous species of darkling beetles (Tenebrionidae) endemic to the Namib Desert in Africa will scavenge on a wide range of dead matter. Here,* Onymacris rugatipennis *strip a grasshopper corpse.*

Concealment is perhaps the commonest form of defense against vertebrate predators, with immobility playing a very important part; once the beetle moves, it may reveal itself. Those that live under stones, under bark, and in soil are generally plain black or brown, and are remarkably easy to overlook. Those living in more exposed habitats often come to resemble their backgrounds (crypsis). The concealed head and expanded thorax and elytra of members of the darkling beetle genus *Endustomus* make the insect look less like a beetle than the winged seeds among which it lives. Some weevils of the genus *Gymnophilus* have taken crypsis a stage further by encouraging the growth of fungi and algae on their elytra.

Mimicry – resemblance to a poisonous or potentially unpleasant animal – may also give a measure of protection. Many myrmecophiles – beetles that habitually inhabit ants' nests – look like their ant hosts, possibly avoiding predation by animals that might not want to risk a painful bite. One tropical longhorn shows reverse head mimicry; with its deceptive eyespots at the end of the abdomen, it looks at a random glance more like a poisonous frog than a beetle.

they live in tunnels. Plants are composed largely of cellulose, and the enzyme cellulase is needed to break this down to its constituent sugars. Very few beetles are capable of making their own cellulase, so to survive on wood most woodborers (for example, members of the Lucanidae, Scarabaeidae, and Anobiidae families) have to form symbiotic relationships with bacteria or fungi that can produce it. These symbionts live in special pockets in the beetles' gut. They also supply their hosts with a vital source of B vitamins.

Flowers are a rich source of nutrients that are exploited by a wide range of insects. The adults of many beetle species, like the longhorns, feed exclusively on pollen or nectar, while their larvae survive on tougher materials. Rose chafers feed directly on flower petals.

Some beetles are specialists on fungi; Cisidae species, for example, can usually be found inside bracket fungi on dead or dying trees. Members of the Liodidae are true gourmets, feeding almost exclusively on the sought-after black truffle.

Most of the predatory beetles attack other insects. They are fast and have good vision. Adult tiger beetles (Cicindelidae) can reach speeds of up to 60cm (24in) per second. Their larvae lie in wait for their prey, heads wedged into the opening of a tunnel in the ground. Although it possesses only simple eyes, or ocelli, the larva can tell when suitable prey is within range. It springs out, grabs the insect, and drags it down the tunnel to devour it. Large water beetles need more substantial food, and will take small fish and tadpoles.

Many ground beetles of the Carabidae family specialize in eating slugs or snails. *Cychrus caraboides* has an elongated, narrow head that can reach right into a snail's shell as the animal retracts. The beetle secretes enzymes onto the snail's body, predigesting the tissues, which it then sucks out in liquid form.

Dead plants and animals represent a rich source of valuable nutrients, and very few dead organisms fail to attract the attentions of a beetle. Dead trees attract a wide range of woodborers and bark beetles. Fresh corpses attract beetles in successive waves, each "guild" with its own specialization. Burying beetles are flesh feeders, while skin beetles will take on dry materials like feathers, until eventually nothing is left but a few bones. Even insect remains may be sought after; some beetles raid spiders' webs, taking the remnants of their last meals. Others, such as the Silken fungus beetle, specialize in the cast skins of molting caterpillars.

Cannibalism can also be a successful strategy. Among siblings that encounter one another in the same food source, it reduces competition and increases the chances that at least some survive. It is thought to be particularly common among ladybugs, both adults and larvae; they eat both eggs and freshly molted larvae.

Signaling for Mates
SOCIAL BEHAVIOR

To reproduce successfully, a beetle, like any other animal, must ensure that its chosen mate belongs to the correct species, so before copulation or courtship can take place specific signals must be given and received. This mate location may involve sight, sound, scent, or a combination of all three. Wingless female drilid beetles are unable to seek out mates, so must attract males with scent; they climb up low-growing plants and release a fetid odor into the air. The high-pitched squeaks of screech beetles, produced by rubbing the tip of the abdomen against the underside of the elytra, are also thought to be a means of communication between the sexes.

Deathwatch beetles (*Xestobium rufovillosum*) use sound. Deep inside old timbers where it has developed for many years as a larva, the adult beetle calls in spring. It braces its front legs against the sides of the wooden tunnel, then taps rapidly on the floor with the top of its head. Both males and females tap to advertise their position, moving toward the sounds made by other potential mates. The tapping is most noticeable during the relative quiet of the night, so was often heard by those keeping watch at the bedside of the sick, with the result that the sound came to be regarded as a warning of a forthcoming death.

Fireflies use their large eyes to pick up visual signals. The tip of the abdomen contains photoluminescent chemicals that give out a glow that is clearly visible at night. The glow can be switched on and off to produce a regular series of synchronized flashes, each species having its own distinctive pattern. Male fireflies display the light signal, and the wingless, larvalike females (commonly known as glowworms) signal back when they see the appropriate flash sequence (although the size and brightness of the flash may in fact be as important as the sequence itself). The males drop down to the females with remarkable accuracy. Predatory glowworms of the genus *Photuris* can mimic the signals of *Photinus* females, and lure searching *Photinus* males to their death.

Females of the Two-spot ladybug (*Adalia bipunctata*) are very variable in color pattern and seem to select their mates principally on the basis of color. In a largely red population, a female is more likely to accept the attentions of one of the black forms, while in a dark population, the rarer red varieties will be at an advantage. This behavior presumably serves to enhance genetic variability within a population.

A number of beetles produce species-specific chemical signals, or pheromones. Those released

○ **Right** *Representative species of beetles:*
1 Blue ground beetle (Carabus intrica-tus: Carabidae), which hunts slugs, worms, and other insects in oak and beech woodlands. 2 Mealworm beetle (Tenebrio sp.; Tenebrionidae), whose larvae live off stored grain. 3 Diving beetle (Dytiscus marginalis; Dytiscidae), which can extract oxygen from bubbles of air that it carries below its wing cases. 4 Dung beetles (Scarabaeus sacer; Scarabaeidae) rolling a ball of dung in which they will lay their eggs. 5 Sexton beetle (Nicrophorus investigator; Silphidae), which buries the corpses of small animals and lays its eggs on the carcasses. 6 Click beetles (Agriotes ustula-tus; Elateridae) have a peg-and-groove mechanism on their underside that allows them to jump quickly away from predators. 7 Hermit beetle (Osmoderma eremita; Scarabaeidae), which lives in decaying oak and lime trees. 8 Oil beetle (Meloe proscarabaeus; Meloidae), so called because adults produce an oily fluid that can blister human skin. 9 Nut weevil (Curculio nucum; Curculionidae) with its rostrum buried in a nut.

by female chafers and click beetles will draw males from a surprisingly large area. The expanded male antennae, which may resemble combs or leaves, are beautifully adapted for receiving these messages. Skin beetles and bark beetles release aggregation pheromones, which attract both males and females to a site suitable for burrowing and egg laying; this behavior increases the chances of successful mating. In bark beetles, once females are mated and start burrowing, they emit a deterrent signal that inhibits further arrivals. The males usually remain with the females, helping with burrowing and guarding eggs.

In many species there is competition between the males for possession of a female. This rivalry often involves a trial of strength, which helps to ensure that only the healthiest males pass on their genes to the next generation. A male stag beetle will try to grip his rival between his "antlers" and flip him to the ground. Horned beetles displace other males by pushing and shoving or getting the horn under their rival's body.

Once contact has been established, a courtship ritual usually takes place before the male is accepted; it may involve the male tapping the female with his legs or antennae. Among the oil beetles a complex stroking ritual is necessary to make the female receptive. *Malachius* (Melyridae) males produce chemical secretions, which the female chews; she is presumably reassured by the presence of a species-specific chemical. Other males similarly "taste" the female by nibbling her elytra.

Once both insects are sure about their partner's identity, mating may occur if the female is sexually receptive. The male – who is frequently smaller than his partner – mounts the female and grips her elytra and thorax with his feet; male feet are usually larger for this purpose, and some males may even grip with specially-adapted antennae. He inserts his copulatory organ (aedeagus) into her vagina, and deposits either a sperm package (spermatophore) or free sperm that will be stored in a special sac, the spermatheca, until the female is ready to lay her eggs. The female now ceases, either permanently or temporarily, to be sexually receptive. In some species she may mate more than once, and may possibly have some control over which male's sperm fertilize her eggs.

Many chafers and Passalidae species form a monogamous pair and cooperate in providing for their young; typically the sexes in these species resemble one another. More usually, the males are polygamous and play no part in raising their off-spring; in this case, the sexes are more likely to be dimorphic, differing in size, form, or color.

Beetles undergo complete metamorphosis from egg to adult, with an intervening resting pupal stage (in other words, they are holometabolous). The wings develop internally and are only present in the adults. The mouthparts are usually very different in the larval and adult stages, due to differences in diet. The amount of time larvae take to develop depends on their final size, the environmental temperature, and the nutrient value of their food source. Large woodboring beetles, which live on fairly poor food lacking in protein, can take an unusually long time – up to 45 years in some cases.

The eggs may be laid in the soil (rove beetles of the family Staphylinidae) or else inserted into

⊙ **Right** *Warningly-colored blister beetles* (Mylabris tiflensis; Meloidae) *from India in a courting ritual. The male (left) strokes the female with his front legs.*

STREPSIPTERANS: STRANGE PARASITES

Strepsipterans are highly specialized internal parasites of other arthropods. In the past, they have been included in the Coleoptera, or were at least thought to be closely allied to the order. Today, however, characteristics once thought to show close relationship to other insect groups (beetles, hymenopterans, scorpion flies) are believed rather to derive from strepsipterans' special lifestyle, and the 300 or so species are placed in a separate order, the Strepsiptera, comprising five families.

Adult females are typically grublike, wingless, and never leave their host. Only the fused head and thorax project from the host's body. An exception is the family Mengeidae, in which females are active, free-living, and usually found under stones, although sometimes they are parasitic on bristletails.

The active, short-lived adult males are 0.5–4mm (0.02–0.16in) long, black or brown, with a large, transverse head, bulging eyes, and fan- or comb-shaped antennae. The club- or plaitlike forewings

gave rise to the name "twisted-winged parasites". Borne on large, fanlike hind wings with reduced venation, the body held vertically with the abdomen turned horizontally, males seek out virgin females, which emit a sex pheromone.

Insemination takes place through a "brood passage" between the female's cephalothorax and last larval cuticle. Up to 1,000 eggs mature in her inflated abdomen, to hatch, via the brood passage, as six-legged, triungulin larvae. In late summer this free-living, "infective" stage enters its host, usually an immature stage. After winter, and five or more grublike stages, the mature larva extrudes its front end between the host's abdominal segments and pupates. The adult male emerges by pushing a cap off the pupa, but the adult female remains in the puparium formed by her last larval cuticle. Her position on the host helps to identify the species (here, a female *Halictophagus* on a leafhopper). Strepsipterans are very host-specific: the Elenchidae are found on grasshoppers, Halticophagidae on tree- and leafhoppers, spittle bugs, and mole crickets, and stylopids on certain bees and wasps.   GCM

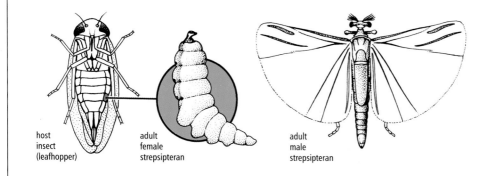

host insect (leafhopper)   adult female strepsipteran   adult male strepsipteran

plant tissues (weevils, Curculionidae). They are usually placed where they are least likely to dry out or be found by predators. Some are deposited singly (as in chafers), others in batches of several thousand (oil beetles). Many beetles give their eggs the added protection of an egg case. The Great silver diving beetle (*Hydrophilus piceus*) lays its eggs in batches in a silk cocoon that is attached to a floating leaf. Other water beetles, such as *Helochares* species, carry their eggs with them, bound in strands of silk beneath the abdomen.

The Beech leaf-roller (*Deporaus betulae*) makes a complicated series of cuts in the margins of a leaf, allowing it to form a central inner funnel in which it lays a number of eggs. The rest of the leaf is wrapped around it to form a protective outer funnel, and "sewn" in place; the larvae can feed unseen inside the leaf. Weevils and seed weevils (Bruchidae) often cause the soft tissues of a plant to form a gall, inside which their larvae develop. *Bruchus pisorum* produces galls on laburnum seed pods, while *Smicronyx* causes swellings on the stems of *Cuscuta*.

Females do not usually remain behind to protect their eggs, but instead place them near a source of food. The Hazelnut weevil (*Curculio*

nucum) uses her long snout to drill a hole in a developing nut, and deposits the egg safely inside. Large scarabaeid beetles may dig deep vertical shafts, which they provision with food; they then lay a single egg on top.

In the majority of species, the females get no help from the male in raising the young, but sometimes there is cooperation between the sexes. With the dorbeetle *Geotrupes stercorarius*, the female digs a brood chamber, using her powerful, spiny legs, while the male collects a ball of dung on which the female lays her eggs. The dung provides the sole food source for the developing larvae. By giving his assistance, the male is helping to ensure the survival of his offspring.

Hatching larvae break through the eggshell using their mandibles and body spines, or "egg-bursters." They feed and grow, passing through several more stages (instars), each of which ends with a molt or change of skin. They do not resemble the adults, except in the case of female fireflies, whose adults retain a larval form (as glowworms). Instead, they may take the form of legless grubs (in the case of furniture beetles), may resemble sawfly larvae (leaf and flea beetles), may be long-bodied and long-legged (rove beetles) or, in the

◐ **Above** In most beetles, such as these Orange ladybugs (Halyzia sedecimguttata; Coccinellidae) from Europe, males and females look very similar. Male ladybugs sometimes get confused and attempt to mate with females of a different species or even family.

◑ **Below** Attempted mating between Batanota *sp.* tortoise beetles (Chrysomelidae; Cassidinae). They are aptly named, being able to retract their head and legs and lower their pronotum and elytra when molested.

◁ **Left** *A small number of bee-tles are viviparous, giving birth to live young. This* Eugonycha *leaf beetle (Chrysomelidae) from Brazil is depositing a batch of babies rather than laying eggs.*

▷ **Right** *Of more than 3,000 species of tortoise beetles (Chrysomelidae: Cassidinae) found around the world, only four exhibit maternal care. This is* Acromis sparsa, *a common species in Central and South America, sitting on her batch of dark-colored larvae.*

◔ **Below** *Four types of larvae:* **1** *ground beetle (active, preda-tory);* **2** *leaf beetle;* **3** *chafer (lives in soil, rotten wood);* **4** *weevil (lives in plant material).*

case of chafers, even C-shaped. Most aquatic lar-vae are air-breathers, rising to the surface to take in oxygen through spiracles. Screech beetles remove oxygen directly from the water, using a gill system. Some larvae, particularly among the dung beetles, communicate by making soft, chirping noises, using stridulatory structures.

A few beetle species exhibit parental care, look-ing after their larvae until they are partly or fully grown. The burying beetles of the genus *Nicropho-rus* initially cooperate in mating pairs, after which the female is left on her own to complete the task. First, the corpse of a small mammal like a mouse is located. The beetles dig away the soil beneath it until it is completely buried in a subterranean chamber; it is stripped of its skin on the way down. After mating the male leaves, and the female lays her eggs in separate egg chambers close by. When the larvae emerge, they make their way to the food chamber, where the female feeds them on regurgitated, predigested flesh. She will leave when they are able to feed themselves.

Many beetles have highly specialized, often bizarre, life histories, particularly those that are parasitic. For example, the larva of the Bacon bee-tle (*Dermestes lardarius*) is an occasional parasite on newly-hatched chickens, boring into their flesh. It is normally associated with dead matter.

Eight families are known to contain species that are either exclusive (obligate) or facultative (optional) parasites; these last mainly attack the eggs or pupae of other insects. The larvae of oil beetles of the genus *Mylabris* burrow into the soil to feed on grasshopper eggs. The first larval stage of the rove beetle, *Aleochara*, is very active and goes out in search of a fly pupa, attracted by a chemical scent. Once found, it enters the fly's body and the second stage is spent as a virtually blind, legless grub, feeding on the host tissues. The third stage has fully-developed legs and

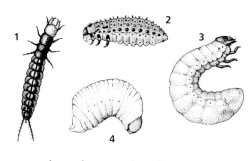

eyes, and goes down into the soil to pupate.

All members of the Rhipiphoridae are parasitic as larvae, although the adults feed on flowers. *Metoecus paradoxus* larvae are found in nests of common wasps (*Vespula* species). The female bee-tle oviposits on flowers, and the eggs hatch into minute, bristly planidium larvae with a thick, spiny cuticle and suckers. This is a nonfeeding stage, specialized for transport by the host adult to its nest. There the larvae await the arrival of a wasp, and then hitch a lift back to its nest; few will be successful, so large numbers are produced. In the nest, each larva goes through several differ-ent forms (hypermetamorphosis). First it pene-trates a wasp grub and feeds internally as an endoparasite. Later it emerges, molts to become a legless grub, and then wraps itself around the body of the wasp larva, on which it continues to feed, this time as an ectoparasite. After pupation it becomes a fully winged adult.

Some types of dung beetle, including *Aphodius* species, are brood parasites. They do not collect their own dung, but instead lay their eggs in the nests of larger dung beetles. Members of one genus of tiny bark beetles (*Crypturgus*) are not capable of penetrating bark by themselves; instead they enter through existing holes and excavate within the tunnels of other bark beetles.

Adults of some chafer species have adopted a semiparasitic way of life, clinging to the fur of

mammals in the anal region – a tactic that allows the female to drop her eggs in a ready food source. *Macropocopris symbioticus* lives in the intestine of kangaroos, feeding on the feces. The African *Zonocopris gibbicollis* lives inside the shell of the large *Bulimus* snail, where it also feeds on fecal material.

Well over 1,000 beetle species live in close association with ants, either as predators or parasites or else as commensals, obtaining food from their hosts but otherwise neither damaging nor benefiting them. Some are actively welcomed, while others avoid attack by mimicking the chemical odor and behavior of their hosts. A number of rove beetles share the nests of ants both as larvae and adults, and many species produce attractive secretions that the ants lick from special glands.

Larvae of the rove beetle *Lochmechusa pubicollis* are so attractive to *Formica polyctana* ants that they are adopted and taken into the brood chamber. They probably give off a pheromone that stimulates the ants' brood-rearing behavior, and also mimic the begging behavior of young ants by rearing up and tapping the mouthparts of the ant

"nurse": she responds by regurgitating a droplet of digested prey juices. The beetle larvae will also prey upon any nearby ant or other beetle larvae. In the fall, the adult beetle, not yet sexually mature, once more begs food from its *Formica* hosts, then flies off in search of a nest of ants of a different genus (*Myrmica*) that carry on raising their brood through the winter. The beetle offers the *Myrmica* ant a secretion from the tip of its abdomen that forestalls any aggressive behavior. Secretions produced by glands behind the elytra contain chemicals that then cause the ant to adopt the beetle, carrying it into the brood chamber, where the beetle finishes its development. Mating and egg-laying take place near a *Formica* nest in the spring.

Friend and Foe
CONSERVATION AND ENVIRONMENT

Beetles have been associated with people and their dwellings since humans first began to establish a settled way of life; they often feature in myths and legends. The ancient Egyptians used scarabs (dung beetles) to symbolize rebirth and

immortality. They saw the adult bury itself underground, only to return in the form of its offspring the next year. The beetle became associated with good fortune, and even today is worn as a protective amulet. The familiar red and black ladybugs, *Adalia* and *Coccinella*, have similar associations with luck, the "lady" in question being the Virgin Mary. Other beetles, like the Devil's coachhorse (*Staphylinus olens*) have a bad reputation, being credited with the power to curse and kill. *Lucanus cervus*, a stag beetle, is believed to draw lightning to the thatched roof of a house.

Insect remains from archeological sites indicate that many of the species we consider pests today have been with us for a long time. A pest species is simply a beetle going about its normal business in a place that has been annexed by humans. The Golden spider beetle (*Niptus hololeucus*) originally from Asia, is a supreme generalist; it can eat virtually any dead organic matter, and will happily take on leather, feathers, hair, and dried plants, so is not welcome in the home or the warehouse. Another generalist, *Stegobium paniceum*, which

○ **Right** *The grotesquely elongated neck of the male Giraffe-necked weevil (*Trachelophorus giraffa; Attelabidae) from Madagascar is the kind of "over-the-top" result of sexual competition found in widely varying families of beetles.*

attacks many stored products, is reputed to bore its way even into tinfoil and lead.

Woodboring beetles break down dead trees, so that the nutrients locked up in the wood can be recycled and support new life. People use wood for structural timbers and furniture, and both are subject to internal attack by beetles. Longhorn beetle larvae will feed on roof timbers, often taking several years before emerging as adults; the Old house borer or beetle is commonly found in pine. Old oak timbers are more likely to be infected by the Deathwatch beetle. Furniture and floors will be attacked by the woodworm beetles *Anobium punctatum* and *A. inexspectatum*, detectable by the presence of tiny round holes in the wood. These are the adults' flight holes, from which they emerge after spending their lives as legless larvae chewing tunnels through the wood.

Bark beetles are more of a problem for living trees. The Elm bark beetle has had a drastic effect on the character of the British countryside, once dominated by tall elms. In itself, the beetle does little harm, the larvae chewing out tunnels in surface wood directly beneath the bark, but it transports a virulent fungus (*Ophiostoma novo-ulmi*) that spreads into the tree's transport vessels, causing a blockage that kills the tree. The disease entered the country in the 1960s in imported American timber and destroyed over 80 percent of British elms. As the tree population declined, the fungus found it more difficult to spread, and became dormant. It reemerged with the new, young elms in 1990, and once more killed large numbers of trees. Many attempts have been made to bring an end to this repeating cycle; these rely either on killing the beetle or the fungus, but neither method has been successful so far.

Now biotechnology has entered the arena. Trees are being created with additional genes allowing them to manufacture their own chemicals either to deter bark beetles or with antifungal properties. If the technology works, it may be needed in the future to protect other species. An American oak-wilt fungus is just an airplane-ride away; there are fears that if it enters Britain, it could be passed on by the native Oak bark beetle and decimate ancient oak forests.

Other beetles attack crops, causing heavy losses. A wide range of weevils (Curculionidae, Bruchidae) feed on the seeds, flowers, and leaves of legumes, fruits, and root crops. Larvae of the Boll weevil feed inside the flowers of the cotton plant, so that the valuable cotton fiber, which normally surrounds the seeds, fails to form. Another species of the same genus, *Anthonomus pomorum*, lays its eggs in apple blossom, preventing proper development of the fruit. Indian corn (maize) may be badly affected by the larvae of several species of click beetles, which feed on its roots; among weevils, Maize billbug larvae attack the soft pith of corn stems. Other villains include the Mexican bean beetle and its close relatives, which attack

Above The Bearded weevil (Lixus barbiger; Curculionidae) is a large and bizarre species from the rain forests of Madagascar. Like all weevils, it feeds on plant matter, which can lead to direct competition with farmers when commercial crops are the target. Conversely, many rainforest beetles are threatened by destruction of their habitat by forestry and ranching.

Left The leaf beetles (family Chrysomelidae) are a highly speciose group, containing around 35,000 representatives. Some, like the destructive Colorado beetle, are familiar, others less so, for example Fulcidax violacea, a strange member of the subfamily Chlamisinae from Brazil.

legumes such as the soybean, the forage plant cowpea, and solanaceous plants such as the tomato and aubergine.

Among the leaf-feeding Chrysomelidae is the well-known Colorado beetle, much feared by potato growers. The brightly-colored adults and larvae feed on the potato haulms (stems), so preventing the production of tubers, and a heavy infestation will devastate a whole crop. Genetic engineering techniques have created plants with their own inbuilt toxins that successfully deter the beetle. However, there are fears that these toxins are being passed on to useful insects like ladybugs through the food chain – a side-effect that will in turn create a whole new set of problems.

Some crop damage may be accelerated by the transmission of pathogenic microorganisms by beetle visitors. Among leaf beetles, the cucumber beetles carry the bacterium that causes wilt disease; the insects deposit it with their feces, from where it may be washed into a fresh plant wound. Any insect that subsequently feeds on the infected plant will help to transmit the pathogen further. In a similar manner, the Corn flea beetle transmits the bacterial wilt disease of Indian corn.

Not all beetles found on crops are harmful.

Predatory ladybugs feed, as adults and larvae, on aphids and scale insects, and can, in large enough numbers, save a crop from destruction. Several species, such as *Aphidecta obliterata*, which feeds on fir tree aphids, have been deliberately introduced into new areas and have become permanently established there. Others may be periodically applied in large numbers as eggs, larvae, or adults to particular crops; the Seven-spot ladybug is used to control potato aphid in parts of the United States.

Dung beetles are currently being used in Australia to solve a different farming problem. The existing insect fauna cannot deal with the large amounts of dung produced by the non-native cattle, so beetles have been imported from Africa and South America. Meanwhile, species imported into Hawaii and Puerto Rico have been very successful in controlling the numbers of dung-feeding horn flies (*Haematobia*, of the family Muscidae), which, as adults, suck the blood of cattle.

In Britain, there has been concern that chemicals fed to cattle to stop them picking up parasites may be slowing down the breakdown of cowpats. The pats may now remain untouched for several months, because dung beetles and other insects avoid them. The result is a marked deterioration in quality of the pasture available to the cows.

Ground beetles are very important predators of pests. Their numbers can be devastated by overuse of pesticides, and they have declined in recent years. At the same time, the cost of the pesticide erodes farmers' profit margins – significantly so in poorer countries. In the 1990s, a study showed that farmers in the Philippines who were given training in how to increase the numbers of ground beetles and spiders around their crops, largely by giving up the use of pesticides, produced the same amount of crop but were financially much better off.

Global warming is already causing changes in insect distribution. Many beetles that previously found northern Europe too cold and damp, particularly in the winter months, are now able to

survive and breed there. This development can have devastating effects on the existing ecosystem.

In Britain, two beetles that have entered the country in the last few years could have as devastating an effect on areas of woodland as the Elm bark beetle has already done. The large black and white Asian longhorn beetle (*Anoplophora glabripennis*) is thought to have been imported in wooden pallets carrying a consignment of slate from China. It was first sighted in Cumbria, but has now spread to many other locations. The larvae will attack a wide range of trees including sycamore, horse chestnut, willow, apple, and pear, boring into the heart of the tree and destroying it. The longhorn has already caused widespread damage in the USA, where it arrived in the 1980s. The larvae were brought into America in wooden packing cases holding new pipes for the New York

sewage system. Longhorn larvae have already spread to native maple, elm, and poplar.

The tiny Eight-toothed spruce beetle (*Ips typographus*) is originally from southern Europe. It only attacks the bark of a tree, but, like other bark beetles, carries a fungus that causes serious damage. The bark eventually falls off, exposing the tree to other diseases, which kill it. Commercial forestry operations in the USA are already under serious threat from this pest. Measures have been taken in Britain to prevent any more packaging materials containing bark from coming into the country, but the beetle may already be spreading.

New invaders probably enter countries all the time but, not finding conditions to their liking, fail to get established. This is known to have occurred in the case of the Douglas fir beetle, which entered China from the USA in logs.   LJL

PARTNERS IN DESTRUCTION

Inside the gut of a number of beetles that feed on very dry foodstuffs, such as hair, skin, wood, or feathers, live symbiotic organisms (symbionts), usually bacteria or protozoans. These secrete enzymes that enable the beetles to digest such unpromising material, allowing them to attack material too dry to support bacterial or fungal growth. As a result, the beetles form a major threat to stored products, and many are common household pests.

The young beetles are infected with the symbionts by their parents. In the wood-feeding powderpost beetles, the symbionts migrate into the egg before it is laid, while in *Rhizopertha dominica* (fami-

ly Bostrychidae), a grain weevil that also feeds on wood and paper, they are transmitted by the sperm. In the furniture beetles, the female's anus infects the outer egg surface, and the larvae themselves become infected when they eat the empty egg cases.

The tiny, hairy larvae of *Anthrenus verbasci* and *A. flavipes* (family Dermestidae) are the notorious "woolly bears," or carpet beetles, which attack woollen fibers and chew holes in expensive carpets. *Anthrenus museorum* will gradually reduce dried museum specimens of animals to dust. When about to pupate, *Anthrenus* larvae enter firmer materials, such as wood or cork, on which they do not feed.

The adults are pollen feeders and cause no damage.

Among the furniture beetles, there are several pests of materials other than wood. The Cigarette or Tobacco beetle can cause serious economic loss by attacking all types of tobacco products. Among weevils, the Biscuit or Drugstore weevil was the bane of early sailors, feeding on the hard tack that formed their staple food.

Many pests of stored products take a varied diet and are consequently difficult to control. The Bamboo borer seems to eat almost anything of plant origin; it specializes in bamboo products, particularly furniture, but has also been found in dried fruit, avocados, ginger, cinnamon, and various types of wood. The quaintly named Red-legged ham beetle prefers materials with a high fat or oil content, such as smoked bacon, cheese, nuts, or copra, but will attack other insects and their eggs, bonemeal, and even guano.

◗ *Above and right* Insect pests of the home and crops: *1* Carpet beetle (Anthrenus verbasci; Dermestidae) and its larva – the woolly bear – which feeds on woollen fibers. *2* Woodworm or Furniture beetle (Anobium punctatum; Anobiidae). *3* Colorado beetle (Leptinotarsa decemlineata; Chrysomelidae), feared by potato growers. *4* Mint leaf beetle (Chrysolina menthasthri; Chrysomelidae). *5* Deathwatch beetle (Xestobium rufovillosum; Anobiidae), a wood-borer so called for the tapping noise it produces in timber at night.

TARGETED INVADERS

Beetles as agents of biological control

WHEN AN ALIEN PLANT IS INTRODUCED INTO AN area, either deliberately or accidentally, it usually comes without the natural control agents that keep it in check. This immunity gives the plant the opportunity to undergo a population explosion and overtake native ecosystems. Beetles are increasingly being used to combat these invaders.

The Floating fern (*Salvinia molesta*) has been carried by humans from its native South America to Africa, Asia, and Australia. Once introduced, it spreads vegetatively through rice-paddies, lakes, rivers, and irrigation channels. In 1972, one or two plants were brought into Papua New Guinea, and by 1980 they had spread to form a number of mats covering an area of 250sq km (100sq mi) and weighing 2 million tonnes. A search was made for native insects that feed on the weed, and the weevil *Cyrtobagous salviniae* was discovered in Brazil. It was distributed worldwide, wherever the fern was causing problems, and found to be an extremely effective control agent. The adult weevils eat the buds of the fern, while their larvae attack the roots and rhizomes; typically, fern populations are rapidly reduced down to 1 percent of their original size. In Queensland, Australia, where the weevil was released in 1980, 30,000 tonnes of *Salvinia* were destroyed within a year. Control was so effective in Papua New Guinea that people were able to reoccupy villages that had been abandoned because of problems caused by the weed.

Water hyacinth (*Eichhornia crassipes*) is said to be one of the fastest-growing plants in the world. Originally found in a river in Brazil and admired for its beautiful flowers, it has now been introduced to waterways in 53 different countries. Rapidly covering the water surface, it stops light penetrating and destroys the existing ecosystem, causing the fish to die. It reached Lake Victoria, Uganda, in 1989, and formed such dense mats that small boats were unable to move through it. Thousands of fishermen lost their jobs, and death rates due to crocodile attack also increased because the weed offered such good cover for the predators. Two species of South American weevil, *Neochetina eichhornia* and *N. bruchi*, were introduced to attack the plant in 1996. The adult beetles eat the leaves, while the larvae tunnel into the stem and ultimately destroy the plant. Unfortunately, the water hyacinths were already so well-established that the weevils could not keep pace with their rapid growth. Eventually, the authorities were forced to resort to herbicides, despite the fact that these bring the risk of adding toxic chemicals to the water supply and also kill fish.

Now, the plant is overwhelming Lake Malawi, one of Africa's largest lakes. The infestation is having a major effect on the local economy, but the

available chemical weapons are expensive and not very efficient. Instead, a number of water-hyacinth beetles have been imported and are being bred locally in their thousands for release onto the lake vegetation. Biological control is inevitably a slower process than chemical control, but here it seems to be the only safe, longterm method available.

There is a catch, however. Introducing a non-native insect into a country can cause a new set of problems. The beetle cannot be guaranteed only to attack the targeted weed; it may well turn its attentions to native plants. A weevil introduced into the USA in 1969 has done just that. *Rhinocyllus conicus* was brought in to control non-native thistles, which were becoming a problem in cattle country. The weevil is now also attacking at least four native thistles, and may drive them to extinction. In addition, it is competing for resources with native insects, which may also die out. There is no knowing how far this ripple effect will spread, or which other organisms may ultimately be affected.

○ **Above** *Voracious feeders on aphids, Seven-spot ladybug larvae are effective control agents, as shown in the USA in the 1980s. Now, though, they have become too successful, outcompeting local species.*

Similarly, the Seven-spot ladybug (*Coccinella septempunctata*) was released in the wheatfields of America as part of a campaign to control the Russian wheat aphid, which was devastating crops in the 1980s. Now there are fears that it has spread into areas where it was not present before, and is outcompeting the local ladybugs.

Even when the beetles cannot fly, they are still able to spread. In France a technique for producing flightless ladybugs has been developed. Asian ladybugs (*Harmonia axyridis*) are exposed to radiation and mutagenic chemicals to produce flightless mutations, which are then used as breeding stock. They are just as effective as winged ladybugs at killing pests, and are widely used in the USA to protect melon crops. Yet even without wings, they appear to be taking over in certain areas and are becoming the dominant ladybug species.   LJL

Scorpionflies

SCORPIONFLIES

Class: Insecta

Subclass: Pterygota

Order: Mecoptera

Fewer than 400 species in 8 families, among them true or common scorpionflies (Panorpidae), including the Common scorpionfly (*Panorpa communis*); snow scorpionflies (Boreidae); and hanging scorpionflies (Bittacidae).

DISTRIBUTION Worldwide; generally in cool, moist conditions.

SIZE Adults mostly 12–26mm (0.5–1in) long, usually with two pairs of similar long, membranous wings with span up to 5cm (2in) across.

FEATURES Slender, small to medium-sized, with downward-projecting "beak." Adults have threadlike antennae and male genitalia that, in the Panorpidae family, are upcurved like a scorpion's tail.

LIFE CYCLE Larvae caterpillarlike, usually with prolegs, and characteristic compound eyes. Pupae have moveable mandibles and appendages free from the body. Development features complete metamorphosis (holometabolous); the wings develop internally (endopterygote).

CONSERVATION STATUS Not at risk.

SCORPIONFLIES TAKE THEIR NAME FROM A *feature found in the true scorpionflies of the family Panorpidae – an upturned and enlarged tip to the abdomen, reminiscent of a scorpion's tail. In fact the resemblance ends there: scorpionflies do not bite or sting humans.*

Of the eight recognized families of scorpionflies, five – the Choristidae, Nannochoristidae, Notiothaumidae, Austromeropeidae, and Meropeidae – are represented by a total of only 11 species, living almost exclusively in the southern hemisphere and possessing very archaic features, seemingly unchanged since the Jurassic period more than 144 million years ago. The other three – the Boreidae or snow scorpionflies and the Bittacidae or hanging scorpionflies, as well as the true scorpionflies of the family Panorpidae – are much more common and widely distributed.

Slender Carnivores
FORM AND FUNCTION

Scorpionflies are slender, small to medium-sized carnivorous insects with primitive biting mouthparts that project down at right angles to the body to form a beaklike rostrum. The beak is formed by elongation of parts of the head capsule. The adults have long, threadlike antennae with many segments, well-developed compound eyes, and usually three simple eyes or ocelli.

Adult scorpionflies generally have two pairs of similar, long, membranous wings – the order's name comes from the Greek *mekoptera*, meaning "long wing" – with many cross-veins. The wings may be carried horizontally or longitudinally at rest, and are usually transparent or semitransparent, but often conspicuously spotted or banded. The Californian genus *Apterobittacus* lacks wings, while males of the family Boreidae have a pair of slender, bristlelike vestiges instead of wings, and the females have scalelike lobes on the middle segment of the thorax.

The legs are long and slender and generally adapted for walking, with the claws usually paired. The abdomen is elongated, with short cerci and prominent genitalia (in the male), and it usually comprises 10 segments.

The larvae are caterpillarlike (cruciform) with a well-developed head, sharp mandibles, and short, three-segmented antennae. Compound eyes on either side of the head are formed by groups of simple eyes and are a distinguishing feature of the order. Some larvae are very similar to sawfly larvae, while others are covered with branched projections

arising from the body segments. The larvae all live on plant remains or on dead insects. The number of molts is not known, but some members of the family Panorpidae have seven. Pupation occurs in the soil, and the pupae are able to escape from the cocoon by means of mandibles.

The scorpionflies first appear in the fossil record before the end of the Permian period (295–248 million years ago). The order is one of the most primitive to have a pupal stage.

A Preference for Cool, Moist Places
DISTRIBUTION PATTERNS

Out of fewer than 400 species in the order, some 85 occur in the United States, 20 in Australia, and four in the United Kingdom. Most adults prefer moist, cool situations, and some are never found far from swamps, pools, or small streams.

The true, or common, scorpionflies are widely distributed. About 15–20mm (0.6–0.8in) long, they are usually yellowish-brown with brownish bands and spots on the wings. *Panorpa communis* is a very common species throughout Europe, with a wingspan of 30mm (1.2in).

The snow scorpionflies, characterized by their vestigial wings, are found in Europe and North America, where they live and feed on moss. These unusual insects are often found on the surface of the snow in winter, and are 2–5mm (0.08–0.2in) long and dark-colored.

The hanging scorpionflies are so called for their method of capturing prey with their hind legs while hanging from twigs or vegetation by their

◑ *Below Scorpionflies owe their common name to the bulbous, reddish genital capsule of Panorpidae males, which bears a marked resemblance to a scorpion's sting. The capsule is turned conspicuously upward at the rear end of this Common scorpionfly.*

◗ **Right** *Following the normal courtship strategy adopted by male hangingflies, this Australian representative of the genus* Harpobittacus *(Bittacidae) has presented the female with a plump, nutritious fly. He has little choice, as females will not accept males that arrive empty-handed.*

forelegs, although some species do actually catch prey on the wing. Most adults are yellowish-brown with long legs and look superficially like crane flies.

Scorpionfly adults, like their larvae, feed on plant or insect remains or hunt live prey, although some occasionally feed on pollen, nectar, or flowers. Both sexes of the Common scorpionfly have been seen raiding spiders' webs for insect prey, seeming to be able to walk safely over the web, which they do without attracting the spider's attention. Some species can be cannibalistic, although this is extremely rare.

Courting with Gifts
SOCIAL BEHAVIOR

The complex courtship of scorpionflies involves an exchange of "nuptial gifts" and the production by the male of pheromones to attract females, which mate more than once and are receptive in cycles; courtship in hanging scorpionflies of the genus *Harpobittacus*, for example, depends on temperature, the majority of matings occurring around midday. The male grasps a prey item with his hind legs, then punctures it with his beak before flying to a resting place, where he holds the nuptial gift of prey in his mouthparts. Females of the species are attracted by a secretion produced from a special glandular area behind the seventh and eighth dorsal plates (tergites) of the male's abdomen. After seizing an approaching female, the male transfers the gift to her, and she feeds on it while mating takes place. After several minutes the couple separate, and the male may finish eating the nuptial gift before leaving to forage once more. Only males with nuptial gifts are attractive to females. Several females may be attracted to the same male, which may use the same prey item as a nuptial gift for several mates.

Female hanging scorpionflies are not often observed to feed, and it is thought that the prey offered by the male is a valuable food source enabling the female to produce mature eggs. Some males seek out other males in order to steal their gifts. Others have been observed forcibly ousting mating males before sperm transfer has been completed, but the terminal structures of most species are adapted for maintaining a grip on the female, thus reducing this possibility.

After mating, eggs that are ovoid (*Panorpa*) or cuboidal (*Bittacus*) are dropped or laid in batches in soil crevices or on the ground. In *Panorpa* species the larvae emerge in a week or so and forage over the ground for food, which may be eaten from below or dragged into a burrow.   KP-M/GCM

MATING GIFTS AND "RAPE" IN TRUE SCORPIONFLIES

Adult males of most *Panorpa* species can choose from three available options to promote sexual encounters. The first is to provide the female with a gift consisting of a dead arthropod such as an insect. As these are often garnered from spiders' webs, there are risks involved, as suggested by the fact that males are more often found dead in such webs than females. Alternatively, the male may offer a gift consisting of a pillar of saliva, generated from the salivary glands that make up a large proportion of the male's total body weight. Only males that are themselves well-fed through a successful search for food can provide such gifts, and as this food in turn may also be substantially derived from spider's webs, the same risks apply as in the first option. Finally, they can engage in "rape," using a clamp-like structure on the third and fourth abdominal terga to secure the female's wings and prevent her from escaping. This option avoids the hazards inherent in the first two courses of action, but suffers from a disadvantage of its own, in that females that have engaged in forcible copulations lay fewer eggs than those that have received gifts. In practice, males only resort to this desperate tactic when they have lost out in the intense competition to secure genuine arthropod resources.   KP-M

Fleas

FLEAS ARE DISTINCTIVE, BLOODSUCKING insects, highly specialized for their ectoparasitic life on warm-blooded hosts. They are laterally flattened and streamlined, with a keel-shaped head for "swimming" rapidly through the fur or feathers of their host. As an essential adaptation to life on hosts that can fight back with teeth, claws, or beaks, they have extremely tough bodies and are very hard to kill by crushing.

The nearest relatives of the fleas are the scorpionflies, with which they share similarities in skeletal structure, muscle arrangements, and chromosome complements. Probably, mecopteran ancestors gave rise to fleas, butterflies, moths, and flies (together known as the panorpoid group, or the Antliophora) about 160 million years ago, with the newly-evolving mammals serving as flea hosts.

Clinging Bloodsuckers
FORM AND FUNCTION

In addition to having many backward-pointing bristles all over the body, most fleas possess two sets of spines that form combs (ctenidia): a genal comb on the head and a pronotal comb on the first thoracic segment. Combs and bristles protect delicate joints and the eyes, and also anchor the flea in the host's fur. Hedgehog fleas and porcupine fleas, living on spine-covered hosts, exhibit convergent evolution in both having short, stout, widely-spaced spines in their combs that are thought to catch around the host's spines. Fleas with winged hosts such as birds and bats must cling to the host at all costs or be lost, so they possess well-developed combs with many spines, or even extra combs.

Fleas undoubtedly evolved as mammalian parasites, since only about 10 percent of species are found on birds (mostly seabirds and small perching birds). Only aquatic mammals (whales, seals, muskrats, platypuses) and certain land mammals including flying lemurs, primates, zebras, elephants, rhinos, and aardvarks are normally untroubled by fleas. Fleas are unusual among parasitic insects in having complete metamorphosis, and because of the resulting separation of adult and immature stages, they are forced to rely mainly on hosts that build nests or live in burrows or dens – habitats that enable the newly-emerged adults easily to colonize a resident host (or, in the case of many birds, a host returning to the same nest site a year later). Despite often being blind or virtually so, the adult flea's powerful jumping

3 The pupa forms within the cocoon and hatches into an adult.

1 Adult flea finds host to feed on. Female lays eggs on host or in nest.

2 Eggs drop to the ground. After 2–12 days, a larva hatches from each egg.

Pupa

Adult flea

Cocoon

Eggs

Larvae

⬗ **Above** Details of the flea's life cycle are known for only a few species, but the pattern is clear. Female fleas lay eggs from which legless larvae hatch within 2 weeks. After two or three molts, the larva spins a cocoon and enters the pupal stage, from which it emerges as an adult sometimes in days, although the process can be delayed for a year or more.

⬗ **Right** A rabbit flea of the family Pulicidae sucks blood through the skin of a rabbit's ear. Rabbit fleas are major vectors of myxomatosis.

ability and extreme sensitivity to nearby vibrations, heat sources, or exhaled carbon dioxide enable it to detect and colonize hosts very effectively, even in a non-enclosed situation.

Environmentally cushioned on its (generally) warm-blooded host, the adult flea's range may be limited by the tolerance of its more exposed larvae, and so may fall short of the host's range. Widespread host species may therefore support several different flea species separately in different areas. Conversely, some fleas infest a wide variety of hosts. Cat fleas will feed on nearly every kind of host, even lizards, and only rodents appear immune, although this flexibility in host choice may severely reduce their fertility. Humans come well down their list of preferences, however, since human blood represents a poor source of nutrition for them. The size of a flea is not necessarily correlated with host size, so that *Hystrichopsylla talpae*, one of the largest fleas, is found on small mammals such as moles and shrews.

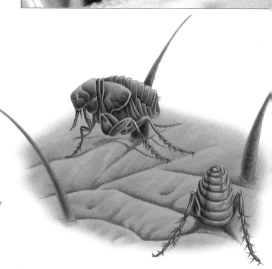

⬗ **Above** Female chiggers (Tunga penetrans), also known as chigoes or Sand fleas, burrow into areas of soft flesh on humans and other mammals, leaving the tip of the abdomen exposed. After mating, their bodies swell to the size of peas as the eggs develop, causing intense irritation to their hosts.

How Fleas Bite
FOOD AND FEEDING

Unlike many bloodsucking flies, in which only females take a blood meal, both sexes in fleas regularly feed on blood. Although the bite and the resulting skin irritation are unpleasant for their victims, the flea's method of reaching the blood is nonetheless fascinating.

Inside the head is a special membrane made of resilin, the same material as in the pleural arch (see Flying with their Legs). Embedded in the head next to the resilin is a hammerlike bar attached to the piercing stylets. As soon as the hungry flea reaches an appetizing patch of host skin, the stylet muscles press the hammer hard against the resilin. The flea prepares to feed by tilting its head down and backside up. When it suddenly relaxes the muscles, the resilin membrane springs back, plunges the hammer down, and drives the stylets into the victim's skin. This is repeated rapidly until blood capillaries in the skin are reached, usually painlessly unless the flea touches a skin nerve-ending.

Waiting for a Host
DEVELOPMENTAL STAGES

The full breeding cycle in fleas tends to be adapted to the sleeping or breeding habits of their hosts. Many flea larvae feed on host blood that has dried, having been passed out by the adult flea as feces while the host is in its lair. The larva of the European rat flea will beg for food by grasping an adult by a bristle on its posterior, thus stimulating it to release a drop of blood from its anus, which the larva then drinks. Being so small, flea larvae are very vulnerable to climatic change, and they may drown in a droplet of water, yet they succumb equally easily to very dry conditions. This fact may explain why the nests of swallows and martins, which are relatively constant in environmental terms, are very popular with fleas: as many as 19 species are commonly associated with these birds worldwide.

The basic life cycle of fleas is simple: the adults are ectoparasites, while eggs, larvae, and pupae develop freely in the nest or habitat of the host. Pupae can remain viable for long periods until a host becomes available. When an empty house once more becomes inhabited, the new owners may suddenly be plagued by hordes of adult cat fleas; vibrations caused by walking on the carpet or by vacuuming lead pupae that may have been dormant for a year or more to hatch instantly.

In some exceptional species, among them the Arctic hare flea, the larvae live alongside the adults in the fur of the host, while in the Tasmanian devil flea the female sticks her eggs to the fur of the host and hatching larvae burrow into and develop in the host's skin. By contrast, the eggs and larvae of the alakurt, which is parasitic on deer, yaks, goats, and horses throughout central Asia, are scattered wherever the hosts have roamed.

FACTFILE

FLEAS

Class: Insecta

Subclass: Pterygota.

Order: Siphonaptera

About 1,800 species in 200 genera and 16 families, grouped into 3 superfamilies

DISTRIBUTION Found worldwide as ectoparasites, mostly of mammals and birds.

SIZE Small; adults 1–9mm (0.04–0.33in) long.

FEATURES Wingless, generally dark brown or black, laterally flattened and streamlined, with piercing and sucking mouthparts for exclusive diet of blood; eyes when present simple ocelli; short antennae lie in grooves (foveae) on each side of head; body covered in shiny, tough integument, colored yellowish-brown to black, bearing backward-pointing bristles and combs; abdomen composed of 7 typical segments, the remaining 3 terminal segments modified as

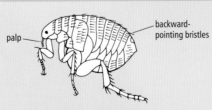

uniquely complex reproductive organs; extensive adaptations for jumping include powerful rear legs and pleural arch; skeletal locking mechanisms.

LIFE CYCLE Development holometabolous (complete metamorphosis), with egg, larva (3 stages or instars), pupa (enclosed in a silk cocoon), and adult. The wormlike larvae are free-living, legless, and eyeless, but with well-developed head; feed on organic debris (such as flakes of dead skin from the host) and dried host blood, derived with mouthparts and head muscles modified for grinding and sucking.

CONSERVATION STATUS Not threatened

See superfamilies table ▷

Fleas that as adults live mostly on the host (for example, cat and dog fleas) are termed fur fleas, while those found mostly in the nest, jumping onto the host for brief periods of feeding, are termed nest fleas. Fur fleas lay shiny, smooth eggs, which fall out of the host's fur into its lair or other parts of its habitat, but nest fleas deposit sticky eggs in the nest material. Fleas in the superfamily Ceratophylloidea tend to be nest fleas, with the adults spending only a short part of their life in contact with the host and often migrating considerable distances. Within the Pulicoidea, females of the Sand flea or chigger bury themselves in the host's skin (often between the toes in humans) and lay all their eggs while embedded.

Fleas are remarkably adept at colonizing new hosts. Mice that have had all their fleas removed may sometimes regain their full complement (or even more) within as little as 24 hours of being released into their natural habitat. Bird fleas are equally quick off the mark.

■ Transmitting Plague
ENVIRONMENT AND HEALTH
Plague caused by the bacterium *Yersinia pestis* is primarily a rodent disease, but it is spread from rats to humans by fleas such as the Oriental rat flea. Throughout history, plague, or the "Black Death," has been virulent and dramatic in its

effects: in 14th-century Italy, the great cities lost every second citizen to its ravages. Even now plague is still with us, breaking out periodically in human populations in central and southeast Asia as well as the United States of America.

As a flea feeds on the blood of a plague-infected host, the bacteria stick to the spines of the blood filter chamber (proventriculus) that leads into the flea's stomach. Here the plague organisms multiply until they block the gut completely. The hungry flea subsequently bites a new host repeatedly, but the blood sucked up by the powerful esophagus muscles cannot pass the blockage and shoots back into the wound, carrying with it some of the plague bacteria, and so transmitting the disease to the next victim. The most virulent strains of plague bacteria are very sticky and form a block easily. Blocking is reduced as temperatures rise above 28°C (82.4°F), so incidence of plague corresponds closely to seasonal temperatures.

A potentially dangerous situation arises when flea-infested rats live in towns, feeding on rubbish tips and refuse scattered near dwellings. Nowadays, pesticides are used to control the reservoirs of the disease (rodents and fleas), while vaccinations and modern drugs serve to reduce its virulence. Even so, the World Health Organization continues to describe plague as "an enemy in ambush."   KP-M/BW

⊙ Right *The frontal view of the notorious Cat flea (Ctenocephalides felis; Pulicidae) admirably illustrates the side-to-side flattening of its body, designed to enable it to slip easily through the dense fur of its host. The genal comb on the head is also conspicuous.*

Flea Superfamilies

Superfamily Pulicoidea

1 family, about 180 species, including the **Arctic hare flea** (*Euhoplopsyllus glacialis*), **Cat flea** (*Ctenocephalides felis*), **hedgehog fleas** (*Archaeopsylla* species), **Human flea** (*Pulex irritans*), **Oriental rat flea** or **Plague flea** (*Xenopsylla cheopis*), **porcupine fleas** (*Periodontis* species), **Rabbit flea** (*Spilopsyllus cuniculi*), and **Sand flea, chigoe,** or **chigger** (*Tunga penetrans*).

Superfamily Malacopsylloidea

3 families, about 170 species, including the **alakurt** (*Vermipsylla alakurt*) and **penguin fleas** (*Parapsyllus* species).

Superfamily Ceratophylloidea

12 families, about 1,580 species, including the **Beaver flea** (*Hystrichopsylla schefferi*) – the largest known flea – the **European rat flea** (*Nosopsyllus fasciatus*), **Tasmanian devil flea** (*Uropsylla tasmanica*), **bird fleas** (*Ceratophyllus, Callopsylla, Frontopsylla* species), and *Palaeopsylla* species.

FLYING WITH THEIR LEGS

Fleas have been described by the entomologist Miriam Rothschild as "insects which fly with their legs." Despite being wingless (a secondary condition), they have exceptional mobility thanks to a special structure, the pleural arch, which is a modification of the wing-hinge of the fleas' winged ancestors. The arch, made of the elastic protein resilin, is the powerhouse for the flea's remarkable jump.

To jump effectively in a wide range of temperatures from arctic cold to equatorial heat, fleas cannot rely exclusively on muscle, which has a slow twitch and becomes less efficient at low temperatures. Instead, they achieve their extraordinary acceleration during the jump by making use of a triggered click mechanism.

When compressed, the helmet-shaped pleural arch generates and stores energy needed for jumping: resilin is extremely efficient and may release as much as 97 percent of its stored energy when

required. As the flea gathers itself to jump, muscles associated with the second segment of the rear leg (trochanter depressor muscles) distort the cuticle, and "flight" muscles compress the pleural arch. A series of link-plates on the flea's hard exoskeleton interlock to clamp the three segments of the thorax together. The rear legs are raised and the flea, now resting on its trochanters, is poised for take-off.

As soon as a poised flea is stimulated by, say, the carbon dioxide breathed out by a potential host, the muscles relax to release the pleural arch and a

sudden burst of energy is sent down a cuticular ridge and into the trochanters. The recoil of this force, which arrives with an easily heard "click," accelerates the flea away from the substrate faster than the eye can follow, at the equivalent of about 60 gravities, and the descending rear legs hit the substrate to provide an extra boost up to 140 gravities' acceleration. Hungry fleas may jump 600 times an hour for three days in their attempts to find a host. Cat fleas readily achieve a height of 34cm (13.4in) when they jump.

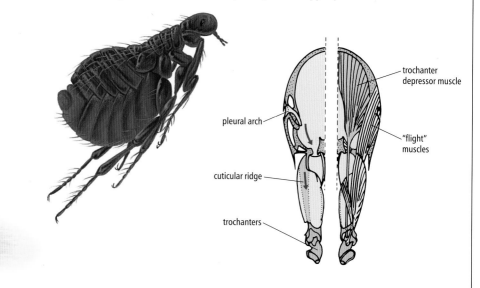

trochanter depressor muscle

pleural arch

"flight" muscles

cuticular ridge

trochanters

Flies

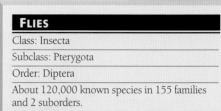

FLIES

Class: Insecta

Subclass: Pterygota

Order: Diptera

About 120,000 known species in 155 families and 2 suborders.

DISTRIBUTION Worldwide, in all possible habitats.

SIZE Adults 0.5mm–5cm (0.02–2in) long; maximum wingspan 8cm (3.2in).

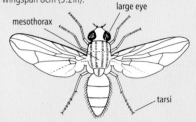

FEATURES One pair of membranous wings; hindwings modified as clublike balancers (halteres); 2nd segment of the thorax (mesothorax) much enlarged, 1st and 3rd reduced; mouthparts for liquid feeding, but highly adaptable for piercing, sucking, lapping.

LIFE CYCLE Development with complete metamorphosis (holometabolous); pupal stage between larvae and adult. Larvae (maggots) legless.

CONSERVATION STATUS The IUCN currently lists 1 dipteran species as Critically Endangered, 2 as Endangered, and 1 as Vulnerable. In addition, 3 species including the Volutine stonemyian tabanid fly (*Stonemyia volutina*) are thought to be recently extinct.

See suborders table ▷

t RUE FLIES ARE NOT POPULAR; THEY LACK *the beauty of butterflies or the intricate societies of some social ants and bees. Yet the Diptera is nonetheless one of the most fascinating orders of insects. The beneficial effects of the many flies that visit and pollinate flowers, kill pests, control weeds, or recycle organic nutrients should certainly outweigh our distaste for the relatively few flies that irritate us by biting , infecting our foodstuffs, or eating crops.*

In warmer parts of the world flies can be a genuine scourge, carrying some of the most dangerous diseases of man and livestock and spreading pathogens in areas of poor hygiene. In these cases, study of the flies' biology has revealed much about coevolution between different types of animal, and about the ecology of insects as a whole.

Diverse, Versatile, and Never Far Away
FORM AND FUNCTION

In many temperate countries flies make up about a quarter of all insects, although worldwide they are second in numbers to the beetles, which abound in the tropics. The 120,000 known species make their living in almost every imaginable manner, in all climatic zones right through to the polar fringes. Although they live and breed in almost all habitats, there are comparatively few species in marine environments. Adult flies have varied dietary habits including feeding on flowers, predation on other animals, scavenging dead tissues, and sucking blood. Larvae usually have different feeding habits to the adults; many feed in decaying plant and animal tissue, but others are filter-feeders in water, feed in plants, or are parasites or predators.

Much of the diversity of flies is based on three main features: their mouthparts, flight machinery, and larval forms. The adult mouthparts are essentially suited to liquid feeding but have proved highly adaptable for piercing, sucking, and lapping. Borne on a large and mobile head, they can extract fluids from almost any living or decaying source, with the aid of one (or sometimes two) highly muscular pumps within the head. Almost all adult flies can feed, the exceptions being some species that are parasitic on mammals (Oestridae) and small midges with very short adult lives.

The flight machinery consists of just two wings that are usually quite short but strong; the name

⊙ **Below** *This adult Banana fly (Nerius nigrofasciatus; Neriidae) has come to lap up the juice from a decaying papaya. Neriid larvae generally breed in decomposing plant matter, especially rot-holes in trees.*

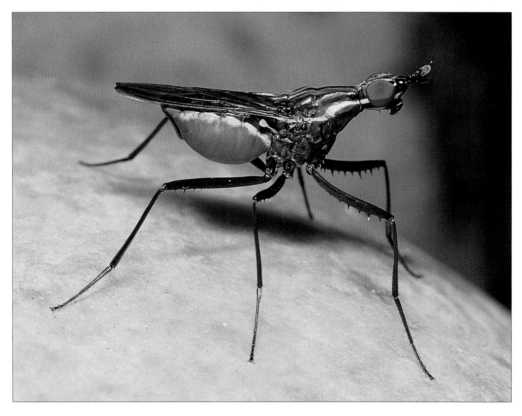

Diptera means "two-winged" in Greek. The second pair are reduced to small halteres (as proved by the fruit fly genus *Drosophila*, in one mutant form of which the halteres revert to a winglike structure). This adaptation distinguishes the true flies (Diptera) from the many other orders of insects with "fly" in their name – dragonflies, caddisflies, and others. Having a single pair of wings allows for a simpler structure of the thorax: the fore and hind segments are virtually lost, while the middle segment is huge and entirely packed with wing muscles. This condition also permits a high degree of maneuverability, with very high speeds and wingbeat frequencies (up to 1,000 beats per second in tiny midges), and a control of direction and position that permits access to every possible landing site, even upside down on ceilings!

Many flies can hover, rotate on their own axis, fly through spaces little wider than their wingspan, and even fly backward. All these abilities are aided by the sensory information provided by the halteres, which act like tiny gyroscopes. The sense organs at the base of each haltere form three groups at right angles to one another, an arrangement that enables a fly to sense how fast it is flying and turning, and whether it is being

Above *Flies come in many shapes and sizes. This Pantophthalmus comptus (Panthophthalmidae) from Costa Rica is one of the world's largest, reaching a length of 4.75cm (1.9in). Its huge larvae breed in fallen rainforest trees.*

Below *Most flies have large eyes, to aid maneuverability in flight. In females like this Notch-horned cleg (Haematopota pluvialis; Tabanidae) they are generally widely separated; by contrast, many males are holoptic, with the eyes meeting on top of the head.*

blown off course. Also associated with maneuverability are flies' relatively large eyes, whose acute vision results from the separation of the individual, sensitive elements of the rhabdome in the nervous supply to the eye facets (a feature unique to flies), as well as the elaborate claws and pads on flies' feet, which can grip on any surface.

In all the main divisions of flies there are, surprisingly, many species in which the wings have been secondarily lost, and sometimes the halteres as well. In some of the parasitic flies (Hippoboscidae), this may be an adaptation to life on the host animal. Some scuttleflies (Phoridae) have fully-winged males and wingless females; since mated pairs have been seen flying around, it is presumed that the male carries the female from one habitat to another. Other scuttleflies live in termite's nests, and the female is fully winged until she enters the nest, when she sheds her wings. Loss or reduction of wings in both sexes is particularly common in species that inhabit windswept oceanic islands, where wings would increase the risk of the fly being blown away, or that live deep in caves or the burrows of other animals, confined spaces in which wings would be a disadvantage. Many higher flies with reduced

or lost wings also show a reduction in the size of the thorax due to loss of wing muscle; in addition, they have reduced eyes and enlarged antennae, because touch is more important to them than sight.

Maggots and Others
DEVELOPMENTAL STAGES

There is a typical endopterygote or holometabolous pattern of development in true flies. Larvae are usually quite different from adults in form and habits. Fly larvae lack thoracic legs, but may have secondarily developed false legs for locomotion. It has been written that fly larvae have been recorded from almost every medium capable of supporting life. They can survive in a vast range of microhabitats, and they have an extraordinary diversity of appearance, far surpassing that of any other order. They occur in ponds, lakes, saline water, hot mineral springs and oil pools, and in water caught in the leaf-bases of plants and rotholes in dead wood. In running water they are found in slow and fast rivers and even in the fastest waterfalls, clinging to rocks and plants.

On land larvae live in desert sands, soil, compost, the muddy edges of water bodies, and highly polluted sludge. They exploit decaying vegetation, fungi, and the dung and corpses of almost all other animals, and are scavengers in the nests of mammals, birds, and other insects. Plant-feeding has evolved many times, and almost any part of a plant from the root to the seeds may be attacked. Others are predators or parasites of worms, snails, most large orders of insects, other arthropods, amphibia and their eggs, reptiles, birds, and mammals. Some larvae feed on their own parents, or are fed to maturity by the female fly.

In the Nematocera the larva has a complete head capsule and the mandibles move horizontally, as in most other insects; the Garden leatherjacket – the larva of the Crane fly – is an example. In many nematocerous families the larvae are aquatic, as in black flies, mosquitoes, and many midges. These flies have a "free" pupa, without a surrounding puparium. The Brachycera have mouthparts that move vertically and show a progressive reduction of the head capsule from the least to the most developed forms. The four infraorders included in the Orthorrhaphous Brachycera have larvae with an incomplete head capsule, and the pupa is again free; there is great diversity of form in the larvae of these species, some of which can breed in extremely dry conditions. An unusual feature of the pupae of some Nematocera and Orthorrhaphous Brachycera is that they may be highly mobile, whereas in almost all endopterygote insects the pupa is immobile. Mosquito pupae can swim actively – they have to, because they often live in still and oxygen-poor water where they need to come to the surface to collect air and then swim down again for safety. Beefly and robberfly pupae develop underground, often

many inches down, but before emergence they work their way close to the surface, using a fearsome array of body spines and processes.

The larvae of higher flies are the familiar maggots, which appear simple and featureless but in fact have a wide range of physiological adaptations. In contrast with the Nematocera and Orthorrhaphous Brachycera, the pupa of higher flies is contained within the last larval skin, which serves as a "puparium." This is generally well protected and impermeable, able to resist inclement conditions in unpredictable climates; and it may require precise cues, such as the correct temperature, day length, or humidity to trigger it into further development and thus allow the adult to emerge. The

◁ **Left 1** *Robberfly* (Machimus atricapillus) *seizing a lacewing in flight.* **2** *Dung fly* (Scathophaga steroraria). **3** *Bluebottle* (Calliphora vomitoria). **4** *Two male* Diopsis *stalk-eyed flies (Diopsidae), using their eye-stalks as yardsticks to assess their relative sizes in a territorial contest.*

○ **Right** Looking like a pair of miniature drumsticks, the halteres of this Common orange tipula cranefly (Tipula lunata; Tipulidae) are clearly visible at the rear of the single pair of wings. In many families of flies the halteres are covered.

○ **Left** Maggots are the legless, wingless larvae of flies. These fungus gnat maggots (Mycetophilidae) are crawling en masse across a fungus-ridden log. Such communal migrations are typical of this family.

LARVAE THAT LIVE UNDERWATER

Many flies have freshwater larvae. Such insects face two main physiological problems: respiration and osmotic control.

Many fly larvae are not strictly aquatic when it comes to breathing: they use "siphons," tubes extending from their own spiracles to the water surface. Mosquito and gnat larvae (BELOW) hang from the surface film by the unwettable hairs on their abdominal siphons, and can breathe directly from the air. The rat-tailed larvae of the Drone fly have long, telescopic siphons and can reach the air even with their bodies buried 6cm (2.4in) deep in the stream bed. Some dipterans even get oxygen by thrusting sharp siphons into pond weed, tapping the plant's air spaces!

Smaller larvae can survive on dissolved oxygen, which diffuses through their thin cuticles. The bloodworms are almost unique among insects in containing hemoglobin, which enables them to carry and store extra oxygen. In blackflies oxygen diffusion is assisted by a fine network of tracheae just beneath the cuticle, or sometimes by special "tracheal gills."

In fresh water, salts leach out of animals and must be replaced. Many dipterans have special salt-uptake tissues, especially on tracheal gills; although this uptake requires energy, it prevents loss of essential ions, or swelling and bursting due to excess water inflow. Such control mechanisms allow flies to survive and breed in highly variable freshwater habitats (even transient puddles), and also to cope with intertidal pools.

Some larvae can survive even when their freshwater pools totally evaporate. African midges of the genus *Polypedilum* survive for years in a shriveled state until the rains return: these dehydrated larvae can withstand temperatures of as low as −190°C (−310°F) or as high as +100°C (212°F) for brief periods!

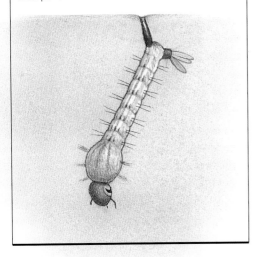

hard, protective puparium also comes with a disadvantage, however; in order to escape from it, the adult fly has to inflate with blood a special sac in its head, rather like a car airbag, in order to push the top off, allowing the fly to emerge. The sac then deflates, and the adult fly is left with a groove above the antennae.

Given the diversity of life-history noted above, it comes as no surprise that the eggs of Diptera show great diversity. Most female flies have a relatively simple, tubelike ovipositor for laying eggs. Species that lay eggs in plants or that are parasitic on animals have in many cases evolved a hardened ovipositor, or else an elongate one to insert the eggs deep within the substrate. The egg may be a simple oval or highly complex. Species laying eggs in wet microhabitats may have eggs with a ridged or reticulate surface, which functions as a plastron, holding a thin film of air close to the surface, through which the egg is able to absorb oxygen. If the substrate is more liquid, the egg may have respiratory horns projecting above the surface, as in *Drosophila* (which lay eggs in fermenting yeasts) or *Sepsis* (in dung). Some mosquitoes have more elaborate flotation devices on their eggs, and the eggs may be stuck together in a raft, as in *Culex*.

Beeflies, whose larvae live in solitary bee's nests, have some very curious adaptations; in some species the female fills an abdominal pouch with sand, which is used to coat the egg. The egg,

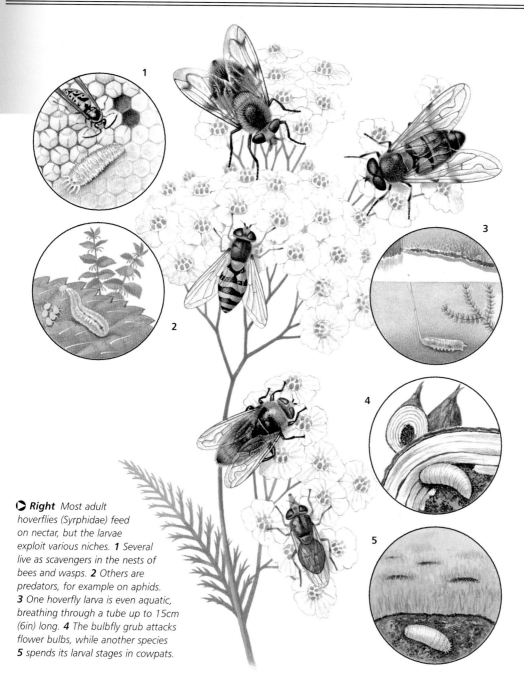

> ◗ **Right** Most adult
> hoverflies (Syrphidae) feed
> on nectar, but the larvae
> exploit various niches. **1** Several
> live as scavengers in the nests of
> bees and wasps. **2** Others are
> predators, for example on aphids.
> **3** One hoverfly larva is even aquatic,
> breathing through a tube up to 15cm
> (6in) long. **4** The bulbfly grub attacks
> flower bulbs, while another species
> **5** spends its larval stages in cowpats.

plus sand, is then flicked away by the female, either onto suitable ground or directly into a bee's nest. Strangest of all, however, is the Human bot-fly (*Dermatobia hominis*; Oestridae), in which the female lays an egg on the underside of a mosquito. When the mosquito bites a mammal, the warmth of the host causes the egg to hatch, and the larva burrows into the skin of the host.

The larvae of true flies are structurally less diverse than the adult stages, but they vary in appearance more than any other insect order and they live in a vast range of different habitats. Adult females, when ready to lay their eggs, seek out every conceivable niche where food supplies and a moist, protected atmosphere can be found. They usually insert their mobile and often telescopic egg guide (ovipositor) deep into the chosen substrate, so that the larvae hatch and grow secure from predators or parasites with little danger of desiccation or starvation.

Larvae of higher flies tend to be "terrestrial," but nearly always occur in almost liquid habitats, whether in the soil, within plants (as galls, or in leaf mines), or in association with other animals. In the last category come not just the many parasitic flies but also the dwellers in dung and many scavengers around bird or bee nests – or, indeed, around human habitations. Generally all these flies have simple maggot larvae, with no legs and very limited sensory organs. The maggots pursue a wriggling, wormlike existence in whatever semi-liquid site their mother selected for them, feeding voraciously with a strong suction action until they are large enough to pupate. In only a few cases, such as the aphid-feeding hoverfly larvae, do genuinely free-living terrestrial larvae occur.

Among the nematoceran flies especially, truly aquatic larval forms are found. Egglaying females rest on the surface film, using their ovipositor either to reach down and attach eggs to under-

water stones or weeds or to assemble a floating "egg raft" on the water's surface. Most resulting aquatic larvae are freshwater forms, preferring still ponds, puddles, and lakes: midges and mosquitoes in particular will rapidly colonize any standing water in summer.

Many species can tolerate low levels of oxygen in the water, or have evolved methods of obtaining oxygen. Larvae of some midges (Chironomidae) are red in color because they have an analog of hemoglobin, used to collect oxygen from the upper layers of water and to store it while the larva descends to lower, anoxic layers to feed. The rat-tailed maggot of *Eristalis* (Syrphidae) has a simpler adaptation; a very long tail, which reaches from the mud in which the larva feeds to the surface of the water, where it obtains air. Even more bizarre are the larvae of some syrphids and ephydrids in which, independently, the last pair of spiracles (breathing tubes) are mounted on sharp stylets. The stylets are driven into the stems of water plants, and oxygen is obtained from the plant. The larvae of a few species, notably the blackflies or buffalo gnats, inhabit fast-running streams and rivers, where they hang on to stones by means of a suckerlike pad, and filter small particles of food from the current with special mouth-brushes. The shore-fly (*Helaeomyia petrolei*) has "aquatic" larvae that reside in pools of gasoline! The larvae ingest the oil, but are not damaged by it, while they live on other invertebrates that may fall into the oil.

Transition from an aquatic larval and pupal stage to a terrestrial flying adult condition is not easy, and here the flies have again achieved some strange adaptations. Blackfly pupae become inflated with air, and when the pupal case splits the incipient adult fly rises to the surface in a bubble, thus avoiding being wetted. In a few cases, emerging flies are actually catapulted clear of the water surface by the sudden splitting of their pupal cases. Thus a new, dry, and pristine fly leaves its protected larval environment for its brief and hazardous flying existence in pursuit of a mate.

Flies that Visit Flowers
POLLINATION AND FLOWER FEEDING

As pollinators of wild flowers and crops, flies are second only to the bees, wasps, and ants of the order Hymenoptera. Flies are most commonly "generalist" flower visitors, taking nectar or pollen from many different species of flowers as a supplement to their main diet, or using floral products as the main "top-up" fuels for their rather brief adult lives after food stored in the body from the larval stage has been exhausted. Representatives of almost all dipteran groups can thus be found at flowers – especially those with shallow corollas, like umbellifers (hogweed or cow parsley), composites (daisies), or rosaceous plants such as hawthorn and bramble. For these unspecialized flowers, often white or yellow and with nectar and pollen readily available even to a short-tongued visitor, flies may be the principal pollinator. Some rather surprising flies are very frequent visitors: mosquitoes and midges, whose males feed on nectar (only the females, needing protein for their eggs, irritate us by blood-feeding); or dung flies and blowflies, which we normally associate with less aesthetic food sources! In high arctic and alpine environments, where bees and their relatives are poorly represented, flies are the principal pollinators of flowering plants.

The flies also include some more specialized flower visitors that make their adult living from pollen and nectar, and these are amongst the most attractive of all insects. They include the hoverflies (Syrphidae), also known as flowerflies. Most of these are medium- to large-sized and brightly decked in yellows, bronzes, and golds in a variety of striped patterns that mimic bees and wasps. Many are also furry or hairy, and their bodies pick up a dense dusting of pollen. Hoverflies are often abundant in gardens, where their hovering and darting flights between flowers are characteristic. They even seem to mimic the bees in their behavior patterns; the drone flies (*Eristalis*) in particular are excellent and cosmopolitan honeybee mimics

◐ **Below** *Hoverflies (Syrphidae) are common visitors to garden flowers. Many people mistake some of the commonest species, such as this Yellow-footed drone fly* (Eristalis pertinax) *for hive bees.*

that must have often evaded capture for fear of their (non-existent) sting!

The subject of mimicry in flies is complex, possibly because humans do not have the visual acuity necessary to appreciate the resemblance between model and mimic. Some hoverflies, among them *Volucella* species, closely resemble wasps, in whose nests their larvae are scavengers, suggesting a double payoff for the fly; it benefits from resembling an insect with a sting, and may also be mistaken for another wasp when it enters the nest to lay eggs. Other hoverflies have different strategies, living in daffodil bulbs (*Merodon*), rot-holes (*Criorhina*), or feeding on aphids (*Eriozona*), but are nonetheless excellent mimics of bumblebees, even having forms that resemble different bee species. These flies are conspicuous visitors to flowers, and may gain advantage by being mistaken for bumblebees. Many species of flies in several families have striking black and yellow color patterns that appear to give them a general resemblance to wasps.

Specialized flower feeders generally have long tongues that can penetrate tubular corollas. A few hoverflies come in this category, as do the beeflies (Bombyliidae). In temperate regions these flies visit primroses and periwinkles and are adept hoverers, while some tropical examples have enormously elongated tongues and resemble miniature delta-wing jet planes. Such flies may have a critical role in pollinating flowers inaccessible to more conventionally proportioned insects.

Flies may visit flowers for reasons other than nectar collection. Many of those to be seen on umbellifers have more sinister motives – they are on the lookout for pollinating insects, which they use for their own ends. The brightly-striped wasp flies (Conopidae) frequent flowers to wait for wasps and bees on which to deposit their eggs. Danceflies and dung flies may similarly use flowers as patrolling stations when seeking prey. A few flies lay their eggs in flower heads. Yet others use flowers for sunbathing, as a cup-shaped corolla can be considerably warmer than its surroundings, especially in rather cool climates. Arctic mosquitoes use white flowers that track the sun as favored places in which to warm up, sitting on the "hot spot" in the center of the corolla until their wing muscles have heated up enough for flight.

All these flower-visiting activities involve benefits to the fly: but sometimes the plants benefit, and flies are exploited instead. Certain flowers, including cuckoo pints (*Arum*), attract flies by producing odors suggestive of carrion or dung, then trap the flies until pollination has been ensured. Some of the largest and most curious flowers in the world, such as species of *Stapelia* and *Aristolochia*, are carrion-scented and rely on pollinating flies for their continuing success. Cocoa, the main ingredient of chocolate, is fertilized by a tiny midge. Other flowers trap small flies with sticky exudations and devour them slowly to extract nitrogenous food; familiar examples include sundews and butterworts.

A walk through woods or among trees in almost any part of the world may well show that certain tree leaves are particularly attractive to flies of many different families. In many cases the appeal lies in the fact that they are covered in honeydew, a secretion of homopteran species (aphids and their allies) that is particularly rich in sugars. Flies run around on the leaves until they find a good concentration of honeydew, then regurgitate a small amount of liquid from their crops to dissolve the sugars, which they suck up. This particular behavior does no harm, but other dipteran feeding habits may be less salubrious; houseflies and others can feed on less savory media like rotten meat, dung, or infected sores, then visit houses or humans and regurgitate water containing bacteria onto human food or perhaps a fresh wound, thereby spreading infections.

Hunters and Bloodsuckers
PREDATION

Predators and blood-suckers are less common than flower feeders among adult flies (although larvae are often predacious). Several families of short-horned flies of the suborder Brachycera come in this category – notably danceflies, long-legged flies, and robberflies – and a few of the higher flies related to dung flies and house flies are also predacious. The robberflies have proved to be highly opportunist, taking almost any small creature that is available – often another fly!

A few more specialist examples are known. Some flies prey on insects trapped in the surface film on ponds, swooping low to "net" the victim with their trailing feet; others are specialists at stealing trapped prey from spiders' webs. Some minute midges of the Ceratopogonidae family specialize in living on larger insects, including dragonflies and beetles; they insert their mouthparts between the hard parts of the insect or into the wing veins to suck blood. Even more bizarre is the mosquito genus *Malaya*, in which the adult fly

WHEN FLIES FLY

Nearly all insects depend on sunny conditions for flight, since (unlike many vertebrates) they cannot themselves generate sufficient body heat to operate the wing muscles. But larger insects can absorb more radiant heat than smaller ones, and dark-bodied insects absorb heat quicker than pale or shiny forms. So small, bright flies are rarely seen around dawn or dusk, when they are too chilled for effective flight; whereas larger, dark-bodied drone flies, flesh flies, or muscids can be abundant at these hours. In hot summer conditions, however, larger flies may risk overheating, and the small, colorful hoverflies, soldier flies, and long-legged flies come into their own. At sites frequented by many flies, such as the flower head of an umbellifer such as hogweed, or on convenient resting perches like sunlit twigs or large leaves, the sequence of fly visitors through the day correlates neatly with the body temperatures resulting from microclimatic conditions at the site.

Watching such activity patterns also highlights interesting anomalies – some flies appear at times when, on the basis of their size and color, one would predict they should be either chilled into inactivity or dangerously overheated. For example, some hover-flies and botflies can warm themselves up without significant heat from the sun, simply by "shivering" their thoracic muscles; other flies can control the distribution of heat between the hairy thorax and the uninsulated, radiatorlike abdomen by special blood-shunting mechanisms. However, we still do not understand how the tiny winter gnats manage to fly efficiently even on days when snow is lying!

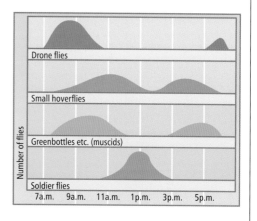

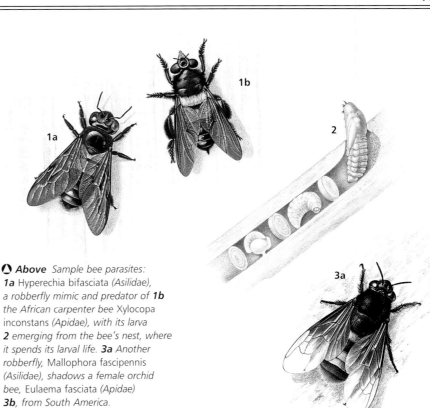

❶ **Above** *Sample bee parasites:*
1a *Hyperechia bifasciata (Asilidae),*
*a robberfly mimic and predator of **1b***
the African carpenter bee Xylocopa
inconstans (Apidae), with its larva
2 *emerging from the bee's nest, where*
*it spends its larval life. **3a** Another*
robberfly, Mallophora fascipennis
(Asilidae), shadows a female orchid
bee, Eulaema fasciata (Apidae)
***3b**, from South America.*

◀ **Left** *The long, stiletto-like proboscis*
of this Dark-winged beefly (Bombylius
major; Bombyliidae) from Europe is
adapted for probing into long-tubed
flowers such as the bugle (Ajuga
reptans) seen here.

❼ **Below** *A Long-headed fly*
(Dolichopus wahlbergi; Dolichopodidae)
eats an aquatic worm – a relatively rare
sight, since the adult flies are seldom
observed feeding on prey.

is associated with ants living on tree trunks. This mosquito intercepts ants carrying honeydew from aphids; landing in front of them, it removes the honeydew from their mouths.

Predation in flies is closely allied to the blood-sucking habit, and it requires similar mouthparts and behavior. But bloodsuckers usually use larger animals for their food source, exploiting vertebrates in particular, and take only a little of their juices. Many families have evolved this habit: midges, mosquitoes and gnats, blackflies, horseflies, deerflies, and stable flies are the best known, and in most cases only the female fly bites. Midges and mosquitoes have elongate, needlelike mouthparts, while horseflies and the bulkier muscid biters, including stable and tsetse flies, have shorter, bladelike mouthparts. Many of these flies carry diseases to animals and even to man.

Predation in flies is far more important in the larval stages, and the larvae of many species are extremely useful in controlling crop pests. Some fly larvae consume the young stages of beetles. More important are their attacks on homopterans, the hoppers and aphids that can plague farmers and horticulturalists. In this role the larvae of many

Living off Others
PARASITISM

With the exception of the hymenopterans, flies are the most abundant and influential of all insect parasites, laying their eggs in or on a vast range of other animals, but especially on other insects and vertebrates. The Tachinidae are the most important family of internal parasites; along with some flesh flies they form a group of rather bulky adult flies with larvae that live especially off the flesh of beetles, bugs, wasps, caterpillars, and grasshoppers. The mechanisms by which the female parasitizes the host are remarkably varied; eggs may be injected into an adult bug by a heavily hardened piercer, or laid on the host plant for the host larva to eat, or laid either directly on the skin of the host or else in its environment, so that the emerging larva has to search for a suitable host and burrow into it, like the triungulin larva of *Strepsiptera*. True parasitism has evolved many times in the Diptera, in all the major divisions of the order.

Various other groups of flies have specialized associations with vertebrates. Some Pupipara families, like louseflies and keds (Hippoboscidae) and bat flies (Nycteribiidae), are strict external parasites of birds and mammals, and have remarkable structural adaptations as a result. Hippoboscids live on birds and some large mammals, feeding on the host's blood; their wings are often tiny, while their claws are greatly enlarged and used to move sideways in a crablike fashion. Nycteribiids are even more peculiar – tiny, wingless insects, they live exclusively on bats, having heads so reduced that they can be tucked back into a groove on the thorax, and with feet again much enlarged.

The warble flies and botflies are intermediate between external and internal parasites. Eggs (or sometimes live larvae) are laid on the outside of a large mammalian host, and the larvae burrow into the flesh, or enter the host's body via openings such as the nostrils. The maggots then live for some time either just within the skin, breathing via a tube, or in the nasal passages or mouth area. They drop off (or are sneezed out) when ready to pupate and complete their life cycle. Such parasitic flies can be irritating, and are often a source of secondary infections, but they rarely do much harm directly (except by soiling the fleeces and hides of livestock) unless infestation is heavy.

Dining on Decay
SCAVENGING

Flies are preeminently scavengers. Since they are essentially liquid feeders, with mouthparts appropriate to sucking and lapping, it is not surprising that decaying matter of all kinds provides perhaps their most important foodstuff. As a result, they play an immensely important role in the processes of decomposition and in recycling nutrients through an ecosystem; their habits may not endear them, but without fly maggots the world would be a much less clean and pleasant place!

◐ **Above** *Many fly larvae are active predators. The Throdiplosis persicae midge larva, seen here (top) feeding on a diapausal mite, is put to commercial use in glasshouses as a biological agent employed to control spider mite pests, which feed on growing plants.*

◑ **Below** *Displaying the strikingly patterned eyes that are typical of its family, this Richard's fly (Richardia podagrica; Richardiidae) is feeding on a bird dropping. As a general rule, flies prefer mammal dung to bird excreta, but are opportunistic feeders.*

types of hoverfly and a few gall midges are especially beneficial. Hoverfly larvae are regularly recorded as scourges of aphids in market gardens; these mobile, flattened, cryptically-colored creatures can work their way through aphid colonies at rates of up to 80 aphids an hour each. Some syrphids specialize on root aphids, or on the woolly aphids found on conifers. In several large families of flies, including the Empididae and Dolichopodidae, whose population levels are very high in temperate regions, the larvae are almost all predacious and presumably have a considerable effect on the populations of some pest species of insects; yet little is known for sure, because the larvae mostly live in soil or debris and are difficult to find and study.

A few larval flies have even stranger predatory habits. One family (the Sciomyzidae) specializes in consuming slugs and snails, while certain species of long-legged flies (dolichopodids) that live on the seashore have larval stages that have adapted to eat barnacles!

Flies have complex associations with all kinds of decaying matter. Some are linked with fungi, especially in woodlands; one group lives on fresh fungal material (which itself is hastening the breakdown of green plants), while another group invades the fungus after it has fruited and begun to decay in its turn. The larvae of fungus gnats grow on a wide range of fungal species and often fly up as clouds from rotting wood when disturbed. A great many other flies feed on naturally decaying plants once the dead matter has begun to liquefy; many of the acalyptrate families are of this type, and the fruit flies are classic examples, being able to sense the vinegarlike substances produced when green plants decay and being adapted to feed as larvae on the yeasts that produce these fermentation products.

Larvae that live in compost or similar habitats form part of a very large and varied guild of species from many arthropod groups. Like aphids, some have evolved ways of increasing the speed of reproduction. Some gall midges can produce eggs in the larval stage. The female fly produces several large eggs, which develop into large larvae. Within these larvae other larvae are developed, which feed on the parent larva and then emerge to produce more larvae in their turn. Later, male and female adults are produced. Perhaps most conspicuous of all are the flies that live on either the excreta of animals (dung flies and others) or their

dead bodies. These flies get ideally nutritious liquid food, and by laying their eggs in such places they also ensure a moist and relatively safe microhabitat for their youngsters to grow up in.

Among flies that feed on and recycle the dead and decaying remains of other organisms there is a characteristic sequence of interrelated species, which has been studied on vertebrate corpses. Generally the first arrivals to exposed (unburied) corpses are blowflies, especially the familiar "greenbottles," which can detect a corpse when flying more than 35m (115ft) above it. Once decay has begun, members of certain muscid genera and of some acalyptrate families arrive; and once decay is well advanced and the dead tissue is liquefying, many more flies begin to appear and lap up the juices, including fruit flies and other generalists. The corpse then becomes ammoniacal, and as it dries out the scuttleflies (Phoridae) are characteristic visitors. Dessicated skins and bones containing marrow are finally utilized by piophilids and related families. This succession of species has been carefully timed at different temperatures and can be used in forensic work to determine the interval between death and the discovery of a corpse – and whether the corpse has been inside or outside a building since death.

When the corpse is buried, the fauna is different. The scuttle fly *Conicera tibialis*, also called the coffin fly, has the ability to enter human graves,

breed for several generations in the corpse, and successfully emerge from the grave.

Similar successions of insects occur on dung, where there may be considerable competition between dung flies, beetles, and others to lay eggs on a fresh dungpat while it still warm and soft, so that the larvae can develop below the protective crust that soon forms. In both carrion- and dung-feeding species there are myriad adaptations that enable quicker usage of the resource. Although from the human point of view dead animals and dung are an unpleasant feature of the environment, they are a rich source of nutrients that are scarce in nature and there is great competition for them. Some flies lay a few large eggs that hatch quickly, so the insect has a start on more slowly developing species. Large female flesh flies (Sarcophagidae), which are early visitors to corpses, retain their eggs until they hatch and lay living maggots into the flesh. These sarcophagid larvae then release an agent that liquifies the corpse, and the larvae develop in the resulting "soup." The maggots of *Lucilia* have been used to clean infected wounds in humans, since they have a natural antibiotic effect to reduce competition. Other

◐ **Below** *The odor of fermenting fruit soon attracts fruit flies (Drosophilidae), which arrive to feed and to lay their eggs. With their high reproductive rate, fruit flies are favored subjects for genetic research.*

◁ **Left** In the permanent gloom of the rainforest understory, these stilt-legged flies (Ptilosphen insignis; Micropezidae) rely on the conspicuous white tips of their front legs for sexual signaling. The abdomen of the female of this mating pair from Trinidad is clearly distended with eggs.

Lucilia species cause the condition known as sheep strike. The female fly locates a sheep with an open wound and lays eggs in it; the emerging larvae cause a large lesion, which may prove fatal. These flies will also feed in decaying corpses, but two species (one in the New and one in the Old World) have specialized in this habit. These screw-worm flies are able to locate animals (including humans) with a small wound from great distances and lay a batch of eggs beside the wound; the resulting larvae produce a lesion the size of a man's fist, and may kill the animal. So efficient are the flies at finding a host that they can maintain a viable population at levels of only a few flies per square kilometer.

Apart from the specialist dung- and carrion-feeders, yet other flies have larvae that appear to be generalized scavengers. A garden compost heap will be home to many species of flies, but recent work has shown that some of these are more specialized than they appear. Dead plant material in particular is broken down by a complex succession of micro-organisms, and the fly larvae may specialize on a particular component, such as bacteria or fungi. Examples include scavengers in nests, whether of mammals, birds, or bees (this last category often involving bee-mimic flies); the seaweed flies (Coelopidae and others),

frequenting shoreline debris; and many larval flies living in mud around the edges of ponds, puddles, and in damp ruts, feeding on algae and detritus. Some of these species have cuticles that can resist desiccation when necessary, and await re-wetting in the mud, while others just burrow deeper into their mud-patch in dry weather. Some, especially the larvae of Nematocera (thread-horned flies), are genuinely aquatic (see Larvae that Live Underwater), and these are generally opportunistic feeders, preying on small insects, filtering micro-organisms, or scavenging, as appropriate.

Swarming and Courtship Dances
MATING AND REPRODUCTION

It is among scavenging and saprophagous flies (those that feed on dead or decaying organic material) that some of the most interesting examples of dipteran behavior have been recorded. Most notable among these are interactions with mating strategy.

The fly species that is probably best-known to scientists is the fruit fly *Drosophila melanogaster,* one member of a genus that has long been favored for genetic research because its chromosomes are readily visible, its reproductive rate is high, and many mutants occur. But *Drosophila* is also renowned for its courtship displays. Small, yellowish flies with bright red eyes, they congregate wherever fruit is stored and where fermentation occurs naturally (for example, in fallen fruit or sap

from tree wounds). A male approaches a stationary female and taps her with his forelegs, extending his tongue and confronting her face to face. Both then "dance," employing a series of side-to-side steps. As they do so, the male gradually opens and waggles one or both of his wings until the female stands still again, when he circles round and mounts her from behind.

A somewhat similar dance can be observed in long-legged flies that frequent muddy puddles in woodland. In their case, the male has two conspicuous white wing spots, which he flashes at the female by vibrating the wings prior to leaping right over her, twisting in mid-air to land neatly with his chosen female still in view. Many flies with wing spots and patterning seem to use their wings in sexual signaling of this type. Dolichopodids are also remarkable for their elaborate male genitalia and leg adornments that are presumably also important in courtship.

Two other examples do not involve courting dances. The stalk-eyed flies (diopsids and some other acalyptrates) are remarkable for having immensely broadened heads with the eyes (and sometimes antennae) set on stalks. These mostly tropical flies feed on decaying plant matter, and will compete for occupancy of a small patch of such material by threatening any intruder. The stalked eyes give a good resolution up to a distance of 60cm (2ft) away and are used in ritualized fights, between males in particular: two males will "measure" each other's size by comparing their eye separations, and the fly with closer-set eyes normally retires! Similarly, male flies with particularly long eyestalks seem to be preferred by female diopsids.

Male fruitflies of the peculiar *Phytalmia* genus have facial processes that resemble the horns of deer or moose and are used similarly in territorial battles; the fly that drives the intruder away gets to mate with the female. These flies live as larvae under the bark of newly fallen trees, and the males hold territory on the tree trunk of their choice.

Finally, the fascinating story of the dung flies (*Scathophaga*) should be considered. The golden male dung flies wait for the females around new pats of dung, since they must come there to lay their eggs. Males will compete for each arriving female, and she may be mounted by a tussling heap of several individuals; it pays the males to put a lot of effort into this struggle, since the last mating before egg-laying occurs will secure about 80 percent of the fertilizations. (In *Scathophaga*, as in many other flies, "sperm displacement" occurs, each successive male displacing the sperms of previous copulations with its own sperm mass.)

Females, by contrast, seek to lay their eggs as quickly as possible, since the dung rapidly cools and solidifies and is soon unsuitable for ovipositing. Males also recognize this fact; they leave older dung pats for newer ones, balancing the chances of a few females still coming to older, harder dung, where there may be fewer competitors, against the chances of competing successfully for the last mating at a new and crowded pat.

Some hoverflies also exhibit intricate mating behavior; males may hold solitary territories around a plant or along a woodland ride, chasing

○ **Above** *Curving her abdomen forward between her legs, this female* Empis trigramma *(Empididae) dips her proboscis into a droplet of fluid donated by the male during mating. In other empidids the male's gift consists of a dead insect.*

◑ **Below** *Male* Cyrtopogon *robberflies (Asilidae), which inhabit the mountains of Europe and North America, perform an elaborate courtship "dance" in front of the females. Here a male Red-horned robberfly (C. ruficornis) – a European species – is seen at right bobbing his abdomen up and down.*

off other flies and even hovering inquisitively in front of encroaching humans. They have developed a clever "computing" system that allows them to set an interception course for an approaching intruder, flying at exactly the right speed and angle to meet and repel the invader. In this way they are able to protect their territory as a mating ground.

One thread running through Diptera mating behavior is male swarming. It is not universal, because many species exhibit non-aerial mating, but it is found in families in all the major groups. Male flies form dancing swarms, usually using some object as a marker; the swarm may form above or under a tree, over water, or even over a stationary human. Probably the most extraordinary marker of all is that of smoke flies (*Microsania* spp., Platypezidae), in which the males are attracted to, and swarm within, the smoke of fires. Almost all other insects avoid fires and smoke.

Whatever the marker, females are attracted to the swarm and enter it to be courted by the males; they usually leave the swarm to mate. Different species use different markers for their swarms, and sometimes gather at different times of day, making it easier for females to locate suitable males; closely related species are separated in space or time, reducing the number of unsuccessful mating attempts. In most groups in which the males swarm, the males have larger eyes than the female; they often meet on top of the head and have facets of differing sizes.

The danceflies (Empididae) are a good example of swarming flies. They are fiercely predacious, and males risk being treated as prey rather than potential mates by the females. In some species males swarm while carrying appropriate prey objects (often another fly) to present to the female to eat during mating. In certain species the prey is wrapped in silk, while in others still a nonedible object may be wrapped in silk and presented as a gift; finally there are even species that present the female with an empty silk case.

The two large genera of danceflies found in temperate regions form swarms either over land (*Empis*) or water (*Hilara*), and the many closely related species in each one have swarming behavior that uses subtly different markers. Such mating swarms are conspicuous in most countries, either as clouds of flies over trees, church steeples, and similar landmarks, or at ground level, in which case they may become a hazard to humans walking or cycling in the vicinity. There are cases of midges causing an allergic reaction in humans through inhalation of adults from swarms. Swarming depends on flies' highly-developed flight mechanism and acute visual senses to control it.

Flies may also produce mass aggregations in which both sexes occur in equal numbers, and these may not be associated with mating. An example of this is the mass aggregation of *Sepsis*

(Sepsidae) on vegetation; the reason for these aggregations is not understood. A few species of fly in the Calliphoridae and Chloropidae families overwinter in large aggregations of both sexes. Such groupings occur partly because there are a limited number of suitable places for the flies to go, but it has also been shown that aggregation pheromones play a part; flies from one year leave behind a chemical marker that attracts the same species the following winter, often causing a nuisance to householders affected by the swarms.

In mating swarms and on flowers, syrphids and other flies often use humming noises or changing wingbeat frequencies as sexual signals. The use of increasingly sophisticated sound-detection devices has shown that many flies (and also other insects) produce sound or vibrations of the substrate as part of mating behavior. There are even differences in the songs of individuals of the same species from different localities, rather in the way there are regional dialects in human languages.

Both male and female flies may use pheromones to communicate with the opposite sex. These include the longrange attractants produced by females that are so familiar in moths. Fruit-fly males are strongly attracted by artificial lures analogous to the female's natural pheromones, and these chemicals can be useful for monitoring or controlling pest species. In other species the

males exude short-range chemicals to induce the female to mate. Many flies have glands of uncertain function on the abdomen, some of which have been shown to produce these short-range pheromones.

Crops at Risk
CONSERVATION AND ENVIRONMENT

The ability to consume green plants (phytophagy) has evolved many times in fly larvae, probably from saprophagous ancestors, and it is a common way of life found in all the major divisions of the order. In many cases the plants involved are crops, and damage by fly larvae is one of the main constraints on agricultural production, especially in the tropics. Damage from fruitflies alone was estimated to amount to $400 million annually several years ago. Gall midges (Cecidomyiidae) cause distortions of plant tissue, often noticeable as galls, and heavy infestations can destroy a crop; many major cereal crops, for example wheat and rice, may be affected. Frit flies (Chloropidae) and some Muscidae are shoot flies. The egg is laid on the leaf or stem of a cereal crop and the larva hatches and burrows into the stem, severing the growing point. The later larval instars feed on the rotting center of the stem, and the plant, if it survives, has to grow a new shoot from root level. Leaf-miners (Agromyzidae) produce conspicuous damage, as

the tiny larvae tunnel within the living tissue, leaving their pale "trails" through leaves or through the stem of the plant, weakening it until it falls. The leatherjacket of the northern hemisphere (Tipulidae) is damaging to grasslands as the larva eats roots and can occur in huge numbers, killing the sward. The Carrot fly (Psilidae) and the Cabbage root fly (Anthoymiidae) both damage the roots of their respective hosts. The fruit flies (Tephritidae) are associated with plants or their fruits, and the females have a specialized, hard ovipositor to pierce plant tissue and lay eggs within the plant. Some species form galls on plants, in which the larvae develop. Others pierce the developing fruit and lay an egg, which hatches into a larva, feeding on the fruit. The female may leave a chemical signal to prevent other females from ovipositing on the same fruit. The presence of the larva may hasten ripening of the fruit, which becomes damaged and unsaleable as a result of the feeding of the larva and the associated rot.

The majority of fruit flies are specialized on one or a few non-economic plants, but there are a few species that may live on any of several hundred species, many of them fruit or vegetable crops. The Med fly (*Ceratitis capitata*), which originated not in the Mediterranean but in East Africa, is an example. Equally worryingly, leaf-miners and fruit flies have proved particularly adept at establishing colonies in new environments, some a continent away from their natural distribution. They are therefore one of the main targets of quarantine regulations, and areas with known infestations are unable to export their produce overseas. These flies are the reason why many countries prohibit the import of fresh fruit by travelers. As with most insects, there are also beneficial fly species that attack weeds, and some of these have been moved around the world as biocontrol agents.

With about 120,000 known species, it is not surprising that flies have also been used to assess the state of the environment. The midges (Chironomidae) include some species that are able to tolerate polluted water as well as others absolutely confined to pure water; the range of species found in a water body is an excellent indication of the degree of pollution. The guild of flies whose larvae live in dead wood and associated habitats includes species that are very conservative in their distribution, so their presence in a woodland indicates that the area has been untouched for a long time; their value as indicators is second only to that of the Coleoptera (beetles). Wetlands also have aquatic or semi-aquatic species in several families (for instance soldier flies) that are good indicators of pristine environments; they are unable to tolerate pollution, so their presence indicates a long history of good management.   PGW/JWI

◐ **Above** *Enigmatic swarming in the Spot-winged manure fly (Sepsis fulgens). Despite much speculation, no convincing function for these large aggregations of intensely active flies has yet been proposed.*

◗ **Right** *A Carrot fly larva (Psila rosae) feeds on a damaged carrot. The larvae are serious agricultural pests, tunneling through root crops, which also provide them with a winter home. Besides carrots, parsnip, celery, and fennel may also be attacked.*

Fly Suborders

Thread-horned flies
Suborder Nematocera

35 families. Delicate, often with long, thin body, long legs, and wings. Antennae also long and slender, like body, often bearing long, fine hairs, and with many (more than 8) segments. Larvae (usually 4 instars) have hardened head capsules and biting jaws with mandibles that move horizontally; often aquatic, as are pupae. Families include: **blackflies** or **buffalo gnats** (Simuliidae), **crane flies**, **leather-jackets** (Tipulidae), **fungus gnats** (Mycetophilidae), **gall midges** (Cecidomyiidae), **midges** (Chironomidae and Ceratopogonidae), **mosquitoes**, **gnats** (Culicidae), and **winter gnats** (Trichoceridae).

Short-horned flies
Suborder Brachycera

120 families. Short, stout antennae (less than 8 segments); varied in size and shape. Larvae have partially hardened or reduced head capsule, with mouthparts that move vertically. Includes 5 infraorders divided between 2 main groupings:

Orthorrhaphous Brachycera
(4 infraorders and 21 families)
Well-built, rarely very small. Short, stout antennae; body often brightly colored. Larvae (5–8 instars) with partially hardened head capsules, sometimes aquatic. Families include **beeflies** (Bombyliidae), **horseflies** and **clegs** (Tabanidae), **long-legged flies** (Dolichopodidae), **robberflies** (Asilidae), and **soldier flies** (Stratiomyidae).

Higher flies
(Infraorder Muscomorpha)
Pupate inside the last larva skin (puparium). Usually with short, 3-segmented antennae; larvae are simple maggots feeding with "mouth-hooks." Divided into 2 series:
SERIES ASCHIZA (8 families) Includes **hoverflies** or **flowerflies** (Syrphidae) and **scuttle-** and **coffinflies** (Phoridae).
SERIES SCHIZOPHORA (91 families in 2 sections)
The **acalyptrates** (75 families) are mostly small, undistinguished flies, including **carrot** or **rust flies** (Psilidae), **fruit flies** (Drosophilidae, Tephritidae), **leaf-mining flies** (Agromyzidae), **shore** and **seaweed flies** (Ephydridae, Coelopidae), **stalk-eyed flies** (Diopsidae), **wasp flies** (Conopidae).

The **calyptrates** (16 families), more familiar, stouter, and generally more heavily bristled, include the **blowflies** and **bluebottles** (Calliphoridae), **bulb-** and **root-eating flies** (Anthomyiidae), **dung flies** (Scathophagidae), **flesh flies** (Sarcophagidae), **houseflies** and **stable flies** (Muscidae), **parasite flies** (Tachinidae), and **warble flies** and **botflies** (Oestridae and Gasterophilidae).
Within the calyptrates, the **Pupipara** (3 families) have flattened bodies and are parasites on birds and mammals; the females bear live young. They include **bat flies** (Nycteribiidae), **deer flies**, **keds**, and **louse flies** (Hippoboscidae).

FLY-BORNE DISEASES
Scourge of human societies

FLY-BORNE DISEASES HAVE HAD AN INCALCULABLE impact on human history; the two-winged flies are the worst insect scourge of mankind. For example, within 50 years of Christopher Columbus and his men bringing mosquito-borne smallpox to Haiti, the disease had wiped out the entire indigenous population, estimated at 5 million people. By the 17th century, European colonists had transmitted so much fatal disease to inhabitants of the New World that the British perversely came to regard the ensuing mortality as proof that God had granted the colonists rights to the land! Despite advances in the fields of insecticides and drug treatment, fly-borne diseases continue to mold the organization and distribution of many human societies.

Flies impinge on human health in three major ways. First, they act as simple, mechanical transporters of disease organisms. Houseflies (*Musca* and *Fannia* species) and bluebottles (*Calliphora*

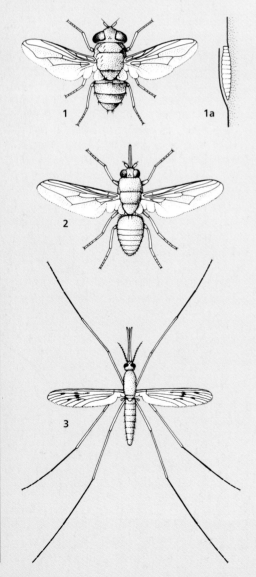

1   **1a**

2

3

species), which feed and breed in feces or rotting organic matter, may contaminate food. A huge range of bacterial, viral, and protozoan infections are transmitted in this way. In developing countries, they account for millions of infant deaths per year due to dehydration associated with severe diarrhea.

The contaminated mouthparts of blood-sucking flies may result in a "flying pin" type of mechanical transmission. Thus, mosquitoes may transmit the virus of serum hepatitis after feeding on an infected person. Horseflies and mosquitoes may also be transmitters to humans of the bacillus of pseudo-plague (tularemia), which is normally transmitted between rodents by ticks. When humans become indirectly involved in this way in an animal disease cycle, the disease is called a zoonosis.

The second type of impact of flies on humans and animals (notably domesticated breeds) is via a condition called myiasis, in which the larvae of certain flies feed on living tissues beneath the skin. Examples are the Human botfly (*Dermatobia hominis;* Oestridae) in the tropical Americas and, in Africa, the Tumbu fly (*Cordylobia anthropophaga;* Sarcophagidae). The wounds caused by the feeding larvae are an entry route for infections.

◖ *Left* Three types of dipteran flies that cause disease in other animals: **1** The Tumbu fly, whose larvae **1a** leave wounds where they enter the skin. **2** The tsetse fly, which infects humans with a protozoan that causes sleeping sickness. **3** The bloodsucking Anopheles *mosquito, which carries malaria.*

The third and most important effect occurs with the biological transmission of disease organisms. In biological transmission, the pathogen has a complicated development cycle, part of which is spent in the body of a blood-sucking fly and part in the human victim. Malaria, the most prevalent and widespread of these diseases, is carried by some 30 species of *Anopheles* mosquito, the most important being the African species *A. gambiae.* The disease organisms of malaria are four species of *Plasmodium*, a genus of unicellular protozoans. *Plasmodium falciparum*, the most dangerous species, has a pantropical distribution.

The war against malaria has to be fought on a broad front. Adult mosquitoes and their aquatic larvae can be killed with insecticides, the *Plasmodium* stages in man can be treated with drugs, and people can help themselves by using insect repellents and mosquito nets. But attempts at total eradication have been successful only in the

COMBATING DISEASE ON THE PANAMA CANAL

In 1881, a French company under the control of Ferdinand de Lesseps, renowned constructor of the Suez Canal, began the huge task of cutting a canal across the Panamanian isthmus. Eight years later the venture collapsed; the single most important factor in its failure was the terrible toll claimed by insect-borne diseases – over 20,000 men (two-thirds of the labor force) died of yellow fever or malaria.

In the same year this ill-fated attempt began, the Cuban physician Juan Carlos Finlay first posited a link between the spread of yellow fever and a mosquito vector (*Culex fasciatus*, later renamed *Aëdes aegypti*). Traditionally, such diseases had been attributed either to immoral living or to so-called "miasmas" – vaguely defined atmospheric imbalances.

More than a decade was to pass before Finlay's theory was vindicated. In 1894, the Scot Patrick Manson, port surgeon on the island of Formosa, showed that the local strain of the gnat *Culex pipiens* injected into humans minute worms that migrated to the lymph glands, causing the massive swellings known as elephantiasis. This was the first non-circumstantial evidence that flies transmit diseases,

especially those in which vital stages in a parasite's life cycle take place in both fly and human host.

Six years later, a US medical commission under Walter Reed was sent to Cuba to combat a yellow fever epidemic. Embracing Finlay's views on the cause of the disease, Reed wiped out the breeding grounds of *A. aegypti* by covering all standing bodies of water with oil, fumigated against the adult mosquito, and isolated infected patients under netting. The death rate fell dramatically.

Reed's pioneering work took place under the supervision of US Army physician Colonel William Gorgas (who was also well aware of Manson's studies). In 1904, when the USA took over the Panama canal project, Gorgas was made chief sanitary officer of the Canal Zone, and, in the face of official skepticism, instantly applied Reed's methods. Their efficacy is reflected in the statistics; in the seven years from 1906 onward, the incidence of malaria among canal workers fell from 80 to 7 percent. In the same period, yellow fever was totally eradicated. Gorgas left Panama in 1913, just before the triumphant completion of the canal.   CO'T

◁ **Left** *The Banded mosquito (Culiseta annulata) is one of the largest mosquitoes, measuring 8mm (0.3in) in body length, excluding the proboscis and antennae. It owes its name to the distinctive white banding on its abdomen and legs.*

▷ **Right** *Colored electron micrograph showing the head of a horsefly (family Tabanidae) magnified 90 times. Horseflies are a major pest worldwide; females are bloodsuckers whose piercing mouthparts (shown in red) can inflict a painful bite and are responsible for transmitting several blood-borne diseases.*

warm, temperate fringes of the malarial zone. Despite numerous control programs and the best efforts of international bodies such as the World Health Organization, more than 120 million clinical cases of malaria (80 percent of them in tropical Africa) and over 1 million deaths occur annually.

Although it is easy to cite political instability in some regions as a cause, the failure to eradicate malaria is due in large part to the ease with which both *Anopheles* mosquitoes and the malaria parasite have developed resistance to the battery of chemical weapons deployed against them by entomologists and physicians. The ability of the malarial parasite rapidly to change the chemistry of its outer coat has made the development of a vaccine virtually impossible. Recent developments in the artificial culture of the parasite, however, in conjunction with new techniques in genetic engineering, offer some hope.

The total eradication of *Anopheles* is now recognized as an impossible dream. Rather, current efforts to counter malaria center on integrated control. By judicious timing of insecticide applications, in concert with drug treatment and the screening of populations at risk, it is hoped to keep the level of the disease down to acceptable levels – namely, ones at which mortality is reduced substantially and the number of people experiencing the debilitating and economically damaging recurrent fevers is kept as low as possible.

Complete success in disease eradication, if it were to be achieved, would bring its own problems. This is especially true of sleeping sickness, a malady confined to Africa and caused by trypanosome protozoans (*Trypanosoma gambiense*) in the blood, transmitted by five species of tsetse flies (*Glossina* species). The sickness (nagana) is found also in cattle, and is endemic in the large herds of wild grazing animals. The disease has profound effects on human ecology. Cattle-ranging is impossible in many parts of Africa because of the transfer of nagana from game to domestic stock. In colonial times, this resulted in whole peoples being forcibly relocated to disease-free areas.

Control of sleeping sickness could be effected by large-scale slaughter of wild game, which acts as a reservoir. Another method, already used to a limited extent, is to clear vegetation belts that provide specific resting places for tsetse flies. Yet both methods risk serious damage to the environment and, ultimately, to human populations.

Moreover, other problems would arise if tsetse flies and sleeping sickness were eradicated. Cattle raising would be extended further, resulting in competition with game animals and an increased likelihood of desertification through overgrazing. Game animals also provide many countries with a valuable income from tourists that would be lost if the herds were slaughtered. The major fly-borne diseases therefore raise pressing and immediate problems. Their solution will present new ones to challenge us in the future.   CO'T/AWRM

Caddisflies

○ **Right** *Representative species of caddisflies, also showing the protective larval cases that are a distinctive feature of this order:* **1** *Limnephilus rhombicus, one of the Limnephilidae, a large family found across the northern hemisphere.* **2a** *The larva known to anglers as the Great red sedge (Phryganea grandis; Phryganeidae) peers from its case;* **2b** *an adult form.* **3a** *A Limnephilus lunatus emerges into adulthood, leaving the case* **3b** *in which it has spent its larval stages. The larvae, which build their cases out of plant debris, can be pests in watercress beds.*

aLMOST EVERY PLACE WHERE FRESH WATER *flows or collects has its caddisfly larvae. The typically drab-colored adults are somewhat mothlike in appearance, but the order is better known for the often elaborate cases constructed and inhabited by the larvae of many species. These resemble small stone tubes that are camouflaged against the background of the caddisflies' habitat.*

The ancestors of the caddisflies first appeared during the Permian era, 295–248 million years ago. The Trichoptera are in fact closely related to the butterflies and moths, but they have long maxillary palps and lack the butterflies' and moths' coiled proboscis and overall covering of wing scales. Caddisflies might be confused with lacewings, but have fewer crossveins; they differ from stoneflies and mayflies in, among other features, the way they hold their wings at rest.

Hairy Wings
FORM AND FUNCTION
The forewings of caddisflies generally bear a small, semitransparent, horny spot (the nygma or thyridium), and are usually a little longer than the hindwings. They are also normally hairy – hence the scientific name for the order, from the Greek *trikhos*, meaning "hair," and *pteron*, "wing." In addition to longitudinal veins, the wings of many groups have some crossveins, and occasionally scales along some of the veins. The head has well-developed compound eyes. The outermost

○ **Above** *Caddisfly wings are covered in hairs, rather than the scales seen in the related butterflies and moths. This* Halesus radiatus (Limnephilidae) *from Europe is resting in typical fashion, with its wings held in a rooflike manner above its body.*

segments of the five-segmented maxillary and three-segmented labial palps are sometimes long and flexible. The three segments of the thorax are well developed, and the upper surface bears warts.

The best fliers have a strong coupling between front and rear wings, narrow forewings, expanded hindwings, and long antennae. The wings are coupled by means of curved hairs (macrotrichia) along the veins and simple overlapping of the margins. The abdomen has quite distinct segments, with breathing vents (spiracles) on segments 1 to 7. The legs are relatively long and slender; the lower legs (tarsi) each have five segments, and above these the femora and tibiae may be equipped with dense spines, or alternatively with strong bristles and long spines.

Adult caddisflies are chiefly active in the evening and at night; they rest in cool, dark places during the day. Some species swarm in daylight. The mouthparts are adapted for licking fluids, but adults have rarely been observed feeding and it is certain that some species do not feed at all. Some are known to visit flowers.

The adults are to be found near fresh water, although there is an Australian species, *Philanisus plebeius* (Chathamiidae), that breeds by the sea in rockpools near the low-tide mark. Newly emerged

adults can be seen in large numbers dancing, often in vertical swarms. Mating occurs on the wing. Males locate females by using their large eyes and antennae; the flight movement of males in swarms may also serve to attract females.

Life among the Larvae
REPRODUCTION AND LIFE CYCLE
Caddisflies reproduce once a year. They overwinter as larvae, pupate in the spring, and emerge as adults in early summer. The females lay small, more or less spherical eggs, measuring 0.3mm (0.1in), that are normally pale blue-green or whitish. The eggs are usually deposited in masses or strings covered in a sticky secretion that attaches them to stones and other objects in or near the water, or else on vegetation overhanging the water. The females of many families, especially those whose larvae do not make cases, enter the water to lay their eggs on submerged objects.

The generally omnivorous larvae are caterpillarlike, with a well-sclerotized head and thorax (in other words, with a hardened cuticle) and a soft abdomen. The larva's head bears small antennae,

FACTFILE

CADDISFLIES

Class: Insecta

Order: Trichoptera

7,000 species in 43 families and 3 subfamilies: **Hydropyscoidea** (9 families, including Hydropychidae); **Limnephiloidea** (30 families, including Phryganeidae, Limnephilidae); and **Rhyacophiloidea** (4 families, including Rhyacophilidae)

DISTRIBUTION Worldwide, except polar regions.

SIZE Adults slender, elongated; body length from 1.5–35mm (0.06–1.4in).

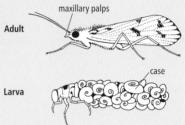

FEATURES Filiform antennae; mouthparts reduced or vestigial; long maxillary palps; 2 pairs of membranous wings, clothed in hairs; wings held rooflike over abdomen when at rest; mostly nocturnal. Larvae have threadlike gill along abdomen and one pair of hooked prolegs at tip of abdomen.

LIFE CYCLE Holometabolous (complete metamorphosis); larvae caterpillarlike, usually inside a case.

CONSERVATION STATUS 3 US and 1 German species have recently been classified as extinct.

🌢 **Above** *Glued by the female to waterside vegetation with the aid of a gelatinous secretion, these caddisfly eggs are well protected from desiccation. On hatching, the larvae will drop to the water below, where they will build protective cases. As the larva grows, the case may be increased in size; alternatively, the larva may leave it to make or adopt a larger case.*

a patch of simple eyes (ocelli) on each side, and chewing mouthparts. The three pairs of legs arising from the thorax are used for walking or crawling, for capturing prey, and for constructing the larval case. The abdomen has nine segments and a pair of prolegs at the tip, which serve to anchor the larva in its case, into which it can withdraw completely when disturbed or at rest. There are no functional spiracles, but most species have external, filamentous, tracheal gills attached to the respiratory tubules on the segments of the abdomen and thorax. Some species respire through the cuticle; others have a tuft of anal blood gills.

The larvae are fairly active, and the members of many families construct a portable case made of various small objects fastened together with a gluelike substance or with silk from the tip of the labium. Each species of caddisfly larva is to be found in a particular kind of habitat (slow-running or fast streams, ponds, small lakes) and constructs its own specific type of case. The micro-caddisflies make purse-shaped cases; snail-case caddisflies make snailshell-shaped cases, as their name implies; large caddisflies make cases of spirally-

arranged strips of plant material; while northern caddisflies make cases of various kinds.

Some larvae do not make cases at all, but instead construct silken nets stretched between underwater plants, debris, and stones. The nets are made to face upstream and serve to catch prey items such as small crustaceans and plankton. Most larvae feed on plant material – algae, moss, or decaying vegetation; carnivorous larvae take their prey with their forelegs.

Caddisfly larvae are very important in the food chains of freshwater streams and pools; they are eaten by many species of fish and by birds and frogs, as well as by some predacious insect larvae. In consequence, the larvae are used as models for human anglers' lures, as are the adults, and many have attractive names such as Black silverhorns, Great red sedge, Grouse wing, and grannom. The larvae and pupae may be parasitized by an ichneumon wasp, *Agriotypus armatus* (Hymenoptera: Ichneumonidae), whose females submerge and pull themselves down to lay eggs near their prospective hosts. The larvae of some species in the family Leptoceridae are pests of paddy fields.　　　DM

Butterflies and Moths

bUTTERFLIES AND MOTHS ARE INSTANTLY *recognized by people the world over as attractive, harmless insects. They are found in every habitat from mountaintops to the darkest jungle, in deserts and even in our homes – a truly cosmopolitan group. They include some of the most colorful insects, many with incredible stories attached to them. Among an otherwise frightening collection of creepy-crawlies, adult butterflies and moths do not sting or bite and are viewed with pleasure by people across the world.*

Butterflies and moths belong to the order Lepidoptera, a name that provides a clue to the main characteristic of this group: it derives from the Greek words *lepis*, meaning "scale," and *pteron*, "wing." The presence of overlapping scales on the wings and body helps distinguish the Lepidoptera from other insect orders. Their closest relatives are the caddisflies (order Trichoptera), whose wings are actually covered by scalelike hairs. The Lepidoptera also exemplify the concept of metamorphosis, as the transformation from caterpillar to pupa and then to a large-winged, often brightly-colored butterfly or moth is dramatic, sudden, and stunning.

The moths and butterflies are one of the biggest orders of insects (beetles are the largest), with an estimated 200,000 species. Yet despite their spectacular variety of size, from the tiniest nepticulid moths with a wingspan of 3mm (0.1in) to the massive 32cm (12.5in) wingspan of the South American noctuid moth *Thysania agripina*, both adults and larvae of the order Lepidoptera all share the same body plan. As a group, their fossil record dates back some 100 million years to the Middle Cretaceous. This reckoning may in fact be an underestimate of the age of the order, as fossils of Lepidoptera are rare and mostly occur as fragments of whole insects preserved in amber; the earliest known are wingscales. The butterflies and moths are now strongly associated with flowering plants, and it is likely that the evolution and subsequent explosion of these in the Middle Cretaceous were mirrored by an increase in the diversity and number of Lepidoptera species.

Scales on their Wings
FORM AND FUNCTION

Scale-covered wings are the most notable characteristic of Lepidoptera, as is readily seen when a butterfly or a moth is handled. The fine dust that rubs off is actually composed of tiny scales. Scales also clothe other parts of the body. Those on the head are often hairlike and stand erect to form a tuft; alternatively, they may be scale- or platelike, and flattened on the head-capsule. The legs often also appear hairy, but again these "hairs" are in fact modified scales. The wing scales in most lepidopterans have a cavity (the lumen) between the upper and lower surfaces, but in the most primitive moths they are solid.

Underneath the covering of scales, the wings are glassy, transparent structures, as in other insects, with a strong

○ **Above** *Butterflies are the display artists of the insect world. The spectacular livery of this Royal blue pansy (*Junonia rhadama*; Nymphalidae) from Madagascar is structural in origin, resulting from light-refraction in specially shaped scales.*

◑ **Left** *"False-head mimicry" is common in the Lycaenidae. Slender projections from the hind wing-tips, allied to adjacent dark spots, give an impression of a "head," complete with eyes and antennae. These are given lifelike movement by constant shuffling of the wings. This is* Hypolycaena liara *from Uganda.*

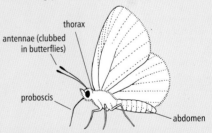

● **Above** *Characteristic overlapping scales on the wing of a tropical moth (family Uraniidae). Wing scales are modified hairs and are responsible for the colored wing patterns of moths and butterflies.*

FACTFILE

BUTTERFLIES AND MOTHS

Class: Insecta

Subclass: Pterygota

Order: Lepidoptera

180,000–200,000 species, grouped in 127 families and 46 superfamilies.

DISTRIBUTION Widespread wherever there is vegetation, up to the snowline.

SIZE Wingspan in adults 0.3–32cm (0.1–12.5in).

FEATURES Adults usually have wings covered in overlapping scales; modified scales (often hairlike) also clothe the rest of the body and legs; most species have a long, sucking proboscis, or "tongue," for nectar feeding. Common defenses include vivid warning or camouflage markings; spines or irritant hairs; poisons or repugnant taste; or mimicry of poisonous species.

LIFE CYCLE Complete metamorphosis via egg, larva, pupa (chrysalis), and adult (imago); the wingless larvae (caterpillars) usually have chewing mouthparts adapted for a plant diet.

CONSERVATION STATUS 6 Lepidoptera species, including the Piedmont anomalous blue and the Sri Lankan rose butterflies and the Prairie sphinx moth, are currently listed as Critically Endangered; a further 36 are Endangered, and 116 are Vulnerable.

See superfamilies table ▷

network of veins that are pumped full of air and fluid after the adult emerges from the pupa. Once the wings have hardened, the veins function as struts to help maintain their shape and rigidity when flapped; timelapse photography reveals that the wings flex considerably when in flight, and the tubular veins perform a valuable mechanical purpose. Lepidoptera fly by beating both sets of wings at the same time, with the fore and hindwings beating as one in the same direction (unlike those, say, of dragonflies). The way in which the forewings are linked to the hindwings has been used as a classification tool to divide the order into two groups. The most primitive species have a simple lobe of membrane on the back of the forewing that catches the front edge of the hindwing. The majority of Lepidoptera, however, have a special structure consisting of a group of tough bristles that form a spine, or frenulum, on the front edge of the hindwing, which is held by a special catch structure under the hind edge of the forewing. Most butterfly species lack a frenulum.

Special scales, called androconia, are found on males of many Lepidoptera species. These scales, modified to hold chemical scents or pheromones, help to disseminate scent from glands on the wings, and are scattered over the female during courtship. Modified scales are bunched together in some species to form brushes or "pencils," which serve the same purpose. These brushes are often held within a pouch on the side of the abdomen and are raised to disseminate the scent during courtship. Scent is also used by many female moths to attract mates, in which case it may either be disseminated through a tuft of special scales at the tip of the body or by extruding a special scent gland. This behavior is called "calling" or "assembling," and a single female may use it to attract many males.

The head of an adult lepidopteran has a common form across all species. The three most obvious features are the antennae, the tongue or proboscis, and the large, compound eyes. The antennae are a characteristic of the group and

⬤ *Above* **1** *The resilient Buckthorn hawkmoth (Hyles hippophaes; Sphingidae) can easily survive on the sparse vegetation of deserts. **2** The long-tongued Madagascan hawkmoth (Xanthopan morgani; Sphingidae) hovers while it feeds, whereas butterflies come to rest on flowers. **3** Attacus edwardsi (Saturniidae) is one of a small number of Atlas moths, all from Asia, which are giants of the moth world. **4** The Venus swift moth (Leto venus; Hepialidae), restricted to South Africa, whose larvae feed in tree trunks. **5** The brilliant irides-cent wings of this East African day-flying moth (Chrysiridia croesus; Uraniidae) were much used in Victorian costume jewelry. **6** The Gulf fritil-lary (Dione vanillae; Nymphalidae) belongs to the subfamily Heliconiinae; members of this group are unique for collecting pollen in their proboscis. **7** The Monarch (Danaus plexippus; Nymphalidae) is the only butterfly that migrates annually both north and south. **8** When this male Morpho butterfly (Morpho menelaus; Nymphalidae) folds its blue wings, predators are fooled by the bark-colored underside.*

function as noses and taste buds. In adults they vary in structure and length. In primitive families they are composed of short, simple segments, but in more advanced groups they may bear fine hairs (in other words, they are "ciliated") or have their segments extended into long filaments to give a comblike (pectinate) appearance, so that the antennae resemble feathers. Pectinate antennae occur in many species of tussock and emperor moths. These groups have refined the scent-aided mate-location system; the males have very large pectinate antennae while their female partners have simple antennae, a sexual dimorphism that reflects the need for the male to be able to detect extremely small amounts of pheromones at some distance downwind of a virgin female. Experiments with the European emperor moth (*Pavonia pavonia*) have shown that males can detect females from 1.6km (1mi) or more away. The female scent of some species of moth pests has been artificially manufactured and is used in orchards to lure males to their death.

Next to the scales, one of the most characteristic features of adult lepidopterans is the sucking proboscis, or "tongue." The proboscis is generally rolled up underneath the head when at rest, but when the insect feeds it is extended. A channel runs through the proboscis so that the organ functions as a flexible drinking straw up which liquid, particularly nectar, is sucked. The length of the proboscis varies. In the primitive family Micropterigidae it is entirely absent; instead, these tiny moths have chewing mandibles that they use to eat pollen grains. For this reason the Micropterigidae are excluded from the order Lepidoptera by some taxonomists.

In other families such as the tussock moths (Lymantriidae), the proboscis has been lost, and the adults do not feed at all; or it may be present but short, as in the tiny Nepticulidae. The longest tongues are found in the hawkmoths, enabling them to suck nectar from the deep-seated nectaries of tubular flowers. Hummingbird hawkmoths hover while they draw nectar; the genus to which they belong is appropriately called *Macroglossum* ("great tongue"). The length of tongue is related to the adults' preferred source of nectar. Those with short tongues are restricted to feeding on open flowers such as the Ranunculaceae. This association between tongue length and lepidopteran enabled Darwin in 1822 to predict the existence of a moth that could pollinate

151

the Comet orchid (*Angreacum sesquipedale*) with its 30cm/12in flower spur. This prediction was proved correct by the discovery of the hawkmoth *Xanthopan morgani*, which does indeed have a proboscis to fit the spur. The coevolution of Lepidoptera and flowering plants has created an enormous number of close relationships between adult moths and butterflies and flowers.

The eyes of adult Lepidoptera consist of 12,000–17,000 individual facets, or ommatidia. Each facet is a discrete optical unit that sees part of the scene; the more complex the eye, the better the vision. Many day-flying moths and butterflies have excellent vision and can detect movement and a wide range of colors. Their visual range extends into the ultraviolet, but is generally poor at the red end of the spectrum, so moth collectors use red light to watch moths feeding at night without disturbing them. The eyesight of adult Lepidoptera is well developed to enable them to recognize pattern, shape, and color for feeding, courtship, and predator avoidance. In addition to the obvious compound eyes, the adults also have a few simple eyes toward the back of the head, often hidden by scales. Their function is not so clear, but it may be related to assessing overall light level.

The adult's thorax bears three pairs of legs and two pairs of wings. The legs are not simply walking mechanisms, but also have a role to play in detecting tastes and sounds. The terminal segments of each leg are adorned with sensory pits, which specialize in detecting moisture and the presence of sugars or certain chemicals in a host plant; the best way to persuade a butterfly to extend its proboscis in order to feed is to touch its "feet" with a pad moistened with sugar solution. A female butterfly, intent on egg-laying, can be seen to test the leaves with her feet to check that she has in fact chosen the correct foodplant and that it is in a suitable condition to support caterpillars. Most Lepidoptera species have a very restricted range of foodplants, each differentiated by their chemical makeup.

The bulk of the thorax houses the powerful flight muscles, which act to flex the elastic outer skeleton of the thorax and beat the wings up and down. In cool climates, many species regularly thermoregulate by basking in the sun or shivering in order to maintain a high temperature in their flight muscles. The remainder of the adult body has a typical insect body plan, with a segmented abdomen and a tubular gut and system of nerves and tracheae.

Caterpillars and Chrysalises
DEVELOPMENTAL STAGES
The immature stages of Lepidoptera have a very different set of structures and behaviors, befitting their differences in shape and function. With few exceptions, the larvae, or caterpillars, have chewing mouthparts, which is only appropriate since

they spend most of their time feeding. This is the growing stage in the life cycle, and the larvae are designed as eating machines. Consumption is related not only to the growth of the larvae but also to the needs of the winged adult. Since many adults do not feed at all, food reserves have to be built up by the caterpillar.

Most caterpillars have both true and false legs, although in some species some or all of these have been lost. There are three pairs of true legs, which are found on the three segments behind the head – a part of the caterpillar technically known as the thorax. In addition there are usually five pairs of fleshy false legs, or prolegs, one pair on each of segments 3–6, and a terminal (anal) pair on segment 10. The larvae of sawflies (Hymenoptera) look very similar to those of Lepidoptera, but they always have a pair of legs on the second abdominal segment and also always have more than five pairs of false legs. Each false leg can grasp stem or leaf surfaces by means of a ring of hooks, called crochets, around its base. Prolegs are absent in slug caterpillars, which instead have an adhesive "sole" with suckers. In the geometrid moths, two or three of the central pairs of prolegs are lost, to leave only the hind pairs, and the caterpillars walk by "looping." This larval behavior gives the group its name, as *geometrein* in classical Greek means "to measure the earth."

The majority of caterpillars can produce silk, using a pair of specialized glands near the mouthparts. According to species, they use the silk for a variety of purposes, from helping hold together a feeding tube to making pupal cocoons. A careful look at the head of the caterpillar reveals that it has a pair of tiny, stublike antennae and a group of simple eyes, or ocelli, on either side. Larvae do not need the good vision of adult moths or butterflies, and use these simple eyes merely to detect the level and color of light.

Caterpillars are very vulnerable to predation, and most use any of a variety of strategies to protect themselves: either by merging into their surroundings, by concealing themselves inside plant

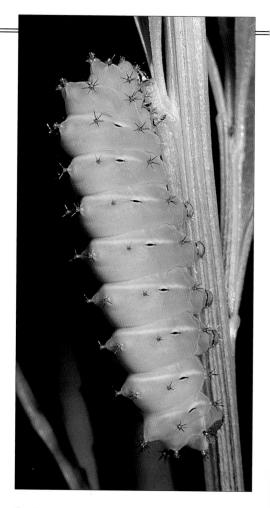

⬆ **Above** The three pairs of true legs of this Molippa moth caterpillar (Saturniidae) from Argentina are inconspicuously grouped near the head (at top). The stumpier false legs (prolegs) are clearly visible in the middle of the body and at the rear.

▶ **Right** Black-and-white striping or banding is a common form of aposematic (warning) coloration. By forming a kinship-based group, these "looper" moth caterpillars in a Ugandan rainforest reinforce the "keep off" message.

▼ **Below** Many swallowtail butterfly caterpillars (Papilionidae) resemble bird droppings. This half-grown Great mormon swallowtail caterpillar from Asia (Papilio memnon) is protruding its osmaterium – a forked defensive organ that emits noxious odors.

tissues, or, as in the bagworms (Pyschidae), by using cases of silk or plant material. They also achieve concealment by using color or shape, or else a mixture of the two. One of the most common methods is simply to use shades of green to countershade their outline, so that the undersides of the caterpillar are a lighter green than the uppersides. This stratagem cancels out the shadow effect when they sit on leaves, making it difficult for bird predators to recognize them as solid objects. Larval colors are generally formed below the external layers of the skin, using pigments derived from foodplants, and they can change as the larva grows and molts the old skin to the next instar. Some of these changes are spectacular, as in the swallowtail butterfly, *Papilio machaon*; its young caterpillars are cryptically colored to resemble bird droppings, but they grow and molt into extremely gaudy large caterpillars that are banded black and yellow. Such changes reflect the risks of retaining a particular defensive strategy as a caterpillar grows in size: concealment as a bird dropping seems to work for a small caterpillar, whilst a much larger one needs a more credible defense from predators, such as distastefulness.

Shape, in combination with color, is an excellent means of concealment. The geometrid moths have larvae that resemble twigs, even to the extent of having blemishes and knobs that match the real thing. These larvae are night feeders and spend most of the day concealed in twig form.

A common form of defense for caterpillars is to be covered in sharp hairs or spines; these are known to be extremely irritating to many bird and lizard predators, which will in consequence generally avoid these types of caterpillars. Yet the most effective strategy of all is to use the natural phytotoxins of their foodplants for defense. This tactic carries some risks, in that each individual bird or lizard has to learn that certain behaviors or bright color patterns warn of danger, and one or two caterpillars may be eaten, and vomited up, before the message is understood.

In the pupa or chrysalis, the chewing, wingless larva undergoes its transformation into a winged adult. The most primitive pupae have functional mandibles that help to break open the cocoon before the adult emerges. In the family Eriocraniidae, the pupal mandibles are very large. In most groups the pupa is simply a hard, brown, spindle-shaped case, with movement limited to the occasional wiggle of the abdominal segments. This pupal stage may last for a year or more in some species. In moths the pupa is often protected by a silken case, or by being formed underground or within plant tissue.

In butterflies the pupa is generally exposed, and relies on shape and color to avoid predators. Most species of butterflies have pupae that hang suspended from a set of hooks on a pad of silk on the last segment of the pupal case. These hooks are attached as the caterpillar sheds its final skin by means of an acrobatic flick, revealing the case underneath. Many chrysalids are adorned with bright metallic markings, spines, horns, and other structures that help disguise them. The emerging moth or butterfly first breaks through the hard case and inhales air into its digestive tract; once clear of the case, sometimes after a lengthy crawl out of the ground or up into a bush, the adult uses the air to inflate its wings and then to allow them to "dry." During the transformation from caterpillar to adult, a quantity of waste products accumulates, and these are discharged at emergence as a liquid called the meconium.

Overcoming Plant Defenses
DIET

Lepidoptera have evolved alongside plants, and a continual battle has raged between these and the insects that eat them. Plant defenses are sometimes obvious and physical, such as spines or tough leaves. The real battle, however, is unseen, operating at the level of plant chemistry.

Most species of Lepidoptera rely on a relatively small number of larval food plants, and they will starve to death if deprived of these. This response is partly behavioral and partly physiological. Caterpillars will not begin to feed unless they detect the correct mixture of plant compounds. They can be fooled into eating artificial substances if the host plant compounds are added to a nutrient base – a method used to rear large numbers of larvae in experimental studies where sterile conditions are needed, as in virology. All plants contain one or more compounds intended to be toxic to animals. These compounds may block the digestive process or otherwise adversely affect herbivores. Different species of Lepidoptera have evolved to cope with different types of plant compound, and they have ways of either coping with the toxin or storing it within their bodies for use in their defense. Without their foodplant, they either will not eat or will be unable to digest a substitute.

The link between plant compounds and foodplants is well illustrated by a European species, the Marsh fritillary (*Eurodryas aurinia*). The foodplant for this species in the United Kingdom is a plant called Devil's-bit scabious (*Succisa pratensis*). This plant is known to contain a range of secondary compounds called iridoid gylocosides,

*Above left and right Flower nectar offers poor nutrition to butterflies that feed on nothing else; this Malay lacewing (*Cethosia hypsea*) will need a great deal to fuel its daily activities. Similarly, leaf-eating caterpillars like these Buff-tip moths (*Phalera bucephala; Notodontidae*) must eat large volumes of their poor-quality food to derive enough protein for growth.*

and these are believed to be used to make the adult butterfly distasteful. These same compounds also occur in a few other plant families and, if tested in the laboratory, the larvae of the Marsh fritillary will eat, and thrive on, a range of other species not used in the wild. This elaboration of plant toxins is a common defense mechanism against butterflies and reflects the close coevolution between plant and butterfly in a chemical "arms race."

Caterpillars derive all the necessary nutrients from their foodplant, but need to eat large volumes of vegetation in order to extract sufficient protein. In some species, the caterpillar has to accumulate reserves to take it through to the egg stage. Few adult butterflies obtain much in the way of protein from their food; when developing eggs or repairing body tissues, they rely upon reserves laid down by the caterpillar. Certain species of *Heliconius* butterflies are exceptions to this rule; these denizens of Central and South American tropics eat amino acids and proteins derived from pollen grains, which they rupture by means of their specially modified tongues. They may live for up to 130 days, producing eggs for much of that time. By contrast most butterflies, particularly those of temperate regions, have a protein-free diet and rarely live for more than a week or two.

Protecting the Eggs
BREEDING AND REPRODUCTION

Lepidoptera eggs are extremely varied in form and shape. The strategies for laying eggs range from the random broadcast of thousands of small eggs to the careful placing of a small number of large eggs. The hepialid moth *Abantiades magnificus* is known to lay up to 18,000 tiny eggs, whilst the skipper *Quinta cannae* lays only 20 to 30. Most Lepidoptera have a simple ovipositor that enables the eggs to be placed on or near a foodplant, but some have long, flexible ovipositors that enable eggs to be placed in cracks (in geometrid moths such as *Biston betularia*), or even inserted inside plant stems (as in many small Incurvariid moths). A few species have eggs that hatch inside the female oviduct, and these females effectively "lay" live larvae. This trait was first noted in the Australian tineid moth *Monopsis meliorella*.

The eggs of Lepidoptera can be very resistant to climatic change, and many species in temperate countries have eggs that overwinter and hatch in the spring. In some, such as the apollo *Parnassius apollo* and the High brown fritillary *Argynnis cydippe*, the larvae hatch within the shell of the egg and remain in a torpid state through the winter.

The egg stage is a very vulnerable one for Lepidoptera, and a range of defenses are commonly used. A common cause of death for an egg is attack by a parasitic wasp. The eventual emergence of the adult parasites leaves a small hole in the egg, and at least one moth, *Automeris io*, fools other predators into thinking its eggs have already been parasitized by placing a round black spot on each one. The most common ploy, however, is to

The caterpillar feeds voraciously, shedding its skin between each instar

The caterpillar eats its way out of its ribbed egg

The adult develops inside the pupa, which is attached to the substrate

The female lays her eggs on selected leaves, often specific for the species

After emerging from the pupa, the adult pumps up its shriveled wings

During mating the male passes the female a sperm package

The male flutters around the female during courtship, showering her with androconia (pheromone-rich scales)

⊙ **Above** *The life cycle of butterflies is a sequence of extraordinary transformations. From the egg a caterpillar emerges, growing through a series of molts. The last stage (instar) "pupates," shedding its final larval skin, and the adult issues from the immobile pupa. Here a Large cabbage white is shown.*

⊙ **Below** *During mating, male butterflies deposit in the female's body a sperm package (spermatophore) that sometimes represents a substantial proportion of their total body weight. These* Atrophaneura antenor *(Papilionidae) from Madagascar are connected end-to-end, a typical position in butterflies.*

camouflage the egg, either by means of its natural coloration or else by coating it with other materials for disguise. The lackey moths of the genus *Malacosoma* lay their eggs in batches on twigs and coat them with a hard secretion that cements them into a solid mass. Two lappet moths, the European *Gasteropacha quercifolia* and the North American *Epicnaptera americana*, both lay small batches of disruptively-colored eggs. Their strongly contrasting black-on-white markings are believed to break up the round outline, thereby confusing searching predators.

Many Lepidoptera eggs are simply poisonous. These include the large, brightly-colored eggs of several families of butterflies, and also those of the burnet moths of the family Zygaenidae. The larvae of these species feed on plants known to contain toxic compounds, and these are passed from caterpillar to adult and on to the egg – an especially good defense against ants.

Rather than place poison inside the egg, however, many species of moth make the eggs unpalatable by other means. The example of the Brown tail moth (*Euproctis phaeorrhoea*) is well-known; the female protects her egg batches by leaving a thick coating of stinging hairs over them. This tactic is particularly potent in moths of the family Agrotidae, whose larvae contain a lethal toxin within specialized, barbed hairs; the female moth carries these from the pupal case and deposits a layer on her egg batch.

The presence of eggs similar to their own will deter females of most butterfly species from laying on a plant. This trait is exploited by certain species of passionflower, which produce small, raised yellow blisters on their tendrils and leaves; these mimic eggs, and may deter female *Heliconius* butterflies from laying there. (The poisonous *Heliconius* adults are themselves also mimicked by palatable members of the butterfly family Pieridae.) The Amaryllis azure butterfly of Australia selects food plants that are visited by a certain species of ant. The caterpillars of this butterfly live in mixed-age groups, and the ants protect them from small insect predators; in return, the caterpillars secrete a sweet liquid that the ants eat.

Butterflies all over the world visit patches of mud or damp ground – a behavior known as "puddling." This trait is particularly common among tropical species and is restricted to males. At first entomologists assumed that the butterflies were seeking water, but they could not explain why only males were involved. It has recently been suggested that in fact swallowtails and whites puddle in order to absorb sodium. When the adults emerge, both sexes have enough sodium in their bodies for the functioning of their muscles and nerves. On mating, however, many males deposit into the female's body a sperm package that contains much of the male's free sodium. The female uses the sodium to replace that which she has put into egg production, and the males in turn make up for the deficiency by absorbing sodium salts where evaporation of ground water has concentrated this element. In a little-known variation on puddling behavior, some male butterflies extract sodium from perfectly dry stones, gravel, or even the dried carcasses of animals. Species from a wide range of families use their proboscises to daub dry surfaces with saliva and then drink the dissolved salts.

Each butterfly species has its own unique approach to reproduction. Most females mate several times during their lifetime and develop eggs when necessary food is available. Others, such as the apollos of the genera *Parnassius* or *Euphydryas*, mate only once, after which the male deposits a secreted plug in the genital aperture of the female, in this way preventing matings by other males.

Leaf Miners and Mimics

SMALLER MOTHS

Lepidopterists are often divided into those who study the small moths ("Microlepidoptera") and those who study the larger species ("Macrolepidoptera"). This division is a useful colloquialism, even though it does not closely reflect evolutionary relationships. Nevertheless, primitive moths are generally small, and more advanced species generally larger. Also, size reflects lifestyle: small moths, not surprisingly, develop from small larvae, and small larvae are able to occupy habitats quite different from those occupied by large ones. Small larvae tend to feed as leaf miners inside seeds, galls, fruit, stems, flowers, or leaves. Larger larvae are generally external feeders: they are what we think of as typical caterpillars, and they spend

○ **Above** *This "micro" moth (Micropterigidae) resembles a crinkled, dead leaf – one of many ploys evolved by insects to avoid predation. The accuracy of such mimicry reflects the acute vision of birds and lizards, and the intense selection pressures they exert.*

○ **Left 1** *The Yellow underwing moth (Noctua pronuba; Noctuidae) uses its brightly-colored underwings to startle attackers.* **2** *When disturbed, the Eyed hawk moth (Smerinthus ocellata; Sphingidae) opens its wings to reveal a pair of large eyespots that scare off predators.* **3** *The Bordered white moth and larva (Bupalus pinaria; Geometridae) rest in spruce and pine trees.* **4** *Burnet moths (Zygaenidae) are day-flying, and their brilliant red markings warn enemies that they are poisonous.* **5** *The larvae of the Case-bearing clothes moth (Tinea pellionella; Caleophoridae) feed on fabrics and create the familiar holes found in clothes.* **6a** *Black Peppered moths (Biston betularia; Geometridae) flourish in polluted environments where the tree trunks are dark; in cleaner environments, mottled members of the same species* **6b** *are dominant.* **7** *The Peppered moth's larva, the inchworm, resembles a twig.* **8** *This prominent moth (Epicoma melanostica; Notodontidae) inhabits parts of Australia.*

this stage of their life cycle eating leaves. This ecological division is reflected not only in larval (and usually adult) size, but often in structure and habits as well – for example, internal feeders tend to have reduced legs.

The most primitive species of moths alive today are small, and the belief that the first moths were small too received confirmation a few years ago when a specimen was found preserved in Lebanese amber dating from the early Cretaceous period, at least 100 million years ago. What made the find so exciting was that the fossilized specimen belonged to the Micropterigidae, considered on grounds of structure to be the most primitive family of moths. The adults of this widespread family are remarkable in having chewing mouthparts instead of the typical adult lepidopteran's sucking proboscis. They visit flower heads and feed on pollen grains, which they grind with their mandibles. The components of the mouthparts destined to evolve into the proboscis in more advanced members of the Lepidoptera are only tiny vestiges in the Micropterigidae. Micropterigid larvae are found in leaf litter, where they probably feed on detritus or fungal hyphae.

There are two other groups of moths that have not developed a proboscis: the Australian kauri moths (family Agathiphagidae), and the recently-discovered South American genus *Heterobathmia* (family Heterobathmiidae). The larvae of both groups feed inside plant tissue, those of the kauri moths in the seeds of the Kauri pine (*Agathis*) and those of *Heterobathmia* as leaf miners within the leaves of southern beeches (*Nothofagus*).

Leaf mining is widespread among the lower Lepidoptera. Since leaf miners live between the two outer (epidermal) layers of leaves, their appendages are usually reduced or absent. Leaf mining is characteristic of the pygmy moths (Nepticulidae). Although not frequently encountered, the family occurs all over the world. Close examination of the leaves of such trees as oaks and beeches will often reveal the signs of leaf-mining larvae at work. As the insect eats the tissue of the plant, a channel or blotch is formed that becomes visible when the caterpillar eats the chlorophyll-bearing cell layers that give the leaf its green color. Many leaf miners restrict their feeding to a particular host plant, so that, with a correctly identified leaf bearing the marks of a larva, it is often possible to identify the species of leaf miner from an empty "mine."

The leaf-mining habit has probably evolved more than once in the Lepidoptera. In one family

8

7

6a

6b

of case bearers (Coleophoridae), the larvae are often leaf miners at first, but in later stages (instars) they construct protective silken cases and feed externally. Larvae of the family Heliozelidae cut oval pieces from the leaf at the end of their mining life and make them into a case within which they pupate.

The family Incurvariidae, which is related to the Heliozelidae, includes the remarkable yucca moths of the genus *Tegeticula*. These moths, which occur in North America and Mexico, have developed a close association with the yucca plant. The female moths lay their eggs in the ovaries of yucca flowers before fertilizing the plants with pollen that they have collected. As a result of this pollination, the plant produces seeds, some of which germinate while others are eaten by the moth larvae. Thus plant and insect depend on each other for survival.

Although some ghost or swift moths (Hepialidae) are among the largest lepidopterans, the affinities of the group lie within the small members of the order rather than with the larger ones. Hepialid larvae feed in or among the roots or in the trunks of trees. The family is well represented in Australia, where one species, *Aenetus eximus*, forms tunnels as long as 50cm (20in) in the stems and roots of certain trees. One of the most beautiful hepialids is the Venus or Silver-spotted ghost (*Leto venus*), a species confined to the coastal forests of the southern Cape region of South Africa. The larvae tunnel in the trunks of the keurboom tree (*Virgilia oroboides*). Shortly before the time for emergence, the pupa protrudes from the tree trunk. The moth, when freshly emerged, is a rich, deep purple, covered with silver patches.

Many of the smaller moths are rather drab. For example, members of the enormous family Tineidae, to which the notorious clothes moths belong, are often yellowish-brown or gray, although some are exquisitely colored. The delicate little moths that belong to the Gracilariidae (the leaf blotch miners) often have their long-fringed wings adorned with eyespots and colored bands. It is difficult to imagine the function of the complex patterns and variety of colors in this group of tiny moths, if indeed there is one.

There is little doubt about the function of pattern in the clearwings (family Sesiidae), which mimic wasps and bees. Their wings are largely devoid of scales, leaving them transparent, as in wasps. The bodies of clearwing moths bear wasp- or beelike stripes and are usually similar in shape to their models; the insects may even make a buzzing sound when they fly. Clearwings do not sting, of course, but by mimicking insects that do they usually escape the attentions of predators.

Another colorful group of moths is the family Zygaenidae, which include the burnets or foresters. Like clearwings, they are day-flying; but while clearwings are harmless mimics, zygaenids are colorful in order to advertise their distastefulness. Some species store toxins of great potency, such as hydrogen cyanide, in their tissues. As in the case of other poisonous lepidopterans, these toxins are derived from their food plants.

○ **Above** Dysphania contraria (Geometridae) from Sulawesi is a member of a large genus of warningly colored moths from Asia and Australasia. This specimen on the rainforest floor had probably just inflated its wings after emerging from its pupa.

◁ **Left** Many moths are cryptic, and often select a suitable matching background. This Angle-shades (Phlogophora meticulosa; Noctuidae) from Europe is spending the day on a dead leaf, thereby increasing the effectiveness of its camouflage.

Fluttering Giants
LARGER MOTHS

One of the most primitive families of larger moths is the Cossidae, the carpenters. The larvae generally bore into trees – hence their colloquial name. *Cossus cossus* is known as the Goat moth because the larvae are said to smell like goats. The species is widespread, being found in Europe, North Africa, and central and western Asia. It takes 3 to 4 years to mature.

The larger emperors (Saturniidae) are among the most dramatic moths. All bear prominent eyespots on the wings. The enormous Giant atlas moth is among the largest of all lepidopterans, with a wingspan of up to 30cm (12in). Emperor

moths lack a proboscis; each antenna resembles a comb (bipectinate). The larvae bear fleshy protuberances called scoli. The larva of the Mopane moth is a staple food of humans in southern Africa. It is an attractive caterpillar with bright red, yellow, and black markings on a white background, and it feeds on leaves of the Mopane tree. "Mopane worms" are often sold dried for food, and they have a rather nutty flavor. A family closely related to the emperors is the Bombycidae, which includes the well-known Silkworm moth. The copious quantities of silk spun by the larva when it makes its cocoon have been used for 2,000 years in the commercial production of silk.

Some of the large species look less like moths

than butterflies. The Castniidae is a fairly small family found in the tropics and subtropics, excluding Africa. In some species the hindwing has a bright "flash" coloration, while the forewing is camouflaged; others are believed to mimic unpalatable species of butterflies. Like butterflies, the Castniidae have clubbed antennae, and the two groups may be closely related. Day-flying species of the swallowtail moths (Uraniidae) are startlingly similar to swallowtail butterflies: not only are they brightly colored, but the hindwings bear the typical papilionid "tails."

Nearly all moth larvae are herbivores, but occasionally a truly carnivorous lifestyle has arisen. Some species feed on scale insects or other homopteran bugs. The only larvae known to ambush prey are certain species of pug moths (*Eupithecia* species), a genus belonging to the enormous family Geometridae, to which the Uraniidae are related. Many geometrid larvae are cryptic and resemble twigs. Normally this gives them a measure of protection from predators, but some species of *Eupithecia* take advantage of their camouflage to actively hunt prey. By gripping the substrate with the claspers at the end of the abdomen and keeping the rest of the body erect, a *Eupithecia* caterpillar remains motionless until suitable prey comes within range: then it strikes. Although the genus is widespread, only the species on the Hawaiian Islands have adopted the predatory habit.

The moths most noted for their powerful flight are the hawkmoths (Sphingidae). Some are known to fly considerable distances, and certain species have an intercontinental distribution. One of the most widespread is the Death's-head hawkmoth (*Acherontia atropos*) so called because of the skull-like markings that decorate its thorax. The adults of this species are known to raid beehives for honey. Like many hawkmoths, they have a long proboscis. Sphingid larvae (hornworms) have a prominent horn that projects from a position near the end of the abdomen.

Among the most serious lepidopteran pests are the cutworms and the armyworms, which are larvae of the enormous family Noctuidae. The

African armyworm *Spodoptera exempta* attacks the leaves and stems of cereals, sometimes in immense swarms. Except for some of the colorful Ctenuchidae (handmaidens), all the Noctuoidea species have "ears" on the thorax. These structures basically comprise a membrane that picks up sound vibrations. Noctuoid moths probably use the ears to pick up the high-pitched, ultrasonic sounds of hunting bats, thereby permitting them to take evasive action when they hear one. Certain species of the tiger moth family (Arctiidae) actually produce ultrasonics themselves. Many arctiids are distasteful, and these auditory signals probably function to warn bats of the fact in much the same way that day-flying insects advertise distastefulness with bright colors.

Although the Noctuoidea include thousands of rather similar-looking moths, two particularly curious habits have arisen – one larval, the other adult. Processionary caterpillars such as *Thaumetopoea processionea* set off at night in a long line, one following the other, to feed. The remarkable adults of the genus *Calpe* (Noctuidae), instead of using their tongues to suck nectar, pierce fruit and, in one Asian species, *Calpe eustrigata*, actually suck blood from cattle.

The Most Beautiful Insects
BUTTERFLIES

We generally think of butterflies as day-flying insects with clubbed antennae and brightly colored wings, and moths as drab insects with variably shaped antennae that fly at night These distinctions have been used as the basis for splitting the order into Heterocera (moths) and Rhopalocera (butterflies), but this is an artificial division. Firstly, some moths, such as burnets and foresters (family Zygaenidae) and the South American Castniidae, are day-flying and brightly colored, and also have clubbed antennae. Secondly, a detailed study of structure demonstrates that many "moths" (even without those features) are in fact more closely related to butterflies than they are to other moths. It is best to regard the split as being of colloquial value rather than as a natural primary division of the Lepidoptera.

Of all insects, the colorful and highly visible butterflies have always attracted naturalists and laymen alike. The Victorian mania for cataloging the natural world was enthusiastically directed toward the butterflies, and as a result of this interest there are now over 17,700 species (including skippers) described, with more being added each year. Yet despite this vast body of knowledge, we still know relatively little about living butterflies and their early stages.

The family Papilionidae contains some of the most impressive of all insects, including the swallowtail, birdwing, and apollo butterflies, all renowned for their beauty and size. The smallest members of the family, the Southeast Asian genus *Lamproptera*, have a wingspan of around 50mm (2in), while at the other end of the scale is Queen Alexandra's birdwing (*Ornithoptera alexandrae*) whose females have a wingspan of 280mm (11in), making them the largest known butterflies. All species are brightly colored and often sequester toxins, derived from their food plants, that make

◁ **Left and below** 1 *The Queen Alexandra's birdwing (Ornithoptera alexandrae; Papilionidae) is the largest butterfly in the world. 2 When traveling long distances, this Poplar admiral (Limenitis populi; Nymphalidae) glides with the wind instead of using its usual flapping motion. 3 The Apollo butterfly (Parnassius apollo; Papilionidae) can survive at high altitudes, but is endangered. 4 Also at risk, the Hermes copper (Lycaena hermes; Lycaenidae) is restricted to San Diego and Baja California. 5 The prominent streamers on the wingtips of the Zebra butterfly (Colobura dirce; Nymphalidae) resemble antennae, distracting the attention of predators. 6 When the Kallima butterfly (Kallima inachus; Nymphalidae) folds its wings, it resembles a dead leaf. 7 The Orange sulfur (Colias eurytheme; Pieridae), a common North American species. 8 The Red admiral (Vanessa atalanta; Nymphalidae) is a widespread species whose larvae feed on nettles.*

SKIPPER BUTTERFLIES

The skippers, which form the superfamily Hesperioidea, are distinct from other butterfly families
and have been regarded by some authors as a
group apart from the "true" butterflies. Their
common name alludes to their rapid, darting
flight. They are distinguished by many structural
features, including the mothlike antennae with
tapering clubs that set them apart as "primitive"
butterflies. The link between moths and skippers
is close, and the South American skipper subfamily Megathyminae has in the past been treated
as part of the moth family Castniidae. In general,
skippers are somber-colored but with notable
exceptions such as the metallic Neotropical genus
Pyrrhopyge, which consists of iridescent blues.

Many species have larvae that feed within vegetation tubes held together with silken threads
and that pupate in loose silken cocoons. These are
both characteristics that distinguish the skippers
from the rest of the butterflies, whose larvae and
chrysalids are usually exposed on their foodplants.
In general the skippers are grass feeders, and this
may reflect the coevolution of the skippers with a
plant group that arose before the more advanced
plant families.

⬤ **Above** *The Brown-tipped skipper*
(Netrobalane canopus) *is one of a number
of African members of the Hesperiidae
family that resemble bird droppings when
their wings are splayed out.*

them distasteful or poisonous. The swallowtails occur worldwide and typically have long "tails" on their hindwings. These tails are part of an elaborate deception, for on resting adult butterflies they resemble antennae. At the base of the tail in many species is an eyespot marking that reinforces a perceived resemblance to the head end of the insect. Any attacking bird or lizard will go for its prey's head first, and thus it is common to see wild swallowtails with damaged tails, indicating that their deception has fooled a would-be predator. Other species rely upon bold black, yellow, red, and white markings to warn of their poisonous qualities. Not all that is boldly marked is poisonous, however, and some edible species specialize as mimics of truly venomous species.

The birdwings have always been highly sought after by collectors and are now protected by stringent international laws that forbid trade in these increasingly rare and beautiful insects. In many species males and females show a striking sexual dimorphism, with the bright, metallic colors of males playing a key role in courtship with the larger but somber-colored females. Birdwings are restricted to southeast Asia and Australasia, and are often inaccessible in their jungle homes except when attracted down to feed on dung or carrion.

The apollos' *Parnassius* species are the papilionid representatives in cold climates. These robust, leathery butterflies are slow, ponderous flyers that live in the mountains of northern Eurasia and America. Their rounded, pale wings are characteristically marked with red or yellow blotches that warn of their unpalatable nature. One species, *Parnassius acco*, has been found 5,640m (18,500ft) up on the slopes of Mount Everest and must take the record for the highest-living species of butterfly.

The family Pieridae has some of the most abundant and familiar butterflies worldwide, including the whites, brimstones, sulfurs, jezebels, and orange-tips so familiar to children everywhere. As the names suggest, white and yellow are dominant colors in their wing patterns, with plants of the cabbage and pea families (Brassicaceae and Fabaceae) being major food plants. The larvae of pierids are largely hairless and rely upon their cryptic coloration for defense. The males and

Left *As its name suggests,* Acraea natalica *(Nymphalidae) is a South African species. The Acraeinae to which it belongs are a pantropical subfamily noted for their bright warning coloration. This specimen is feeding on flowers.*

females of most species have some form of sexual dimorphism in their wing markings, but the most interesting differences are invisible to our eyes. Butterflies can see into the ultraviolet end of the spectrum, a faculty put to use in some species of brimstones and sulfurs, whose apparently solid yellow colors conceal a hidden pattern that enables the sexes to distinguish one another by using ultraviolet reflecting pigments. The Pieridae also contain some of the world's greatest travellers. The Large white (*Pieris brassicae*) is a well-known migrant in Europe, with adults reaching far into the north each year. The genus *Catopsilia* occurs across the tropical regions and contains several familiar migrant species that move in huge "flocks" many thousands strong.

The "blues" or Lycaenidae form a large family of small, colorful butterflies, occuring worldwide, that are loosely divided into three main groups; the blues, the hairstreaks, and the coppers. All are small insects, often with metallic or bright pigments. The hairstreaks practice the same deception as the swallowtails in having one or two pairs

Above *Members of the large family Pieridae are often among the most abundant of butterflies locally. It is common for certain members of the family to form large groups drinking on riverside sand, as in these* Phoebis *species from Argentina.*

of fine tails and associated eye spots on the hind wing. It is rare to find a wild specimen with all its tails intact, demonstrating the effectiveness of this decoy tactic against predators. Puddling occurs among adult blues and hairstreaks, with adults gathering in clouds to imbibe salts at the edge of muddy waterholes.

The larvae of many lycaenids have a symbiotic relationship with ants. Some species have developed special larval glands that exude honeydew, a sugary liquid that is extremely attractive to ants. The relationship resembles that between ants and some aphids, in that the ants in both cases provide protection from predators in return for the sweet food. In extreme cases, the relationship has evolved to such a degree that the caterpillars of some species now live within ants' nests, feeding

◀ **Left** *South American Batesian mimicry: The non-poisonous* Dismorphia amphione *(Pieridae) **1** mimics the highly poisonous* Heliconius isabellu *(Nymphalidae) **2**.*

1

2

Female Mocker swallowtail mimicking the Common tiger butterfly

Common tiger butterfly (Danaus chrysippus)

on grubs. A similar relationship has developed in another group closely related to the Lycaenidae, the metalmarks or Riodinidae. Lycaenid larvae are generally sluglike, with broad, flattened bodies that merge into their surroundings using a hair fringe. The food plants of this group include a wide range of herbs, bushes, and trees.

The final, and probably the largest, grouping of butterflies is the family Nymphalidae. The popular name for this group is the brush-footed butterflies, in reference to the reduced size of the adults' forelegs. These do not function as legs and are often covered in dense tufts of scales, rather like brushes. This family includes many groups that are best recognized by their common names, such as the browns, fritillaries, emperors, vanessids, and heliconids. The most typical examples of this group are in the subfamily Nymphalinae, which includes some of the most colorful of all butterflies, with a huge variety of wing shapes and sizes. Foremost amongst them are the *Agrias* and *Callicore* butterflies of South America, whose striking, metallic, splashed uppersides are countered by swirling rings of black, yellow, and white on their undersides. Metallic colors are common among tropical nymphalids, never more so than in the male *Morpho* butterflies, whose electric blue colors flash like strobe lights as they cruise along

Male Mocker
swallowtail butterfly

Friar butterfly
(*Amauris niavius*)

Female Mocker
swallowtail mimicking
the Friar butterfly

◖ **Left** *When a non-noxious butterfly species evolves to resemble a poisonous one, employing the defensive strategy known as Batesian mimicry, its population must remain smaller than that of the species it mimics; if it becomes more numerous, predators may come to regard the edible variety as the norm and protection may be lost. In Africa, the female of the Mocker swallowtail butterfly* (Papilio dardanus) *has avoided this constraint on population size by developing three forms (two are shown here), each mimicking a different noxious species of danaid butterfly. Males, however, retain a single pattern, since variation would reduce their chances of mating successfully.*

tracks and river banks in their South American jungle home. Sharing these tropical and neotropical jungles are the huge owl butterflies (Brassolinae), with extremely large, realistic "eyes" on their under hindwings. Among the largest South American butterflies, they use the eyes as a startle device if disturbed, reinforcing the effect with loud rustling sounds as they flap their wings.

The most impressive African nymphalids are species of *Charaxes*, whose bright patterns and multiple "tails" can lead to them being mistaken for swallowtails. These are very robust butterflies with a fondness for rotting fruit, a fact used by lepidopterists to trap specimens. A characteristic of many African savanna species is seasonal dimorphism, with different color forms occuring in the wet and dry seasons; in some species such as *Precis octavia*, the two forms are totally different in color and pattern. Africa is also the principal home of the subfamily Acraeinae, whose adults are distasteful to birds and animals – a fact that has led many groups of *Acraea* butterflies to evolve similar

◖ **Left** *This* Callicore sorana *feeding on damp ground in the Brazilian rain forest owes its colloquial name of "80" to its prominent, figurelike wing markings. Like all the brush-footed butterflies* (Nymphalidae), *it uses only two pairs of legs for walking.*

color patterns in order to reinforce the message with predators (Müllerian mimicry). These patterns are in turn mimicked by butterflies of other groups, such as the Satyridae or Pseudacraea, in order to fool predators into thinking that they also are distasteful (Batesian mimicry).

The Nymphalidae also includes groups once regarded as distinct families. The Danaidae, commonly called tiger, crow, or milkweed butterflies, are virtually all poisonous to predators. Their larvae generally feed on asclepiads, a group of plants known to contain powerful heart poisons.

The Monarch (*Danaus plexippus*) has all the characteristics of the Danaidae. Its larvae are brightly colored and toxic, adults are large, slow-flying, and warningly colored, and their bodies are very tough, to allow a bird to peck them and learn its mistake. These butterflies are regular migrants, traveling huge distances across oceans and continents, a trait that has allowed the New World Monarch to spread throughout most tropical and subtropical regions of the globe. In North America the Monarch undertakes regular movements from south to north in spring, a subsequent generation returning again in the fall. Only recently have we appreciated where these butterflies spend their winter. It has long been known that communal wintering roosts existed in selected trees in the

southern USA, but no-one had anticipated the immense congregations of these butterflies that have recently been discovered roosting in the pine forests of northern Mexico. The migratory behavior of the Monarch is especially interesting to biologists because of the species' apparent ability to return to hibernate in the same roost after traveling vast distances. Such abilities are normally only associated with higher organisms such as birds or mammals. Individual Monarchs that have been tagged have traveled 1,900km (1,200mi) in a few days, attaining average speeds of up to 130km (80mi) per day: there have been some suggestions that the mass return to communal roosts in Mexico is a recent phenomenon, and the direct result of largescale deforestation by man.

Perhaps the largest group within the Nymphalidae are the browns or satyrs, the Satyridae. These generally somber-colored butterflies are represented worldwide and are almost all grass feeders. Eye spots are taken to an extreme in this group, being used very effectively to deflect the attacks of birds and lizards. Many species are associated with the Palearctic region, where the *Erebia* species are the dominant group in alpine habitats. These small butterflies use their dark brown colors to absorb heat from the sun, giving them an advantage over other butterfly species. KP/MJS

Butterfly and Moth Superfamilies

THIS TABLE FOLLOWS COMMON USAGE IN dividing the Lepidoptera between moths and butterflies. Unless otherwise stated, all superfamilies are distributed worldwide.

MOTHS

Mandibulate archaic moths
Superfamily Micropterigoidea

1 family of c.120–150 species. The most primitive group of moths. Adults very small, with chewing mouthparts for feeding on pollen; larvae live in leaf mold and feed on detritus.

Kauri moths
Superfamily Agathiphagoidea

2 species in 1 genus (*Agathiphaga*). Australia and SW Pacific. Caterpillars feed in seeds of kauri pines (*Agathis* species); adults have not developed "tongues."

Valdivian archaic moths
Superfamily Heterobathmioidea

Around 9 species in 1 genus (*Heterobathmia*). Temperate S America. Caterpillars mine leaves of southern beech (*Nothofagus* species); adults lack developed "tongues."

Eriocranioid moths
Superfamily Eriocranioidea

About 24 species, most in family Eriocraniidae. Holarctic. Very small moths; larvae usually leaf miners.

Archaic sun moths
Superfamily Acanthopteroctetoidea

At least 4 species of small moths. Palearctic and S America. Larvae are leaf miners.

Australian archaic sun moths
Superfamily Lophocoronoidea

6 species of small moths. Australia. Adults with nonfunctional mouthparts; larvae unknown.

Archaic bell moths
Superfamily Neopseustoidea

10 named species of medium-sized moths (up to 27mm/1in wingspan). Disjunct distribution, with one group in SE Asia and the other in Australia and S America.

New Zealand primitive moths
Superfamily Mnesarchaeoidea

14 species of small moths. New Zealand. Larvae live in silken structures on damp soil and eat detritus.

Ghost and swift moths
Superfamily Hepialoidea

Around 520 species of small to large moths, with nonfunctional mouthparts; larvae often feed in roots or stems. Includes **Venus** or **Silver-spotted ghost** (*Leto venus*; Hepialidae). Unusual lekking behavior in males of some species.

Pygmy moths, eyecap moths, and relatives
Superfamily Nepticuloidea

Approximately 900 species of minute moths; larvae generally leaf miners. Includes **pygmy moths** (family Nepticulidae) and Opostegidae.

Leafcutters, yucca moths, and relatives
Superfamily Incurvarioidea

Over 590 species of small to very small moths, frequently "metallic" in coloring; larvae are often leaf miners (e.g. Heliozelidae); also includes **yucca moths** (*Tegeticula* species; Prodoxidae) and **longhorn moths** (Adelidae).

Gondwanaland moths
Superfamily Palaephatoidea

Around 60 species of small moths. S America and Australia. Larvae are leaf miners in early stages, and spin leaves together in later instars to form feeding "tents."

Trumpet leaf miners
Superfamily Tischerioidea

Over 80 species of small moths. N America, Australasia, Oceania.

Simaethistid moths
Superfamily Simaethistoidea

4 species of micromoths. Australia, China, India.

Clothes moths, bagworms, and relatives
Superfamily Tineoidea

Around 4,200 species of small or very small moths. Includes **clothes moths** (Tineidae), **bagworm moths** (Pyschidae), and several other families with leaf-mining larvae.

Leaf blotch miners
Superfamily Gracillarioidea

Over 2,000 species of small moths; larvae are leaf miners in a wide range of plants, bushes, and trees.

Ermine moths and relatives
Superfamily Yponomeutoidea

Over 1,500 species of small micromoths. Larval behavior includes leaf mining, stem boring (*Ochsenheimeria vacculella* is a serious pest of cereal crops), and communal silk web feeding (*Yponomeuta* species).

Case bearers and relatives
Superfamily Gelechioidea

Over 16,250 species of small moths, divided into 15 families; includes case bearers (Coleophoridae) and species with larvae that mine grass stems (Elachistidae).

Burnets, forester moths, and relatives
Superfamily Zygaenoidea

Over 2,600 species of small to medium-sized moths; adults often day-flying, with bright, often metallic colors to warn of toxic qualities. Larvae similarly brightly-colored, with chemical (Zygaenidae) and physical (Limacodidae) defenses. Families include **burnets** and **foresters** (family Zygaenidae) and "slug" larvae (Limacodidae).

Clearwings and relatives
Superfamily Sesioidea

Over 1,350 species of small to medium-sized moths; usually day-flying, with clear, patterned wings and body colors that mimic wasps; larvae root-feeders or borers. One family (**giant butterfly moths**: Castniidae) resemble butterflies. Includes **clearwings** (family Sesiidae).

Carpenter worms and relatives
Superfamily Cossoidea

A group of around 680 species of small to very large moths (up to 236mm/9in wingspan in genus *Endoxyla*); larvae are stem- or wood-borers, such as the **Goat moth** (*Cossus*). Includes **carpenters** (family Cossidae).

Leaf roller moths
Superfamily Tortricoidea

Over 6,200 species of small to medium-sized moths; larvae mostly internal feeders in stems, or inside leaf tubes held together by silk.

Metalmark moths
Superfamily Choreutoidea

Over 400 species of small moths, often with metallic markings on the forewing. Larvae often pests of fruit trees (*Choreutis* species).

False burnet moths
Superfamily Urodoidea

Over 60 species; adults small to medium-sized micromoths; larvae known to feed freely on trees.

Galacticoid moths
Superfamily Galacticoidea

Around 17 species of small moths, closely related to the Urodoidea; larvae live in community silken webs on plants of the pea family (Fabaceae).

Bristle-legged moths
Superfamily Schreckensteinioidea

8 species of small moths; larvae feed on a range of herbs.

Fruitworm moths
Superfamily Copromorphoidea

Over 310 species of small moths, whose larvae are typically internal feeders in seeds, fruits, shoots, or galls; most use tree species as host plants.

Fringe-tufted moths
Superfamily Epermenioidea

Over 80 species of small, narrow-winged moths, closely related to fruitworm moths; larvae feed on herbaceous plants.

Plume moths
Superfamily Pterophoroidea

Around 1,000 species of small moths, characterized by their strange, featherlike, divided wings; a few families have "normal" wings (Macropiratinae); group includes species with external and internal feeding larvae.

Many-plumed moths
Superfamily Alucitoidea

Around 150 species of small moths with deeply divided wings, closely related to the plume moths. Larvae generally borers of buds, seeds, and fruits, with some species creating galls.

Imma moths
Superfamily Immoidea

Over 245 species of small to medium-sized moths. Larvae are external feeders on a range of plants, including conifers in pantropical regions.

European gold moths
Superfamily Axioidea

6 named species of medium, brightly-colored, gold-blotched moths in 1 family (Axiidae). N Africa–Mediterranean region.

Teak moths
Superfamily Hyblaeoidea

Around 18 species of medium-sized, robust moths. African and Asian tropics. Larvae feed openly or in silken leaf "tents" on a range of plants; *Hyblaea puera* is regarded as a pest of several species of tropical hardwood trees.

Picture-winged leaf moths
Superfamily Thyridoidea

Over 1,000 species of medium to large moths; adults generally well-patterned and some species resemble dead leaves; larvae feed within stems or inside leaf "tents" on a range of plant families.

Picture-winged leaf moths
Superfamily Whalleyanoidea

2 species of medium-sized moths, closely related to Thyridoidea. Madagascar. Larvae unknown.

Pyraloids and plume moths
Superfamily Pyraloidea

Over 16,000 named species, with possibly the same number undescribed. Adults with tympanic "ears" on their abdomen; generally small to medium-sized; larvae typically feed inside, or on, plant tissues in a wide range of ways, but a few are scavengers.

Sack bearer moths
Superfamily Mimallonoidea

Some 200 species of stout, medium to large moths; larvae, often brightly colored, move from living within folded leaf "tents" to constructing portable cases of leaf fragments and silk when in later instars.

Lappet moths
Superfamily Lasiocampoidea

Over 1,600 species of small to large dark-colored moths with broad wings and large, "furry" bodies; males of some species are day-flying; larvae large and often hairy, or with "lappets" of strong bristles along their segments.

Geometrid moths
Superfamily Geometroidea

Over 20,500 medium to large species; includes wide range of color forms and wing shapes, from dull and cryptically colored to very bright with "tails" (Uraniidae). Larvae classically have strong, "looping" gait, and often bear a strong resemblance to twigs. Includes **swallowtail moths** (family Uraniidae), **pug moths** (genus Eupithecia).

Hook tips
Superfamily Drepanoidea

675 species closely related to the Geometroidae; adults are small to large, and include some colorful, day-flying species; common name derived from the recurved wing tip; larvae external, or concealed feeders within leaf "tents."

Silkworms, emperors, and relatives
Superfamily Bombycoidea

Over 3,500 species of medium to very large moths (including *Attacus atlas*, one of the largest of all moths); larvae free-feeding, sometimes gregarious; pupa often within a cocoon involving silk or in a loose, silk-lined subsoil cell. Families, genera, and species include **emperor moths** (family Saturniidae), **hawkmoths** (family Sphingidae), **hummingbird hawkmoths** (genus *Macroglossum*), **Death's-head hawkmoth** (*Acherontia atropos*), **Giant atlas moth** (*Attacus atlas*), **Silkworm moth** (*Bombyx mori*), **European emperor moth** (*Pavonia pavonia*), and the critically endangered **Prairie sphinx moth** (*Euproserpinus wiesti*).

Old World butterfly moths
Superfamily Calliduloidea

60 species of medium to large moths, often day-flying and resembling butterflies. Oriental regions and Madagascar. Known larvae include species feeding on ferns.

American butterfly moths
Superfamily Hedyloidea

About 40 species in 1 family (Hedylidae). C and S America. Adults small and mainly nocturnal; closely related to butterflies.

Noctuid moths
Superfamily Noctuoidea

The largest group of moths, with over 70,000 species; adults small to large, and extremely varied in shape, color, and ecology. Key characteristic is the tympanal organs on the adult thorax; this is an "ear" used to detect ultrasound from hunting bats. Larvae diverse in form and ecology, often polyphagous. Families and species include **prominent moths** (family Notodontidae), **tiger moths** (Arctiidae), **owlet moths** (Noctuidae), **tussock moths** (Lymantriidae), **handmaidens** (Ctenuchidae), **Giant agrippa moth** (*Thysania agrippina*), **Processionary caterpillar** (*Thaumetopoea processionea*).

BUTTERFLIES

The five families of butterflies are grouped in two superfamilies, the Hesperioidea and the Papilionoidea.

Skippers
Superfamily Hesperioidea

1 family (Hesperiidae). About 3,500 species of small to medium-sized butterflies with stout bodies, narrow, sharp-angled wings, and pointed antennae; flight short, darting; some have short "tails;" wings often have metallic markings. Subfamilies include the Hesperiinae (over 2,000 species), Pyrginae (1,000 species), Heteropterinae (150 species), Pyrrhopyginae (150 species in the neotropics), Coeliadinae (75 species in Africa, India to Australia), and Trapezitinae (60 species in Australiasia). Larvae generally live in leaf "tents" on grasses and related plant groups. The "worms" in bottles of mescal are larvae of *Megathymus* species.

"True" Butterflies
Superfamily Papilionoidea

More than 13,600 species in 4 families (Papilionidae, Pieridae, Lycaenidae, and Nymphalidae).

Swallowtails and relatives
Family Papilionidae
About 600 species. Includes the swallowtails (550 species, including *Papilio dardanus*, *P. machaon*, and *P. polyxenes*, all of the subfamily Papilioninae); the apollos and festoons (54–76 species, including the *Parnassius* species of the subfamily Parnassiinae); and a monotypic group consisting of the rare Mexican species *Baronia brevicornis*. Medium to large, conspicuous and powerful fliers, usually with large "tails" and bright markings. Species include **Queen Alexandra's birdwing** (*Ornithoptera alexandrae*), the largest known butterfly, and the endangered **Sri Lankan rose** (*Atrophaneura jophon*).

Whites, sulfurs, and relatives
Family Pieridae
About 1,000 species. Includes the **whites** and **jezebels** (700 species in the subfamily Pierinae), including *Pieris* species, among them the **Large white** (*P. brassicae*); the **sulfurs** and **yellows** (250 species in the subfamily Coliadinae), including *Colias* species; the **whites** of the neotropics (about 100 species in the subfamily Dismorphinae); and the African subfamily Pseudopontiinae, with just a single species, *Pseudopontia paradoxa*. Medium-sized; wing ground color usually white or yellow, some very colorful; many are migrants.

Brush-footed butterflies
Family Nymphalidae
About 6,000 species, roughly one-third of all the butterflies. This family is currently recognized as containing 10 subfamilies: the Nymphalinae (about 350 species), including the **tortoiseshells** (*Aglais* species) and the **Checkerspot** (*Euphydryas editha*), as well as the S American *Agrias*, *Morpho*, and *Callicore* species; the Brassolinae (neotropics), including the **owl butterflies** (*Caligo* species); the Satyrinae (the largest subfamily, with 2,400 species), with **browns** and **satyrs** and the Palaeacrtic *Erebia* genus; the Libytheinae (12 species); the Heliconiinae (400 species), including both the typical heliconids of S America, some fritillaries of northern temperate regions, and the acraeids of Africa; the Limenitinae (1,000 species), including the **Viceroy butterfly** (*Limenitis archippus*); the Charaxinae (400 species), a mainly African group of robust butterflies; the Apaturinae (430 species), including the **European purple emperor** (*Apatura iris*); the Morphinae (230 species), in New World tropical regions and the Asian/Australasian tropics; the Calinaginae (8 species), restricted to the Far East; the Danainae (470 species), including the **Monarch** (*Danaus plexippus*) and **Queen** (*D. gilippus*) butterflies, the neotropical **glasswing butterflies**, and the **tiger**, **crow**, and **milkweed butterflies**. Predominately N temperate, but also well represented in the tropics. Medium to large in size, and very colorful; lifestyles varied, but all with forelegs modified with brush-like hairs acting as chemoreceptors.

Blues, metalmarks, and hairstreaks
Family Lycaenidae
Over 6,000 species, currently classified in 5 subfamilies: the Lycaeninae (4,000 species), which includes the **blues** (Polyommatini, including the endangered **Piedmont anomalous blue**, *Polyommatus humedasae*, and the **Amaryllis azure butterfly**, *Ogyris amarillis*), **hairstreaks** (genus *Thecla*), and **coppers** (genus *Lycaena*); the Riodininae (1,250 species), called **metalmarks** in reference to the metallic spots and dashes in their patterns; the Poritiinae (530 species), "blues" of Africa and China; the Miletinae (150 species) of the Old World tropics, whose larvae eat aphids; and the Curetinae (18 species) of the Far East. The lycaenids are typically small and predominantly tropical, often in association with forest trees; many with metallic blue wing colors; larvae with varied habits, including aphid eating, lichen eating, and symbiosis with ants.

PREDATORS BEWARE!

The defenses of caterpillars

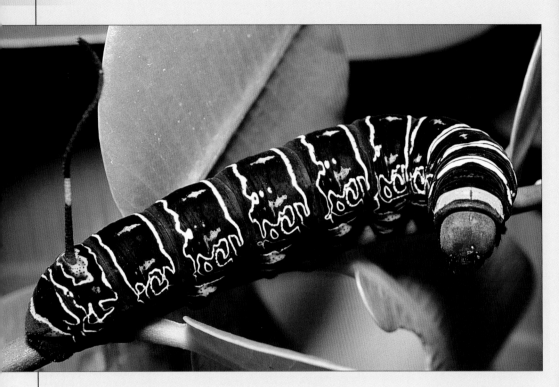

CATERPILLARS ARE VULNERABLE. THEY ARE NEARLY always slow-moving, are often exposed, and present an often readily available plump morsel to birds and other predators. It is not surprising, therefore, that they have developed a wide range of defenses.

Many of the small species gain indirect protection from their concealed lives within roots, stems, galls, seeds, and other plant tissue. Some large species similarly benefit from the shelter they choose; for example caterpillars of the ghost and swift moths (family Hepialidae) live in tree trunks or roots, while the larvae of carpenter moths (Cossidae) bore into tree trunks.

The "bagworms" (family Psychidae) construct cases in which larvae live (along with the usually wingless adult females). The bags are made of silk to which the larvae stick grains of sand, twigs, or leaves. In some of the larger species, such as those in the African genus *Eumeta*, the bags are extremely tough and difficult to tear apart, giving the vulnerable larvae considerable protection. The larvae of many species of the family Yponomeutidae live colonially, concealed in the large thick silken webs which they spin.

Camouflage is very common among animals of all kinds, and lepidopterans are certainly no exception to the rule. Some of the most remarkable examples occur among the "looper" caterpillars of the Geometroidea superfamily, many of which uncannily resemble the twigs of the plants on which they feed. The ability to remain motionless

◑ **Above** *Set against a matt-black background, the swirling white doodle-style pattern sported by this* Isognathus caricae *hawk moth caterpillar (Sphingidae) from Brazil is a particularly effective use of black-and-white as a "warning" color.*

◐ **Right** *Many caterpillars combine bright warning colors with an array of protective spikes, spines, and hairs that are often capable of inflicting a painful and long-lasting sting. For additional protection, such caterpillars often form defensive aggregations, as seen here in these moth larvae (Saturniidae).*

while anchored only by the hind claspers perfects the twiglike effect.

Other caterpillars resemble bird droppings, among them the early larval stages (instars) of the swallowtail butterfly *Papilio machaon*, which have a white patch in the middle of an otherwise black body. The same disguise is employed by the early instars of the Alder moth.

Some insects protect themselves from predators by looking alarming. The caterpillar of the Elephant hawkmoth bears "eye-spots" on its body. When disturbed, it draws in its head, suddenly exposing the spots. There is some evidence that this kind of behavior may startle predators into leaving the insect well alone.

Certain caterpillars combine this so-called "flash" coloration with an unpleasant odor. The larva of the European Puss moth not only assumes a threatening posture but is also capable of ejecting a strong irritant (formic acid) from glands on

its thorax. The battery of defenses is completed by a pair of bright red filaments that can be extruded from the "tails" at the end of the abdomen and waved about. These are believed to deter approaches from parasitic hymenopterans.

Those who have unwittingly handled certain hairy caterpillars will know that they can cause unpleasant skin rashes. Sometimes symptoms can be very severe and acute. Indeed, a clinical term – "erucism" – has been coined for the adverse effects of the lepidopteran caterpillars on humans. The hairs that are responsible for such reactions are called urticating hairs. There are two main kinds: those that have a poison gland at their base and discharge venom into an aggressor, and those that are non-poisonous but barbed and extremely irritating. In the Yellowtail moth, there are said to be 2 million urticating hairs on a single last-stage caterpillar. The moth belongs to the family Lymantriidae (tussock moths), a group noted for

Left When molested, the caterpillars of many hawk moths (Sphingidae) display prominent eyelike markings and begin swishing their head from side to side. This display, which is remarkably snakelike, presumably serves to intimidate and thwart smaller and more nervous predators.

its hairy caterpillars. The caterpillar of the Venezuelan emperor moth (*Lonomia achelous*) can inject a powerful anti-coagulant, which may result in serious hemorrhage.

The "slug" caterpillars of the family Limacodidae often bear tufts of sharp, stinging spines, sometimes loaded with toxic compounds. The name "slug" refers to both their squat, broad shape and their undulating or gliding motion. Contact with the spines may cause acute pain and swelling. Limacodid caterpillars are generally green, but are often bedecked with bright colors, probably as a warning to potential predators.

There is little value in being toxic or distasteful if the fact is not advertised. If a predator does not learn to associate particular colors with unpleasantness, the prey, albeit toxic or distasteful, may suffer fatal damage while the predator finds out. Hence many larvae have developed warning colors. The caterpillars of the burnet moths are black and yellow – two of nature's most widespread warning colors. Cyanide compounds have been found in the tissues of these larvae.

Among the butterflies, the predominantly black and yellow caterpillars of the Danainae (to which the migratory Monarch belongs) store heart-toxins derived from their food plants – for instance milkweed (*Asclepias*) – and pass them on to the adult.

The caterpillars of swallowtail butterflies bear a forked process (the osmeterium) on the thorax that releases a pungent odor when everted. It is said to be used to defend the caterpillars particularly from the attention of parasitic insects. MJS

A KALEIDOSCOPE OF COLORS

How butterfly wings retain their brilliant tints and patterns

FEW GROUPS OF ANIMALS CAN RIVAL THE brilliant colors found in the wings of butterflies and moths. Each species has a unique combination of pattern; some even have more than one, with differences between broods and between the sexes. The fact that these colors generally do not fade after death has made the Lepidoptera one of the best-studied insect groups; butterfly collecting dates back to the early 1500s, when Conrad Gestner, a Swiss zoologist, established a zoological museum. The oldest existing specimen is of a Bath white (*Pontia daplidice*) caught in 1702, and its impressive state of conservation suggests that dried insects can be preserved with their original colors almost indefinitely.

These colors and patterns are directed at two audiences. The first is members of the same species, either to challenge a rival male or to impress a potential mate. In this respect humans are at a distinct disadvantage to the insects themselves, in that our eyesight is restricted to colors in the indigo to red section of the spectrum; Lepidoptera and some other insect orders, in contrast, can see into the ultraviolet, and so can distinguish "colors" that are outside our visual range.

The second audience is the horde of animals that attack and eat Lepidoptera. For this target group, the colors and patterns send signals about distastefulness, or else help to camouflage the insect from vertebrate predators.

The secret of the stability of lepidopteran scale color is that the scales either contain pigments that are permanent or else have a microscopic surface structure that produces interference hues. Such durability stands in stark contrast to the ephemeral colors of insect orders such at the dragonflies (Odonata), whose brilliant patterns fade after death. The most common pigment is melanin, which produces the black color in all insects and is derived from a chemical released to harden the skin, or cuticle, of insects after a molt; this is the same pigment that gives humans black hair and dark skin. Other pigments are derived from the larva's foodplants or are produced by the caterpillars themselves.

Plant pigments, an obvious source of colorings, are absorbed by the caterpillars and passed on to the adults. Carotenoids – red, yellow, and orange plant pigments – are commonly used by butterflies and moths, often in combination with melanin, to produce browns and deeper shades. Xanthophylls produce bright yellow colors. The anthocyanins, responsible for blue, purple, and scarlet in flowers, can give these same shades in wing scales. Finally, grasses contain large amounts of flavones, which produce colors ranging from ivory through to

🔺 Above *The shimmering blues of butterflies such as this* Lasaia agesilas *metalmark (Riodinidae) from Brazil are structural in origin. They are created by microscopic ridges on the surface of the scales.*

🔻 Right *This* Acraea zitja *(Acraeidae) from Madagascar displays the kind of rich orange coloration that is produced by pigmentation. This species is chemically defended, so the bright uniform is aimed at an audience of potential enemies.*

yellow. These colors are used by species whose larvae feed on grasses, such as the European marbled white (*Melanargia galathea*), which can turn from pale to bright yellow on exposure to ammonia. The chemical interacts with flavone pigments to temporarily modify the color.

Internally-produced pigments made from amino acids, the building blocks of proteins, are also commonly put to use in the Lepidoptera. Ommochromes are responsible for the browns and reds familiar in nymphalid butterflies. A second group of pigments, called pterines, are likewise common in the Pieridae, producing their white and yellow coloration.

These basic pigments can also be used to create an illusion of color: the green, dappled coloring of the underside of orange-tips of the genus *Anthocaris* is created by combining yellow scales over a background of black scales – the same optical device used to create colors in printing or on computer screens, where each pixel can have a different tone. Similarly, a black-scaled edge to a pale eye spot can give emphasis to a wing pattern, or even create an impression of three-dimensional depth on a flat wing.

The wings of some butterflies incorporate pigments and patterns that are invisible to our eyes, and presumably also to those of many potential predators. These patterns reflect ultraviolet light,

which is invisible to vertebrates but visible to insect eyes, enabling members of the same species to communicate visually without giving any clues to vertebrate predators. Many apparently plain white or yellow pierids in fact bear distinct ultraviolet patterns that enable the two sexes to recognize one another.

The most spectacular colors of all are the shimmering blues, violets, and reds present across many families of Lepidoptera. These colors disappear if the scales are wetted with a liquid, reappearing once the liquid evaporates. They are structural colors, created by microscopic ridges on the scales' surface and on fine layers of cuticle underneath. These structures create iridescent colors that change according to the angle of view. The ridges and layers combined within the scales of the *Morpho* butterflies interfere with light rays, which strike them to create reflection patterns rich in blue and ultraviolet light; a similar effect can be seen by looking across a compact disc, where light is refracted from the tiny grooves and ridges. Each species has a subtly different hue, due to the microscopic differences in scale structure. While this spectacular electric coloration is obvious to us – flying males of *Morpho* species are visible even from low-flying aircraft – the effect on other males is believed to be far greater. The reflected light is rich in the ultraviolet, and the eyes of *Morpho* are very sensitive to this wavelength; the butterflies probably see the mirrors of blue as intense, stroboscopic flashes of light.

A less well-known use of wing color is in the regulation of body temperature by basking. Dark pigments absorb radiant heat from the sun more efficiently than pale colors, and therefore accelerate the warming up of a butterfly's body before flight. In butterflies such as the clouded yellows (*Colias* species) and some whites (*Pieris* species), the amount of dark pigment (melanin) in the pattern varies with season, altitude, and latitude. The cooler the environment, the darker the pattern, so that the insect's mobility is enhanced.

This effect is helped by the chemical process that creates the melanin; in cold conditions, the process of cuticle hardening is slower and more melanin is produced than in warmer conditions. The resulting color change has been graphically demonstrated by experiments exposing chrysalids to cool temperatures that have created spectacular, dark-patterned varieties of many species. In nature things are rarely what they seem, however, and at least one tropical butterfly with black wings has been shown to avoid overheating by wingscale pigments that, although black in appearance, in fact do not absorb infrared rays.   KP

Wasps, Ants, and Bees

WASPS, ANTS, AND BEES

Class: Insecta

Subclass: Pterygota

Order: Hymenoptera

Probably at least 280,000 species (120,000 described) in about 106 families, grouped into two suborders: Symphyta and Apocrita.

Distribution All continents except Antarctica

Size Length 0.17–50mm (0.007–2in)

Features Highly specialized insects with chewing mouthparts and 4 membranous wings, coupled by a row of hooks called hamuli; forewings larger than hindwings.

Life cycle Males haploid (derived from unfertilized eggs). Wings develop internally (endopterygotous), metamorphosis complete. Larvae caterpillarlike in externally feeding Symphyta, legless maggots in Apocrita.

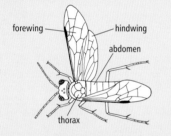

forewing — hindwing — abdomen — thorax

SAWFLIES AND WOOD WASPS Suborder Symphyta Some 10,000 species in 14 families. Worldwide except Antarctica. Most primitive of living hymenopterans; wing venation complex, generalized; abdomen broadly attached to thorax (no "wasp waist"); ovipositor usually sawlike for inserting eggs in plant tissue. Larvae (except in wood borers) have segmented legs on thorax and abdomen and segmented labial and maxillary palps.

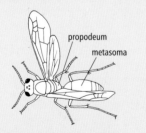

propodeum — metasoma

PARASITIC WASPS, WASPS, ANTS, BEES
Suborder Apocrita
Some 110,000 species described in about 92 families. First abdominal segment incorporated into rear of thorax to form propodeum; marked "wasp waist" constriction between propodeum and rest of abdomen, which forms metasoma. Larvae legless. **Conservation status:** 3 ant species, including the Australian ant (*Nothomyrmecia macrops*) and the Sri Lankan relict ant (*Aneuretus simoni*) are currently listed as Critically Endangered; a further 142 are Vulnerable.

See superfamilies table ▷

THE UBIQUITOUS HYMENOPTERA ARE HIGHLY *specialized insects second only to the beetles in numbers of species; many thousands more probably remain to be discovered, especially among the parasitic wasps. Their tremendous diversity reflects the order's ecological importance. In the temperate forests of North America, ants recycle as many soil nutrients as earthworms do. In tropical South America the biomass of ants, together with termites, exceeds that of all other animals put together, including capybaras, tapirs, and people! The parasitic wasps can exert tremendous pressure on their insect host populations, and many species are used as biological control agents against pests. As pollinators, the Hymenoptera (especially bees) play a vital, economically important role in maintaining much of the earth's vegetation.*

The order Hymenoptera divides into two suborders. One, the Symphyta, is made up of sawflies and wood wasps, both sometimes refered to as horntails. The other consists of the wasp-waisted Apocrita, and it too splits into two parts. One division, the Parasitica, is mainly composed of the parasitic wasps; the other, the Aculeata, includes the "true" wasps, ants, and bees, in which the ovipositor is modified as a sting, having lost its egg-laying function.

How the Wasp Waist Developed
EVOLUTION

The oldest known fossil hymenopterans are sawflies of the superfamily Xyeloidea, dating from the Triassic period 248–205 million years ago. The order with which hymenopterans share the most recent common ancestor is that of the scorpionflies (Mecoptera), dating from the Permian, 295–248 million years ago, by which time the Hymenoptera must also have been established.

The bodyplan of sawflies has persisted for at least 248 million years. By the Jurassic (205–144 million years ago), however, a major new evolutionary trend had appeared. It is from this period that the first fossils of the "wasp-waisted" Apocrita are known. Instead of the abdomen being broadly attached at its base to the thorax, in these insects the first abdominal segment is incorporated into the thorax to form the propodeum, and the latter is separated from the apparent first abdominal segment by a highly flexible hinged joint. The flexibility allowed by the development of the wasp waist is still a vital part of apocritan lifestyles; it allows precise movement in egg-laying female

parasitic wasps, and permits solitary hunting wasps and bees to turn around in the confined spaces of the nest burrow.

The Apocrita show two other structural advances over the sawflies. The mouthparts are retractable into the mouth cavity, and the forelegs are armed with a neat device for grooming the antennae. In the larvae, moreover, the mid- and hindgut are not united until the larval stage, thus delaying defecation until just before pupation. By this means the larvae avoid fouling their food, an adaptation of obvious importance for parasites living in their food and for bee larvae feeding in their natal cells on a mixture of pollen and nectar.

In the Jurassic period and the Cretaceous (144–65 million years ago), the wasp-waisted Apocrita diversified into the Parasitica, a vast assemblage of wasps. In some forms (the Aculeata) the egg-laying function of the ovipositor was lost, to be replaced by the evolution of the sting, with which hunting wasps paralyze their prey by injecting venom. Also in the Cretaceous flowering plants began to diversify, providing new sources of food. Some hunting wasps gave up preying on insects in favour of pollen and nectar as food for their larvae, evolving a range of structures for handling and transporting the new food. So flowering plants and bees invented each other.

Boring Holes for Eggs
SAWFLIES AND WOOD WASPS

Sawflies (suborder Symphyta) owe their name to the sawlike blades of the egg-laying tube (the ovipositor) with which the females insert eggs into plant tissues. In the wood wasps, whose larvae feed inside dead or dying wood, the ovipositor is a tough drilling tool that protrudes from the apex of the abdomen, and insects of the family Siricidae are therefore often called horntails (the ovipositor sometimes being mistaken for a sting).

In most sawfly species, the short-lived adults are active in spring and early summer. Some species appear not to feed, but most visit flowers for nectar and some eat small insects. Females lay eggs in leaves, stems, or wood, although some members of the family Pamphilidae glue their eggs onto the surfaces of leaves, which the larvae of some species roll up and live inside.

▷ **Right** *A queen paper wasp* (Polistes dorsalis; *Vespidae) from Mexico exhibits the characteristic "wasp waist". The nest she is attending to was built in the spring by several females and is made from wood pulp and saliva. The short stalk bearing a single horizontal comb has a shiny black ant-repellent coating.*

◁ **Left** Themos olfersii *(Argidae)* from Brazil is unusual among sawflies in staying to guard her eggs. These are exceptionally large, and are deposited in a group on the leaf, rather than within it.

The larvae of most sawflies resemble the caterpillars of moths and butterflies. They differ in having only one pair of simple eyes (ocelli) and more than five pairs of abdominal prolegs. Those that feed internally, such as the larvae of wood wasps, have only vestiges of thoracic legs and resemble the larvae of other hymenopterans. Wood-feeding larvae may take several years to complete development, but the external, leaf-eating species take about two weeks. The eggs of some species such as *Pontania* induce tumorous growths (galls) in the host leaf, and the larvae feed inside these.

One sawfly family, the Orussidae, has abandoned plant feeding. Instead, the larvae are internal parasites of wood-boring beetle larvae. It is also thought that some species feed on the fungal-infected larval feces of boring beetles.

Sawflies often achieve pest status in dense, single-species stands (monocultures) of forest trees. The European Pine sawfly is a major problem in young plantations, where the larvae may completely strip the trees of needles. The wood wasp *Urocerus gigas* is a pest of spruce, the larvae transmitting a fungus that may eventually kill the tree. Some sawflies, however, are allies rather than enemies of man. *Uncona acaenae*, for instance, has been introduced into New Zealand from Chile to control a pernicious weed of the rose family, *Acaena*, which was an accidental introduction. CO'T

Killer Larvae

PARASITIC WASPS

Most parasitic wasps are neither parasitic nor predatory. Unlike true parasites, the larval stages invariably kill the host on which they feed, and unlike predators they require only one host ("prey") individual for their complete development. Members of the division Parasitica are therefore more accurately referred to as "parasitoids."

The adult female forages for hosts. Using her ovipositor, she deposits eggs either in or on the host, or nearby. Thereafter, she displays no further involvement with either offspring or host. After hatching, the larvae begin feeding, but cause little damage. Toward the end of their development, however, they feed extensively on host tissues, causing the host to die. The larvae finally pupate, either within or outside the host's remains.

Endoparasitoids develop within the host, whereas ectoparasitoids develop externally, feeding through a lesion produced by the larva in the host's cuticle. Ectoparasitoids are associated particularly with hosts that live in concealed situations, such as leaf mines or galls. A distinction is

also made between those parasitoids that develop singly in hosts (solitary) and those that develop in groups (gregarious).

Some endoparasitoids complete their development in the host stage that was originally attacked – that is, they utilize a nongrowing host, such as the egg or pupa – whereas others (egg–larval, egg–pupal, larval–pupal, and larval–adult parasitoids) use a growing host, completing their development in a later stage. In contrast, most ectoparasitoids complete their development on the stage originally attacked, because the female parasitoid paralyzes the host when she lays her egg, and also because the larvae grow very rapidly.

Parasitoids tend to be host-species specific. For example, among ichneumon flies that attack western Palearctic aphids, about half the parasitoid species are restricted to one aphid species, while most of the remainder will only attack closely related species that belong to a single genus or subfamily. By contrast, many other species of ichneumon fly, along with some chalcid wasps, attack a diverse array of unrelated hosts in a distinct microhabitat – they are microhabitat- or "niche"-specific.

Female parasitoids forage for hosts in a two-phase search, first for the host's habitat and then for the host itself. In both phases, they respond to two sorts of stimuli: "attractant" stimuli, which cause them to orient to host-containing areas (patches), and "arrestant" stimuli, which bring

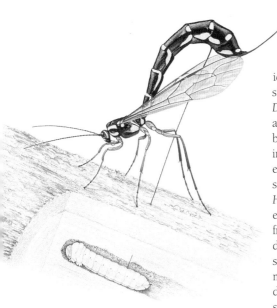

⏶ Above *Alerted by the smell of droppings contaminated with symbiotic fungi, this female ichneumon wasp,* Rhyssa *species (Ichneumonidae), has found a wood wasp larva on which to lay an egg.*

⏵ Right *Some wasps act mainly as "kleptoparasites." The larvae of this minuscule* Eurytoma brunniventris *wasp (Eurytomidae) ovipositing in a pea gall on oak will mainly feed on the nutritious tissues of the gall, as well as on its occupants, larvae of the wasp* Cynips divisa *(Cynipidae).*

⏷ Below *Having fed inside this moth caterpillar, at least 50 parasitic wasp larvae (Braconidae) have burst out to spin white cocoons and pupate on the host's skin. This is the final phase of metamorphosis, when the larvae transform into adults. The caterpillar often dies before adult wasps emerge from their cocoons.*

about a reduction in the distance or area searched within a patch.

Some "attractant" stimuli emanate from the host's food medium. Parasitoids such as the ichneumon flies *Diadromus pulchellus*, which parasitizes the Leek moth (*Acrolepia assectella*), and *Diaeretiella rapae*, which attacks the Cabbage aphid (*Brevicoryne brassicae*), are initially attracted by odors from the host's food plant (mustard oils in the case of *Diaeretiella*). Feeding by insects, especially on plants, produces chemical or visual stimuli that attract parasitoids. The chalcid wasp *Heydenia unica* of the family Pteromalidae, for example, responds to a volatile terpene released from conifers as a result of feeding by its host, the dark beetle *Dendroctonus frontalis*. Some attractant stimuli arise directly from the host itself. These are mostly chemicals, such as those released through defecation, molting, or feeding (for instance, in saliva). Parasitoids are also attracted by host aggregation and sex pheromones.

"Arrestant" stimuli are visual, tactile, or chemical in nature. Walking parasitoids commonly concentrate their search in response to chemicals deposited by hosts. Being of low volatility, these "contact chemicals" cause parasitoids to respond only upon contact. For example, when a female ichneumon fly of the *Venturia canescens* species meets a deposit of mandibular gland secretion from larvae of the meal moth *Plodia interpunctella*, she stops and begins tapping the tips of her antennae rapidly on the substrate (usually milled and stored grain products). She then moves over the patch at a reduced walking speed, occasionally stopping to probe with her ovipositor. When she contacts the edge of the patch, she turns back sharply into the secretion-contaminated area.

Once a host has been located, the female parasitoid examines it in order to identify its species and stage of development, performing a series of "tests," usually with her antennae and ovipositor, which bear sense organs of various kinds. *Telenomus heliothidis*, of the family Scelionidae, for example, recognizes the eggs of its host, the moth *Heliothis virescens*, by means of a chemical substance present on their surfaces. The substance is derived from the accessory gland of the female moth's reproductive organs. Host eggs that lack this substance are not attacked by *Telenomus*, whereas glass beads resembling the eggs and coated with accessory gland material stimulate the female parasitoid to drill with her ovipositor.

The final stimuli for the release of eggs are received when the female probes the host with her ovipositor. At this point, egg laying may depend on whether or not the host is already parasitized. If a solitary parasitoid lays more than one egg, the excess progeny will die as a result of competition. Larvae of many species eliminate rivals with their mandibles. In gregarious species, if more eggs are deposited than the host can support, some or all of the brood will perish, or the larvae will develop

into undersized adults. Not surprisingly, superparasitism – egg laying into an already parasitized host – is usually avoided.

The number of eggs produced per parasitoid female may vary considerably from species to species, even within the same family. Such differences can be viewed as adaptations to the abundance and distribution of hosts. Parasitoids that attack the advanced larval or pupal stages of the host tend to carry fewer eggs than those that attack its early stages. Parasitoids of concealed hosts – for example, those found in mines, tunnels, or silk webbing – likewise tend to be less fecund than those attacking exposed hosts.

Parasitic wasps belonging to the families Eucharitidae, Perilampidae, and Trigonalidae deposit their eggs on foliage, often at some distance from the host. In the former two families, the first-stage larvae (planidia) remain near the site where the eggs were laid, awaiting the arrival of a potential host. Eucharitid planidia attach themselves to foraging worker ants, and are then carried to the ants' nest, where they transfer to the ants' offspring. In the Trigonalidae, the eggs have to be eaten by a caterpillar host before they hatch. In these parasitoids, the chances of first-stage larvae becoming established in hosts are very low. Females therefore tend to lay very large numbers of eggs during their lifetime. Total egg production in the Eucharitidae ranges from 1,000 per female in some species to 15,000 in others. One female was observed to lay 10,000 eggs in six hours!

Some female parasitic wasps emerge from the pupa with their full complement of eggs, while other species are able to produce new eggs during their adult life, provided that they can obtain

suitable food, such as host body fluids or even honeydew and nectar. Some parasitoids of hosts concealed in, for example, plant tissues, cocoons, or puparia, being unable to reach the host directly with their mouthparts, construct a special feeding tube. *Pteromalus semotus* (family Pteromalidae) stings its host, the larva of the grain moth *Sitotroga cerealella*, then withdraws its ovipositor until only the tip protrudes within the cavity surrounding the larva in the grain. A clear, viscous fluid oozes from the ovipositor and is molded, before hardening, into a tube by movements of the ovipositor. When the tube linking the puncture in the cuticle to the exterior is complete, the ovipositor is reinserted into the original puncture and then carefully withdrawn. The female then applies her mouthparts and imbibes the fluids, which pass up the tube by capillary action. Many parasitoids, in the absence of hosts and suitable food, are able to resorb eggs. The eggs' energy and materials can then be used for adult maintenance.

Parasitic wasps usually inject glandular secretions (venoms) into their hosts during or before oviposition. Often these venoms, particularly those produced by ectoparasitoids, paralyze the host, enabling the female to lay eggs and feed unhindered. The venoms of many endoparasitoids, by contrast, do not cause paralysis, but they may nevertheless have major effects on host physiology. Endoparasitoids of growing hosts commonly cause alterations in their host's condition – in food consumption rate, growth rate, development, reproduction (for example, parasitic castration), morphology, behavior, respiration, and other physiological processes. Symbiotic,

◗ *Right* The parasitic wasp Cotesia aglomerata (Braconidae) is a naturally occurring parasite of the destructive Cabbage white butterfly (Pieris brassicae). Here, a newly emerged adult wasp stands on its cocoon, on the caterpillar of its host species.

AGENTS OF BIOLOGICAL CONTROL

The accidental introduction of an insect species into a new geographical region where its natural enemies are not present may result in its becoming a serious pest. Many parasitoid wasps are used in biological control programs that involve the importation and release of these natural enemies of pest insects in an attempt to reduce pest numbers and the ensuing crop damage.

Such a program begins with a search for suitable parasitoid species in the pest's native country. The parasitoids are imported and then investigated under quarantine conditions, with particular attention paid to their life cycles and reproductive and searching behavior, so that their mortality effects upon host populations can be predicted. If the introduction of more than one species is contemplated, competitive interactions between them are also studied. Great care is taken not to introduce hyperparasitoids, as they would drastically reduce the

effectiveness of the primary parasitoids. Finally, one or several species are chosen and released. They may become established, increase in abundance, and reduce pest numbers.

Biocontrol is used not only to reduce pest numbers, but also to keep them at the new, reduced level. An example of such an interaction is the control in Barbados of the Sugarcane stem borer (*Diatraea saccharalis*), a moth larva, by two introduced parasitoid species, the braconid wasp *Cotesia flavipes* and the tachinid fly *Lixophaga diatraeae*. Following their introduction in 1966–67, the three populations (the host and the parasitoid species) fluctuated very little, and the percentage of cane plants damaged remained at around one-third of previous levels.

To date, over 180 species of parasitoid wasp, fly, and beetle have been successfully established against insect pests.   MAJ

viruslike particles are present in the calyx and calyx fluid of various parasitoids (the calyx is the region between the ovary and oviduct). When injected along with an egg, they invade certain host tissues and then apparently suppress the host's immune response to parasitoid eggs and larvae, diverting energy and materials. Parasitoid wasps therefore resemble platyhelminth and other true parasites in manipulating their hosts.

Each host species can support a number of parasitoid species that together form a structured community. The parasitic wasps are often organised into groups of species that utilize the host in similar ways, such as egg parasitoids, larval parasitoids, and pupal parasitoids. The community can also include several trophic levels: parasitoids that attack the nonparasitoid host (primary parasitoids) and secondary and tertiary parasitoids (or hyperparasitoids), which are parasitoids of parasitoids. Many hyperparasitoids, including nearly all tertiary species, are able to develop either hyperparasitically or in the primary role. These facultative hyperparasitoids are largely responsible for the extremely complex structure of food webs found within many galls and leaf mines.

The division Parasitica contains many non-parasitoid species, the vast majority of which have secondarily reverted to a plant diet. Many Gasteruptiidae, together with a few ichneumon flies (for example, *Grotea* and *Macrogrotea* species), kleptoparasitize solitary bees. The first-stage larva devours the host egg or young larva, and then develops on the food store in the host's nest cell. Larvae may also move to either one or a succession of cells in the nest, eating the contents.

Large numbers of plant feeders occur within the families Eurytomidae and Torymidae. Some develop in seeds, while others – some members of the Pteromalidae and most, if not all, Tanaostig-matidae among them – produce galls. The best known gall-causers, however, are members of the family Cynipidae. In Britain, at least 31 species of cynipid gall-causers are associated with oaks alone. Most of them have an alternation of sexual and parthenogenetic generations during a year,

and the galls produced by the two generations of each species differ markedly, both in structure and in their position on the oak tree. Associated with these species are about half as many species of "inquiline" Cynipidae, which do not form their own galls but develop in the galls of other species, eventually taking them over (most of them destroy the gall-maker).

Another group of plant-feeding Parasitica is the family Agaonidae, members of which have symbiotic relationships with fig plants, which they pollinate. Larval agaonids develop within the ovules of the fig fruit, inducing gall formation.   MAJ

Totalitarians of the Insect World
ANTS

The ants (Formicidae) are just one of over 40 families in the division Aculeata. All ants are social, forming perennial societies that parallel those of the honeybees, but have workers that are wingless.

Ant queens shed their wings after a single mating flight. Males also fly, and mating takes place on the wing or on special surfaces such as bare soil patches where members of the same species gather. The mated queens may then attempt to rear workers and hence start a new nest, or may adopt another strategy (see below).

Ants commonly indicate the position of food sources by scent trails, laid by satiated ants using

visual orientation to return to the nest. Scent trails are readily seen in species like the Jet black ant (*Lasius fuliginosus*) of temperate Eurasia. *Leptothorax* species and others avoid attracting more aggressive ants by not emitting odors. An ant returning to a large food source is followed closely by a second nest mate. Further doubling can be rapid.

The food is regurgitated and passed to other ants or fed to larvae back in the nest. Mutual antennal tapping precedes food transfer (trophallaxis) between two adults. In Wood ants and other *Formica* species, the begging ant may also stroke the cheeks of the donor ant. Rather more violent antennal strokes may be used to alert others to potential danger, but the main alerting signal in most species is a chemical secretion that may contain several components of different volatility to provide progressively stronger stimuli nearer to the site of the disturbance, as in the Old World tropical weaver ants of the genus *Oecophylla*. Larger quantities of chemicals may be sprayed out as a defense against predation. The formic acid produced by Wood ants can easily be seen and smelt by humans – or felt painfully in the eyes.

The chemical messengers (pheromones) usually differ between species, although in closely related species the difference is often only in the proportions of constituents. An ant will therefore generally recognize a member of a different ant

detail of brood chamber

eggs

larvae

pupae

◀ **Left** The internal structure of the nest of the Black garden ant (Lasius niger; Formicidae), showing detail of the brood chamber. Eggs are laid in late spring and worker ants tend the brood through the stages to adulthood.

◐ **Below** Large numbers of pupae litter the nest of the Black garden ant. The smaller, wingless ants are workers, while the large, fully winged individuals are new queens ready to make their nuptial flight.

species; furthermore an ant of the same species from a separate nest is usually recognized as a stranger and attacked. However, some ant societies have "slaves" from other species; for example the Slave-maker ant of Europe (*Formica sanguinea*) normally has *F. fusca* workers as auxiliaries. These slaves hatch from pupae robbed from their parent nests, and they behave and are treated as normal members of their adopted nests.

Ant societies have been looked upon as "super-organisms," in which component parts (meaning individuals, as opposed to the head or limb of an individual) may be lost without disabling the organism as a whole. The apparent altruism of ant and other hymenopteran workers has attracted much attention (see "Altruism" – A Paradox Resolved?). Many activities can take place simultaneously in societies, while ordinary individuals cannot usually do two things at once, or not at any rate if they involve elaborate behavior. Some ant species have one or more special subcastes – for example, workers with very large heads for seed crushing, as in *Pheidole* species – while special soldiers or nest-entrance blockers have been evolved in others, such as *Colobopsis* species.

Most species, however, retain a more flexible system whereby workers can transfer from one task to another according to demand. Weaver ants are unique in that their silk-emitting mature larvae are employed by workers as "shuttles," enabling them to weave leaves together for nests in trees.

Ant societies are very successful, if success is measured by ecological dominance. The tropical driver or army ants made famous by writers of fiction, such as *Eciton* in South America or *Anomma* in Africa, are certainly spectacular examples. With

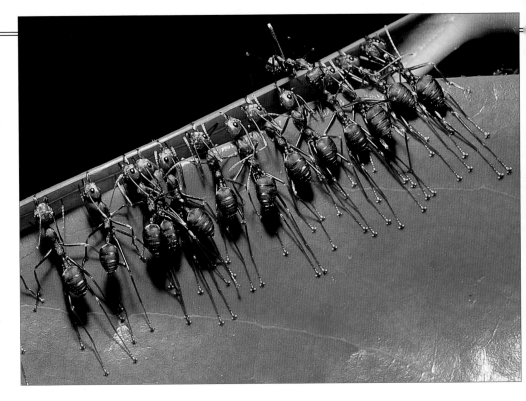

up to several million individuals per society, driver ants need to move on to new areas, as they use up the prey in a locality in a few days. Most animals (notably other ants) must either move out of their way or else be eaten.

Ants that reach high numbers but remain in static nests must adopt more advanced ecological strategies. Continuous food supplies that are not so easily overexploited by the ants include the sweet feces (honeydew) of sap-sucking insects such as aphids. The tropical American parasol or leafcutter ants and their relatives carry into their nests pieces of leaf on which they cultivate a fungus

(the species differs for different ant species) that is the ants' main food, found only in nests of the ant genus *Atta*. Seed-eating enables some harvester ants to survive harsh semidesert conditions by storing dormant seeds in their nests for use during very long periods of drought. The "honeypot" ants use the abdomens of immobile workers as storage vessels for liquid honeydew or nectar.

The ants' saturation of tropical and temperate

◁ *Left* **1** *Fire ants* (Solenopsis geminata; *Formicidae*) *are serious crop pests; their name derives from the burning sensation caused by their venomous bites.* **2** *Workers of a* Myrmecocystus *species in the USA never leave the nest but are fed with nectar and honeydew, becoming "living storage jars" for the colony in times of drought.* **3** *Underground nest chamber of the Australian Bulldog ant* (Myrmecia gulosa; *Formicidae*) *with larvae and eggs;* **3a** *a winged male,* **3b** *queen, and* **3c** *two workers tending pupal cocoons.* **4** *Black garden ant workers* (Lasius niger) *tend aphids. In return for the ants' protection against predators, the aphids provide the ants with sweet honeydew.*

◁ **Left** *In Thailand, workers of the weaver ant species Oecophylla smaragdina (Formicidae) use their jaws as temporary clips to hold together the edges of two leaves, destined to form their pouchlike nest.*

habitats has resulted in many interactions between different ant species, and in highly evolved associations with other organisms. One example of ant interaction is temporary social parasitism as an alternative strategy of nest founding. Pioneer species such as *Lasius flavus* or *L. niger* invading disturbed land have normal, queen-founded nests, but saturation of an area by these species makes entry of further queens impracticable, because they are eaten. Species such as *L. umbratus* and *L. mixtus*, which follow the pioneers, therefore produce larger numbers of smaller queens, which do not found colonies alone but instead seek adoption in nests of the pioneer species. A third stage in this sequence is provided by the Jet black ant, a woodland species that is in turn adopted by *L. umbratus*. Most of the invading queens are killed, but some are successful, perhaps in queenless host nests, and nests with a mixture of workers result. Slave-makers maintain this mixture by raiding, but *Lasius* nests soon consist entirely of the takeover species.

In ant/plant interactions, the plants may gain either protection from defoliators such as moth larvae (in the case of *Cecropia* species in tropical America) or else nutrients from the ants' rubbish dump (as, for example, in some epiphytes), and the ants may be positively catered for by the plants. For example *Cecropia* trees produce special, Müllerian bodies that are eaten by ants

(*Azteca* species) for their glycogen, protein, and lipid content, and have no other apparent function. The evolutionary arms race has been taken a stage further by some lepidopteran larvae that have evolved defenses against the ants. Plants exploit ants in other ways, notably for seed dispersal. Many non-seedeating ants carry certain plant seeds (for example *Viola* species) that have edible outgrowths (elaiosomes) but very hard, smooth coats; the seeds are discarded eventually on the ants' rubbish dumps, which may provide a fertile growing medium. AJP

Sting in the Tail
TRUE WASPS

Most "true" or aculeate wasps are solitary hunters, but some are social and others (the bees, here treated separately) vegetarian, while the parasitoid aculeates have a lifestyle similar to that of the division Parasitica.

None of the aculeate parasitoid wasps build nests. Instead, the female lays one or more eggs in or on the host. Although biologically they are parasitoids, they are nonetheless true aculeates in that the ovipositor functions as a sting and has lost its egg-laying function.

Ruby-tailed wasps, of the superfamily Bethyloidea, are beautiful, metallic green or blue insects with only three visible abdominal segments. Females have neither sting nor ovipositor; instead, they lay eggs via a retractable tube formed by the fused segments of the tip of the abdomen. Ruby-tailed wasps parasitize other wasps and bees. Some are true parasitoids, and their larvae feed on the fully-grown host larva; others are cuckoos

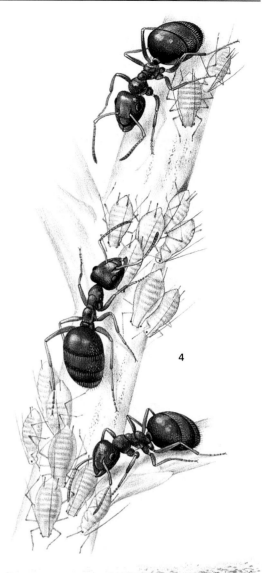

4

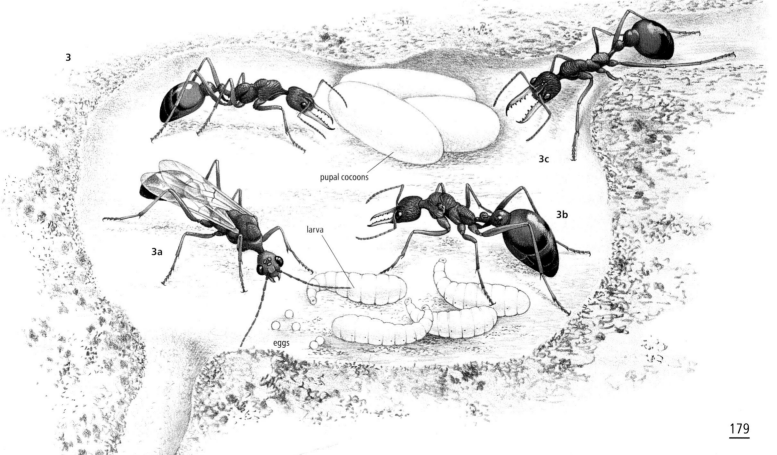

pupal cocoons

larva

eggs

3

3c

3b

3a

(kleptoparasites) that eat the host egg or larva and then feed on the stored food.

The principal parasitoid families in the superfamily Vespoidea are the Scoliidae, Tiphiidae, and Mutillidae. All scoliids and most tiphiids develop as external parasitoids of the subterranean larvae of chafer beetles (family Scarabaeidae). The tiphiid genus *Methocha* parasitizes the larvae of tiger beetles (*Cicindela* species) in their burrows; the females are wingless and resemble ants. Wingless females are characteristic of an entire tiphiid subfamily, the Thynninae, found in Australia and South America. The Australian *Diamma bicolor* parasitizes mole crickets, but most thynnines are assumed to attack scarabaeid larvae. Courtship and mating in thynnines involves the females being carried in flight by the males, attached by the genitalia (phoretic copulation). The male feeds the female ritually with nectar.

The females of the so-called "velvet" ants (Mutillidae) are also wingless. They run about on the ground, in leaf litter, or on tree trunks, with an agitated, antlike gait. Mutillids always parasitize the prepupae or pupae of other insects. Most attack other wasps and bees and are fairly host-specific. Two African species, *Chrestomutilla glossinae* and *Smicromyrme benefactrix*, parasitize the

puparia of tsetse flies, and are currently under investigation as potential control agents against these vectors of sleeping sickness. Female velvet ants have an extremely painful sting and, not surprisingly, are warningly colored. Males are fully winged and usually larger than the females. Some species indulge in phoretic copulation like the thynnines. In others, the males carry females in flight clasped in their mandibles, braced against a modified area of the head. Wingless females have evolved many times independently in the order Hymenoptera, for instance in worker ants, and are presumed to be adapted for host or prey searching underground or in confined spaces, where wings would be a hindrance.

The evolution of nest-building behavior was a major evolutionary advance in the aculeate wasps. In the superfamily Vespoidea, it is found in varying degrees in the spider-hunting wasps, reaching its most complex developments in the social species of the family Vespidae. Nest building is also well developed in the superfamily Sphecoidea.

In its simplest form, a nest is a space prepared by the female wasp or bee in which to store food for her offspring, and which provides physical protection for the developing larva. Primitively, the female wasp finds and stings a single insect

⚫ *Above* **1** *A weevil-hunting wasp (Cerceris arenaria; Sphecidae) at her nest.* **2** *This female African mud-dauber (Sceliphron spirifex; Sphecidae), left, is watched at her nest by two enemies, the wingless female of a "velvet ant," (Dolichomutilla guineensis; Mutillidae), above, and a female ruby-tailed wasp (Stilbum cyanurum; Chrysididae), below.* **3** *A fly-hunting wasp (Mellinus arvensis; Sphecidae).* **4** *American thread-waisted wasp (Ammophila alberti; Sphecidae) returning with prey to her nest.* **5** *A Digger wasp (Astata boops; Sphecidae) stings a shieldbug nymph.* **6** *Hornet (Vespa crabro; Vespidae); the sting of this social wasp species is especially virulent.* **7** *Wasps (Vespula species; Vespidae) feeding on an apple; though commonly regarded as a nuisance, wasps benefit gardeners by preying on pests.*

prey, and only then excavates a simple nest in the ground into which she drags her paralyzed victim before laying an egg on it. This is the situation in many spider-hunting wasps and in the primitive sphecoid subfamily Ampulicinae.

In the more advanced spider-hunting wasps, solitary vespoids, and the remaining sphecoid families, the nest is built before any prey is captured. This behavior requires the ability to return again and again to the nest site. Wasps and bees do this by memorizing visual clues close to the nest, such as the relative positions of pebbles, grass tussocks, and similar landmarks. More distant structures on the horizon, such as trees or hilltops, are also used. The landmarks are memorized during short orientation flights around the nest entrance. Wasps and bees also use the position of the sun as a reference point in orientation, remembering the angle between it and their outward flight path. An internal clock enables them to adjust for the sun's positions.

According to species, the nest may be excavated in the ground or dead wood, or the wasp may use existing cavities such as hollow stems or beetle borings in dead wood. Mason and other wasps collect mud and build exposed nests on rocks or the undersides of leaves. Whatever the architectural details, the nest comprises one or more cells,

and a single larva develops in each. The female provides each cell with several prey insects (mass provisioning), sufficient for the complete development of the larvae. She usually dies before her offspring emerge.

The best-known hunting wasps are the nine subfamilies in the superfamily Sphecoidea. They comprise just over 7,600 species, and hunt a wide variety of insect prey; a few isolated species collect spiders. Some advanced *Bembix* species (family Nyssonidae), such as *B. texana* in North America, practice progressive feeding of their developing larvae, providing the fly prey as and when the growing larva needs it, rather than through mass provisioning. Females of the American caterpillar-hunting wasp *Ammophila azteca* not only practice progressive feeding, but also maintain several nests at once, in varying degrees of development.

The sphecoid wasp families were probably established by the early Cretaceous period (soon after 144 million years ago). Other groups of insects diversified at this time and provided new sources of prey. The prey of modern sphecoids reflects this history: primitive wasps tend to hunt primitive prey, while the more advanced hunting sphecoids hunt more highly evolved insects.

The complexity of social wasp society ranges from loose associations of egg-laying females that cooperate only in nest construction to the highly social paper wasps or yellowjackets, with their well-defined worker caste of sterile females. Most species of social wasps are in the family Vespidae, but the superfamily Sphecoidea includes (as well as the bees) hunting wasps that have a simple social organization. In the Central American sphecid *Trigonopsis cameronii*, up to four females cooperate in constructing the mud nest, but each provisions its own cells with cockroach prey – behavior classed as attaining a communal level of social organization. There is very little aggression between nest mates, and prey-stealing is rare. The nest mates are likely to be closely related. Two obvious advantages of such communal societies are that the labor of nest building is shared and nest defense is improved, because the nest is rarely left unattended.

A more complex form of social behavior occurs in another Central American sphecoid wasp, *Microstigmus comes* (family Pemphredonidae).

In this species, up to 11 females share a single, thimble-sized nest. They cooperate in building the nest and in provisioning the cells with springtails; only one cell is mass-provisioned at a time. Although the females are morphologically identical, there is a reproductive division of labor: only one female has developed ovaries and lays eggs, while the others function as a worker caste. Moreover, it is believed that more than one generation is present in the nest. The society of *M. comes*, while small in numbers, is an example of eusociality, the most developed level of sociality in hymenopterans, which is typical of, for example, ants, paper wasps, and honeybees.

Many vespid wasps (and also bees) are of an intermediate level of social development. Three of the six currently recognized subfamilies of the Vespidae (Stenogastrinae, Polistinae, and Vespinae) consist entirely of social species. All provision their nests with chewed insect prey rather than whole insects. As in all vespids, the egg is laid in the cell before any food is provided. The Stenogastrinae are communal, except for one unnamed species of *Parischnogaster* that appears to be semisocial. The nests of polistine and vespine wasps are made of tough paper, comprising wood fibers mixed with saliva.

Polistine colonies may be founded by either one female (haplometrosis) or several females (pleometrosis). Although there is no morphological distinction between females, one always emerges at the apex of a dominance hierarchy. She is the sole or major egg-layer, or queen, and seldom leaves the nest. The ovaries of subordinate females more or less atrophy, and these insects function as workers, foraging for food and feeding

the queen and the larvae. In the African genus *Belonogaster* and in some *Ropalidia* and many *Polistes* species, the female that manages to eat most eggs laid by nest mates eventually assumes dominance. In other *Polistes* species, dominance is asserted by outright aggression.

The exchange of food between adults and larvae is characteristic of polistine and vespine wasps. Larvae solicit food from workers by exuding from their mouthparts a droplet of liquid, which contains carbohydrates and possibly enzymes the adults cannot make themselves. Workers and queens consume this liquid; it seems that the latter require it for continued egg production.

Species of the South American polistine genus *Polybia* have the beginnings of a morphological caste distinction. There may be one or several queens in a colony, and colonies may have up to 10,000 workers. As well as having developed ovaries, *Polybia* queens are usually larger than the workers, although this distinction is not always clear-cut. With such large colonies, it is obvious that the queens(s) cannot assert dominance by mere aggression alone or by differential egg eating. Instead, they and vespine wasps secrete a "queen pheromone," a scent that inhibits the development of the workers' ovaries.

Polybia is also more advanced than *Polistes* in its nest architecture. A mature nest comprises several horizontal combs, connected by vertical pillars and enclosed in a durable paper envelope. The colony is perennial, and may persist for up to 25 years. A colony is formed through swarming: one or more queens and several hundred workers leave the old nest and set up a new one.

The subfamily Vespinae is characterized by a clear-cut size distinction between the larger queen and smaller workers. Colonies are

⬥ **Above** In Polistes *wasps the colony members are visually indistinguishable, although one will always head the dominance hierarchy. Here three members of a* Polistes cavapyta *colony (Vespidae) from Argentina are sharing out a food bolus that one of them has recently brought in; they will then feed it to the larvae.*

⬥ **Left** *Ruby-tailed wasps of the family Chrysididae have a brilliant metallic coloration. As with most species, the larvae of this* Chrysis ignita *from Europe are solitary ectoparasites of bee and wasp larvae.*

⬥ **Right** *Although spiders are highly efficient predators, usually equipped with formidable poison fangs, they are seldom a match for the superlative hunting tactics exhibited by female spider-hunting wasps of the family Pompilidae, such as this species from Argentina. Paralyzed by the wasp's sting, the spider is dragged to the nest-site and used as larval food.*

always established by a single queen, which behaves as a solitary and then as a subsocial wasp, until the first generation of workers emerges. Nests are either suspended under branches or made in cavities in the ground. Although vespines are often a nuisance and frequently are pests of bee hives, they are beneficial insects as they kill a wide range of pest species for their larval food.　　　CO'T

Vegetarian Hunters
BEES

Bees are sphecoid hunting wasps that have become vegetarians; they collect pollen and nectar from flowers. The change in diet probably occurred in the middle of the Cretaceous period (144–65 million years ago), soon after flowering plants appeared. The earliest known fossil bees, from late in the Eocene (55–34 million years ago), already include members of specialized, long-tongued families such as the honeybees and stingless bees. Today, many bees specialize on one plant species, or a group of related species, as a source of pollen. Examples are *Macropis* species, which visit only *Lysimachia* flowers, and the economically important *Peponapis*, which pollinate melons. These bees, termed oligolectic, are most abundant in dry, warm regions, where they may account for over 60 percent of bee species. In such areas, where the climate induces the simultaneous flowering of many flower species, oligolecty reduces competition between bees and probably results in more successful pollination.

The vast majority of bees have a solitary lifestyle. They are most abundant and diverse in regions such as the deserts of southwestern North America and in the Mediterranean basin. From their sphecoid ancestors bees inherited the nesting habit, including the ability to find their way back to the nest. Superimposed on this inheritance are structures such as longer tongues, branched body hairs, and scopae ("brushes") adapted to deal with the collection and transport of nectar and pollen; some specialists (for example, *Macropis* and some *Centris* species) are adapted for collecting plant oils.

There are two main types of nest-building behavior in bees. The females of short-tongued

◖ Right On the dorsal side of its abdomen, the worker honeybee possesses the Nasonov scent gland which it exposes by flexing the tip of the abdomen. The pheromone produced attracts other bees to the site.

◗ Below Though apparently a wasp, this is in fact a nomad bee (Nomada flava; Anthophoridae). Nomad bees behave rather like cuckoos, laying their eggs in other bees' nests, where the larvae eat the rightful occupants' food.

◖ Above As in all leafcutter bees of the family Megachilidae, this female Megachile willughbiella, *having cut her semicircular section of leaf, lands briefly in order to fold and adjust it into a more comfortable position beneath her.*

mining bees line their underground brood cells with the secretions of the abdominal Dufour's gland. The resultant waterproof, fungus-resistant lining is important in maintaining the right level of humidity inside the cell, and prevents the cell and its contents from being inundated if the soil becomes waterlogged. In only a few species with cell linings of this type does the larva spin a cocoon before pupation.

The second type of nesting behavior is found mainly in one family, the Megachilidae, whose members use collected materials rather than glandular secretions in nest construction. Moreover, most species use existing cavities – old insect borings in dead wood, hollow twigs, snail shells, or often the crumbling mortar of old walls – rather than digging nests in the soil. Some species also build exposed nests on rocks or shrubby plants. According to species, the building materials include mud, resin, a mastic of chewed leaves, petals, pieces of leaf and plant, and animal hairs, or a combination of these. Those that use soft, malleable substances are often called mason bees. Megachilid larvae spin a tough, silken cocoon.

Because megachilids nest in almost any suitable cavity, especially in wood and stems, many species have been accidentally dispersed from their normal range by human commerce. Thus, a mason bee, *Chalicodoma lanata*, common in the southeastern United States and islands of the Caribbean, originated in Africa and is thought to

have been brought to the New World by the slave trade. The leafcutter bee *Megachile rotundata* is another accidental introduction. A native of Eurasia, it first appeared in the United States in the 1930s, and is now managed by American farmers as the major pollinator of alfalfa or lucerne.

The family Megachilidae includes the largest bee in the world, *Megachile pluto*. Until recently, the biology of this remarkable bee was unknown. In fact, it was known only from the single type specimen, a female collected by Alfred Russell Wallace on the island of Batchian in the Moluccas, Indonesia. This specimen is now housed in the Oxford University Museum of Natural History. Apart from its large size – it is 39mm (1.5in) long – the female is notable for its very large jaws.

Recent research has shown that this bee lives on several of the Moluccan Islands, where the females use their large mandibles to excavate nest burrows in the compacted mud forming the sides of termites mounds. The females nest communally, with several sharing a nest entrance. They also use their massive jaws to scrape up wood chips, which they mix with resin from tree wounds to make a lining for their brood cells and nest burrows.

Like the vespine wasps, bees show all the grades of sociality. The Halictidae are of particular interest because a single genus, *Lasioglossum*, contains communal, subsocial, primitively eusocial, and eusocial species, as well as many that are solitary.

Bumblebees (*Bombus* species) are the most

◑ **Above** *A solitary mining bee (Colletes succinctus; Colletidae) and her cluster of cells, each with an egg attached to the cell wall. On hatching, the larvae drop into the liquid mixture of honey and pollen below.*

THE LANGUAGE OF DANCE

Worker honeybees communicate information about food sources to their nest mates by "dancing." The dance is performed within the darkness of the hive on the vertical surfaces of the wax honeycomb. The dancer is always attended by several "followers."

Foragers returning from a food source within 25m (80ft) of the hive perform a "round dance" of circular runs with more or less frequent changes in direction. The greater the frequency of direction changes, the greater the calorific value of the nectar at the food source indicated.

To indicate a food source 25–100m (80–330ft) away, a bee performs a figure between the round dance and the "waggle dance." The latter, used for longer distances, is a contracted figure-of-eight in which the bee waggles her abdomen from side to side during the straight run between the two semicircles at the ends of the figure. Distance is indicated by the duration of the straight run and the frequency of the waggles; indication of direction is explained in the diagram RIGHT. Waggling, and the high-frequency buzzes that accompany it, may together impart information on food quality.

The followers perceive all this information by touching the dancer with their antennae and by their sensitivity to airborne vibrations (sound). The specific scents of flowers on the dancer's body may also be important. Thus, the dance language is a multi-channel system of communication.   CO'T

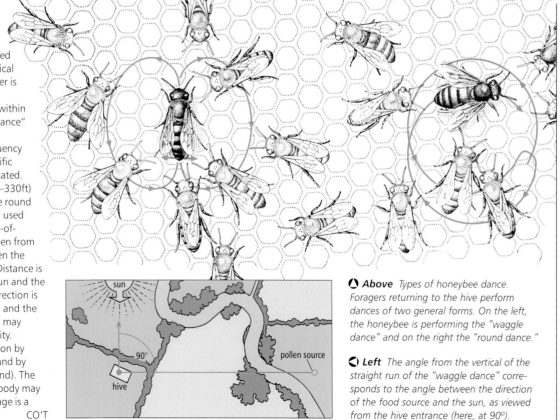

◑ **Above** *Types of honeybee dance. Foragers returning to the hive perform dances of two general forms. On the left, the honeybee is performing the "waggle dance" and on the right the "round dance."*

◐ **Left** *The angle from the vertical of the straight run of the "waggle dance" corresponds to the angle between the direction of the food source and the sun, as viewed from the hive entrance (here, at 90°).*

familiar social bees in temperate regions. There are a little over 200 species, with only a few found in the tropics. Each colony is founded in spring by a lone queen, which was mated the previous season and then it hibernates. Bumblebees are at the primitively eusocial level of organization, with no clear morphological difference between queen and worker. Indeed, in some species there is little or no difference in size, and the queen apparently asserts her dominance by aggression.

The advanced eusocial bees in the family Apidae comprise the pantropical stingless bees, *Melipona* and *Trigona*, and the eight species of honeybees (*Apis*). They differ from the bumblebees in that their large colonies are perennial, there are clear-cut morphological differences between castes, and workers can communicate the direction of food and other resources and recruit additional bees from the hive to exploit them.

Stingless bees usually nest in hollow trees or in cavities in the ground. A few species nest in termite mounds. A large colony of *Trigona* may contain 180,000 bees, including one to several queens. Brood cells and food storage pots are kept separate and are made of wax, secreted by the bees, mixed with resin and/or animal feces. Stingless bees practice mass provisioning of brood cells. Foragers communicate the source of food by laying a scent trail between it and the nest. Although they do not sting, meliponines are not helpless. They attack vertebrate nest intruders by biting their skin; some species also secrete a corrosive fluid via the mandibular glands. In all the stingless bee genera except *Melipona*, queens are derived from larvae reared in larger than usual cells, along with extra food. In *Melipona* species, by contrast, "queenness" is determined by genetic factors.

In the honeybees (*Apis* species), larvae destined to be queens are reared entirely on royal jelly (or "bee milk"). This is a mixture of sugars, proteins, vitamins, RNA and DNA, and the fatty acid trans-10-hydroxy-decenoic acid, and is secreted by the mandibular and hypopharyngeal glands of young workers. Larvae destined to be workers are deprived of royal jelly after about three days, thereafter feeding on pollen and honey.

Worker honeybees use secreted wax to build double-sided, vertical combs of hexagonal cells. Pollen and honey are stored in cells the same size as those used to rear worker larvae. Males (drones) are reared in larger cells, and queens develop in large cells suspended from the comb. Honeybees also use resin, but unlike stingless bees they do not mix it with wax. Instead, they use the resin only to stop up gaps or to reduce the

◑ **Right** *Many bumblebees (Apidae) nest below ground, but the Small garden bumblebee (Bombus hortorum) from Europe builds its nest on the surface in dense grass tussocks. Note the typically haphazard collection of brood cells (occupied by larvae or pupae) and the storage cells containing honey.*

size of the nest or hive entrance. Like the stingless bees, however, the honeybees collect resin from plant sources and carry it to the nest in the pollen basket (corbiculum) on the tibia of the rear leg.

A healthy colony of the Western honeybee will contain some 40,000–80,000 workers, 200 drones, and one queen. The queen may lay up to 1,500 eggs a day, and exerts physiological dominance over the workers by means of a pheromone called "queen substance" (as do vespine and some polistine wasps). This is trans-9-keto-2-decenoic acid; it is produced in the mandibular glands, and not only does it inhibit the development of the workers' ovaries but it also suppresses the building of special queen cells for potential rivals. The queen may live from one to five years. Either when her powers wane or when the number of workers is very large, there is proportionally less queen substance to go round and the workers begin to build queen cells. A swarm may then ensue, and the old queen will leave the colony to be taken over by the first of the young queens to emerge who usually kills any other young queens.

The activities of worker honeybees are age-related. Their first three days are spent as cleaners. Then, from days 3 to 10, a worker is a nurse; her mandibular and hypopharyngeal glands become active and she feeds the larvae. At about day 10, these glands atrophy and the abdominal wax glands become active: now she is a builder. From about day 16 to day 20, she receives pollen and

⊃ **Right** Honeybees have achieved the acme of social behavior. The exposed nest of the small oriental honey-bee (Apis florea; Apidae) from Southeast Asia consists of a single vertical comb, usually built in a tree.

"ALTRUISM" – A PARADOX RESOLVED?

The existence of social insects was felt by Charles Darwin to seriously challenge his theory of natural selection. How could selection have favored "altruistic" traits (such as caring for the young of others) in a worker caste if the workers themselves did not reproduce and pass on these traits? Darwin covered this dilemma with an escape clause: social insects were a special case with selection acting on the colony as a whole rather than on individuals.

Highly social behavior has evolved independently at least 11 times in the Hymenoptera, but only once in all the rest of the insects (in the termites). It now seems, however, that the "selfless" behavior of worker hymenopterans is in fact not really altruism, but instead has a lot to do with a most unusual method of sex determination. In most insects and other animals, males and females are derived from fertilized eggs. They have two sets of genes, one from each parent, and are consequently said to be "diploid." Sons and daughters share, on average, one half of their genes with each other and with either of the parents. In the Hymenoptera, however, while all females are diploid, the males arise from unfertilized eggs and have only one set of genes; they are haploid (Males therefore have a

single, maternal grandfather, but no father.)

Because a male hymenopteran is haploid, all his sperm are genetically identical. Assuming that a female mates only once (not always the case in highly social species), then all her female offspring will receive an identical set of genes from their haploid father. However, since their mother is diploid her daughters have in common only one half of the maternal genes. Adding up the genes received from father and mother, it is clear that hymenopteran sisters share, on average, 75 percent of their genes by common descent (50 percent from the father and 25 percent from the mother). They share only 50 percent of their genes with their mother or, if they have any, with their daughters.

In terms of the numbers of genes identical with her own that pass into the next generation, it pays a female hymenopteran not to have daughters, but to help her mother rear sisters, some of which will become queens and reproduce. The pay-off is the extra 25 percent of genes identical with her own that are perpetuated in this way. This "kin selection" theory offers the most elegant explanation to date for the evolution of insect sociality; and it also solves Darwin's dilemma.   CO'T

nectar loads from returning foragers and places them in the comb. At about day 20, she guards the nest entrance and thereafter, for the rest of her 6 weeks or so of life, she is a foraging field bee.

The allocation of duties is not inflexible, however. If the age structure of a colony is disrupted, whether experimentally or by a large predator, duties are reallocated among the survivors.

Colony defense is the hallmark of eusociality and in *Apis* is triggered by an alarm pheromone, secreted from glands in the sting. This recruits additional workers to a point of danger. The barbed sting and the venom gland are left behind as the bee struggles free. The bee soon dies, in apparently "altruistic" self-sacrifice, but the venom sac continues to pulsate and inject venom.

Concerted defense strategies of this kind evolve where a bee (or ant or wasp) colony has valuable resources to protect. With the honeybee species, the large numbers of larvae and the stored pollen and nectar attract predators. It is the honey, an energy-rich mixture of plant sugars (nectar) modified by the bees, that attracts man. Honeybees, particularly the Western honeybee, have been managed in hives for at least 3,000 years.   CO'T

Hymenoptera Superfamilies

SAWFLIES & WOOD WASPS

Suborder Symphyta

About 10,000 species in 14 families, including: Pamphilidae (**web-spinning sawflies**, with larval stage either solitary or else gregarious in silk web or rolled up in leaf held by silk); Pergidae (S America and Australia, where there are at least 136 species; some eucalyptus-feeders, e.g. *Perga*, *Pergagrapta* species, may be serious defoliators); Argidae (over 800 species; cosmopolitan); Tenthredinidae (most commonly-seen **sawflies**, with over 5,000 species; N temperate regions; some, e.g. *Pontania*, induce galls); Siricidae (about 85 species of **wood wasps** or **horntails**; worldwide excepts America; larvae are wood-borers in conifers, e.g. *Urocerus gigas* in spruce); Diprionidae, including the **European pine sawfly** (*Neodiprion sertifer*); Orussidae (66 species of **parasitic sawflies**; cosmopolitan; larvae parasitic on larvae of wood-boring beetles and wood wasps); Cephidae (100 species of **stem sawflies** whose larvae bore into grass stems, e.g. *Cephus pygmaeus* in wheat).

PARASITIC WASPS

Suborder Apocrita
Division Parasitica

An estimated 200,000 species (many still to be described) in 51 families, grouped into 6 superfamilies. Probably not a monophyletic grouping. Comprises mainly parasitic wasps or parasitoids, in which the ovipositor retains its egg-laying function, and larvae develop as internal or external parasites of insects and other terrestrial arthropods. Includes ichneumon flies, gall wasps, fairy flies.

Trigonalyoidea

Consists of family Trigonalidae, parasitic on caterpillars.

Ichneumonoidea

Includes Braconidae (**bracon flies**, probably 40,000 species); Aphidiidae, parasitic on aphids; Ichneumonidae (**ichneumon flies**, probably 60,000 species).

Evanioidea

Includes Gasteruptiidae, with many species kleptoparasites of solitary bee eggs and larvae.

Chalcidoidea

Possibly 80,000–100,000 species, including Agaonidae (**fig wasps**), gall makers in figs; Pteromalidae; Eurytomidae, with larvae of many species seed-eaters; Eulophidae; Encyrtidae; Mymaridae (**fairy flies**) and Trichogrammatidae, both parasites of insect eggs; Eucharitidae, parasitic on ant

larvae; Perilampidae, including some species that are hyperparasites of caterpillars; Torymidae, containing many plant feeders; Tanaostigmatidae, mostly gall makers.

Cynipoidea

Parasitic and gall wasps, including Ibaliidae, whose larvae parasitize those of wood wasps; Anacharitidae, with larvae parasitic on lacewing pupae; Eucoilidae, with larvae parasitic on pupae of dipteran flies; Cynipidae (**gall wasps**), including many species in galls made by other cynipids, e.g. the **Oak marble wasp** (*Andricus kollari*).

Proctotrupoidea

Includes Diapriidae, parasites of flies; Proctotrupidae, whose larvae are internal parasites of beetle larvae; Scelionidae, parasites of insect and spider eggs; Platygasteridae, parasites of flies and mealybugs.

WASPS, ANTS, AND BEES

Suborder Apocrita
Division Aculeata

Some 70–85,000 species in 41 families, grouped into 3 superfamilies. Comprises mainly non-parasites, in which the ovipositor is modified as a sting for defense and for immobilizing prey. Larvae of most species feed on maternally provided food. Includes ants, hunting wasps, paper-making wasps, and bees.

Bethyloidea

At least 3,500 species in 9 families, including Bethylidae, whose larvae are gregarious ectoparasites of beetle and moth larvae; Cleptidae, parasites of mature sawfly larvae; Chrysididae (**ruby-tailed wasps**), whose larvae are cuckoos in nests of other wasps and bees; Dryinidae, parasites of leaf hoppers.

Vespoidea

Some 40–50,000 species in 12 families, including Scoliidae and Tiphiidae, whose larvae are parasitic on those of scarabaeid beetles; Mutillidae (**velvet ants**), 4,000 species parasitizing the larvae and pupae of bees and wasps and the pupae of tsetse flies, or else hyperparasitizing scarab beetles; Pompilidae (**spider-hunting wasps**); Vespidae (solitary **hunting wasps** and social **paper-making wasps**), including **hornets** (*Vespa* species), **yellowjackets** or **common wasps** (*Vespula*, *Dolichovespula*), and *Polistes* and *Polybia* species; Formicidae (**ants**), about 14,000 species including **army** or **driver ants**, e.g. *Eciton*, *Anomma*, **honeypot ants** (*Myrmecocystus*), **leafcutter** or **parasol ants** (*Atta*), **weaver ants** (*Oecophylla*), **Jet black ant** (*Lasius fuliginosus*), **Slave-maker ant** (*Formica sanguinea*), **Wood ant** (*F. rufa*).

🜂 **Above** *An* Ectatomma *ant from the rain forest of Trinidad displays a typical alert ambush posture.*

Sphecoidea

Some 29,600 species in 20 families, 9 of hunting wasps (7,600 species) and 11 of bees (about 22,000 species).
Hunting wasp families include: Ampulicidae (**cockroach-hunting wasps**); Sphecidae (**thread-waisted wasps**), preying on spiders, cockroaches, crickets, caterpillars including *Ammophila* and *Sphex* species; Pemphredonidae, preying on springtails, thrips, and aphids; Larridae, preying on orthopterans, some on bugs; Mellinidae, preying on flies; Crabronidae, preying on flies, some on beetles; Nyssonidae (**sand wasps**), including *Gorytes* species preying on plant hoppers and their cuckoos *Nysson*, and *Bembix*, fast-flying hunters of flies; Philanthidae, including *Philanthus triangulam*, the European **bee wolf** pest of honeybees, and the weevil- and bee-hunting genus *Cerceris*.

Bee families include: **mining bees** in the families Colletidae (e.g. *Colletes* and *Hylaeus*), Halictidae (e.g. *Halictus*, *Lasioglossum*, including some social species), Oxaeidae (e.g. *Oxaea*), Melitidae (e.g. *Melitta*, *Dasypoda*), Andrenidae (e.g. *Andrena*, *Panurginus*, *Perdita*), all with short to medium-length tongues; Fideliidae, with pollen scopa on underside of abdomen, not hindlegs; Megachilidae, long-tongued bees with abdominal scopa, including **mason bees** (e.g. *Osmia*, *Hoplitis*, *Chalicodoma*) and **leafcutter bees** (*Megachile*); Apidae, including **digger bees**, subfamily Anthophorinae (e.g. *Anthophora*, *Centris*, *Melissodes*, *Eucera*, *Ceratina*, *Xylocopa*) – long-tongued, fast-flying, mainly ground nesters, some primitively social and others cuckoo genera (e.g. *Epeolus*, *Nomada*, *Melecta*); also including **orchid bees** (*Euglossa*, *Eulaema*), **bumblebees** (*Bombus*) and their cuckoo *Psithyrus* species, **stingless bees** (e.g. *Melipona*, *Trigona* species), and eleven species of honeybee, including the **Western** or "**Domestic**" honeybee (*Apis mellifera*).

THE BEES' VITAL GIFT TO HUMANKIND

The economic importance of pollination

AS POLLINATORS, BEES OCCUPY ONE OF THE keystone positions on which life on earth depends: from the equatorial rain forests to the deserts of North America and the Middle East, from the flower-rich shrublands of the Mediterranean to the hedgerows of rural England, much of the visual impact of the world's habitats results from networks of interlocking relationships between plants and pollinating bees.

When our ancestors left their forest habitat to colonize the east African savannas, they found ecosystems based on the evolved codependency of bees and plants that made the hunter–gatherer lifestyle a viable possibility. Quite literally, bees made our humanity possible. This fact is of more than theoretical, ecological interest: today, every third mouthful of human food is dependent on the pollination services of bees.

Like us, flowering plants are sexual organisms, and a high proportion of species are self-sterile: they need to receive pollen (male cells) from another individual of the same species if they are to set seed and reproduce. Being literally rooted to the spot, however, they require some second party to act as an agent to effect mating by proxy. Many species, such as the conifers, oaks, and grasses, are pollinated simply by the wind. They produce billions upon billions of light, dry pollen grains from simple, exposed flowers, and these are easily picked up and transported by the wind. But the majority of plants are insect-pollinated, and most of these are specialized to be attractive to, and therefore pollinated by, bees.

Bee-pollinated plants produce pollen in amounts excessive to those required for reproduction, the extra pollen being a protein-rich attractant to foraging bees. Flowering plants also provide an additional reward in the form of nectar, an energy-rich mixture of sugars that is a highly efficient fuel for bees. And the bright colors of flowers, which we find so attractive, are, together with scents, advertising ploys competing for the attention of foraging bees.

The experience of farmers in New Zealand dramatically demonstrates the economic importance of bees as pollinators. Nineteenth-century settlers found a climate ideal for rearing sheep and dairy cattle, with clover as a forage crop. However, the native bee fauna of New Zealand is impoverished and comprises primitive, short-tongued species that cannot pollinate clover, with the result that for much of the century New Zealand had to import hundreds of tonnes of clover seed each year. Then, in the 1880s, someone had the idea of introducing four long-tongued species of bumblebee (*Bombus*) from Britain to perform the task of pollinating the native clover. Within five years, New Zealand was not only freed from the need to import clover seed each year but actually became a net exporter of clover to other countries.

Worldwide, about 150 crop species depend largely or entirely on bees for pollination. In North America alone, the annual value of such crops is at least US$19 billion. Some of the pollination is performed by honeybee colonies managed for the purpose. Indeed, it can be argued that the honeybee is the ideal managed pollinator: it is possible to move hives into target crops as and when they are required, and this migratory beekeeping enables farmers to enjoy the pollination services resulting from the commanding presence exerted by enhanced populations of honeybees. The farmers pay the beekeeper a fee for pollination, the beekeeper exploits the honey and wax crops, and everyone enjoys a win–win situation.

Although honeybees are of great economic importance via the honey, wax, and propolis they produce, the annual value of the world's honey crop is estimated to be only one-fiftieth of the value of the crops pollinated by them. Yet only one-third of the land area of North America that is devoted to bee-pollinated crops is thought to be actually supplied with honeybees for pollination purposes. As a result, the majority of North American crops are dependent on the adventive pollination services of honeybees and native bees;

the same is almost certainly true of agriculture in many other parts of the world, with potentially serious consequences. Evidently, we need to know more about our native bee faunas and their potential as managed pollinators of crops.

There is strong evidence from parts of North America and Western Europe to suggest that intensive agriculture and habitat destruction or fragmentation are having adverse affects on the wild bee faunas. For example, 25 per cent of the 254 species of bees native to Britain are now on the IUCN's British Red Data Book list of endangered species; in parts of central Europe the situation is even worse, with about 45 percent of 500-plus species now on local at-risk lists. The implication is that each year we are making a bet with the planet that, despite the habitat destruction associated with intensive agriculture and the resultant reductions in nest sites and floral diversity, we can still expect the bees to be there next season to perform the pollination services on which we all depend.

Bee Populations at Risk

There is now another very important reason why we should conserve our wild bees as potential managed pollinators: the *Varroa* mite, which has devastated honeybee populations around the world. This mite only attacks honeybees, and it is possible for beekeepers to fight it by combining enhanced hive hygiene with the use of specially designed pesticides (acaricides); but the cost in time and money has made beekeeping a more expensive and labor-intensive activity. In Britain, between 40 and 45 percent of beekeepers have given up their craft in the last 10–15 years, and

Above *The* Varroa *mite has had a huge impact on the beekeeping industry, devastating honeybee populations worldwide. Varroa is an external parasite of both brood and adult bees. Here the mite is infecting the pupal stage of two drone honeybees.*

⬤ *Above* Honeybees (Apis mellifera) *like this individual on an oilseed rape flower play a vital part in maintaining ecosystems by helping plants to reproduce. They do so by transferring pollen – the golden grains snagged on hairs along the length of the bee's body – from plant to plant. The payoff for the bee comes in the form of energy-filled nectar, as well as surplus amounts of the protein-rich pollen itself.*

similar declines have been reported from much of Europe and North America. Moreover, very recently, the first evidence of mite resistance to acaricides has been reported.

While *Varroa* adds urgency to the need to find alternatives to the honeybees as managed pollinators, there has also been a growing realization that the honeybee is not, in any case, always the best pollinator for particular crops. Alfalfa (*Medicago sativa*), which is widely cultivated as an important forage crop for cattle in large areas of North and South America, is a classic example. The plant is a member of the pea family, and hence has a spring-loaded pollination mechanism: the weight of a bee on the lower (keel) petal "trips" the bundle of pollen-bearing stamens and the female stigma, which strike the underside of the bee with some force, depositing pollen. When the bee visits another alfalfa flower, the stigma picks up pollen from the previous flower and the anthers deposit more pollen. Honeybees react badly to this treatment, however, and either avoid the flowers altogether or force their way in to the nectaries via the base of the side petals without tripping the flower – and this in turn does not further the process of pollination.

So honeybees, for behavioral reasons, are poor pollinators of alfalfa. Other bees, however, are excellent pollinators of this important crop, and none more so than the Alfalfa leafcutter bee (*Megachile rotundata*). Unlike the honeybee, the leafcutter bee is undeterred by the alfalfa flower. Like alfalfa itself, this bee is not native to North America, having originated in the steppes and semideserts of Eurasia. It nests in ready-made cavities such as beetle borings in dead wood or hollow plant stems, and was almost certainly accidentally introduced into North America in the 1930s via occupied nests.

Leafcutter bees are so called because the females line their nest cells with pieces of leaf cut to size and glued together. They are solitary rather than social, and will nest readily in manmade nests. Mass propagation of this bee is now a multimillion-dollar business in North America, where trailers full of drilled wooden boards or blocks occupied by thousands of leafcutter bees are towed out into alfalfa fields each year, just before the bees are due to emerge and the crop is about to flower. It is likely that in its native Eurasia *Megachile rotundata* is a specialized pollinator of alfalfa. This useful little bee's pollen-collecting apparatus is in the form of a dense brush of stiff hairs on the underside of its abdomen, so it is anatomically predisposed to receive the alfalfa pollen when it trips the flower.

The Quest for Managed Pollinators

The success with *Megachile rotundata* led American entomologists and agriculturalists to explore the idea of developing other wild bees as managed pollinators, and several species are now being actively researched or propagated in artificial nests. One success story is the Blue orchard mason bee (*Osmia lignaria*). Like *Megachile rotundata*, it is a solitary bee that nests readily and gregariously in blocks of wood drilled with holes of the right diameter. It is called a mason bee because, instead of cut leaves, it uses collected mud to build partitions between the cells.

Osmia lignaria is an excellent pollinator of orchard fruits, especially apples and cherries. In fact, the potential for mason bees as fruit pollinators is so great that researchers at the US Department of Agriculture have combed the world for other related species. They have imported *Osmia cornuta* from Spain for almond pollination in California, and *O. cornifrons* has been introduced from Japan for apple pollination. Another species, *O. ribifloris*, a native American bee, is considered to have potential as a managed pollinator of highbush blueberries in California.

Research in Europe has shown that, in addition to *O. cornuta*, the Red mason bee (*O. rufa*) is a very efficient pollinator of apples. *O. rufa* is widespread and common in Britain, and nest kits are now available to gardeners to attract them. All species of *Osmia* are docile and safe with children and pets: they only sting if handled roughly.

Left Commercial beekeepers in the USA rent their hives to farmers for pollination. Over 1.1 million colonies of honeybees are rented annually to pollinate around 50 different crops. Here a beekeeper delivers hives to a cherry orchard. Delivery is carefully planned for the time when the cherry buds are just bursting.

Right Managed beehives are a common sight in England. Beekeeping regulations usually require bees to be kept in hives with movable combs rather than fixed ones, which would mean destroying the hives to harvest honey.

Below Female Alfalfa leafcutter bees (**left**) in wooden block nests provided for them by farmers in Utah. Completed nests are sealed with pieces of leaf, while those of the Red mason bee (**right**) are sealed with mud. This bee takes readily to artificial nests, which are now available to those who want to take advantage of this bee's efficient pollination services.

All the species of *Osmia* that have been studied as fruit pollinators share certain features that make them more efficient pollinators than the honeybee. Firstly, they can fly at temperatures at which the honeybee is grounded. In addition, at any given temperature, *Osmia* visits more flowers per minute. On foraging trips, *Osmia* are more promiscuous in terms of the number of trees visited, so they affect more cross-pollination. Then again, *Osmia* females carry their pollen dry on a dense brush of hairs under the abdomen, and are inefficient at grooming themselves; by contrast, the honeybee compacts its pollen loads onto the hind legs, moistened with nectar, and is very good at grooming itself. Thus, for anatomical and behavioral reasons, there is a greater chance with *Osmia* of loose pollen being transferred from one fruit blossom to another than there is with the honey-

bee. Finally, *Osmia* is almost entirely pollen-driven: mason bees do not store honey, and so actively scrabble for pollen at flower visits. Honeybees, however, are equally interested in collecting large amounts of nectar and often land on the sides of fruit flowers to gain access to nectaries; there is minimal contact with the pollen-bearing anthers.

Research has shown that about 500 females of *Osmia rufa* will adequately pollinate 1ha (2.5 acres) of apples at commercial densities, while the recommended density of honeybees for the same area is 3–4 colonies, each with about 20,000 bees. Thus one female *Osmia rufa* does the pollination work of between 120 and 160 honeybees!

For all of these reasons and many more, there are sound economic grounds for conserving our native bee faunas and increasing our knowledge of their natural history and behavior. CO'T

BUILDING NESTS OF MUD AND PAPER

1 *Constructing nests of mud to protect their larvae, the non-social potter wasps of the subfamily Eumeninae are the master-builders of the Vespidae. Here a female Delta dimidiatipenne, working with delicate precision, adds a slightly flared lip to a nest on a rock in the Israeli desert. Using her front legs and mandibles, she "dribbles" a ball of mud into place, checking the dimensions with her antennae.*

2 *Some potter wasps collect dry building materials and then mix them with water from their crop. Others, such as this Eumenes fenestralis in South Africa, visit the margins of ponds and puddles to collect a ball of mud ready-made for construction work.*

3 *In many potter wasp species, the female builds a series of mud cells, side by side and one at a time. Once the first cell is finished, she sets off in search of caterpillars, which she paralyzes with her sting. When the nest is stocked with several prey items, she lays a* *single egg, suspended from a stalk, and seals the nest with mud. She then proceeds to build a second, adjacent cell and repeats the process until she has a series of 4–6 cells in a row. Meanwhile, the egg hatches and the larva feeds on the stored prey.*

6

5 6 In the most highly developed social wasps, such as the European Common wasp (Vespula vulgaris) *below*, an overwintered, inseminated queen labors alone to construct a new nest in springtime. Note the plump larvae in their cells. By late summer the nest can grow to a sizeable structure, as shown at left. The inner cells containing the brood are protected by a capacious outer shell of paper that often has a scalelike texture, as here.

5

7

4

4 In most social wasps (Vespidae) the nest is fashioned from "paper" fashioned from wood fiber mixed with saliva. There is often no outer covering to the nest, leaving the cells open to the sky. These Parasol wasps (Apoica pallens) *in Brazil are nocturnal, spending the day clustered on the nest.*

7 The nests of social wasps come in all shapes and sizes. In Mischocyttarus vaqueroi (Vespidae) from Peru the individual cells are placed in an offset, end-on-end orientation to form a string that is suspended beneath a rock or the roof of a house.

KP-M

ARACHNIDS

tHE ARACHNIDA BOASTS SOME OF THE BEST *known but least loved animals, including the spiders, scorpions, mites, and ticks. Apart from a few families of mites and some spiders that have returned to an aquatic way of life, arachnids are primarily land dwellers. They have been so successful that members can be found in just about every land, freshwater, and marine habitat.*

For the most part, arachnids are free-living predators, mainly of other arthropods. Harvestmen, however, will also eat such things as fungi and decaying plants and insects, while mites are unique in that they include plant and detritus feeders as well as parasites of vertebrates and invertebrates. The ticks are exclusively blood-sucking parasites of vertebrates.

The Arachnida is an economically important group. Certain scorpions and spiders have venom that is highly toxic to humans, while the mites and ticks include species that transmit human diseases or are pests of domestic livestock; a number of species of mites cause damage to horticultural and agricultural plants. However, many other species are beneficial as they feed on harmful arthropods, while the large numbers of detritus-feeding mites in the soil play an essential part in the breakdown of organic material and the consequent recycling of nutrients.

The Differences from Insects
FORM AND FUNCTION

The class Arachnida is an ancient group. The earliest fossil arachnid, a scorpion, dates back to the Silurian period, some 400 million years ago. Fossil evidence suggests that the ancestral arachnids were scorpionlike, primarily marine animals, the Eurypterida, belonging to the class Merostomata, whose only living members are five species of horseshoe or king crabs. Arachnids are grouped with horseshoe crabs and sea spiders (class Pycnogonida) in the phylum Chelicerata, distinguished from other arthropods by differences in the appendages at the front of the body. In chelicerates, the first are a pair of feeding organs, the chelicerae, the second a pair of leglike pedipalps. (The other arthropods have one or two pairs of antennae in front of a pair of "chewing" mandibles.)

Arachnids are often wrongly referred to as insects, but they have many differing characters. For example, arachnids lack antennae, mandibles, wings, and compound eyes, while, perhaps most obviously, they (usually) have four pairs of legs,

○ **Above** *Scorpions, such as this* Buthus occitanus *(Buthidae) from Europe, have no waist; the front part of the body (prosoma) is joined to the back (opisthosoma) across their entire width.*

○ **Left** *This splay-legged harvestman (Dicranopalpus ramosus) displays the long, spindly legs characteristic of this arachnid subclass. As in this specimen, harvestmen often shed legs as a defensive ploy (autotomy).*

not three as in insects. Also, instead of the three body divisions of insects (head, thorax, abdomen), arachnids have only two regions – the anterior cephalothorax, or prosoma, and the posterior abdomen, or opisthosoma.

The two parts are joined along their whole width in scorpions, pseudoscorpions, ticks, mites, and harvestmen, whereas whip spiders, spiders, and ricinuleids have a narrow connecting waist (the pedicel) between them. In spiders, the pedicel is particularly marked, while in ricinuleids it lies hidden below an extension of the abdominal exoskeleton. The remaining subclasses are all broad-waisted.

External signs of segmentation are often hidden by chitinous plates. In most subclasses, the back of the cephalothorax is entirely covered by a shield (carapace). Schizomids, microwhip scorpions, and sun spiders, however, have a divided carapace. Abdominal segmentation is evident in all groups apart from spiders, ricinuleids, ticks, the vast majority of mites, and some harvestmen. In ticks and mites fusion is so extreme that there is no distinguishing boundary between the cephalothorax and abdomen.

Scorpions also differ, as the abdomen narrows in the posterior half to form the "tail," ending in the familiar sting. At the end of the abdomen of the whip scorpions, the microwhip scorpions, and the schizomids, there is a slender, articulated

extension, the flagellum. In the first two subclasses it is about as long as the body and consists of some 15 articulations, but in schizomids the flagellum is short and comprised of only three.

In spiders and whip spiders the chelicerae are fanglike for piercing, while in plant-parasitic mites they are long and needlelike for penetrating the plant cells. Apart from feeding, the chelicerae are sometimes used for burrowing, as defensive weapons, and to transfer sperm to females during mating. Spiders and pseudoscorpions have respectively a poison and a silk gland opening into the tips of their chelicerae.

○ **Above** *The abundantly hairy nature of a sun spider's body is clear from this frontal view of a* Solpuga sp. *from South Africa. Note also the relatively long, stoutly-built fangs protruding from below the face. Sun spiders have no poison glands.*

CLASS: ARACHNIDA
11 subclasses; about 80,000 species.

Distribution Worldwide; some subclasses more restricted. Primarily terrestrial, but 45 families of mites (and 1 spider species) aquatic. Practically all habitats, including forests, woodland, grassland, desert, seashore, caves, mountains.

Size Body length 0.08mm–18cm (0.003–7in)

Features Body divides into two regions – the cephalothorax (or prosoma), with 6 segments, and the abdomen (opisthosoma), with 12 segments. Externally, segmentation is often not visible. Cephalothorax bears 6 pairs of appendages: piercing, pincer- or fanglike chelicerae, leg- or pincerlike pedipalps, and 4 pairs of walking legs. The abdomen has no appendages apart from pectines (in scorpions) and spinnerets (spiders). Arachnids lack the antennae, mandibles, and wings of insects. Excretory system includes coxal glands; book lungs present in many groups. Most species are predators, but some mites and all ticks are parasitic, and harvestmen and some mites are plant-eaters.

Life cycle Fertilization usually indirect; newly hatched nymph resembles small adult.

Conservation status The IUCN currently lists 1 Araneae species – the Kauai Cave wolf spider – as Endangered; in addition, 7 spiders, 1 harvestman, and 1 pseudoscorpion species are listed as Vulnerable.

SUBCLASSES:

SPIDERS Aranae		p200

About 35,000 species in 3 suborders and 106 families. Families include Tarantulas (Theraphosidae), Funnel-web spiders (Dipluridae), Money spiders (Linyphiidae), Wolf spiders (Lycosidae), and Jumping spiders (Salticidae)

MITES AND TICKS Acari		p214

About 35,000 species (850 of them ticks) in 7 orders. Species include Follicle mite (*Demodex folliculorum*), Flour mite (*Acarus siro*), Scabies mite (*Sarcoptes scabei*), Wood tick (*Dermacentor andersoni*), and Fowl tick (*Argas persicus*)

SCORPIONS Scorpiones		p220

1,500 species in 9 subclasses

PSEUDOSCORPIONS Pseudoscorpiones		p221

2,000 species

SUN SPIDERS Solifugae		p221

900 species

WHIP SCORPIONS Uropygi		p222

85 species

MICROWHIP SCORPIONS Palpigradi		p222

60 species

SCHIZOMIDS Schizomida		p222

80 species

WHIP SPIDERS Amblypygi		p222

70 species

RICINULEIDS Ricinulei		p222

35 species

HARVESTMEN Opiliones		p222

4,500 species

The second pair of appendages, the pedipalps, flank the mouth and are also variously modified. They can be leglike, sometimes flexed for grasping or, as in scorpions and pseudoscorpions, ending in a large pincer. A poison gland opens into the pedipalps of pseudoscorpions; those of certain plant mites have silk glands; while the end segment of the pedipalps of male spiders is adapted to store sperm and impregnate the female. The pedipalps are sometimes also used to keep the chelicerae clean. The only arachnids not to have four pairs of legs occur in young ricinuleids, larval ticks and mites, and the mites of the family Podapolipodidae, all of which possess three pairs of legs, and in the gall mites (family Eriophyidae), which have only two pairs. Arachnid legs end in a maximum of three toothed or smooth claws and, particularly on the end segments, are equipped with sensory hairs. The first pair of legs often act as feelers; in whip scorpions and whip spiders this specialization is carried to extremes as the front legs are exceptionally long and slender and used solely for sensory purposes, the animals walking on just six legs. Other functions of legs include drawing silk threads, manipulating prey, and, in aquatic mites, swimming.

There are no abdominal appendages in most arachnids, with two exceptions: these are the silk-producing spinnerets of spiders and the comblike organs, the pectines, peculiar to scorpions. Most of the internal organ systems and a number of glands open into the abdomen.

The cephalothorax has large bundles of muscles connected to the chelicerae, pedipalps, and legs anchored to special internal projections of the exoskeleton, while the abdomen possesses only narrow muscle strips, needed for the opening and closing of the various orifices and for movements of the gut. Each segment of the appendages has separate extensor and retractor muscles.

Arachnids have an "open" circulatory system, with usually a tubular, pumping heart. The blood is a colorless liquid and, in some spiders and scorpions, is itself poisonous to predators.

The nervous system is generally greatly reduced, comprising a ringlike "brain" through which runs the esophagus, giving rise to nerves that innervate the appendages, the various internal organ systems, and the cuticular sense organs.

Food in Liquid Form
DIET AND FEEDING

Apart from some species of mites that can ingest solid particles such as fungal spores, arachnids take their food in liquid, partially digested form. Once the body of the prey has been pierced (or, in phytophagous mites, the epidermis of the plant), salivary juices containing enzymes pour into the tissues and digestion begins. The resulting "soup" is sucked through a shallow tube, the prebuccal cavity, at the bottom of which is the mouth. In some groups, the wall of the prebuccal cavity has cuticular spines to filter out solid particles. Alternate contraction and relaxation of muscles attaching the pharynx to the exoskeleton sucks food into the pharynx and then pumps it out through the esophagus (the gullet) into the midgut. Blind sacs (diverticula) branching off the midgut fill with the partly digested food, sometimes expanding to fill the whole of the abdomen. The walls of the midgut contain secretory cells that produce the enzymes, and absorptive cells which, when digestion is complete, take up the nutrients and pass them to surrounding storage cells. The waste products are expelled to the outside via the hindgut and the anus, which is usually under the tip of the abdomen.

Other waste products are secreted in the form of guanine by paired coxal glands by the base of the first leg segments and Malpighian tubules emptying into the hindgut – some subclasses have one or other type, but most have both. Each coxal gland consists of a thin-walled, round sac immersed in blood with a long, often partly coiled, tube leading to the outside; the number and position of openings vary between subclasses.

Book lungs and Tracheae
RESPIRATION

In some mites, larval ticks, and microwhip scorpions, respiration is achieved by the simple diffusion of gases through the exoskeleton. More usually, specialized structures are employed in the form of book lungs or tracheae. A respiratory system consisting of tracheae only is found in pseudoscorpions, in sun spiders, harvestmen, ricinuleids, most mites and ticks, and a few spiders. Whip scorpions, whip spiders, schizomids, and a small number of spiders have book lungs only, while scorpions and the majority of spiders have both systems.

Book lungs occur in pairs at the front of the abdomen, each opening onto the underside via a slitlike pore, the spiracle. The maximum number of four pairs is seen in scorpions; but one or two pairs is more usual.

Sieve tracheae are found in ricinuleids, pseudoscorpions, and some spiders. The spiracle opens into an air chamber from which bundles of tracheae arise. The tube tracheae of harvestmen, sun spiders, mites, and most spiders are unbranched or single-branched tubes. The spiracle either opens into a chamber or directly into a trachea.

◗ **Right** *Most true spiders of the order Araneae have eight eyes. In jumping spiders (Salticidae) the anterior-median (front) pair of eyes are exceptionally large, giving a high degree of image resolution and very accurate estimation of distance.*

SENSE ORGANS OF ARACHNIDS

The legs of most arachnids bear conspicuous, usually black, erect bristles – the spines. The base of each spine communicates with a nerve ending. Setae, finer than spines (short ones give arachnids their hairy appearance), are also in communication with a nerve cell. Setae are very variable in shape; they can, for example, be serrated, feathered, or branched. Most are sensitive to touch, but others detect temperature, humidity levels, and chemicals (for example, pheromones). Threadlike trichobothria are considered to perceive air vibrations.

Schizomids, ricinuleids, and certain ticks, mites, and pseudoscorpions are eyeless. Where eyes occur, they are simple and found on the upper surface of the carapace. Harvestmen and sun spiders have just one pair of eyes, but most other arachnids with eyes have four pairs. Some scorpions have six pairs.

Slit, or lyriform, organs on the body and appendages of most arachnids help with orientation of the body. The underside of a membrane covering a fluid-filled, slitlike depression in the cuticle touches a hairlike projection originating from a nerve cell. Any change in tension of the exoskeleton (as during movement) is communicated to the nerve via the membrane.

The Sexuality of Spiders and Scorpions
REPRODUCTION AND LIFE CYCLE

The sexes are always separate. In both male and female the genital orifice occurs on the underside of the abdomen. In the male, sperm passes from the one or two testes along the vas deferens to the genital orifice. Similarly, the female has one or two ovaries, each with an associated oviduct leading to the outside. Most female spiders have separate orifices for the entrance of sperm and the exit of the fertilized egg. Sperm may be passed in a liquid medium or in stalked packets called spermatophores. The shape of the spermatophore is characteristic, even of individual species. The female either takes up the sperm herself, or else it is helped into her orifice by one or more appendages of the male. The males of harvestmen and some mites have a "penis" to transfer sperm directly to the female. There is often an elaborate courtship preceding copulation, enabling the female to recognize the male as a potential mate rather than a potential meal. Stridulatory organs, generally consisting of ridged or toothed areas on the sides of the body and the appendages, have been identified in scorpions, spiders, and whip spiders. In some species, only males have them.

The first active stage (nymph) is immediately recognizable as an arachnid. In most groups it only differs from the adult in size, the absence of secondary sexual characters and reproductive organs, and the smaller number of bristles (setae). The number of nymphal stages varies between the groups. The first active stage of mites and ticks is the highly characteristic six-legged larva, which is then followed by a variable number of eight-egged nymphs. Lifespan ranges from a few weeks in certain mites up to 30 years in females of the largest spiders reared in captivity. However, the expectation in nature is not really known.   RP-M/AB

Spiders

SPIDERS ARE PREDATORY, CARNIVOROUS *arthropods. They play an important part in the balance of nature by helping to control the numbers of insects. They are highly fitted for this role because of their venom, which is used for attack and defense, and because of the many uses they have for silk, which they employ with great skill and ingenuity. Not all spiders actually build webs, but all produce and use silk for a variety of purposes. The large number that do not build webs instead employ a wide range of hunting tactics to catch their prey.*

Spiders are an ancient group and were probably in existence during the Devonian period, more than 400 million years ago. By the beginning of the Carboniferous era (over 350 million years ago), when insects were in their infancy, numbers of highly developed spiders were already in existence. Many of the fossil species described from the Carboniferous are remarkably like the present-day "living fossils," the liphistiomorphs of the suborder Mesothelae. However, in the fossil record there is a long gap before fossil spiders reappear in the Oligocene (34 million years ago). In Baltic amber and other sources in North America and Europe, many well-preserved fossils have been found.

The discovery of the peculiar family Archaeidae is a similar story to that of the much more famous coelacanth fish, but it happened much earlier. First described in 1854 as fossils in Baltic amber, they were found alive in Madagascar a quarter of a century later. These bizarre spiders have an enormously elevated head region and grossly developed fangs, used, apparently, to spear other spiders! Although very rare, they are today known from South Africa and Australasia as well as Madagascar, with relatives in South America.

○ **Above** *This wandering spider (Ctenus sp.; Ctenidae) from Uganda displays features characteristic of a fast arachnid hunter – long legs with fine sensory hairs and multiple eyes (ocelli).*

◐ **Right** *The cryptic coloring of this female Common flower spider (Misumena vatia) provides perfectly camouflage for ambushing a fly. It has the squat, bulky build typical of most crab spiders (family Thomisidae).*

◐ **Right** *Spiders' bodies divide into two main sections, the cephalothorax and abdomen. There are no antennae, but the pedipalps act as feelers. Spiders feed by secreting or injecting digestive juices onto or into their prey, then sucking up the liquid food that results.*

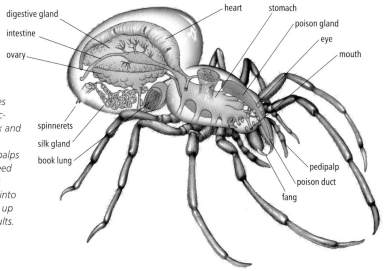

digestive gland
intestine
ovary
spinnerets
silk gland
book lung
heart
stomach
poison gland
eye
mouth
pedipalp
poison duct
fang

Spinnerets and Venom Glands
FORM AND FUNCTION

The largest of all spiders is the Goliath tarantula of South America (*Theraphosa leblondi*), which has a legspan of 26cm (10.2in). The smallest fully-grown spider, the male of a species called *Patu digua*, has a bodylength of just 0.37 mm, which is smaller than a pin-head. Apart from size, spiders also vary greatly in their appearance. While some are brightly colored, others are very inconspicuous and camouflaged. Some are fat-bodied, others are wormlike, and many are bizarrely decorated with strange surface features. Spiders can also be convincing mimics of ants, distasteful bugs, and even bird droppings on a leaf.

The two main parts of a spider's body are the cephalothorax (combined head and thorax) and the abdomen. These two parts are joined by a narrow tube, the pedicel. The cephalothorax is covered by a hardened carapace, and contains the brain, poison glands, and stomach. Six pairs of appendages arise from the cephalothorax: four pairs of legs, a pair of palps, and a pair of jaws (chelicerae) equipped with powerful fangs.

SPIDERS

Class: Arachnida

Order: Araneae

About 35,000 known species are currently recognized in 3 suborders – Mesothelae, Mygalomorphae, and Araneomorphae – and 106 families, although perhaps a similar number may remain to be discovered.

DISTRIBUTION Worldwide, excluding the Antarctic icecap; diverse habitats in forest, heath, grassland, deserts, mountains, caves, buildings, beaches, marshes; mostly terrestrial, but 1 species (*Argyroneta aquatica*) lives underwater in lakes and ponds.

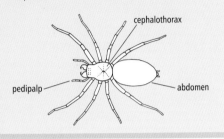

SIZE Body length ranges from 0.37mm–9cm (0.15–3.5in), legspan up to 26cm (10.2in).

FEATURES Distinct from other arachnids in the widespread use of silk, and in having a copulatory organ on the male pedipalp and an unsegmented abdomen (except suborder Mesothelae) joined by a narrow pedicel to the cephalothorax.

LIFE CYCLE Copulation lasts from a few seconds to many hours; courtship is common in species where the male may be at risk of attack from the female. Typically, eggs laid in the fall or dry season hatch in the following spring or wet season. Most spiders live for about 1 year, although, exceptionally, some theraposids (tarantulas) have survived in captivity for up to 25 years.

CONSERVATION STATUS Many species of spider are thriving, but a handful are at risk. Those currently listed by the IUCN include the Kauai Cave wolf spider, which is Endangered, and 7 others considered Vulnerable, including the Great raft spider, the Glacier Bay wolf spider, the Lake Placid funnel wolf spider, the Doloff cave spider, and 3 species of Kocevje subterranean spiders. The Red-kneed tarantula is classed as Lower Risk/Near Threatened.

See suborders table ▷

The eyes lie at the front of the cephalothorax. The eight eyes of most spiders are classed as simple ocelli, unlike the compound eyes found in many insects and crustaceans. The visual acuity of most spiders is very poor, as many are nocturnal and their primary sense is tactile. They "listen" to the world around them through vibrations transmitted by air, the ground, their webs, or the surface of water. However, some spider families, in particular the jumping spiders (family Salticidae) and the ogre-eyed or net-casting spiders (family Dinopidae), have exceptional eyesight. Jumping spiders can visually distinguish mates from prey; and ogre-eyed spiders can see prey in the deep darkness of the rain forest at night.

Below the eyes lie the chelicerae, which are the offensive weapons of the spider. Each chelicera consists of two parts: a strong basal segment and an articulating fang. In spider classification, the two main suborders are separated according to the way their chelicerae move. In the suborder Mygalomorphae, which includes the tarantulas and trap-door spiders, the body rises, allowing the chelicerae to strike downwards like parallel pickaxes. By contrast, in the more advanced Araneomorphae, the jaws close together like sugar tongs, which avoids the need for the body to rise.

The chelicerae are used not only for attack and defense but also for other tasks. For example, trap-door spiders use their chelicerae, which are furnished with a rake of teeth, to dig burrows, and fishing spiders (family Pisauridae) use the chelicerae to hold their large egg cocoons as they run on the surface of the water. Some spiders interlock their chelicerae during mating, and often those of the male are larger, to help restrain the female.

The cephalothorax also bears a single pair of pedipalps ("palps") and four pairs of walking legs. The palps are leglike but have only six, instead of seven, segments. They are not used for locomotion but assist in many tasks such as prey capture. The ends of both palps and legs bear taste receptors. In adult male spiders the tip of the palp is modified into a copulatory organ.

Spiders' legs have seven segments; from the base, these are the coxa, trochanter, femur, patella, tibia, metatarsus, and tarsus. At the tip of the tarsus are either two or three claws. Among araneomorphs, two-clawed spiders are hunters, while web-builders have the additional claw to hold silk threads. Many two-clawed spiders also have a

RL

▶ **Right** Representative spider species:
1 Heather spider (Thomisus onustus) on an orchid, and **2** Misumena vatia, on a daisy, awaiting prey. **3** Black widow (Latrodectus mactans). **4** A water spider (Argyroneta aquatica; Agelenidae) drags a minnow into its diving bell. **5** A Wasp spider (Argiope bruennichi) in its web. **6** Grass jumper (Evarcha llamata) and **7** Four-spot orb-weaver (Araneus quadratus) couples display courting behavior (see box opposite).

dense brush of hairs called "claw tufts" that enable them to walk upside-down on smooth surfaces such as the undersides of leaves. The adhesive forces of the tufts are high because the hairs are split into thousands of microscopic "end feet," thus giving a large surface area.

The pedicel, which carries the nerve cord, aorta, and intestine, connects the cephalothorax to the abdomen. The abdomen itself is usually saclike and quite soft, and is able to expand when fully fed or swollen with eggs. The abdomen contains the heart, digestive tract, silk glands, and the respiratory and reproductive systems. The genital opening is on the underside towards the base and is flanked by the rectangular patches of the book lungs (see below). At the end of the abdomen is the anus, and below that the spinnerets. From the spinnerets, up to six in number, extremely fine strands of silk emerge through tiny spigots.

Spiders breathe air through book lungs and tracheae. A book lung is a chamber containing a number of overlapping folds or leaves (hence the name). Deoxygenated blood is moved by pulsations of the heart through the stacks of leaves, which alternate with air-filled spaces. The organ is visible externally as a patch on the underside of the abdomen toward its base. Araneomorphs have one pair of book lungs, except in the anomalous family Hypochilidae, which has two pairs like the mygalomorphs and liphistiomorphs.

Book lungs present a large surface-to-air area through which water may be lost. Thus, to save water and for greater efficiency, the second pair in most spiders is replaced by a system of tracheae. Like those of insects, the tracheae are branching tubes that carry oxygen directly to the tissues. In most spiders the external opening to the tracheae is positioned close to the spinnerets.

Spiders use venom to quickly immobilize or kill their prey. It is also used in defense. Apart from one family, the Uloboridae, all spiders possess venom glands. Most, however, are not highly venomous, and less than 100 species in the world are considered to be of serious medical importance.

The two venom glands are each connected by a narrow duct to a fang that opens at a pore near its tip. Venom is ejected by contraction of the gland's musculature. Spider venoms are complex compounds that vary from species to species. Venom that has an effect on humans is classed as either neurotoxic or cytotoxic. Neurotoxic venoms affect the neuro-muscular junctions, causing cramp and paralysis. Cytotoxic venoms tend to cause necrosis of the tissues, leaving scars that are difficult to heal. Some cytotoxic venoms, such as those of the

5

6

7

ATTRACTING A FEMALE'S ATTENTION

The predatory nature of spiders limits social behavior generally and can make mating a hazardous business, particularly for the male, which is usually smaller than the female. Before attempting to mate, males will usually take care to signal their intention carefully – literally so in the case of *Evarcha* species (**6** above), since semaphore signalling is the male jumping spider's language of courtship. Males of some orb-web species seek to notify their intended partner by sensory cues transmitted through the web. In *Araneus quadratus* (Araneidae) **7**, for example, the courting male vibrates the web with a specific frequency to signal to the female that he is a prospective mate rather than potential prey. The male will then attempt to coax the female on to a special mating thread that he has previously joined to the web. Usually he will have located her in the first place by the presence of contact pheromones that she had laid earlier on the lines holding the web.

recluse spiders (*Loxosceles* species), may also be hemolytic, leading to kidney failure.

The highly toxic bite of any of the fingernail-sized black widow spiders (*Latrodectus* species) is not immediately painful. The first real pain is felt in the lymph nodes from 10 to 60 minutes after the bite. The muscles then develop severe cramps (known as *facies latrodectismi*), affecting particularly the abdomen and face. Without treatment, symptoms can continue for a week, with the risk of death at any time from respiratory paralysis. *Latrodectus* is found in dry, warm regions of the world. In America it is called the Black widow, in

◁ Left *The black and orange coloration of this female Long-horned orb-weaver (Gasteracantha arcuata; Araneidae) warns would-be predators of the distasteful properties typical of the genus. Most species are elaborately decorated with "horns" and spines, but this Southeast Asian species is the most bizarre of all.*

southern Europe the *malmignette*, in South Africa the Button spider, in Australia the Redback, and in New Zealand the katipo. Fortunately, antivenenes are now available in most of the affected countries.

One of the most dangerous spiders in the world is the Sydney funnel-web spider (*Atrax robustus*) of eastern Australia. The venom is highly acidic and causes immediate pain. Enzymes in the venom break down tissues and assist penetration. The symptoms include nausea, vomiting, salivation, and crying. Uncoordinated muscle activity intensifies, with severe abdominal pain and bizarre heart beats. Paralysis of the respiratory muscles follows, with an accumulation of fluid in the lungs and a severe drop in blood pressure. If delirium and coma occur, death may also follow.

Other poisonous spiders include the fast-moving and aggressive Brazilian wandering spider (*Phoneutria fera*) and the rather delicate recluse spiders (*Loxosceles* species) of South and North

America. Other harmful South American genera include *Lycosa* (wolf spiders), *Trechona* (hunting spiders), and the orb-web spider genus *Mastophora* in addition to *Latrodectus*. Spitting spiders (family Scytodidae) have enlarged venom glands that also produce glue. Their unique method of prey capture relies on squirting the mixture of venom and glue through the chelicerae to paralyze their prey and fix it to the substrate. But they are not dangerous to humans!

Hunters and Web-builders
DIET

Spiders are broadly divided into web-builders and hunting spiders, which do not build webs. There are many examples of hunting spiders that can overpower insects two to three times their own size; for example, quite small crab spiders of the family Thomisidae sometimes grab large bumble-bees on visits to flowers.

The majority of spiders take only living prey. Their food is mainly insects and other spiders. Some take crustaceans and worms, but many refuse ants, wasps, beetles, and distasteful bugs. Diets range from the varied to the highly specific, as, for example, in the tropical bolas spiders (family Araneidae), which feed on males of a single species of moth. The spider lures its prey by imitating the sex pheromone of the female moth.

The Wandering spider of Central America (*Cupiennius salei*) is a typical hunter, although it spends much of its time lying in ambush. It is extremely patient, and highly sensitive to the slightest vibrations. When the prey comes close, it launches a rapid attack, grabbing it in less than 0.2 seconds. Jumping spiders are also hunters, but they are aided by exceptionally good eyesight. Their highly developed main eyes (anterior median eyes) can analyze shapes and recognize motionless prey at distances up to 28cm (11in).

In all spiders, digestion is initiated outside the body. After the prey has been subdued by venom or trussed up in silk, it is held in the jaws while the spider vomits some digestive fluid on to it from the digestive tract. This process alternates with periods when the digested tissues are sucked in. Tangle-web weavers (family Theridiidae) and crab spiders leave their prey almost intact after sucking out the soft tissues because they have no teeth on the chelicerae. Orb-web weavers, on the other hand, with cheliceral teeth, mash up their prey so that it is no longer recognizable. The ability of spiders to survive for months without food is due to their low rate of metabolism.

Spiders are themselves predated by mammals, birds, reptiles, amphibians, and other spiders. Fish, such as trout, eat spiders that fall onto the surface of the water. Even bats can pick up ground spiders and orb-weavers. Ants, assassin bugs, and praying mantises all also prey on spiders. Insect

⚪ **Left and above** *Techniques of prey capture:* **1** *Web-builders like the St. Andrew's cross spider (*Argiope aethereae*) trap flies and other insects in the sticky threads of the web, often cocooning them in silk to eat later.* **2** *Trap-door spiders are ambush hunters, waiting to attack prey that passes near their burrow.* **3** *Net-casting spiders spin a net and drop it over unsuspecting prey.* **4** *The powerful jaws (chelicerae) of spiders are equipped with venomous fangs.*

parasites include minute wasps that parasitize spider eggs, endo- and exoparasitic flies, and large wasps, including the spider-hunting wasps. The larvae of these last feed on the living tissue of the spider, which is paralyzed after being stung. Other parasites simply attach their eggs to the spider's body, or deposit them in the spider's egg sacs. Many species of fungus and nematodes (round worms) also develop on and within spiders.

Besides these direct enemies, there are also parasitic spiders, known as kleptoparasites, which simply steal food from the webs of larger spiders.

Everywhere but the Ice Cap
DISTRIBUTION PATTERNS

Spiders are found all around us, but they are hardly noticed unless they are particularly large or abundant. They live in the house, in the garden, on lamp-posts, in forests, and in most other terrestrial habitats throughout the world. While the greatest diversity of species occurs in tropical rain forest, they are also well represented in temperate woodland, heathland and grassland, and even in some aquatic habitats. They thrive wherever there are plenty of insects. Many species, however, are specialists that inhabit barren and hostile environments such as deserts and mountain tops. Perhaps the only region of the world without spiders is the windswept ice cap of Antarctica. One of the remarkable things about spiders is that some inhabit the most unpromising habitats, such as underground telephone ducts – places that seem to be distinctly lacking in insect prey!

In favorable situations, such as unspoiled meadows and woodland glades, spiders can be present in great numbers. The arachnologist W. S. Bristowe calculated in the 1930s that an undisturbed field in southeast England might contain more than 2 million spiders to the acre (equivalent to almost 5 million per hectare). He went on to estimate that, for the country as a whole, the weight of insects consumed annually by spiders would exceed the total weight of its human inhabitants. Bristowe himself considered that this was a conservative estimate but now, decades later, and following the loss of meadows and the general use of insecticides (not to mention the increased weight of humans), it may no longer be true!

Though many individual spiders may be present in a habitat, it can be difficult to see them. Spiders are masters of the disappearing act because of their camouflage and body posture.

TARANTULAS AND BIRD-EATERS

Bird-eating spiders – known as tarantulas in North America, baboon spiders in Africa, and *araños peludas* ("hairy spiders") in Spanish America – are very large members of the family Theraphosidae. Their size rivals that of the biggest land invertebrates such as giant centipedes, Goliath beetles, and Imperial scorpions. The Goliath tarantula (*Theraphosa leblondi*) of northern South America has a legspan in the male of up to 26cm (10.2in), although its weight is no more than 85g (3oz).

Tarantulas are essentially forest spiders, although in some arid regions such as Mexico and the southwestern USA there are many desert-adapted forms. Typically, tarantulas are black or brown in appearance, although some have vivid coloration.

Despite their formidable appearance, many species of tarantulas are relatively placid and will attack humans only when provoked. Other tarantulas, however, particularly those from Africa and southeast Asia, can be irritable and aggressive. Many are capable of giving a painful bite, although it is rarely serious. To attack, these spiders raise the front of the body with legs held high in the air, and then strike powerfully downwards to drive in the large fangs. With such power, it seems that a potent venom is relatively unimportant. New World tarantulas can also release clouds of hairs from the

abdomen when irritated. Such hairs are highly dangerous if rubbed into the eye, because they are furnished with microscopic barbs that make them impossible to remove.

The name "bird-eating spiders" is somewhat misleading, because the spiders in fact take relatively few birds; their diet is more likely to include small reptiles, amphibians, beetles, moths, grasshoppers, and other spiders. Some species are said to prey on small snakes. Tarantulas have many enemies: mammals dig them from their burrows, and the young are preyed upon by birds, reptiles, and amphibians. They also suffer from the attentions of the tarantula hawk wasps (*Pepsis* species), which sting and paralyze the spider, then drag it to a burrow that is sealed after an egg is laid on it. On hatching, the larvae feed on the still-living spider.

◗ **Right**
Tarantulas have a thick covering of hairs, making them highly sensitive to vibrations.

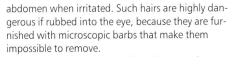

◗ **Below** Jumping spiders (Salticidae) are the keenest-eyed of all spiders and can focus their forward-pointing main eyes to resolve a clear image. This Heavy jumper (Hyllus giganteus) female in Borneo has caught a bug.

Many have carefully concealed silk nests, or even, in the case of the trap-door spiders of the family Ctenizidae, tunnels in the ground that are closed by a trapdoor. An observer should thus look carefully in all the different niches that spiders are likely to occupy. For example, a woodland habitat has a number of different zones, including the ground layer, field layer, shrub layer, woody zone, and canopy, and each one will generally have a different community of spiders.

In Japan, a study of tree species of the orb-web weaver genus *Tetragnatha* (family Tetragnathidae) has revealed the sort of division of habitat, to reduce competition, that is typical of closely related, coexisting spiders. *Tetragnatha praedonia*, *T. japonica*, and *T. pinicola* all build their horizontal orb webs across small streams where prey density is high. *Tetragnatha praedonia* suspends its web from shrubs about 1–2m (3–6.5ft) above the surface. *T. japonica* uses grasses below 1m (3ft), and *T. pinicola* also uses grasses, but its web, below 20cm (8in), lies very close to the water surface.

Among European species that occur only in strictly defined habitats are a wolf spider (*Pardosa traillii*) found on mountain scree slopes, a jumping spider (*Sitticus rupicola*) inhabiting coastal shingle, and a money spider (*Glyphesis cottonae*) that dwells exclusively in sphagnum moss. *Tetrilus macrophthalmus* (Agelenidae) and *Lepthyphantes midas* (Linyphiidae) are species known only from rotten cavities in trees in one or two ancient woodlands; they will be able to avoid extinction only for as long as this unique habitat survives.

Spiders are active colonizers of any new or

unoccupied territory. For example, if any room is left undisturbed, the arachnids will soon move in! Furthermore, spiders are usually among the first creatures to colonize areas devastated by volcanic eruptions. Only one year after the cataclysmic eruption of Krakatau (Indonesia) in 1883, a biologist visiting the island discovered just one solitary form of life – a spider. Fifty years later, more than 90 species of spiders were recorded there. Today, the number has likely doubled.

Spiders populate remote places by flying through the air on long strands of silk, a technique known as "ballooning." Small and young spiders under 5mm (0.2in) long climb to a prominent point and then let out silk on the breeze until they become airborne; when large numbers take off together, their strands may coalesce and form sheets of gossamer. Many of these aerial travellers get no further than the next bush, but others may soar high on the breeze and be transported considerable distances in this way; spiders are often recorded in samples of aerial plankton from heights of up to 5,000m (16,500ft). They are at the mercy of the weather en route, and many individuals find themselves dumped in unsuitable environments such as the sea; others, however, have more luck and may reach that *terra nova*!

Dispersal is necessary to prevent overcrowding and to avoid cannibalism, which is relatively common among the Araneae. Species that have the ability to disperse over great distances tend to have a wide distribution in the world. Other species, however, are unable to disperse over more than a short distance. For example, the islands of the Great Barrier Reef have been colonized by a wide range of spiders of many different families, but not by the large tarantulas that are common on the mainland only a short distance away.

These days, there are many cosmopolitan species that have, with human help, become global travellers. The large and fast-moving Banana spider (*Heteropoda venatoria*) is one such species. For decades it has been transported around the world as a stowaway in company with exports of bananas (among which it sits tight, gripping its egg sac). Today it is widely distributed throughout the tropics and subtropics, including Florida. Most of its close relatives are found in southeast Asia, so we can surmise that this was the region where the species originated. Besides benefiting from modern transportation methods, the global spread of many species is also facilitated by the warmth and shelter afforded by buildings. In Europe, which is generally too cold for the species, the Banana spider inhabits hothouses in a number of botanical gardens.

○ **Right** *In many spiders males are smaller than their female counterparts. This trait is especially marked in species such as* Nephila antipodeana *(Tetragnathidae) in which the tiny male, shown here at the top of the female's web, is dwarfed by his prospective spouse.*

The Dangerous Business of Mating

SOCIAL BEHAVIOR

Spiders begin life as eggs. Eggs laid in the fall or dry season usually hatch in the following spring or wet season. Most spiders have a one-year life cycle, but some tropical jumping spiders have more than one generation per year. Some spiders live for 2–5 years, and theraphosids (tarantulas) in captivity may live up to 25 years. During a lifetime, they typically grow through 4–12 molts of the exoskeleton before finally becoming adult.

Adult males can usually be distinguished from adult females by their smaller size, slimmer body, and relatively longer legs. This sexual dimorphism is most obvious in many tropical web-builders, such as the golden orb-weavers (*Nephila* species), where the females may be giants – up to 45mm (1.8in) in body length – and the males are frequently a dwarfish 4–8mm (0.2–0.3in). The theory is that the advantage that small size confers on the tiny male is that it permits him to enter the female's web with impunity because he is too small for her to bother to eat.

Mating among spiders is a remarkable process that involves a unique method of storage and transfer of sperm. The male's palps carry a pair of bulblike structures that act as accessory sex organs. The bulb and its coiled duct jointly function as a pipette to take up sperm dropped from the genital opening onto a specially-spun "sperm web." When the palps are fully charged with sperm, the male then concentrates on finding a mate. In most cases, this is achieved by following species-specific signals (pheromones) on silk lines laid by the female.

The next stage is courtship, which, if successful, is followed by copulation; this may last from a few seconds to many hours. Among orb-weavers,

courtship is usually lengthy but copulation is brief. In its course the male inserts alternate palps – or, in the case of the more primitive spiders (mygalomorphs), both together – into the female's genitalia. In the relatively advanced spiders (araneomorphs), the structure of the palpal organ has become much more complex than the basic bulb and duct. It combines expandable soft tissue with various hardened (sclerotized) appendages. The appendages project when the palp is inflated by hydraulic pressure and interlock with features on the adult female's genital plate (epigyne). The female has three separate genital openings: two introductory ducts, which receive the tip of the male palp (embolus), and a gonopore, through which the eggs are laid.

The coupling of two predatory and often short-sighted creatures can be a hazardous affair, particularly for the smaller male. Often courtship is essential so that the male can subdue the female's predatory instinct. For example, male orb-weavers attach a mating thread to the female's web and spend many hours plucking the line to coax the female onto it. The Wedding-present spider (*Pisaura mirabilis*), a kind of wolf spider, is famous for its unusual courtship: the male catches an insect, wraps it in silk, and carries it to the female as a "bridal gift." As she feeds on it, the male begins mating. Among the sharp-eyed jumping

◐ **Top** *The European Wedding-present spider* (Pisaura mirabilis; *Pisauridae*) *is unique in being the only spider species in which the male (left) presents the female with a "wedding gift." This consists of a dead insect wrapped in copious amounts of white silk.*

◑ **Left** *The presence of this female Spiny flag spider* (Alpaida bicornuta; *Araneidae*) *from Costa Rica will help to thwart attacks on the egg-sac on which she is sitting. In addition, her warning coloration probably acts as a visual deterrent to birds.*

◑ **Below** *Nursery-web spiders of the Pisauridae family carry their eggs in a silken sac clamped in their jaws. Often, as with this* Dolomedes fimbriatus *specimen, the burden can make walking a difficult task.*

⬛ **Left** *The tiny gray spiderlings of a Meadow wolf spider (Pardosa prativaga; Lycosidae) gather on their mother's back in an urban garden in England. The empty remains of the whitish egg-sac, visible behind the female, will soon be discarded.*

spiders, courtship displays are often performed face to face. The males, usually brightly colored, wave and vibrate their legs and palps.

In most environments, the hazards of life for spiders are so great that females need to produce tens, hundreds, or even thousands of eggs to ensure the survival of the species. Cave spiders of the genus *Telema* (family Telemidae), for example, lay only a single egg, but the tropical forest-dwelling *Cupiennius* (family Ctenidae) lays as many as 2,500 in every egg sac. Spiders' eggs are usually enclosed in a silken egg sac, or cocoon, to protect them from humidity and temperature fluctuations and from egg parasites.

Some spiders guard their egg sac, but those species that produce substantial numbers of egg sacs (up to 20 or more) usually abandon them and rely on camouflage for their protection. Many spiders never see their offspring (often the adults die before the young hatch), but some actively care for the newly hatched spiderlings, providing them with protection and/or feeding.

The very common wolf spiders of the genus *Pardosa* (family Lycosidae) carry their egg sac attached to the spinnerets at the tip of the abdomen. The cocoon is conspicuous and may be as big as the mother herself. She strongly defends the cocoon, and will search for hours if it is removed. After 2–3 weeks she bites open the egg sac, whereupon the brood of up to 100 spiderlings climb onto her abdomen, several layers deep. Living on their own reserves of yolk, they hold on for about a week while the mother continues to hunt prey – but only for herself!

Experiments with wolf spiderlings have shown that there is no mutual recognition. The mother will accept spiderlings from another female, and the spiderlings will climb onto the backs of other spiders, even male spiders of other species, which then often simply eat them.

Nursery-web spiders (family Pisauridae), which are related to wolf spiders, produce a large, globular cocoon that is carefully carried in the mother's jaws. It is often so large that she has to travel awkwardly on extended legs. When the time for hatching is close, she fixes the cocoon to a stem or leaf and surrounds it with a network of silk, forming a protective tent where the spiderlings emerge

to undergo their first molts. In North America and Europe, the mother on guard outside the tent is a common sight during the summer months.

Active feeding of the brood occurs in only a tiny minority of spiders. The level of care ranges from passive provision of prey to direct feeding by regurgitation. Transfer of predigested food is common among social insects but is very rare among spiders; it occurs in only a handful of species in three unrelated families, Theridiidae, Eresidae, and Agelenidae. In some *Theridion* species, newly hatched spiderlings cluster around the mother's mouth to drink from her regurgitate. After their first molt, the mother stops regurgitation but allows the young to share her victims, which she helpfully punctures with her fangs. Later, when the young have grown, she chases them away. In North America and Europe, spiders of the genus *Coelotes* (Agelenidae) carry maternal feeding to the extreme – the mother dies, her tissues break down, and the spiderlings feed on her body.

The great majority of spiders are solitary and cannibalistic, but brood care, as described above, is probably an early stage in the development of sociality. Some spiders are noticeably gregarious, and the extent of their sociability ranges from loose aggregations, such as crowds of webs around a light, to the very few cases of genuine social life. All truly social spiders are web-builders (often cribellates – see Silken Webs), and most live

Spider Suborders

Mesothelae

1 family: **Giant trap-door spiders** (Liphistiidae, 40 species), or liphistiomorphs. Considered to be primitive, with abdominal segmentation (normally, the abdomen of spiders shows no trace of the original segmentation of arthropods); restricted to SE Asia.

Mygalomorphae

15 families, including:
Tarantulas (family Theraphosidae, 800 species). Very large, hairy spiders; eyes small, in compact group; tropical and subtropical. Includes Mexican red-kneed tarantula (*Brachypelma smithi*) and Goliath tarantula (*Theraphosa leblondi*).
Trap-door spiders (family Ctenizidae, 400 species). Rake of teeth present on chelicerae for digging burrows that may be closed with a hinged door; found in most regions with warm climates.
Funnel-web spiders (family Dipluridae, 250 species). Builds webs that incorporate a funnel retreat. Tropical and subtropical. Includes venomous species such as the Sydney funnel-web spider (*Atrax robustus*).

Araneomorphae

Often known as "true" spiders. Over 90 percent of all spiders belong to this suborder. 90 families including:
Tube-web spiders (family Segestriidae, 100 species). Elongated species, with tubular retreat and radiating trigger threads; worldwide.
Spitting spiders (family Scytodidae, 150 species). Only 6 eyes; carapace domed to house enlarged venom/glue glands; squirt a mixture of sticky silk and venom at prey; cosmopolitan except in cold regions.
Comb-footed or **tangle-web spiders** (family Theridiidae, 2,200 species). Usually small spiders with globose abdomens; build tangle webs; worldwide. Includes venomous species such as the American Black widow spider (*Latrodectus mactans*).
Money spiders (family Linyphiidae, 3,700 species). Mostly tiny or small; webs often sheetlike; worldwide. Occasionally discovered landing, as aeronauts, on people.
Orb weavers (family Araneidae, 2,600 species). Usually broad-bodied; webs have sticky silk; worldwide. Includes the common European Garden spider (*Araneus diadematus*) and the tropical bolas spiders, which have greatly reduced webs.

Large-jawed orb weavers (family Tetragnathidae, 250 species). Typical tetragnathids are slim-bodied with large chelicerae; web has open hub; worldwide. Family also includes the large golden orb-weavers (*Nephila* species); tropical and subtropical.
Cobweb weavers (family Agelenidae, 800 species). Fast-moving spiders on large sheet webs; worldwide. Includes Common house spider (*Tegenaria domestica*).
Wolf spiders (family Lycosidae, 2,200 species). Somber-colored ground hunters with 4 large and 4 small eyes; worldwide and often abundant.
Nursery-web spiders (family Pisauridae, 600 species). Like wolf spiders, but eyes smaller; some build nursery webs for the young; many are semi-aquatic (fishing spiders); worldwide.
Night crawlers (family Gnaphosidae, 2,200 species). Nocturnal hunters; dark-colored and often with silvery oval eyes; worldwide.
Sac spiders (family Clubionidae, 1,500 species). Similar to gnaphosids, but usually paler in color; mother sits with young in egg sac; worldwide.
Wandering spiders (family Ctenidae, 350 species). Rather large, fast-moving hunters, often venomous (e.g. *Phoneutria fera* of Brazil); tropical and subtropical.

Huntsman spiders (family Heteropodidae, 500 species). Rather large and fast-moving, with legs extended to the sides (laterigrade); tropical and subtropical. Includes the pantropical Banana spider (*Heteropoda venatoria*).
Crab spiders (family Thomisidae, 2,000 species). Mostly sedentary ambush-hunters; legs crablike (laterigrade); first two pairs of legs longer than last two pairs; worldwide.
Jumping spiders (family Salticidae, 4,400 species). Animated hunting spiders, capable of jumps; often attractively colored, with large front (median) eyes giving exceptional vision; worldwide and especially abundant in tropical regions.
Lampshade weavers (family Hypochilidae, 10 species). Long-legged spiders that make lamp-shaped webs. Two pairs of book lungs. Distribution is disjunct: N. America, China, Tasmania.
Cribellate spiders (main families include Eresidae, Dictynidae, Amaurobiidae, Filistatidae, Dinopidae, and Uloboridae; approximately 1,000 species in total). Produce lace webs, sheet webs, and orb webs of dry, woolly silk. The net-casting spiders of the Dinopidae family uniquely hold their webs between their legs and scoop insects into them.
Telemid cave spiders (family Telemidae, 100 species). Scattered worldwide.

in the tropics, where insects are abundant throughout the year. There, communities can reach as many as 10,000 individuals. The advantages of togetherness are safety in numbers, help in dealing with larger and stronger prey, and plenty of sexual partners, although fights among males often break out. Webs on the outside of the community catch relatively more insects, but those inside get more protection from predators and receive "early warning" vibrations.

The central Mexican spider known as "*el mosquero*" (*Mallos gregalis*; Dictynidae) is one of the most highly social of all spiders. Traditionally, Mexicans installed sections of its web in the home as a protection against flies. The web is a vast sheet of woolly silk that covers bushes with a mass of silken galleries. When an insect becomes trapped in the web, numbers of spiders approach, drag, pull, and bite it, and then feed together. These social spiders live together without territoriality, aggression, or cannibalism, and are remarkably tolerant to outsiders of the same species. Their societies have equality, and all members appear to be fertile, in contrast to the caste systems that are typical of social insects.   PDH

◁ **Left** *The huge webs of the Silk-city spider (Anelosimus eximius; Theridiidae) in Brazil swathe the vegetation on which they are built in curtains of silk. The inhabitants of the nest cooperate to subdue prey.*

SILKEN WEBS

Forming and shaping the spiders' most precious resource

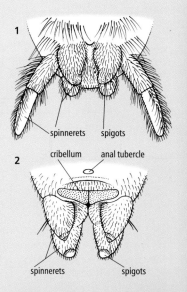

WEB-SPINNING SPIDERS SPEND VIRTUALLY THEIR whole life in contact with silk threads of their own manufacture. New-born spiders are able to build webs – an amazing feat of natural engineering – without the benefit of even a single lesson! From that point on they are constantly making complex calculations, about the size of the space a web must cover, the amount of silk they can produce, the attachment points available for mooring threads, and many other points besides. Indeed, spiders have an impressive ability to act flexibly according to the circumstances. For example, an orb web can be built using just three attachment points, although the spider will use more if they are available. And if a web in one particular place fails to provide enough prey, then the spider will make the decision to move to a new site. Their behavior is all the more impressive when one considers that most spiders cannot see objects, but depend essentially on their sense of touch.

Silk emerges from the spider's spinnerets as extremely fine strands that combine into a single, solid thread. The spinnerets form a group of up to six, each one resembling a showerhead with a number of tiny spigots, and each of these is in turn connected to a particular type of silk gland. Up to seven different glands within the spider's abdomen secrete silk of varied properties for specific purposes, including making cocoons, swathing bands, sticky globules, and safety or draglines, which are anchored to the web or points on the substrate by attachment disks. A disturbed spider will often drop like a stone on a dragline, then wait and climb back up again when the danger has passed.

Orb-weavers possess the full range of silk-producing glands, while hunting spiders, which do not build webs, usually have only four: ampullate glands, to produce silk for the dragline and for the web's dry scaffolding threads; piriform, for the fine silk that bonds between two threads (attachment disks); aciniform, to make the sperm web and swathing bands for wrapping prey, as well as the woolly silk used in the stabilimenta that adorn some webs; and cylindrical (absent in the adult male), to provide silk for the egg cocoon. Orb-weavers additionally have flagelliforme glands, for the thread of the sticky spiral, and aggregates for glue (also found in tangle-weavers of the family Theridiidae).

Of all the different kinds of spider silk, the dragline silk of the golden orb spiders (*Nephila* species) is believed to be the strongest natural fiber known – approximately twice as tough as silk from the silkworm. The thread is more elastic than nylon and stronger than steel of the same diameter. A typical strand of Garden spider silk has a diameter

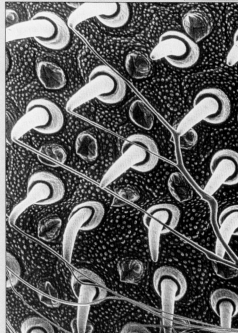

of about 0.003mm (0.00012in), approximately one-tenth the diameter of silkworm cocoon silk. Spider silks are described as fibrous proteins that are insoluble in water. Even so, the silk absorbs water, which causes it to swell (unlike nylon and silkworm silk), and so is affected by rain. As much as 700m (2,300ft) of web silk may be drawn continuously from a well-fed golden orb spider.

In the silk glands within the spider's abdomen, the silk is stored in liquid form. Silk is not squeezed out of the body, like toothpaste, but is drawn out by a leg, or by the breeze, or else by the spider dropping down from an attachment point. It becomes solid, and is transformed from a soluble into an insoluble form, not by drying in air but by

🔹 *Above* A Black widow spider (Latrodectus mactans) *spins a web. The silk can be seen emerging from the spinnerets – a cluster of short, fingerlike appendages on the bottom of the abdomen.*

🔹 *Above left The exit-point for the silk is actually tiny spigots on the spinnerets. 1 Typically there are three pairs of spinnerets, as in cobweb spiders of the family Agelenidae. In cribellate spiders 2, however, the first pair has evolved into a sievelike field, the cribellum, bearing up to 40,000 spigots that produce ultrafine silk with great snagging power.*

🔹 *Left Magnified 170 times, a false-color electron micrograph shows strands of silk emerging from spigots on a spider of the genus* Araneus, *combining at lower right to form a single thread.*

the act of pulling, which changes the orientation of the fibers. The Water spider (*Argyroneta aquatica*), which builds its web underwater, proves the point that silk is not air-dried.

Cribellate spiders (for example those of the Amaurobiidae and Uloboridae families) possess an additional spinning organ, called the cribellum, which produces silk of the finest diameter. Located in front of the spinnerets, it takes the form of a small plate densely covered with many tiny spigots. The threads are combed out by a brush on the hind leg to make silk that is particularly dry and woolly. This cribellate silk is especially good for snagging the legs of insects, and works without the need for glue.

Building an Orb Web

The vertical, two-dimensional orb webs are perhaps the best recognized spider webs. Observing the building process takes luck and patience, especially in the early stages, which are often interrupted by long pauses. To begin construction, the spider takes up a prominent position and uses the breeze to waft out a fine silk line. The spider waits, as if fishing, until this first line (the spanning thread) touches and adheres to some nearby object. Feeling the thread fixed, she tightens it and runs across, creating a stronger cable of many strands – the bridge thread. Then, from the middle of the bridge, the spider attaches a line, drops down it, and moors it to a fixed point below. Under tension, the resulting "Y" provides the first three radii of the future orb web, while the point where the trio join becomes the hub.

The next stage establishes the many radii (the

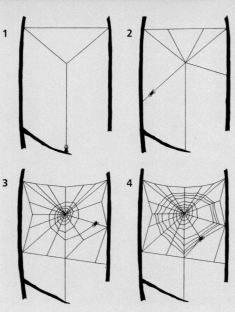

Above A finished web, built by the Four-spot orb-weaver. In building the web, the spider takes account of the developing structural forces, using stronger, thicker threads where the tensions are higher.

Left **1** To build an orb web, a spider must first lay a bridge thread and then drop down from it to create a "Y" shape. **2** The central point of the Y then becomes the hub of the web, from which the radial threads are laid. **3** Once the basic framework has been established and strengthened with mooring threads, the spider will then lay a temporary, non-sticky spiral. **4** The final stage comes when the spider returns to the hub, cutting out the temporary spiral and replacing it with adhesive thread

Continued overleaf ▷

◐ *Left* In a behavior only recently described, a male lynx spider (Oxyopes schenkeli; Oxyopidae) in Uganda twirls the female around on her dragline, and wraps her in a silk "bridal veil" prior to mating.

number ranges from 10 to 80, depending on species) that radiate from the hub of the orb to the edge, which is outlined by the frame threads. Normally, the angles between the radii, measured out by the spider's legs, are very consistent – in the case of the Garden spider (*Araneus diadematus*), the 24 to 30 radii are each placed about 12° apart. The lower half of the orb usually has more radial threads than the upper half, however; this means that the structural forces in the lower half are shared by a greater number of radii, with the result that each one is under less tension.

While the spider is busy placing the radii, a complex of threads develops at the hub, where she may sit later when the web is complete. The hub is reinforced and surrounded by three or four circular threads (the strengthening zone). From this zone, a temporary spiral is laid out towards the edge of the orb, tying the radii together and serving as a non-sticky guideline when the permanent, sticky spiral is put down. This operation is performed as the spider returns to the hub, simultaneously cutting out the temporary spiral. As one of the spider's front legs reaches for the next radius, a

○ *Below* Spiral stabilimenta of shining white silk form the core of the web built by the Variable decoy spider (Cyclosa insulana; Araneidae). These thicker bands make the web conspicuous to birds.

fourth leg pulls a sticky thread from the spinnerets, dabs it against the radius, and gives a tug so that it breaks up into a line of sticky beads. The spiral thread terminates just before it actually reaches the hub, leaving a space (the free zone) in which the spider can dodge from one side of the web to the other.

The entire web may be completed in about an hour, with the sticky spiral being the most time-consuming part of the operation. For a typical Garden spider, the combined length of the threads that go to make up a web is about 20–60m (65–200ft). A spider emitting 36m (120ft) of filament

makes 700 attachments and travels a total distance of 54m (178ft). When the web is complete with all its mooring threads, the spider either settles on the hub or else retires to a nearby retreat, from which she will remain in touch with the web by means of a "signal thread" held by a front leg.

Spiders' webs are designed primarily to catch insects; as many as 250 individuals may be caught in a single web. Their efficiency is influenced by a number of factors including their location and height above the ground (there are more insects lower down), their ability to absorb the momentum of sudden impacts, the quality of the adhesive employed, and the density of the silk threads.

The Development of Webs

Webs are too fragile to feature in the fossil record, so we can only theorize about their evolutionary history – mostly by looking at those in existence today. Undoubtedly, a kind of arms race has always existed between spiders and insects; for example, insects evolved wings to avoid spiders on the ground, but spiders responded by developing aerial webs to catch the flying insects. Many of the earliest spiders, 400–300 million years ago, appear to have dwelt mostly in holes and used silk to weave hiding places, probably with trip wires extending out to detect insects. This kind of simple "tube" web, still found in the family Segestridae, is considered to be a sort of prototype.

A more complex web design is found in the rather thick "tangle" webs of the family Theridiidae, typically found in shrubs or in the corners of rooms. Criss-crossing threads, under considerable tension and studded with gluey droplets, stretch above and below a central tangle, beneath which

BUILDING WEBS ON DRUGS

In 1948, Professor Hans Peters discovered that many of the common drugs taken by humans also have a remarkable effect on web-building spiders. The story goes that the zoologist was bothered by the fact that the Garden spiders that he used in his experiments had the inconvenient habit of always building their webs at around 4 o'clock in the morning. He consequently asked a pharmacologist, Dr. Peter Witt, for a stimulant that, when fed to the spiders, might advance the hour of their work. The resulting "drugged" webs showed crazy distortions, even though there was unfortunately no change in the time of construction. A variety of drugs were then tested, including amphetamines, LSD, caffeine, and Valium. Spiders were found to be sensitive to each of them in low doses, but caffeine, so familiar to humans, caused the severest distortions of all.

 *Above* A male and female Grassland funnelweb spider (Agelena labyrinthica; Agelenidae) mate at the mouth of the "funnel." The male announces his arrival to a prospective spouse by beating a coded message on her extensive sheet web.

the round-bodied spider hangs. Passing insects that break a thread's contact with the substrate find themselves stuck to the gum and lifted into the web as the thread contracts. Struggling only causes further entanglement and, after throwing more gummy silk over the hapless victim, the spider finishes it off with a bite to the nearest leg.

Evolutionary developments beyond the tube and tangle webs may be seen in the hammock or sheet webs of the family Linyphiidae (money spiders). In these webs, the central tangle has become a distinct sheet. When horizontal sheets were transformed into vertical sheets, the first orb webs had arrived, and the most economical and effective trap for aerial prey had evolved.

The design of webs must provide a balance between the time and energy used in their construction and their trapping efficiency. For example, dry, woolly cribellate silk is economical because it weathers well and does not require frequent renewal. Glue-studded silk, on the other hand, catches more prey but loses effectiveness when it becomes wet or dusty, forcing the majority of araneid orb-web weavers to renew their webs every day, often before dawn so as to reduce their exposure to predators. In fact, some tropical orb-weavers may renew their webs up to five times a day, after each downpour. The old web is rolled up and eaten to conserve the protein, so rebuilding is not such an extravagant use of nutrients as it might seem. Destroying the old web also helps to combat the problem of kleptoparasites – small,

uninvited spiders that feed on prey caught in another's web. Spiders get a nutritional bonus when they roll up a web that has many tiny insects or pollen grains caught in it.

The great dome webs spun by members of the genus *Cyrtophora* (family Araneidae) illustrate a number of interesting features. These spiders weave a horizontal, finely radiating sheet, with scaffolding above and below, which, unusually for araneids, lacks stickiness. This robust, semi-permanent construction is often host to numbers of kleptoparasites. The web holds prey less effectively than a sticky orb web of the same general size, and is more conspicuous to insects and so easier for them to avoid, but it requires less maintenance. Its chief virtue, however, may be that it remains in place even after heavy tropical downpours, and so serves to catch the moths and other insects that fly immediately after rain. PDH

Mites and Ticks

IN SPECIES COUNT, BODY STRUCTURE, AND *habits, the mites and ticks are the most diverse groups of arachnids. The number of different habitats they have colonized is almost endless; suffice it to say that they inhabit all terrestrial habitats from alpine to desert, as well as being found as deep as 10m (33ft) below the soil surface.*

Mites and ticks also live in all types of freshwater habitat, including hot springs with temperatures up to 50°C (120°F), as well as the world's oceans, even to great depths. They are significant in veterinary, medical, and agricultural terms, living as they do in, or on, both animals and plants.

The subdivision into mites and ticks is artificial but convenient. Ticks constitute just one order of the mites; these species, however, happen to be distinctively larger in size than most of the rest of the Acari, as well as all being external parasites of terrestrial vertebrates.

Tiny and Teeming
MITES

An idea of the huge numbers and variety of extant mites may be obtained by looking at an area of typical temperate woodland. The woodland floor will be covered with a layer of decomposing plant material in which mites feed on detritus or decomposing organisms, as well as being predators on other litter microfauna. A single square metre (10 sq ft) of such a habitat may contain as many as one million mites from perhaps 200 or more species.

The mite orders Notostigmata and Tetrastigmata are confined to warmer parts of the world, while all other orders are cosmopolitan. The Notostigmata are long-legged predators of other arthropods, and bear a superficial resemblance to the harvestmen. The Tetrastigmata are also predatory.

The beetle mites (Cryptostigmata), whose robust, rounded, dark-colored bodies resemble tiny beetles, are the most abundant mites in soil and leaf litter. Some species feed on decaying wood and leaves of plants, playing an essential role in the recycling of nutrients, while others feed on fungi and algae.

Mesostigmatid mites are mostly large, rapidly-moving, predatory species, equipped with strong chelicerae. They feed on nematode worms and arthropods (including other mites) and their eggs. This group also includes members which are parasitic.

The Prostigmata include sap-sucking plant parasites, especially in the Tetranychoidea and Eriophyidae superfamilies, the most important of which are the gall mites and spider mites that cause damage to a variety of agricultural and horticultural plants around the world. In order to facilitate sap feeding in the Tetranychoidea, the bases of the chelicerae are joined to form a sucking stylophore that can be everted; this structure is pushed into an opening in the plant made by a long stylet, also formed from the chelicerae. Many species of tetranychid

◗ *Right* Large, furry velvet mites of the genus *Trombidium* (Trombidiidae) *are a feature of deserts and savannas in many parts of the world. Huge numbers often emerge and wander around after heavy rain, looking for mates and scattering eggs.*

◗ *Below* With deutonymphs of the mite Parasitellus fucorum *clustered on her thorax, a queen White-tailed bumblebee* (Bombus lucorum) *forages on a heather flower in Europe.*

FACTFILE

MITES AND TICKS

Class: Arachnida

Subclass: Acari

About 35,000 species (850 of them ticks), grouped in 7 orders.

DISTRIBUTION Worldwide, in practically every terrestrial, freshwater, and marine environment.

SIZE Length ranges from 0.08–16mm (0.003–0.6in) in mites and 2–30mm (0.08–1.2in) in ticks.

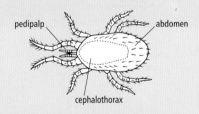

pedipalp — abdomen — cephalothorax

FEATURES Coloration usually black or brown, but reds, greens, yellows also common. No division between the 2 parts of the body – the cephalothorax (or prosoma) and abdomen (opisthosoma) – but a furrow may be present between 2nd and 3rd pairs of legs. Chelicerae variously modified round basic, pincerlike form, for example, for biting, sucking, or piercing; small, leglike pedipalps; usually 4 pairs of walking legs. Abdomen without appendages. Closest arachnid relatives are the Ricinulei.

LIFE CYCLE Development to adult via egg, 6-legged larva, and usually 1–3 (up to 8 in soft ticks) 8-legged nymphal stages. Ticks are ectoparasites of land mammals, birds, reptiles; there are free-living as well as plant- and animal-parasitic mites.

CONSERVATION STATUS Not threatened

mite are able to produce silk, which forms a mat over the plant on which they live and affords a degree of protection. These mites are also able to employ the silk during dispersal, "ballooning" in much the same way as young spiders.

Mites that are pests of stored foods are grouped in the order Astigmata. Some species feed on the food itself, while others prefer the molds that tend to grow on it in storage. Probably the most common and important is the cosmopolitan Flour mite (*Acarus siro*).

▌ Parasites and Helpers
RELATIONSHIPS

Certain members of the orders Mesostigmata, Astigmata, and Prostigmata are found in association with both vertebrates and invertebrates. Parasitic forms generally attack the external parts of their host, while those considered to be endoparasitic invade via the respiratory openings.

A number of species, such as the Red mite of poultry, live in the retreat of their host and only board it to feed. Mites of the superfamily Trombidioidea and most of the freshwater forms are only parasitic as larvae, subsequent stages being free-living predators. The majority of parasitic mites, though, complete their life cycle on the host.

Orders of Mites and Ticks

Order Prostigmata

Diverse in habitat and behavior. Includes Follicle mite (*Demodex folliculorum*, family Demodicidae); quill mites (family Syringophilidae); gall mites (family Eriophyidae); spider mites (family Tetranychidae); family Podapolipodidae; superfamily Trombidioidea; and the water mites (the Hydrachnida, 45 families, including the chiggers or red bugs of the family Trombiculidae).

Order Astigmata

Parasitic, predatory, or feeders on decaying matter. Includes Flour mite (*Acarus siro*); Furniture mite (*Glycyphagus domesticus*); Scabies or Itch mite (*Sarcoptes scabei*); grain and cheese mites (family Acaridae); fur mites (family Listrophoridae); feather mites (family Analgesidae); family Pyroglyphidae; also many free-living forms.

Order Cryptostigmata

Oribatid or beetle mites. Mostly terrestrial in forest humus, tree trunks, foliage; a few aquatic. Feed on algae, fungi, decaying matter.

Order Mesostigmata

Most species free-living in soil or decaying organic matter; also many parasitic species. Includes Red mite of poultry (*Dermanyssus gallinae*, family Dermanyssidae); nasal mites of dogs and birds; also predatory mites on foliage of trees and other plants.

Order Notostigmata

Small, terrestrial order, found under stones and in decaying vegetation in the Indo-Pacific region and the southeastern USA.

Order Tetrastigmata

Small terrestrial order, found in semi-arid habitats in the southwestern USA, Puerto Rico, S America, C Asia, Africa, Mediterranean region.

Order Metastigmata (Ticks)

The largest of the Acari, ranging from 2–30mm (0.08–1.2in) in size. The hard ticks of the family Ixodidae include the Brown dog tick (*Rhipicephalus sanguineus*). Wood tick (*Dermacentor andersoni*). Soft ticks (family Argasidae) include Fowl tick (*Argas persicus*), *Ornithodoros* spp.

Other relationships are mutually beneficial to both parties. For example, the Follicle mite *Demodex folliculorum*, which lives in the hair follicles and sebaceous glands of humans, helps keep the skin clean by feeding on sebum, the fatty matter secreted by the glands. Fur, feather, and quill mites perform similar scavenging duties.

Mites frequently cling to other arthropods, often to beetles and flies. They are not directly parasitizing their "host," merely hitching a lift, a phenomenon referred to as "phoresy." The mite *Parasitus fucorum*, for example, lives, probably as a scavenger, in bumblebee nests. The deutonymphs of the mite then climb aboard the young queens before they leave the nest and disperse. They overwinter on the queens, and are subsequently able to invade the new nests established by the queen bees the following spring. *P. fucorum* is itself pseudoparasitized by an even smaller mite called *Scutacarus acarorum*.

Just as interesting is the relationship between *Dinogamasus* mites and females of some African and Indian species of carpenter bees of the genus *Xylocopa*. These bees have evolved an acinarium, or mite pouch, in the first abdominal segment. The *Dinogamasus* mites that live there are believed to keep the surface of the bees clear of fungi, which develop readily in the tropical conditions in which the bees live. Another fascinating example of "hitch-hiking" occurs when mites living in the flowers of plants pollinated by hummingbirds run up the beaks and into the nostrils of feeding birds, later to disembark onto another flower.

Two species of mite have evolved what appears to be a form of subsocial behaviour. *Myrmonyssus phalaenodectes* lives in the ears of certain species of noctuid moth. The mite bites through the tympanic membranes, providing an entrance into the tympanic air sac for her offspring. She remains with her brood until they mature, often driving off any other female mites that may try to enter, although she may not always be successful in the latter endeavor, and several females with their broods may end up in the ear. The most amazing thing about the whole behavior pattern is that only one of the moth's ears is ever invaded, the other being left intact so that it can listen out for bats, an obvious advantage to the mites as well. Rather different is *Schitzotetranychus celarius*, which builds nests on bamboo stems, where both the male and female guard their offspring from attacks from the larvae of a predatory mite; in defense of their offspring, males have been seen to attack and kill these larvae.

Miniature Blood-suckers
TICKS

The ticks are the largest and therefore the best-known of the subclass Acari, and are exclusively blood-sucking ectoparasites of land vertebrates.

Some species are pests of domestic livestock, while a number transmit human disease.

Ticks are classified into three families, all but one species belonging to the Ixodidae (hard ticks) or to the Argasidae (soft ticks). Hard ticks get their name from the thickened shield (scutum) on top of the front of the body. They possess prominent, well-developed mouthparts, needed to secure themselves to their roving hosts during feeding, which can take several days. A common hard tick is the cosmopolitan Brown dog tick. Soft ticks lack a scutum and have relatively weak mouthparts, positioned inconspicuously on the underside. Soft ticks are "habitat" ticks: they remain in the host's retreat, such as a nest or burrow, only feeding when it returns. Soft ticks are able to complete a meal in as little as two minutes. Their mouthparts do not need to be exceptionally well-armed as the host is generally at rest while feeding proceeds, so reducing the risk of the tick being dislodged. The Fowl tick is a soft tick pest of poultry in warm, dry parts of the world. It lives in cracks and hiding places, emerging at night to feed.

To survive, a tick must find a host on which to feed and, having done so, remain firmly attached until it is replete. Ticks possess special sense organs that can detect a suitable approaching host. Among these, bristlelike setae sensitive to humidity and "smell" are concentrated in special depressions in the cuticle: the characteristic "Haller's organs" are located on the end segment

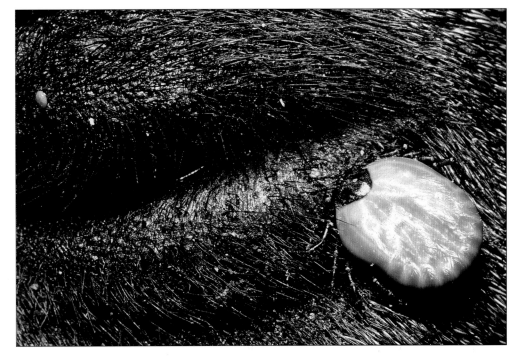

◑ Above *Ticks seek to attach themselves to parts of the body from which they are least likely to be detached. This hard tick of the genus* Amblyomma *(Ixodidae) is fixed to the lower eyelid of a tapir in Peru.*

◑ Left *Abundant springtime rains are often the trigger for swarming in certain mite species, among them these velvet mites (Trombidiidae) assembling on a flowerhead in the Israeli desert.*

of both front legs. When a possible host is eventually detected, a tick climbs to the top of vegetation to "quest," waving its front legs in the air, attempting to home in to the direction of the stimuli and preparing itself to climb onto the animal if it brushes past.

Before feeding begins, the skin of the host is punctured by the serrated pincers of the chelicerae. The hypostome, a conspicuous, toothed, snoutlike projection that lies between the pedipalps, is worked into the wound, the teeth providing anchorage. Blood is sucked up along a groove on the upper surface of the hypostome; anticoagulants in the tick's saliva prevent clotting. After feeding, most ticks drop to the ground, where they molt or lay eggs.   RP-M/AB

VECTORS OF DISEASE

All but two of the seven orders of ticks and mites (the Notostigmata and Cryptostigmata) include species of medical importance. In itself, the blood-sucking habit of ticks causes irritation and malaise in the host, but it is as carriers and transmitters of human disease organisms that ticks are medically most important. The organisms, chiefly viruses or rickettsiae and spirochete bacteria, are transmitted in the tick's saliva during feeding, and any one organism can be carried by a range of tick species.

The viruses cause hemorrhagic fevers or encephalitis; the different types are usually named after the place where they were first identified, as in the case of Omsk hemorrhagic fever or Russian spring-summer encephalitis. They occur in Canada, the USA, Malaysia, India, and eastern, northern, and central Europe. The main human rickettsial infections are the spotted fevers, tick-bite fevers, and tick-typhus fevers, one of the most famous examples being Rocky Mountain spotted fever, which, in the western USA, is carried by the wood ticks. Spirochetes, causing human relapsing fevers, are transmitted by species of the genus *Ornithodoros*, which occur in Africa and the Americas.

Larval mites of the family Trombiculidae, commonly called chiggers or red bugs, are mostly lymph-feeding ectoparasites of vertebrates. About 20 species either transmit human disease organisms or else cause a dermatitis ("scrub-itch") resulting from an allergic reaction to the chigger's saliva. Among

the former is the most important of mite-borne diseases, scrub-typhus or tsutsugamushi disease, which occurs in many parts of eastern and southeastern Asia. The effect chiggers produce on the skin can vary from a simple reddening to the production of huge, fluid-filled blisters 2–3cm (0.8–1.2in) across, which take many days to subside and even longer to heal.

Perhaps the most famous mite infesting humans is the Scabies or Itch mite. Favored sites for infection are the hands and wrists; severe itching and a rash result. House-dust mites are primarily beneficial to humans – they clean up by feeding on dead skin cells and other detritus – but in some people they induce allergic reactions in the form of asthma and rhinitis. In addition, several species of stored food mites cause a dermatitis in people handling infested food. The conditions involved include grocer's itch, caused by the Furniture mite, and baker's itch, associated with the Flour mite.

◑ Right *Engorged with blood after a meal, a female wood tick of the genus* Dermacentor *dwarfs an unfed companion. These ticks are the vectors of Rocky Mountain spotted fever.*

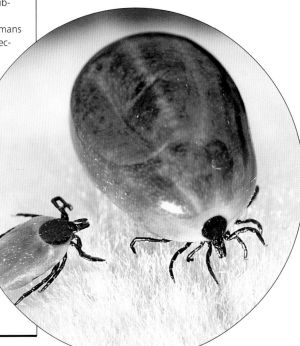

MITES: UP CLOSE AND PERSONAL

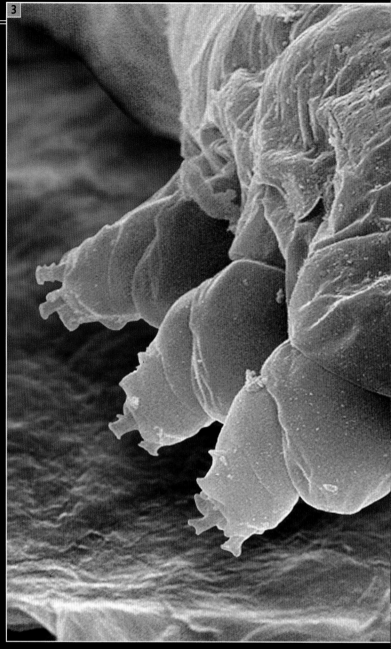

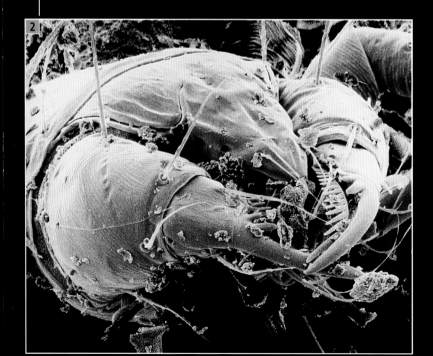

1 Human homes and bodies play host to a variety of arthropod life, with the mites (Acari) playing a prominent part. This electron micrograph shows a Dermatophagoides house dust mite magnified to 250 times its normal size of approximately 0.3mm (0.01in). Every house contains millions of the mites, living in carpets, furniture, and bedding.

2 Dust mites use their palps and mouthparts to feed on detritus – this one is shown in the dust from a vacuum cleaner. In many ways they perform a useful function by eating up dead human skin cells, which constitute the main part of their diet. Their fecal pellets can, however, trigger allergic reactions, causing asthma attacks and dermatitis.

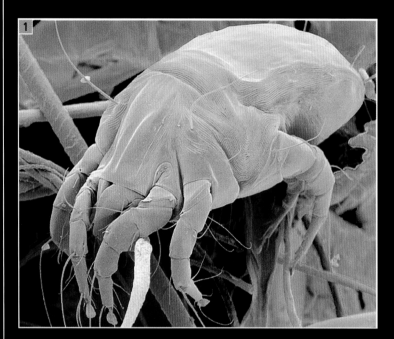

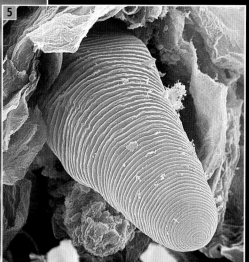

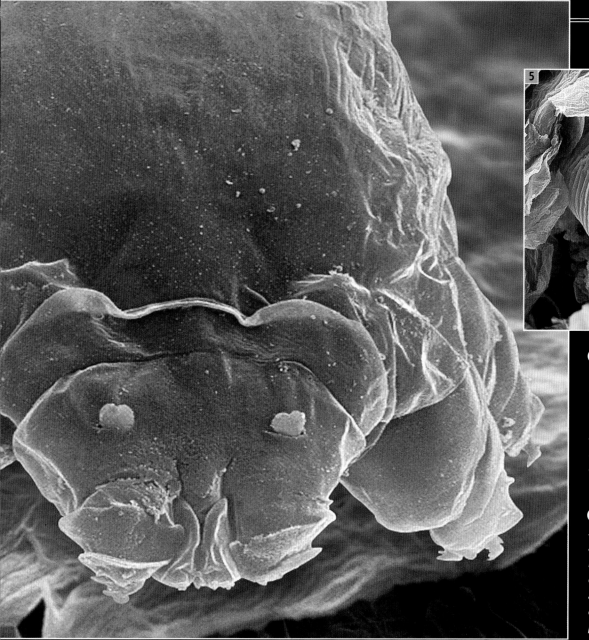

5 *Elegantly ringed, the tail end of a D. folliculorum mite protrudes from a hair follicle. Mobile adults crawl into their new homes headfirst and cannot reverse, so rarely emerge again. They use their needlelike mouthparts to puncture epithelial cells, feeding on oily secretions from the sebaceous glands.*

6 *Hair mites can move across the skin at a rate of about 1cm (0.4in) an hour, usually travelling at night. For their human hosts, the incidence of mite infestation increases with age; about 25 percent of 20-year-olds are affected, but nearly 100 percent of people aged 90 or more.*

3 *Two species of* Demodex *mite inhabit the human body;* D. folliculorum *lives in hair follicles and* D. brevis *close by in the sebaceous glands. Both are for the most part harmless associates. This* D. folliculorum *nymph, shown at more than 3,000 times lifesize, has just six legs rather than the adult mite's eight.*

4 *The heads of four mites protrude from a split follicle. Normally their chosen habitat is the face, particularly the forehead, cheeks, and eyebrows. Females can lay up to 25 eggs. When mature, the mites leave to mate, and then search out a fresh follicle in which to lay their own eggs. The complete life cycle takes about 14.5 days.*

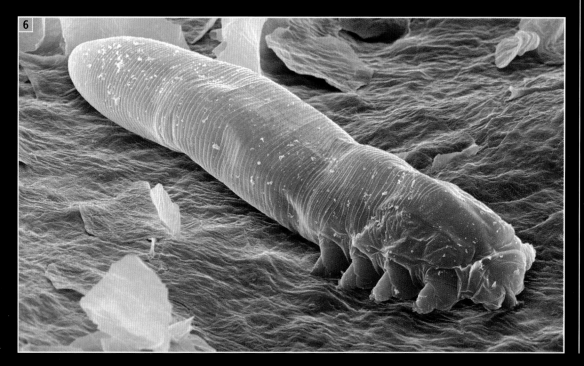

Scorpions and Other Arachnids

SCORPIONS AND OTHER ARACHNIDS INCLUDE a number of groups containing individuals of enormously varying size, the largest 400 times the length of the smallest. They all, however, have one thing in common: they are voracious carnivores, some using stealth, others speed, to catch prey.

The oldest known fossil arachnid is a scorpion, *Palaeophonus nuncius*, dating back some 400 million years. The largest fossil scorpion, *Praearcturus gigas*, measured an impressive 1m (39in) in length, more than five times the length of the biggest extant species.

Scorpions
SUBCLASS SCORPIONES

True scorpions of the subclass Scorpiones can be recognized by their large, menacing, pincerlike pedipalps and by the narrow "tail" arched over the body, bearing at its tip a poison gland opening into a sting. A scorpion uses its sting primarily for self-defense, although it may also assist at times in subduing extra-large prey. Scorpions will, in fact, only sting as a last resort, and as many as 150 species are known to make noises, in one way or another, to warn off possible predators as an alternative to stinging.

FACTFILE

OTHER ARACHNIDS

Class: Arachnida

About 9,230 species in 9 subclasses.

SCORPIONS Subclass Scorpiones
1,500 species in 16 families. Worldwide in tropical and warm temperate regions. From deserts to rain forests, even at high altitudes; under stones, in crevices and burrows, a few cave dwellers, some smaller species in the intertidal zone. Size: 10–200mm (0.4–8in). **Diet:** Other arthropods.

PSEUDOSCORPIONS Subclass Pseudoscorpiones
Pseudoscorpions or false scorpions. 2,000 species. Worldwide except for Arctic and Antarctic. In leaf litter, under bark, in birds' nests, moss, compost heaps, and human dwellings. Size: 2.5–8mm (0.1–0.3in). **Diet:** Small arthropods.

SUN SPIDERS Subclass Solifugae
Sun spiders, wind scorpions, sun scorpions, camel spiders, gerrymanders. 900 species. S Asia, Africa, W Indies, Mediterranean zone, C and S USA, Mexico. In deserts and other arid places; at rest may burrow, or sit under stones. Size: 10–50mm (0.4–2in). **Diet:** Arthropods, small vertebrates, e.g. lizards.

WHIP SCORPIONS Subclass Uropygi
Whip scorpions or vinegaroons. 85 species. Most species in SE Asia, also in India. Japan, New Guinea, Philippines, S USA to S America, introduced locally to Africa. In litter, under stones and logs, will tunnel in soil. Size: 15–75mm (0.6–3in) without "tail." **Diet:** Other arthropods.

MICROWHIP SCORPIONS Subclass Palpigradi
60 species. S Europe, Madagascar, Africa, SE Asia. Texas, California to S America. Litter dwellers, under stones, in soil, some in caves. Size: 0.5–2.8mm (0.02–0.1in) less "tail". **Diet:** Possibly small soil arthropods.

SCHIZOMIDS Subclass Schizomida (Schizopeltida)
80 species. Asia, Africa, Americas. In leaf litter, under stones, (will tunnel into soil) and in caves. Size: 2–15mm (0.08–0.6in). **Diet:** Other arthropods.

WHIP SPIDERS Subclass Amblypygi
Whip spiders or tailless whip scorpions. 70 species. Islands of Aegean Sea to sub-Saharan Africa, W indies, Asia, S USA to S America. In forests, in crevices, litter, under stones and loose bark, some in caves. Size: 5–45mm (0.2–1.8in). **Diet:** Other arthropods.

RICINULEIDS Subclass Ricinulei
35 species. W Africa, Texas to Brazil Tropical forest litter, caves. Size: 10–15mm(0.40–0.6in). **Diet:** Small flies and other small insects, possibly termites.

HARVESTMEN Subclass Opiliones
Harvestmen or harvest spiders. 4,500 species. Worldwide, Grassland, woodland, forests, on vegetation, under loose bark. Size: 1–15mm (0.04–0.6in). **Diet:** Small arthropods, carrion, decaying vegetation, fungi.

The potency of scorpion venom varies from being innocuous to humans in, for example, *Heterometrus cyaneus* from Java to being lethal, as in the case of the Durango scorpion (*Centruoides suffusus*) from Mexico. All dangerous species occur in the family Buthidae. Populations of *Buthus occitanus* in southwestern Europe cause a painful sting with fairly mild toxic effects, but in North Africa and the Middle East the same species' venom can cause death. Symptoms of scorpion poison are similar for a wide range of unrelated species around the world. The patient is initially anxious and agitated, with severe pain where the sting occurred. Salivation and sweating then become excessive, the heartbeat becomes irregular, and body temperature begins to fluctuate. Eventually, breathing becomes difficult, the body muscles begin to twitch, and in a few cases the sequence can lead to convulsions and death.

Scorpions also have a pair of unique, comblike sensory organs, the pectines, on the underside of

○ *Below As night falls across the African plains, a female wind scorpion of the genus* Solpuga *(Solifugae) sets to work to extend her burrow. Having loosened the earth with her large and powerful chelicerae, she scoops it between her long front legs and pushes it clear of the tunnel.*

○ *Right Smaller than a grain of rice, a pseudoscorpion (*Cordylochernes scorpioides*) uses the claws of its pedipalps to hitch a ride on the abdomen of a Harlequin beetle. The pseudoscorpion lives in the beetle's larval tunnels.*

○ *Below Before mating, scorpions (here* Vaejovis boreus*) engage in an elaborate "dance" in which the male seeks to maneuver the female over a spermatophore that he has dropped.*

the abdomen. Male scorpions use these organs to measure the particle size of the substrate on which they stand, and also to detect the presence of female pheromones. Knowledge of the ground's condition is important because a substrate made up of small particles is preferable for the deposition of the spermatophore during courtship.

Ask anyone what they know about scorpions other than their sting, and they will probably mention their "dance." The latter is in fact an elaborate way of ensuring that the male deposits his spermatophore in a suitable place and that the female picks it up successfully.

The initial stages of courtship vary between species, but eventually male and female, facing one another, grasp each other's pedipalpal pincers and the dance begins. The male sweeps the substrate with his pectines before dropping a spermatophore in a suitable spot. He then carefully positions the female so that she can take the spermatophore into her genital opening. Amazingly, the male in some species initially stings the female, the poison seemingly acting as some kind of aphrodisiac. Following their dance the pair may indulge in a bout of wild, reciprocal stinging that culminates in the female picking up the spermatophore.

After fertilization, the female lays from 1 to 95 eggs, depending on species. The newly-hatched scorpions climb onto their mother's back, often along the pincers, which she helpfully turns sideways and rests on the ground to form a ramp. After a single molt the young become independent and disperse.

Pseudoscorpions
SUBCLASS PSEUDOSCORPIONES

With their large, pincered pedipalps held at the ready, pseudoscorpions resemble tiny, tailless scorpions. Vision in pseudoscorpions is very limited, and indeed many, particularly those that live deep down in leaf litter or in caves, are blind. These agile creatures dart backward if threatened from the front. They often cling to flies, beetles, and harvestmen, but they are not parasitizing them, just hitching a lift for dispersal. They use silk from glands in the chelicerae to construct refuges for overwintering, molting, and egg laying.

While in some families there is no contact between male and female, in others courtship may be quite elaborate. In these species the male waves his pedipalps, taps his legs, and quivers his abdomen. If the female responds, the two "dance" in scorpionlike fashion and the female takes up a deposited spermatophore. From 2 to 40 eggs are laid in a silken sac attached to the female's abdomen. After hatching, the young feed on "milk" from the mother's ovaries, but, like scorpions, they become independent after the first molt.

Sun Spiders
SUBCLASS SOLIFUGAE

Mainly nocturnal, sun spiders are very agile and fast. They hold their pedipalps and the long front pair of legs out in front to act as feelers for sensing prey. They then use their enormous chelicerae, which are larger in relation to body size than in any other arachnid group, to manipulate the prey; each chelicera can function independently, one holding the prey impaled while the other cuts it up. The pedipalps lack pincers; they are used to scoop up water and transfer it to the mouth.

There are few niceties before mating; the male literally jumps onto the female, stopping her in her tracks. She allows her partner to topple her on her side, and sperm is transferred to her genital opening by the male's chelicerae. This accomplished, he retires hastily before the female returns to her normal, aggressive state. After fertilization, the female digs a burrow in which to lay 100–250 eggs, sometimes staying to guard them.

Whip Scorpions
SUBCLASS UROPYGI

Whip scorpions have a long, whiplike flagellum that does not, however, bear a sting. They walk with just six legs, as the first pair are slender feelers. The pedipalps are large and pincerlike at the ends for grasping prey, and they then assist the chelicerae in breaking it up as the animals feed. "Scent" from glands at the flagellum base that contains either chlorine or else formic or acetic acid (hence the whip scorpion's common name of "vinegaroon") is sprayed at potential enemies.

The female is fertilized by the male pushing a spermatophore into her genital orifice with a projection of the pedipalps. In some species the process is very simple, but in others there is a long and complex courtship. In *Mastigoproctus giganteus*, for example, the couple "dance" for up to 5 hours before the male finally extrudes the spermatophore, gently guiding his mate over it. For 2 hours or more he then presses the sperm carriers into the female's gonopore, presumably to ensure better dispersal of the sperm. In *Thelyphonus linganus* from Malaysia the complex spermatophore is self-loading, automatically moving up into the female as she presses down on it.

Microwhip Scorpions
SUBCLASS PALPIGRADI

The rare microwhip scorpions are agile and delicate. They lack eyes, the mouthparts are very simple, and they are so tiny that some species lack an internal respiratory system. The pedipalps are simple and used in locomotion. The first pair of legs are adapted to perform a sensory function.

Between the cephalothorax and the abdomen is a narrow waist, formed by the first segment of the latter. The abdomen ends in a flagellum of about the same length as the body, with long, sensory bristles (setae); it is carried vertically to gather information. These scorpions dehydrate very easily, which accounts for their subterranean lifestyle.

Schizomids
SUBCLASS SCHIZOMIDA (SCHIZOPELTIDA)

Schizomids are small subtropical and tropical arachnids with a short flagellum. Some authorities would place them with the uropygid whip scorpions, but the schizomids are in fact much smaller, and there are other important differences too. Prior to mating, the female hooks onto ridges on the male's flagellum and is then dragged over his deposited spermatophore. The female lays between 6 and 30 eggs, which adhere to her genital orifice before hatching.

Whip Spiders
SUBCLASS AMBLYPYGI

Whip spiders have a cephalothorax with both median and lateral ocelli that is noticeably wider than long. It is narrowly joined to the abdomen by a waist formed from the first abdominal segment. The two-segmented chelicerae resemble those of spiders but lack venom glands. The pedipalps end in a claw that opposes the previous segment to form a crude pincer for grasping prey. While all the legs are long and slender, the first pair is particularly so and is only used for sensory purposes.

Whip spiders are somewhat flattened, and characteristically scurry sideways, sliding under pieces of loose bark or stones to escape danger. During mating, the male guides the female over a spermatophore, which she takes into her genital orifice. From 20 to 40 eggs are laid in a sac attached to the female's abdomen. The young are initially carried on their mother's abdomen.

Ricinuleids
SUBCLASS RICINULEI

Ricinuleids are heavily armored, robust arachnids that bear some resemblance to ticks, both in their appearance and in their somewhat sluggish movements. They differ from the ticks, however, in that the cephalothorax and the abdomen are separated by a distinct waist. They possess a unique, hinged flap (the cucullus) at the front of the cephalothorax, overhanging the mouthparts. Before mating, the male climbs onto the female and transfers sperm with the aid of a modified copulatory organ on the third pair of legs. The female lays 1 or 2 eggs, which are carried between her bent pedipalps and the cucullus.

Harvestmen
SUBCLASS OPILIONES

Harvestmen, with their eight legs, can be mistaken for long-legged spiders, but lack the latter's clear division of the body into cephalothorax and abdomen. Unlike all but the most primitive spiders, however, they have an abdomen that shows clear segmentation. The cephalothorax usually bears in the midline a pair of ocelli, carried on either side of an ocular tubercle, or ocularium, that protrudes from its upper surface. In the family Trogulidae the ocularium is flattened or absent, and the ocelli are small. A number of completely blind, cave-dwelling species have been described.

Short-legged species of harvestmen exist, but the most familiar forms are those with long, stilt-like limbs. A pair of defensive scent glands opens into the edge of the cephalothorax. When threatened, harvestmen direct a spray of malodorous liquid at the would-be attacker, or alternatively spread a droplet of the scent over their bodies to create the desired deterrent effect.

Unusually for arachnids, fertilization is direct; the males possess an elongated penis. Courtship, if it exists, is perfunctory, the male merely climbing on to the female and mating with her. Ten to 100 eggs are laid through a long tube, the ovipositor, typically in damp soil or under stones. Exceptionally, males of the Neotropical harvestman *Zygopachylus albomarginis* build a nest made from flakes of bark at the base of a tree or on a log. Using saliva, they build a stockade 1cm (0.4in) high and about 3cm (1.2in) across in which the female lays her eggs, which are then protected and kept clean by the male.   RP-M/AB

▷ **Right** *In the majority of harvestmen (Opiliones), the legs are extremely long and slender. A number of species commonly form aggregations, such as this warningly marked species forming a dry-season assemblage in a forest in India.*

◁ **Left** *Whip scorpions (Uropygi) are generally dark-bodied, with a lengthy, whiplike flagellum. The first pair of legs are extremely long and are used as feelers rather than for walking. Here a pair court at night in a rain forest in Sulawesi.*

Glossary

Abdomen region of the body of an arthropod behind the THORAX, in insects comprising up to 10 SEGMENTS.

Adaptive radiation see RADIATION, ADAPTIVE.

Aerial pertaining to activities that take place in flight, in the air.

Air sac thin-walled expansion of the TRACHEAL system of an arthropod, which boosts the inspiration and exhalation of air. Air sacs also give buoyancy to aquatic insects and in dragonflies provide insulation around the thoracic wing muscles.

Alimentary canal the gut or digestive system.

"Altruism" apparently self-sacrificing behavior performed by one animal for the benefit of others.

Ametabolous of insects having no METAMORPHOSIS, ie the Apterygota, in which larvae hatch from the egg in a form essentially identical to the adult except for the size and undeveloped genitalia. The gonads develop and size increases at each molt.

Amino acid one of about 20 compounds comprising both a basic amino (NH_2) group and an acidic carboxyl (COOH) group, which combine in their hundreds to form proteins.

Amphibious capable of living in both water and on land.

Anaerobic of physiological processes which take place in the absence of oxygen.

Annelid a member of the phylum Annelida which comprises the segmented worms, including the familiar earthworms and leeches.

Aorta the main blood vessel leading anteriorly from the dorsal "heart" of insects.

Apodeme an ingrowth of EXOSKELETON to which muscles are attracted.

Appendage any limb or articulated outgrowth of the body such as antennae or wings.

Arachnid member of the class Arachnida (spiders, scorpions, ticks and mites) of the phylum Chelicerata.

Arthropod "jointed-limbed" invertebrate with a hardened CUTICLE (EXOSKELETON), a condition believed to have evolved independently on several occasions – hence the separate phyla of "arthropods."

Autotomy the process by which a limb can be voluntarily shed if grabbed by a predator. Found in spiders and grasshoppers, where the leg is shed by the sharp contraction of muscles acting on a special fracture point or area of weakness.

Axon long process of a nerve cell; normally conducts impulses away from the nerve cell body.

Bee milk see ROYAL JELLY.

Biological control the use of natural predators, parasites or disease organisms to reduce the number of pest insects or weed plants.

Book gill breathing apparatus in some arachnids, resembling a BOOK LUNG but on exterior of body.

Book lung a paired chamber invaginated into the ventral abdominal wall of arachnids where the gaseous exchanges of respiration take place across folded, leaf-like LAMELLAE, which have a rich blood supply.

Brood cell a specially-prepared space or structure in the nests of bees and wasps in which food is stored, an egg is laid and the larva completes its development.

Calamistrum a row of hairs on the back legs of certain spiders, which are used to comb out silk produced by the CRIBELLUM.

Caste in colonies of SOCIAL insects, any group of individuals that are structurally and/or behaviorally distinct and perform specialized tasks: eg the "SOLDIERS" of termites and ants and the WORKERS of say, hornets and honeybees.

Catalepsy death-feigning.

Cell the basic structural unit of all plant and animal tissues, each comprising a central nucleus surrounded by CYTOPLASM.

Cellulase an enzyme which digests cellulose.

Cephalothorax or prosoma, the 6-segmented head-and-thorax of an arachnid.

Cerci paired, articulated appendages at the end of the abdomen in many arthropods and probably sensory in function.

Chelicerate, chelicerae member of the arthropod phylum Chelicerata (arachnids, horseshoe crabs and sea spiders) possessing a pair of pincer-like mouthparts (chelicerae) in front of the mouth opening.

Chemoreceptor a sense organ of taste or smell reacting to the presence of chemicals, as opposed to other receptors which perceive sound waves, vibrations or touch.

Chitin (adj. chitinous) complex nitrogen-containing polysaccharide which forms a material of considerable mechanical strength and resistance to chemicals; forms the CUTICLE of arthropods.

Chromosome thread-like structure in the nuclei of cells, which carries the genetic information.

Chrysalis the PUPA (pupal stage) in moths and butterflies, often enclosed in a silk cocoon.

Cilia minute hairs which beat with a regular rhythm and are found in many EPITHELIAL tissues which line internal ducts. Cilia also cover the outside of many protozoans and are their means of locomotion.

Claspers a pair of pincer-like appendages of the male genitalia of insects which clasp the female during copulation.

Click mechanism a spring-loaded articulation between THORAX and ABDOMEN of beetles of the family Elateridae which enables the beetle to right itself if it falls on its back. This is accompanied by an audible click, which may surprise predators.

Clypeus the frontal plate or SCLERITE between the COMPOUND EYES and anterior to the antennal insertion.

Cocoon the silk envelope spun by the mature larva (pre-pupa) of many insects immediately prior to pupation.

Colony an aggregation of SOCIAL insects which share a nest.

Comb horizontal or vertical ranks of brood cells in SOCIAL paper-making wasps and the highly social stingless bees and honeybees.

Communal (level of social organization) refers to the situation in insects where members of the same generation share a nest and its construction, but not care of the brood; each female rears her own brood.

Complete metamorphosis where development from the egg goes through a distinct larval and pupal stage before the adult state is achieved. Typically, the larva differs from the adult, not only in structure, but also in diet.

Compound eye type of arthropod eye composed of many long, cylindrical units (ommatidia) each of which is capable of light reception.

Conspecific of the same species.

Convergent evolution the evolution of two or more organisms with some increasingly similar characteristics but different ancestry.

Corbiculum the pollen basket of female bees of the family Apidae, comprising a slightly concave area of the outer face of the hind TIBIA, fringed with stiff bristles.

Corpus allatum see JUVENILE HORMONE.

Cosmopolitan found everywhere.

Courtship dance dance-like actions which precede mating in many arthropods and which enable prospective mates to recognize each other as being CONSPECIFIC and to assess each other's quality.

Coxa basal section of an arthropod APPENDAGE, joining the limb to the body.

Cribellate (noun cribellum) of spiders which have a cribellum, a plate through which a special kind of silk is produced, combed out by the CALAMISTRUM and mixed with ordinary silk from the SPINNERETS to make a bluish, lace-like composite strand.

Crop an enlargement of the foregut in insects, in which food is stored.

Crustacean pertaining to the phylum Crustacea, which includes the crabs, lobsters, barnacles, shrimps and woodlice.

Cryptic (noun crypsis) pertaining to anti-predator adaptations in animals which take up resting positions on backgrounds or among objects to which they have a resemblance – eg moths with a color pattern resembling lichen-covered bark, grasshoppers resembling stones.

Ctenidium a row of stiff spines on the rear of the PRONOTUM in fleas.

Cuckoo see KLEPTOPARASITE.

Cuckoo spit a frothy secretion produced by the NYMPHS of certain soft-bodied plant bugs in which they live and which protects them from desiccation and some, but not all, predators.

Cuticle in arthropods, the external layer formed of CHITIN, which is secreted by the EPIDERMIS; acts as an EXOSKELETON, and as a barrier limiting water loss and preventing entry of microorganisims.

Cytoplasm all the living matter of a cell excluding the nucleus.

Dendrite one of the finest and highly branched ends of a nerve fiber (AXON) which are specialized for the reception of stimuli which initiate nerve impulses.

Dermecos the habitat limited to the spaces between the hairs of a mammal's skin in which ectoparasites such as lice and fleas live.

Diploidy (adj. diploid) the presence within the nucleus of two homologous sets of CHROMOSOMES.

Division of labor the condition in SOCIAL insect colonies where different tasks are allocated to morphological CASTES specialized for carrying them out – eg egg-laying in queens, foraging and colony defense by workers.

Dorsal situated at, or related to, the back of the body, ie the side that is generally directed upward.

Drone a male honeybee (*Apis* species).

Ecribellate of spiders without a CRIBELLUM.

Ectognathous the primitive condition in insects where the mouthparts are exposed (cf ENTOGNATHOUS).

Ectoparasite parasite living on the outside of its host.

Endocrine gland gland whose secretions pass directly into the blood stream (eg the CORPUS ALLATUM of insects).

Endocuticle inner layer of the CUTICLE that is recycled at each molt but remains unhardened, by contrast with the hard EXOCUTICLE.

Endoparasite parasite living within the tissues of its host.

Endopterygote pertaining to (or one of) those insects in which the wings develop internally, and in which METAMORPHOSIS is complete, there being a PUPAL STAGE (holometaboly).

Endoskeleton an internal skeleton, as in vertebrates, or elements of the arthropod EXOSKELETON which, as in larger insects, serve as an internal skeleton (eg sites for muscle attachment, also APODEMES).

Entognathous the condition found in the Collembola, Protura and Diplura in which the pre-oral cavity is enclosed by pleural folds which grow down from the sides of the head (cf ECTOGNATHOUS).

Entomology the branch of zoology devoted to the study of insects.

Enzyme a chemical, usually a protein, which acts as a catalyst in chemical processes such as digestion and tissue respiration.

Eocene the geological epoch which began about 54 and lasted until 38 million years ago: a time of widespread tropical and temperate forests, with an essentially modern flora (except for absence of grasses) and archaic mammals. All modern arthropod groups were well established.

Epicuticle thin outermost layer of the CUTICLE made of proteins and lipids, which in terrestrial arthropods includes a waterproofing waxy layer and usually a tough protective cement layer.

Epidermis or hypodermis, the single layer of living cells which underlies and secretes the arthropod CUTICLE.

Epithelium sheet of cells lining cavities and vessels and covering exposed body surfaces.

Eruciform of insect larvae such as caterpillars and beetle larvae with well-defined segmentation, abdominal legs or PROLEGS and nine pairs of respiratory SPIRACLES.

Eusocial (eusociality) pertaining to SOCIAL insect colonies with the highest level of social behavior, cooperative brood care, a reproductive division of labor, with sterile workers and an egg-laying queen or queens and the overlap of at least two worker generations.

Exarate pupa pupa in which the APPENDAGES are free from the body.

Exocrine gland gland which produces secretions that are ducted directly to the outside of an animal's body (eg salivary gland, scent gland).

Exocuticle the hardened outer layers of the CUTICLE, as compared with the unhardened ENDOCUTICLE.

Exopterygote pertaining to (or one of) those insects in which the wings develop externally, ie with an incomplete METAMORPHOSIS (hemimetaboly).

Exoskeleton the external skeleton of an arthropod, made of CUTICLE.

Facultative parasite parasite capable of a particular type of parasitic behavior or life-style, but not obliged to adopt it for survival.

False legs or prolegs, fleshy outgrowths in insect larvae which function as legs, but are not true articulated limbs.

Femur the 3rd and most muscular of the four components that together comprise and insect's leg (coxa, trochanter, femur, tarsus).

Fitness that part of an organism's reproductive potential which is actually realized.

Flagellum in insects, the outer (distal) series of segments of antennae which are elbowed, ie have a long basal segment (scape).

Flash coloration brightly colored parts of an animal's body which are normally hidden but which can be exposed suddenly to frighten away a predator.

Food chain an hierarchical array of organisms which feed on the next lowest organism(s) or trophic level, eg leaf ? weevil ? robberfly ? bird ? hawk.

Foraging pattern of bees, the pattern of food-gathering behavior which is determined by the local abundance and structure of flowers.

Fundatrix a female member of a generation of plant-feeding bugs, especially aphids, which produce eggs by PARTHENOGENESIS.

Fungus comb a mass of fungus cultivated by macrotermitine termites and leaf-cutter ants, on which the insects feed.

Furca a Y-shaped APODEME of the thoracic sternum in insects.

Fusion the process, in sexually reproducing organisms, in which sperm and egg unite to complete fertilization and initiate the development of a new individual.

Gall a tumorous growth of plant tissues stimulated by the presence of a specific virus, fungus or insect egg. In the case of the latter, the gall increases in size as the insect larva inside it feeds on special "grazing" tissue lining the larval chamber.

Genitalia the terminal, hard parts of an arthropod's reproductive system, which are engaged during copulation.

Gill in insects, thin-skinned outgrowths of the bodies of aquatic larvae across which the gaseous exchanges of respiration take place.

Gland a distinct tissue or group of tissues which secretes a specific substance, eg scent or hormones.

Gonad a gland where gametes, ie sperm or eggs, are produced. Sperms are produced in the testes, eggs in ovaries.

Gonopore the ultimate genital opening in male arthropods through which semen containing sperm are ejaculated during copulation.

Gregarious of animals which live or nest in groups, but which do not cooperate, ie are not truly SOCIAL.

Haltere the modified, club-shaped hind wings of true flies (Diptera), which have a sensory function in flight.

Hamuli the hooks on the leading edge of the hindwings of wasps and bees, which engage a fold on the hind margin of the forewings, so coupling the wings together to make a functional whole.

Haplodiploidy the method of sex determination in Hymenoptera (wasps, ants and bees), where males are derived from unfertilized HAPLOID eggs and females are derived from fertilized DIPLOID eggs, with the normal, diploid, complement of CHROMOSOMES.

Haploidy (adj. haploid) the state of having only one half of the normal complement of CHROMOSOMES and which is found in gametes (sperm and egg) and in male Hymenoptera.

Head capsule the part of an arthropod's EXOSKELETON which encloses the head and associated structures.

Hemimetaboly (adj. hemimetabolous) see INCOMPLETE METAMORPHOSIS.

Hemolymph the blood of arthropods.

Hexapod a member of the superclass Hexapoda, a large group of six-legged arthropods comprising the classes Collembola, Diplura, Protura and Insecta.

Holarctic found in both temperate North America and temperate Eurasia.

Holometabolous see COMPLETE METAMORPHOSIS.

Honeydew the sugary fluid, derived from plant sap, excreted by aphids, leafhoppers and treehoppers.

Hormone a chemical produced in small quantities by a gland in one part of an animal's body, which enters the blood stream and has a physiological effect on other glands or parts of the body. See, eg JUVENILE HORMONE.

Hypermetamorphosis a series of developmental stages beyond the usual larva, pupa and adult stages in COMPLETE METAMORPHOSIS.

Hyperparasitoid a PARASITOID of another parasitoid.

Hypodermis or epidermis, the single layer of cells in arthropods which secretes the CUTICLE.

Hypognathous of those insects with mouthparts and oral cavity on the ventral surface of the head.

Hypostome in ticks, a toothed, snout-like projection between the PEDIPALPS, used in feeding.

Imago an adult, sexually mature insect.

Immature of insects, as a noun, an alternative to "NYMPH" or "larva."

Incomplete metamorphosis or hemi-metaboly, the process of development in the more primitive insects (exopterygotes) which do not have a PUPAL STAGE. Instead, the egg hatches to produce a larva (sometimes called a NYMPH) which resembles a small adult in structure, diet and habitat. Wings develop externally and there is a number of molts before the gonads develop and the final adult stage is achieved.

Inquiline an insect which spends its entire life cycle as a SOCIAL parasite in the nest of another species. Inquiline workers are rare, absent or degenerate in behavior.

Instar the stage between two molts in immature arthropods.

Juvenile hormone (JH) a "hormone" secreted by the corpus allatum of the insect brain which controls METAMORPHOSIS in the young stages and yolk formation in the eggs of females.

Kin selection the selection of genes in one or more individuals favoring the reproduction and survival of close relatives (apart from offspring) which possess identical genes by common descent. Kin selection is believed to have played an important role In the evolution of SOCIAL behavior in wasps, ants and bees.

Kleptoparasitism a form of parasitism where a female wasp or bee (kleptoparasite) seeks out the prey or food store of a different species and uses it to rear her own offspring.

Labellum a pair of soft expansions at the lower end of the LABIUM in flies.

Labium the lower lip in insects comprising the paired mouthparts of one segment fused in the midline.

Labrum a cuticular flap forming the upper lip in insects and hinged to the head above the mouth.

Lamellate any structure comprising a serially repeated array of plate-like elements (lamellae). Often used in connection with the antennae of scarabaeid beetles.

Lateral (adv. laterally) pertaining to the side of a structure or animal.

Leaf miner the minute larva of an insect which tunnels between the upper and lower surfaces of a leaf. Found in beetles, moths, flies and wasps.

Lek an assembly of sexually displaying males which occupies an area containing no resources of interest to females except a choice of males willing and able to mate.

Mass provisioning the habit in solitary wasps and bees and some SOCIAL bees, of supplying and storing all the food required for larval development in a brood cell at the time of egg-laying.

Mechanoreceptors broadly speaking, structures which perceive forces which distort any part of the body. These forces may be air-borne vibrations (sound), water- or substrate-borne vibrations, gravity, and postural effects of the animal's position. Cf CHEMORECEPTOR.

Membranous made of thin membrane.

Metabolism the chemical processes occurring within the living body.

Metamorphosis see COMPLETE METAMORPHOSIS, INCOMPLETE METAMORPHOSIS.

Metatarsus the enlarged basal segment of the TARSUS in aculeate Hymenoptera.

Mimicry the condition where individuals of one species (the mimic) achieve an increase of protection from predators by resembling the appearance of another species (the model). Cases where an innocuous mimic resembles a poisonous or venomous species are called Batesian mimicry. Müllerian mimicry, by contrast, involves the shared resemblance of an assemblage of unrelated species, all of which are poisonous or armed with a sting.

Miner, mines see LEAF MINER.

Monophyletic group a group of species which includes an ancestral species (known or hypothesized) and all its descendants.

Müllerian bodies leaf glands of *Cecropia* trees which provide food for symbiotic ants.

Myiasis disease of man and other animals due to infestation by larvae of flies (Diptera) which are not necessarily parasitic. Most human myiases involve the infestation by larvae of already infected wounds. Others are due to the accidental swallowing of larvae with food, and involve the intestine.

Myriapod member of the UNIRAMIAN superclass Myriapoda, which includes the millipedes and centipedes.

Myrmecophile an organism, usually another insect, which must spend all or part of its life cycle in the nest of ants.

Natural selection mechanism of evolutionary change whereby organisms with characteristics which enhance their chances of survival in the environment in which they live are more likely to survive and produce more offspring with the same characteristics than organisms without those, or with other less advantageous, characteristics.

Nectar a liquid mixture of sugars secreted by plants as an attractant and reward for the pollinating services of insects. Also secreted by some plants from structures remote from flowers (extra-floral nectaries) as a reward for ants which deter plant-eating insects.

Neotropical pertaining to the tropics of the New World, ie Central and northern South America, West Indies.

Neurone a nerve cell.

Nuptial gift a "gift," usually prey, offered to females by some male spiders and insects during courtship.

Nymph an old term for the larvae of an EXOPTERYGOTE insect (though in France it refers to the pupal stage of ENDOPTERYGOTES).

Obligate parasite an animal that must spend at least part of its life cycle as a parasite of another animal.

Ocellus (a) a simple eye consisting of a single cuticular lens and a few sensory cells; (b) an eye-like spot or pattern on the hindwing of a butterfly or moth. Cf COMPOUND EYE.

Oligolectic (noun oligolecty) pertaining to species of bees in which the females collect pollen from only one or a group of related plant species.

Ommatidium a single, optical unit of the COMPOUND EYE of an arthropod.

Öotheca an egg-case or capsule made of a horny substance derived from the colleterial glands of female ORTHOPTEROID insects.

Opisthosoma the abdomen of a chelicerate.

Orthopteroid one of, or pertaining to, a group (Orthopteroidea) of insects with a shared ancestry, and including the orders Opthoptera (crickets and grasshoppers). Phasmatoidea (stick and leaf insects) and Dermaptera (earwigs).

Osmeterium an eversible scent gland found in the caterpillars of swallowtail butterflies (Papilionidae).

Oviduct the duct through which arthropod eggs pass from the female.

Oviparous pertaining to arthropod females which reproduce by laying eggs.

Ovipositor the egg-laying tube in insects, in most groups being derived from elements of the 8th and 9th segments.

Ovoviviparous pertaining to those arthropods in which females retain eggs within the genital tract until the larvae are ready to hatch, Hatching occurs just before or as the eggs are laid.

Palaearctic the biogeographical zone which includes temperate Eurasia and Africa north of the Sahara.

Panorpoid complex the scorpion flies (Mecoptera) true flies (Diptera), butterflies and moths (Lepidoptera) and caddis flies (Trichoptera), which together form a MONOPHYLETIC group with a shared common ancestor.

Pantropical pertaining to organisms or groups found throughout the tropics.

Parasite an animal which feeds on the tissues of another animal, the host, without killing it. The host receives no benefit from the association.

Parasitoid pertaining to those specialized insects whose larvae live as either external or internal parasites of other insects, eventually killing the host.

Parthenogenesis development of a new individual from an unfertilized egg. Occurs in conditions where rapid colonization is important and/or there is an absence or only a small number of males in the population.

Pectinate comb-like, usually pertaining to the much-branched antennae of male moths, such as in the Saturniidae.

Pectine paired, comb-line sensory APPENDAGE unique to scorpions, situated on the ventral side of the 2nd abdominal segment.

Pedipalp appendage on 3rd segment of the CEPHALOTHORAX of chelicerates, variously modified, eg for seizing prey in scorpions, sensory or used by the male in reproduction in spiders.

Phloem sap sap found in the main conducting vessels (phloem) in plants.

Phoresy, phoretic copulation phoresy is the process by which one, usually smaller, animal hitches a ride on the body of another animal; in phoretic copulation, a male insect flies bearing a female with the genitalia of both insects engaged.

Phytophagy (adj. phytophagous) eating plants.

Planidium larva the mobile first INSTAR larva of certain PARASITOID Diptera and Hymenoptera, which actively seeks out its host, using long bristles in locomotion.

Pleuron (pl. pleura) lateral part of a THORACIC segment of an insect.

Pollen grains the male sex cells of flowering plants produced in structures called anthers.

Pollination the process by which pollen grains are transported by various agencies such as wind, water, birds, bats, but mainly insects, to the stigma or receptive female parts of the flower.

Polymorphism the occurrence within a population of several discontinuous genes or phenotypes where even the rarest type has a frequency higher than could be maintained by recurrent mutation and is therefore the direct result of NATURAL SELECTION.

Polyphyletic of a taxonomic group in which the most recent common ancestor is not assigned to the group, that is, a taxon which is based on characters which are not uniquely derived. In other words, a group which is not natural.

Predacious (noun predator) of an animal which preys on other animals for food.

Prepupa the larval phase of an holometabolous insect after feeding has ceased and in which larval CUTICLE becomes separated from its EPIDERMIS (hypodermis) and the developing pupa lies within the persistent larval cuticle. Sometimes called the pharate pupa.

Primary host host in or on which the sexually reproductive forms of a parasite, or a plant-eating insect such as an aphid, are to be found; cf SECONDARY HOST.

Primary parasitoid a PARASITOID which feeds directly on its host's tissues rather than (as in a HYPERPARASITOID) on those of another parasitoid.

Primitive ancestral.

Progressive feeding the habit in EUSOCIAL insects where larvae are provided with food on a regular basis during development, as opposed to MASS PROVISIONING.

Prolegs see FALSE LEGS.

Pronotum the dorsal cuticular SCLERITE covering the first segment of the THORAX in insects, sometimes enlarged to cover the rest of the thorax, as in most cockroaches.

Propodeum the true first abdominal SEGMENT in apocritan Hymenoptera which is incorporated into the rear of the THORAX and separated from the ABDOMEN by a narrow waist.

Proprioceptor a sense organ which receives information, about parts of the body, especially relating to their position. See RECEPTOR.

Prosoma see CEPHALOTHORAX.

Prothorax the first of the three SEGMENTS of the THORAX of an insect.

Proventriculus the "stomach" or gizzard of arthropods, with thick, muscular walls lined with chitinous teeth.

Puddling the habit of male butterflies, especially in the tropics, of congregating at damp soil and the margins of puddles In order to imbibe mineral salts.

Pupa, pupal stage the non-feeding and relatively inactive stage between the larva and adult in holometabolous insects, during which most larval tissues are broken down and reformed into adult structures. See COMPLETE METAMORPHOSIS.

Puparium the hardened, persistent larval CUTICLE in higher flies (suborder Cyclorrhapha), which encloses the PUPA.

Pygidium the rearmost TERGITE of an insect's ABDOMEN.

Queen substance, Queen pheromone a chemical emitted by the mandibular glands of queen honeybees, which inhibits the building of queen cells by workers and the development of the workers' ovaries. Substances with the same function have been found in the queens of SOCIAL wasps (Vespidae).

Quinones a group of chemicals called cyclic diketones emitted as poisonous, repellent secretions by a wide range of insects, including cockroaches, earwigs and beetles, such as the Bombardier beetle.

Radiation, adaptive the invasion, through time, of a wide diversity of adaptive zones and niches by a group of organisms undergoing evolutionary diversification.

Raptorial legs powerful grasping legs found in mantids and mantispids.

Receptor any sense organ which receives input from environmental or internal stimuli. See CHEMORECEPTOR, PROPRIOCEPTOR.

Reflex bleeding the sudden bleeding of brightly colored, noxious blood from special bleed points in limb articulations by insects in response to attack: found, eg, in larvae and adults of ladybirds (Coccinellidae).

Reproductive a member of a social insect colony (males, queens) whose role in the society is reproductive.

Resilin an elastic, rubber-like protein found in the CUTICLE of insects in elastic hinge joints and also involved in the jumping mechanism of fleas. Like rubber, resilin can be stretched under tension, storing the energy involved, and returns to its original length and shape when the tension is released.

Rhabdome sometimes called the retinal rod, this is a structure formed from the united sensory borders of the retinal cells in the COMPOUND EYE.

Rostrum the beak-like piercing and sucking mouthparts of true bugs (Hemiptera).

Royal jelly sometimes called bee milk, a complex mixture of nutrients secreted by the hypopharyngeal glands of worker honeybees and fed to the larvae. Larvae destined to be queens are fed entirely on royal jelly; those destined to be workers receive it only for the first 3 or 4 days of larval life.

Saprophagous feeding on decaying plant or animal material.

Savanna dry, scrub-dominated grasslands with *Acacia* trees and patches of bare earth.

Scale a modified hair, arising from a socket, which has become broad and flattened.

Sclerites thick chitinous plates forming units separated by thinner membranes in the EXOSKELETON of an arthropod.

Scutum the middle and largest of three SCLERITES which form the dorsal cuticular covering or notum of each thoracic SEGMENT of an insect.

Secondary genitalia of male insects, copulatory apparatus remote from the genital opening to which sperm or SPERMATOPHORE is transported before copulation. Pound in spiders, and in dragonflies and damselflies (Odonata).

Secondary host host in or on which the larval, resting or asexually reproductive stages of a parasite, or of a plant-eating insect such as an aphid, may be present; cf PRIMARY HOST.

Segment repeating unit of a body (or of an APPENDAGE) with a structure basically similar to that of other segments; segments may be grouped into TAGMATA, as in the head, THORAX and ABDOMEN.

Semisocial of insect colonies in which females of the same generation cooperate in brood care, with some reproductive division of labor in that some individuals are mainly egg-layers and others are mainly workers.

Sensilla a simple sense organ.

Simple eye see OCELLUS.

Siphuncle a fleshy outgrowth of an aphid's body through which defensive, waxy secretions are emitted.

Slave maker one of several species of ant which steal worker pupae from other colonies, which hatch out and act as "slaves," performing tasks which the behaviorally degenerate workers of the slave maker cannot do.

Slit organ widespread in the arachnids, slit organs are sense organs comprising a slit-like pit in the CUTICLE covered by a thin membrane which bulges inward, making contact with a hairlike process connected to the nervous system.

Social living together in colonies. There are, however, different grades of sociality; see EUSOCIAL, SUBSOCIAL, SEMISOCIAL.

Soldier a member of a worker sub-caste in termites and ants adapted in structure and behavior for a defensive role.

Spermatheca a small, sac-like branch of the vagina in female arthropods which receives and stores sperm.

Spermatophore packet of sperm.

Spinneret a small tubular structure from which silk is extruded by spiders and many larval insects

Spiracle external opening of a TRACHEA or breathing tube in arthropods.

Sternite a plate of CUTICLE covering the underside of an insect body SEGMENT.

Sting the modified OVIPOSITOR of aculeate Hymenoptera (wasps, ants and bees) which has lost its egg-laying function and is used to inject venom into insect prey or attacking predators.

Stridulation the making of a sound by rubbing two specialized body surfaces together, as in, eg, crickets and grasshoppers (Orthoptera).

Style a short antennal APPENDAGE found in some flies (Diptera).

Stylet any sharp, piercing, needle-like organ such as those that form the mouthparts of bugs, fleas and mosquitoes.

Subimago a stage in mayflies immediately before the adult (IMAGO) which is winged, capable of flight and resembles the adult except that it has a thin, dull skin covering the whole body and wings.

Subsocial of insect colonies in which adults share care for their larvae for at least some of the time.

Subtropical of those regions bordering the tropics.

"Superorganism" any highly social (EUSOCIAL) insect colony which has organizational features analogous to those of single organisms, eg workers corresponding to body tissue, exchange of food by TROPHALLAXIS corresponding to the circulatory system, and reproductive CASTES corresponding to the GONADS.

Superparasitism the parasitization of an already-parasitized host by an insect PARASITOID.

Swarming the normal method of colony reproduction in honeybees, whereby the queen and a large number of workers leave the parental nest suddenly and cluster in an exposed site while scout workers seek out another nest site.

Symbiosis (adj. symbiotic) relationship between two organisms (eg an insect and a plant) whereby both derive benefit.

Tagmata (sing, tagma) body regions comprising a number of SEGMENTS, eg THORAX, ABDOMEN.

Tapetum a reflective layer of tracheae behind the retina of the eye.

Tarsus the series of small segments making up the last and 5th region of the leg of insects, the end bearing a pair of claws.

Temperate region the zones outside the subtropics and tropics which do not, as a rule, have marked climatic extremes.

Teneral of adult insects immediately after emergence from PUPAL or final NYMPHAL stage, when the CUTICLE is incompletely hardened and lacks final pigmentation.

Tergite a cuticular plate covering the dorsal surface of an insect body SEGMENT.

Thermoregulation the control of internal body temperature.

Thigmotaxis a locomotory response to being touched. In some insects this results in death-feigning.

Thorax (adj. thoracic) body region of an arthropod behind the head and in front of the ABDOMEN, in insects comprising three SEGMENTS; bears the locomotory APPENDAGES (legs, wings).

Tibia the 4th SEGMENT of an insect's leg, between FEMUR and TARSUS.

Trachea (adj. tracheal) a CUTICLE-lined tubule in uniramians and some arachnids, involved in gas exchange; tracheae open to the exterior via SPIRACLES, and end internally in blind-ending TRACHEOLES.

Tracheole a fine branch of an insect TRACHEA.

Triungulin minute, long-legged parasitic larvae of oil beetles (Meloidae) which hatch from eggs laid In flowers and attach themselves to the bodies of visiting bees. The bees carry them to their nests, when the larvae feed on the egg before eating the stored pollen. Triungulin larvae are also found in Strepsiptera.

Trochanter a short segment of an insect's leg between the COXA and the FEMUR.

Trophallaxis the mouth-to-mouth exchange of liquid food between members of a SOCIAL insect colony.

Tropics the hot climatic zones centered on the Equator and lying between the tropics of Cancer and Capricorn.

Tubercle a small raised area of the CUTICLE.

Tymbal the sound-producing membrane of a cicada.

Uniramian concerning, or a member of, the phylum Uniramia, arthropods comprising the superclasses HEXAPODA and MYRIAPODA.

Urticating hairs detachable hairs containing irritant substances produced by some spiders and caterpillars and which penetrate a predator's skin causing local irritation.

Vector an insect which transmits a disease organism from one host to another.

Venation the pattern of veins in an insect's wing.

Venom a poison produced by arthropods such as spiders and Hymenoptera, which is injected into prey or enemies.

Ventral situated at, or related to, the lower side or surface.

Viviparous giving birth to live young.

Warning coloration conspicuous color patterns found in animals protected by foul-tasting, -smelling or poisonous chemicals, or a sting, which predators learn to associate with an unpleasant experience and so avoid.

Worker a sterile, non-reproductive member of a SOCIAL insect colony responsible for brood care, nest construction and maintenance, defense and foraging. Termite workers can be male or female, but Hymenopteran workers are always female.

Xylem sap the watery sap found in the woody, xylem-conducting vessels which transport water to the leaves.

Zöonosis a phenomenon where an insect-transmitted disease of an animal species enters a human population.

Bibliography

The following list of titles indicates key reference works used in the preparation of this volume and those recommended for further reading. The list is divided into various categories.

GENERAL

Alcock, J. (1973) *Animal Behavior: An Evolutionary Approach*, Sinauer Associates, Sunderland, Massachusetts.

Alexander, R. McNeil (1979) *The Invertebrates*, Cambridge University Press, Cambridge, England.

Askew, R. R. (1971) *Parasitic Insects*, Heinemann Educational Books, London.

Barash, D. (1979) *Sociobiology: the Whisperings Within*, Harper and Row. New York.

Barnes, R. D. (1980) *Invertebrate Zoology* (4th edn), Saunders College/Holt, Rinehart and Winston, Philadelphia.

Barrington. E. J. W. (1979) *Invertebrate Structure and Function* (2nd edn). Van Nostrand Reinhold, Wokingham, UK.

Bell, W. J. and Cardé, R. T. (eds) (1983) *The Chemical Ecology of Insects*. Chapman and Hall, London and New York.

Berenbaum, M. R. (1995) *Bugs in the System*, Addison-Wesley, Baltimore, Maryland.

Birch, M. C. (ed) 1974) *Pheromones, Frontiers of Biology no. 32*, North Holland, Amsterdam.

Birch, M. C. and Haynes, K. F. (1982) *Insect Pheromones, Studies in Biology no. 147*, Edward Arnold, London.

Blum, M. S. and Blum, N. A. (eds) (1979) *Sexual Selection and Reproductive Competition in Insects*. Academic Press, New York and London.

Boror, D. J., de Long, D. M. and Triplehorn, C. A. (1981) *Introduction to the Study of Insects* (5th edn), Saunders College Publishing, New York.

Boudreaux, H.B. (1979) *Arthropod Phylogeny*, John Wiley and Sons, New York and Chichester.

Brackenbury, J. (1992) *Insects in Flight*, Blandford (Cassell), London.

Breed, M. D., Michener, C. D. and Evans, H. E. (eds) (1982) *The Biology of Social Insects, Proceedings of the 9th Congress of the International Union for the Study of Social Insects*, Westview Press, Boulder, Colorado.

Brian, M. V. (1983) *Social Insects, Ecology and Behavioural Biology*, Chapman and Hall, London and New York.

Buchmann, S. L. and Nabhan, G. P. (1997) *The Forgotten Pollinators*, Shearwater Books.

Chapman, R. F. (1998) *The Insects: Structure and Function* (4th edn), Cambridge University Press, London.

Cheng, L. (ed) (1976) *Marine Insects*, North Holland Publishing, Amsterdam and Oxford.

Clausen, C. P. (1940) *Entomophagous Insects*. McGraw-Hill, New York.

Clutton-Brock, T. H. and Harvey. P. H. (eds) (1978) *Readings in Sociobiology*, W. H. Freeman, Reading, UK.

Cott, H. B. (1940) *Adaptive Coloration in Animals*, Methuen and Co, London.

Daly, H. V., Dayen, J. T. and Erlich, P. R. (1978) *Introduction to Insect Biology and Diversity*, McGraw-Hill, New York.

Dawkins, R. (1976) *The Selfish Gene*, Oxford University Press, Oxford.

Dawkins, R. (1982) *The Extended Phenotype: the Gene as the Unit of Selection*, W. H. Freeman, Reading, UK.

Delaplane, K. S. and Mayer, D. F. (2000) *Crop Pollination by Bees*. CABI Publishing, Wallingford, UK.

Edmunds, M. (1974) *Defence in Animals*, Longmans, London.

Eisner, T. and Wilson, E. O. (eds) (1977) *The Insects: Readings from Scientific American*, W. H. Freeman, San Francisco

Emden, H. F. van (ed) (1973) *Insect–Plant Relationships, 6th Symposium of the Royal Entomological Society*, Blackwell Scientific, Oxford.

Evans, H. E. (1984) *Life on a Little-known Planet*, University of Chicago Press, Chicago and London.

Free, J. B. (1971) *Insect Pollination of Crops*, Academic Press, London and New York.

Futuyma, D.J. and Slatkin, M. (1983) *Coevolution*, Sinauer Associates, Sunderland, Massachusetts.

Gilbert, L. E. and Raven, P. H. (eds) (1975) *Coevolution of Animals and Plants*, University of Texas Press, Austin.

Gilbert, P. and Hamilton, C. J. (1983) *Entomology – A Guide to Information Sources*, Mansell Publishing, London.

Gillott, C. (1980) *Entomology*. Plenum. New York and London.

Hennig, W. (1981) *Insect Phylogeny* (trans and ed A. Pont, revisionary notes Dieter Schlee), John Wiley and Sons, New York and Chichester.

Hermann, H. R. (ed) (1979–82) *Social Insects (4 vols)*, Academic Press, New York and London.

Johnson, C. G. (1969) *Migration and Dispersal of Insects by Flight*, Methuen, London.

Kaestner, A. (1968) *Invertebrate Zoology, vol II, Arthropod Relatives, Chelicerata, Myriapoda* (trans H.W. and L.R. Levi), John Wiley Interscience, New York and London.

Kettlewell, H. B. D. (1973) *The Evolution of Melanism: the Study of a Recurring Necessity*, Clarendon Press, Oxford.

Krebs, J. R. and Davis, N. B. (1978) *Behavioural Ecology, an Evolutionary Approach*, Blackwell Scientific, Oxford.

Krishna, K. and Weesner, F.M. (1969–70) *Biology of Termites* (2 vols), Academic Press, New York and London.

Linsenmaier, W. (1972) *Insects of the World* (trans. L.E. Chadwick), McGraw-Hill, New York and London.

McGavin, G. C. (2000) *Dorling Kindersley Handbooks: Insects, Spiders and other Terrestrial Arthropods*. Dorling Kindersley, London

McGavin, G. C. (2001) *Essential Entomology: An Order by Order Introduction*. Oxford University Press.

Manton, S.M. (1977) *The Arthropoda, Habits, Functional Morphology and Evolution*, Clarendon Press, Oxford.

Mound, L. M. and Waloff, N. (eds) (1978) *Diversity of Insect Faunas, 9th Symposium of the Royal Entomological Society*, Blackwell Scientific, Oxford.

Oster, G. F. and Wilson, E. O. (1978) *Caste and Ecology in the Social Insects, Monographs in Population Biology 12*, Princeton University Press, New Jersey.

O'Toole, C. (1995) *Alien Empire: An Exploration of the Lives of Insects*. BBC Books, London.

O'Toole, C, and Preston-Mafham, K. (1983) *Insects in Camera: A Photographic Essay on Behaviour*, Oxford University Press, Oxford.

Owen, D. F. (1980) *Camouflage and Mimicry*, Oxford University Press, Oxford.

Preston-Mafham, K. and Preston-Mafham, R. (2000) *The Natural World of Bugs and Insects*. PRC Publishing, London.

Rainey, R.C. (ed) (1975) *Insect Flight. 7th Symposium of the Royal Entomological Society*, Blackwell Scientific, Oxford.

Richards, O. W. and Davies R. G. (1977) *Imm's General Textbook of Entomology* (10th edn, 2 vols), Chapman and Hall, London.

Rockstein, M. (ed) (1973–74). *The Physiology of Insects* (6 vol), Academic Press. New York and London.

Romoser, W. S. (1981) *The Science of Entomology*. Macmillan, London and New York.

Ross, H. H., Ross, C. A. and Ross, J. R. P. (1982) *A Textbook of Entomology* (4th edn). Wiley, New York.

Sharov, A. G. (1966) *Basic Arthropodan Stock with Special Reference to Insects*, Pergamon Press, Oxford.

Smith, K. G. V. (ed) (1973) *Insects and Other Arthropods of Medical Importance*, British Museum (Natural History), London.

Snodgrass, R. E. (1933) *Principles of Insect Morphology*, McGraw-Hill, New York.

Southwood, T. R. E. (ed) (1968) *Insect Abundance, 4th Symposium of the Royal Entomological Society*, Blackwell Scientific, Oxford.

Speight, M. R., Hunter, M. D. and Watt, A. D. (1999) *Ecology of Insects: Concepts and Applications*. Blackwell Science, Oxford.

Thornhill, B, and Alcock, J. (1983) *The Evolution of Insect Mating System*, Harvard University Press, Cambridge, Massachusetts.

Varley, G. C., Gradwell, G. R. and Hassell, M.P. (1973) *Insect Population Ecology: an Analytical Approach*, Blackwell Scientific, Oxford.

Wickler, W. (1968) *Mimicry in Animals and Plants* (trans. R.D. Martin), Weidenfeld and Nicolson, London.

Wigglesworth, V. B. (1964) *The Life of Insects*, Weidenfeld and Nicolson, London.

Wigglesworth, V. B. (1972) *The Principles of Insect Physiology* (7th edn), Chapman and Hall, London.

Wilson, E. O. (1971) *The Insect Societies*, Harvard University Press, Cambridge, Massachusetts.

Wilson, E. O. (1973) *Sociobiology, the New Synthesis*, Harvard University Press, Cambridge, Massachusetts and London.

REGIONAL

Arnett, R. H. (1983) *American Insects: A Handbook of the Insects of America North of Mexico*, Van Nostrand Reinhold, New York.

Chinery, M. (1976) *A Field Guide to the Insects of Britain and Northern Europe*, Collins, London.

Gertsch, W.J. (1979) *American Spiders*, Van Nostrand Reinhold, New York.

Holm, E, and Scholtz, C. (eds) (1985) *Insects of Southern Africa*, Butterworth, Durban.

Jones, B. (1985) *The Country Life Guide to Spiders of Britain and Northern Europe*, Country Life Books, Feltham.

Main, B. Y. (1976) *Australian Spiders*, Collins, Sydney.

Mani, M. S. (1962) *Introduction to High Altitude Entomology, Life above the Timber-line in the North-West Himalaya*, Methuen, London.

Skaife, S. H. (1979) *African Insect Life* (2nd edn), Country Life Books, London.

Waterhouse, D. F. (ed) (1970) *The Insects of Australia, a Textbook for Students and Research Workers*, Melbourne University Press, Melbourne.

MAJOR GROUPS

Ackery, P. R. and Vane-Wright, R. I. (1984), *Milkweed Butterflies, Their Cladistics and Biology*. British Museum (Natural History), London.

Bristowe, W. S. (1958) *The World of Spiders* (revised edn. 1971), New Naturalist Series, Collins, London.

Butler, C. G. (1934) *The World of the Honeybee*. New Naturalist Series, Collins, London.

Corbet, P. S. (1962) *A Biology of Dragonflies*, Willoughby, London.

Corbet, P .S. Longfield, C. and Moore, N.W. (1960) *Dragonflies*, New Naturalist Series, Collins, London.

Growson, R. A. (1981) *The Biology of the Coleoptera*, Academic Press, London.

Evans, H. E. (1975) *The Life of Beetles*, George Allen & Unwin, London.

Evans, H. E. (1966) *The Comparative Ethology and Evolution of the Sand Wasps*, Harvard University Press, Cambridge, Massachusetts.

Evans, H. E. and West-Eberhard, M. J. (1973) *The Wasps*, David and Charles, Newton Abbot, Devon.

Foelix, R. F. (1982) *Biology of Spiders*, Harvard University Press, Cambridge, Massachusetts.

Ford. E. B. (1957) *Butterflies* (3rd edn), New Naturalist Series, Collins, London.

Ford. E. B. (1972) *Moths* (3rd edn), New Naturalist Series, Collins, London.

Free, J. B. and Butler, C. G. (1957) *Bumblebees*, New Naturalist Series, Collins, London

Frisch, K. von (1967) *The Dance Language and Orientation of Bees* (trans. L.E. Chadwick) Belknap Press of Harvard University Press, Cambridge, Massachusetts.

Heinrich, B (1979) *Bumblebee Economics*, Harvard University Press, Cambridge, Massachusetts and London.

Iwata, K. (1971) *Evolution of Instinct: Comparative Ethology of Hymenoptera*, Amerind Publishing Co New Delhi, for Smithsonian Institution, Washington, DC and Natural Science Foundation.

LaSalle, J. and Gauld, I. D. (eds) (1993) Hymenoptera and Biodiversity. CABI Publishing, Wallingford, UK.

Michener, C. D. (1974) *The Social Behavior of the Bees, a Comparative Study*, Belknap Press of Harvard University Press, Cambridge, Massachusetts.

Michener, C. D. (2000) *The Bees of the World*. Johns Hopkins University Press, Baltimore and London.

Oldroyd, H. (1964) *The Natural History of Flies*, Weidenfeld and Nicolson, London.

O'Toole, C. (2000) *The Red Mason Bee: Taking the Sting out of Beekeeping*, Osmia Publications, Banbury.

O'Toole, C. (2002) *Bumblebees*, Osmia Publications, Banbury.

Owen, D. F. (1971) *Tropical Butterflies*, Oxford University Press, Oxford.

O'Toole, C. and Raw, A. (1994) *Bees of the World*, Blandford Books (Cassell), London.

Preston-Mafham, R. and Preston-Mafham, K (1993) *The Encyclopedia of Land Invertebrate Behaviour*. Blandford Books (Cassell), London.

Preston-Mafham, R. and Preston-Mafham, K. (1984) *Spiders of the World*, Blandford Press, Poole.

Rothschild, M. and Clay, T. (1952) *Fleas, Flukes and Cuckoos, A Study of Bird Parasites*, New Naturalist Series, Collins, London.

Savory, T. (1977) *Arachnida* (2nd edn), Academic Press, London and New York.

Spradberry, J. P. (1973) *Wasps, An Account of the Biology and Natural History of Solitary and Social Wasps*, Sidgwick and Jackson, London.

Stephen, W. P., Bohart, G. E. and Torchio, P. F. (1969) *The Biology and External Morphology of Bees, with a Synopsis of the Genera of Northwestern America*, Oregon University Press, Corvallis, Oregon.

Vane-Wright, R. I. and Ackery, P. R. (1984) *The Biology of Butterflies, the 11th Symposium of the Royal Entomological Society of London*, Academic Press, London.

Witt, P. N. and Rovner, J. S. (eds) (1982) *Spider Communication Mechanisms and Ecological Significance*, Princeton University Press, Princeton, New Jersey.

Index

Picture Credits

t top; **b** bottom; **c** center; **l** left; **r** right.
Abbreviations: HSI Holt Studios International; **NHPA** Natural History Photographic Agency; **OSF** Oxford Scientific Films; **P** Premaphotos Wildlife; **SPL** Science Photo Library

All pictures Ken Preston-Mafham/P except:

7 Ron Brown/P; 10 P.J. DeVries/OSF; 15 Stephen Dalton/ NHPA; 16-17 Dr. Rod Preston-Mafham/P; 28-29 F. Lanting/ Minden Pictures/Frank Lane Picture Agency–Images of Nature; 30-31 OSF; 33 P.J. DeVries/OSF; 34c, 37 Dr. Rod Preston-Mafham/P; 38-39 Robert Thompson/NHPA; 40-41 James H. Robinson/OSF; 41 Melvin Grey/NHPA; 44-45 Dr. Rod Preston-Mafham/P; 60 Jean Preston-Mafham/P; 66-67 Mark Preston-Mafham/P; 70 Dr. Rod Preston-Mafham/P; 73 Gunter Ziesler/ Bruce Coleman Collection; 81 Dr. Rod Preston-Mafham/P; 84 David Scharf/SPL; 85 Vince Smith; 96b Dr. Rod Preston-Mafham/P; 97t Mark Preston-Mafham/P; 100, 104 Dr. Rod Preston-Mafham/P; 126-127 G.I. Bernard/OSF; 129 Quest/ SPL; 138t Nigel Cattlin/HSI; 141b Dr. Rod Preston-Mafham/P; 143 Len McLeod/HSI; 145 Eye of Science/SPL; 149 Stephen Dalton/NHPA; 169 Darlyne Murawski/NGS Image Collection; 176, 190, 190-191 Nigel Cattlin/HSI; 192-193 Marla Stenzel/ NGS Image Collection; 193t Nigel Cattlin/HSI; 193bl Jean Preston-Mafham/P; 193br Chris O'Toole; 195t Ken Wilson/ Papilio/Corbis; 195c, 196, 197t Dr. Rod Preston-Mafham/P; 206 Paul Hillyard; 210t Anthony Bannister/NHPA; 210c David Scharf/SPL; 211 Paul Hillyard; 217b J.H. Robinson/SPL; 218t Andrew Syred/SPL; 218bl Dr. Jeremy Burgess/SPL; 218br, 218-219, 219t, 219b Andrew Syred/SPL.

Artwork

t top; **b** bottom.

Color artwork by Richard Lewington except for the following:
Abbreviations: CS Chris Shields; **SM** Simon Mendez; **LH** Lizzie Harper; **DO** Denys Ovenden; **AM** Alan Male; **JL** Jonathan Latimer; **RL** Ruth Lindsay; **GK** Graham Kennedy; **SR** Steve Roberts; **MW** Michael J. Woods.

18t CS; 18 (1), 19 (7), 51 DO; 54–55 RL; 61 CS; 76–77 DO, 90 CS; 111 (6) SM; 111b GK; 114–115 (1, 5, 7) DO, (2) SM, (4, 6, 8, 9) CS; 126b, 128 JL; 132 (1) SM, (2) CS; 134, 150 (1) DO; 151 (8) SM; 155 DO; 156–157 (1) SR, (2, 6a, 6b) CS, (4) AM, (7) JL, (8) LH; 160–161 (1, 6) SM, (3, 4, 8) DO, (5) AM, (7) MW; 178 (1) CS; 181 (6) JL, (7) AM; 202 (3) AM; 204 (2, 4) AM, (3) SM; 205 AM; 221 SM.

Diagrams by:
Martin Anderson
Simon Driver
Peter Bull Art Studio
Line diagrams in factfiles by Richard Lewington.

All artwork ©Andromeda Oxford Ltd.

2 1982 01315 4020

APR 2 8 2003

APR 2 8 2003